Southerners whose communi~~ties were~~ invaded by the Union army during ~~the war~~ endured a profoundly painful ordeal. For most, the coming of the Yankees was a nightmare become real; for some, it was the answer to a prayer. But for all, Stephen Ash argues, invasion and occupation were essential parts of the experience of defeat that helped shape the Southern postwar mentality.

When the Yankees Came is the first comprehensive study of the occupied South, bringing to light a wealth of new information about the Southern home front. Examining events from a dual perspective to show how occupation affected the invading forces as well as the indigenous population, Ash concludes that as Federal war aims evolved, the occupation gradually became more repressive. But increased brutality on the part of the Northern army resulted in more determined resistance from white Southerners — a situation that parallels the experience of many other conquering forces.

Ash also explains that the ordeal of occupation varied for Southerners according to their distance from the nearest Union army post. Garrisoned towns, the Confederate frontier, and the no-man's-land in between, he argues, represented three distinct zones of occupation. Ash says, "Occupation assumed a different form in each of these arenas and struck with a different intensity. Truly there were three occupied Souths, each with its own story."

When the Yankees Came

CIVIL WAR AMERICA *Gary W. Gallagher, editor*

When the

Conflict and Chaos in the Occupied South, 1861–1865

Yankees Came

· ·

Stephen V. Ash

THE UNIVERSITY OF NORTH CAROLINA PRESS *Chapel Hill and London*

© 1995
The University of
North Carolina Press
All rights reserved
Manufactured in the
United States of America

The paper in this book meets the guidelines for permanence and
durability of the Committee on Production Guidelines for Book Longevity
of the Council on Library Resources.

Library of Congress Cataloging-in-Publication Data
Ash, Stephen V.
When the Yankees came : conflict and chaos in the occupied South, 1861–
1865 / by Stephen V. Ash.
      p. cm. — (Civil War America)
Includes bibliographical references (p.   ) and index.
ISBN 0-8078-2223-x (cloth : alk. paper)
1. Confederate States of America—History. 2. United States—History—
Civil War, 1861–1865—Occupied territories. I. Title. II. Series.
E487.A83   1995
973.7′13—dc20   94-49525
                            CIP

99 98 97 96 95   5 4 3 2 1

For my mother, JUANITA VAUGHAN ASH

Contents

Preface

Historians continue to confound those who insist that everything that can possibly be said about the Civil War has already been said. Even the much-scrutinized military side of the war has been remarkably elaborated in recent years, while the social side has been dragged from a dark and dusty corner of historiography into the light, thoroughly remodeled, and put on prominent display.

This book is intended to fill one of the many remaining gaps in our understanding of the Civil War, and in our understanding of nineteenth-century Southern society. Southerners in the areas invaded by the Union army during the war had a distinctive experience, one that has been ignored by most historians who have written about the Confederate home front. What few studies of the occupied South we have deal with individual cities, counties, or regions, or with selected portions of the populace; there has until now been no comprehensive study of the occupied South.

Such a study is important for reasons beyond the mere fact of historiographical neglect. For one thing, what happened in the invaded sections of the South profoundly influenced Union war policy and thus the war's outcome: civilian resistance, the failure of political reconstruction, the self-emancipation of slaves, and other events in the occupied districts played a decisive role in turning the conflict from a limited war into a revolution.

For another thing, the experience of invasion and occupation was an essential part of the experience of defeat that C. Vann Woodward has identified as a defining element of the Southern mentality, one of the special "burdens" of Southern history. The unique psyche of the South has been shaped, in part, by what happened to the Southern people when the Yankees came.

This study deals principally with Southern whites. Blacks in the invaded regions have been the subject of a number of excellent historical accounts published in the last twenty years or so, most notably those by Leon F. Litwack and Ira Berlin. Because the black story has been so fully and ably recounted by others, I have only sketched its outlines in this volume (I deal extensively, however, with black-white relations). I trust that the reader will understand, my abridged treatment notwithstanding, that blacks were leading players in the drama of invasion and occupation. (I trust, too, given the fact that my focus is primarily on whites, that the reader will not object to my using "Southerners" in the text as shorthand for "white Southerners.")

I have furthermore limited this study to the seceding states, and I have excluded from consideration western Virginia and eastern Tennessee, the two most important centers of persistent Unionism in the Confederacy. Just who the real "invaders" were in those two regions of massive anti-Confederate resistance is debatable, and I think that the story of the people there deserves a separate telling.

Three themes will become apparent to the reader in the chapters that follow. One is the evolution of Northern war aims and policy, and thus of the Southern experience of occupation, as the war went on. Provoked by the continuing resistance of Southern civilians in the invaded regions and by the tenacity of the Confederate armies, the North moved from a conciliatory and conservative policy to a punitive and radical one that brought destruction, disruption, and suffering to the occupied South.

Another theme is the contrasting experiences of the three parts of the occupied South that I have termed the garrisoned towns, the Confederate frontier, and no-man's-land. The afflictions of occupation assumed a different form in each of these arenas and struck with differing intensity. Truly there were three occupied Souths, each with its own story.

The third theme is the array of conflicts that surfaced in the wake of the Union army. The clash of Rebel citizens and Yankee invaders was one of these; the others were all internal, pitting the inhabitants of the occupied regions against one another. The coming of the Northern army encouraged many people, white as well as black, to cast off the chains that bound them. Their insurgency brought them face-to-face with those determined to preserve the world as it was—determined enough, some of them, to resort to bloody violence.

Perhaps it is true, as one inhabitant of the occupied South remarked in 1863, that "the historian will never do Justice to the subject." But even he would probably have agreed that it is worth trying to do so. That is the belief that has inspired this book.

. . .

Everyone who writes a book incurs a multitude of personal and professional debts of the sort that can never be repaid, only acknowledged. I am no exception.

Among those to whom I owe much are the archivists at the various manuscript repositories where I have done research. All those I have dealt with have been unfailingly helpful and courteous, even when deluged by the usual midday flood of genealogists. Regrettably, I cannot name here all those who have aided me. I will, however, mention James Lloyd, Nick Wyman, and William Eigelsbach of the University of Tennessee at Knoxville. They and their predecessors in Special Collections have welcomed me graciously and assisted me generously whenever I have called on them.

I am grateful, too, for the financial support I have received: an American Council of Learned Societies (ACLS)/National Endowment for the Humanities fellowship in 1988 and a Virginia Historical Society/Andrew W. Mellon Foundation fellowship in 1989. I am also indebted to those who wrote letters in my behalf for the ACLS fellowship: Paul H. Bergeron, Catherine Clinton, Pete Daniel, and Eric Foner.

At an early stage in its evolution this book benefited from the comments of Fred A. Bailey, Steven Hahn, and James L. Roark. The completed manuscript was scrutinized—and much improved—by Gary W. Gallagher, George C. Rable, and Paul Bergeron. My debts to Paul continue to mount; he has been both mentor and friend for more than twenty years.

My family is the bedrock on which my professional life has been built. As our marriage enters its twenty-sixth year, my wife Jean remains a cherished source of love and support. Virginia and Landon Miles have opened their home to me and shared my joys and sorrows to an extent far beyond that expected of an aunt and uncle; they have, indeed, made me feel more like a son than a nephew. My mother Juanita, to whom this book is dedicated, has been both inspiration and comfort to me; time and again over the years I have seen that my dependence on her strength and wisdom did not end with my childhood.

....

When the Yankees Came

Prologue *Spring 1861*

The war began, as it would end, in the springtime. Cannon fire in Charleston harbor on April 12, 1861, sent shock waves through the South and the North. An anxious stillness followed, as the nation held its breath and looked toward Washington. The answer came on April 15. This time no olive branch was proffered, but instead a sword.

Across the South, crowds of citizens gathered on courthouse lawns to hear speeches and watch soldiers muster and drill. Most were jubilant, confidently predicting a quick and easy victory; but some looked on in silence and despair. In Gallatin, Tennessee, a schoolmaster stood solemnly among the cheering throng as a Confederate flag was raised on April 18. Turning to one of his young students who stood beside him, he asked if he understood what it all meant. "Music," the little one replied, as a band started playing. "Thoughtless boy," the teacher scolded, "it means war, death and destruction."[1]

How had it happened? How did the Southern people come to find themselves at war in the spring of 1861? And how would they respond once the excitement of those first days had subsided and the war had begun in earnest? Part of the answer to these questions lies in the very nature of those people, in how they understood themselves and their world, and in how they viewed the dramatic events of the years leading up to the war.

. . .

Mid-nineteenth-century Americans of all sections agreed on at least one thing: the South was a realm apart. Whether they celebrated or condemned the South's way of life, they all acknowledged its distinctiveness. But what made the South so different?

It was the presence of large numbers of blacks, and the determination of whites to control and exploit them, that made the South the South. From the twin facts of black presence and white racism flowed many consequences. Slavery evolved as an efficient method of control and exploitation and allowed plantation agriculture to expand. The success of the plantation system gave rise to a powerful planter class that in many ways imposed its will on all of Southern society. Plantation agriculture and planter hegemony impeded urbanization and industrialization and helped preserve traditional ways in the South, while the rest of the nation moved toward modernity.[2]

The image of the South as some sort of feudal relic is exaggerated, however. Democratic reform had come to the South just as it had to the North in the first decades of the nineteenth century. Common citizens (at least those who were white and male) now took part in politics. Nor was the South untouched by the transportation, market, and industrial revolutions that were gathering strength by the mid-nineteenth century. The point is, though, that these changes were not pervasive enough to overthrow Southern traditionalism. Ancient habits and ways of thought lingered on in the South.[3]

One such vestige was a belief that hierarchy was a natural condition of society, that authority and deference were part of God's plan. This article of faith was professed most devoutly by the South's aristocrats (who were mainly identified with, but not confined to, the planter class). Aristocrats assumed the right to rule society and subscribed to a code of gentility befitting their rank. But in assuming authority over those beneath them, white and black, they also assumed paternal obligations. In return they expected obedience and loyalty.[4]

People of lesser rank did not always see things as the aristocrats did— particularly the slaves. Most slaves behaved as their masters expected them to but in their hearts felt no real loyalty to their masters or to the social order as a whole; nearly all of them deeply resented their bondage and longed for freedom. They were careful to keep their true feelings hidden from whites, for the whip inevitably appeared at the slightest hint of black recalcitrance.[5]

Between the aristocrats and the blacks in the Southern social order were the white "plain folk." Broadly speaking, they fell into two categories: yeomen and poor whites. The yeomen were small farmers, artisans, herdsmen—that is, people who owned small-to-middling amounts of productive property (including, in some cases, a few slaves). Poor whites were those with no productive property or any other livelihood save unskilled labor; they were tenant farmers, overseers, farm laborers, shop hands, dockworkers, and the like.

To understand how the yeomen saw things it is first necessary to look at how they got along with aristocrats. Certain matters provoked, if not outright hostility on the part of the yeomen, at least some resentment. One was the elite's lifestyle. The fancy carriages and fine clothes, the private academy schooling, the many slaves, and the leisure of the aristocracy often rankled the plain-living, hardworking yeomen. Moreover, elite ladies and gentlemen could be arrogant, condescending, and standoffish. Economic and political issues, too, could generate friction. Some yeomen feared that the planters' monopoly of land and labor was squeezing out small farmers. Some felt threatened by aristocratic control of courthouse and statehouse.[6]

But the ties that bound the classes were strong. One of the strongest was paternalism. Though some aristocrats acted supercilious and aloof, most really tried to watch over their plebeian neighbors with a fatherly eye, giving advice when it was needed, sending over a barrel of cornmeal in hard times, even putting up money for the education of a promising yeoman boy. The yeomen, for their part, gratefully accepted such favors and in return upheld the social order without demanding social equality.[7]

Why did the yeomen willingly sustain their hierarchical society? Slaves, after all, spurned paternalism and longed for a world of their own. One answer is, obviously, that slaves were at the bottom of the social order and benefited little from it, whereas yeomen ranked high and benefited accordingly.

As white property owners the yeomen were a doubly privileged class. The ascendancy of white over black was the first principle of Southern life: yeomen and aristocrats might dispute other matters, but they—and in fact all whites—were as one in their certainty that blacks were an inferior race, society's permanent mudsill. In that sense yeomen were members of the ruling class, and their recognition of that fact encouraged a sense of oneness with the aristocracy. That identity was reinforced by the yeomen's status as freeholders. Antebellum Southerners were heirs to a republican tradition that saw liberty as perpetually endangered and held that possession of property was a bulwark against tyranny and enslavement. Thus, in an important sense, yeomen stood not only above blacks but also above the propertyless (and thus vulnerable and potentially servile) poor whites.[8]

The benefits of property were, of course, material as well as ideological. Generally speaking, the antebellum South was a land of agricultural prosperity. The climate was mild and the growing season long; arable soil was plentiful, and so was good grazing land. No matter what proportion of the South's productive acreage was held by planters (and in the richest areas it was usually a great proportion), there was plenty left for yeoman farmers and herdsmen. The typical yeoman easily produced a self-sufficiency, and many went beyond that, raising a little corn, cotton, tobacco, or livestock for the market. That individual yeomen were frequently the grateful objects of elite benevolence should not obscure the fact that the yeomen as a class were economically independent.[9]

One last factor that eased social discord was the South's pervasive rural culture. Agrarianism fostered communalism. Few families were wholly self-sufficient in a material sense: the farmer depended on the blacksmith to shoe his horse and on the miller to grind his corn and on the tanner to make his leather, and he paid them in produce that they in turn needed because they did not grow their own; and they all depended on each other when, for example, it came time to raise a house or barn. It was the *community* that was self-sufficient, but that self-sufficiency was a product of mutual assistance.

Rural communalism comprised in effect a second dimension of Southern society, coexistent with the dimension of social hierarchy. Whereas the one followed a vertical axis of rank, authority, and paternalism, the other followed a horizontal axis of neighborliness and mutuality. The communal world extended a broad embrace. It included aristocrats, who often called on their yeomen neighbors for supplies and services. It also included poor whites and slaves, who gathered with the yeomen at camp meetings, barn raisings, logrollings, and the other rituals and festivals of rural life. The country church, in particular, was a key agent of rural communalism, for within its rough log walls gathered planters, yeomen, poor whites, and slaves alike in prayer and Christian fellowship.[10]

In this communal dimension of society, men and women were judged less by their rank than by their fidelity to community mores. The respect of one's neighbors was a greater prize than a big plantation, Christian devotion a finer quality than elegance in dress or speech, sharing work and recreation a higher calling than pursuing fame and power.

Thus, in the South there emerged a society in which the yeoman majority readily acknowledged the preeminence of the aristocratic few. The yeomen did so not only from old habits of deference, but also from a certain identity of interest with the aristocracy and because so much of their world—especially its economic and communal aspects—lay beyond the reach of elite authority. Most yeomen saw no contradiction in using their democratic political rights to put men of wealth and refinement into high office and thereby sustain the aristocracy.

One fact must be underscored, however: the loyalty of the yeomen was, to a degree, contingent. As long as aristocrats displayed paternalist generosity, as long as yeomen perceived a fundamental identity of interests with the elite, as long as the yeomen's economic independence was unthreatened, as long as rural communalism remained intact—just so long would yeomen steadfastly uphold the social order. But let one or more of those props collapse, and no one could predict the result.[11]

What about the poor whites? Although racial ideology incorporated even the most destitute white into the ruling caste, within white society the poor white minority was looked down upon. Aristocrats and yeomen tended to distinguish two classes of poor whites, the "respectable poor" and the "poor white trash." All the poor were regarded with some suspicion by property owners imbued with republican ideals, but the respectable poor were generally objects of compassion whereas the poor white trash were objects of scorn.[12]

This twofold image of the poor actually reflected social reality. One class of poor whites (by far the more numerous) endorsed the prevailing social order and adhered to it. They deferred to the aristocracy and accepted its paternalism; they worked hard, helped their neighbors, went to church, and in other ways tried to live by the standards of the folk community and thereby achieve respectability.

The other class of poor whites lived literally and figuratively on the margins of society, alienated outsiders who spurned social conventions. They squatted on public or abandoned land and eked out an independent living by hunting, fishing, gardening, and gathering, aloof from the communal economy of barter and mutual aid. They stuck to themselves, avoided churches and schools, got as rowdy as they pleased, and ignored the counsel of aristocrats and the tongue clucking and finger wagging of the "respectable" community.[13]

Such deviants could threaten the established order should they get out of hand; they were therefore watched closely and, when necessary, reined in by the arm of the law. But even the "respectable" poor were potentially subversive, for their loyalty to the social order was even more contingent than that of the yeomen. They did not, after all, enjoy any economic independence and did not share much of the South's prosperity. They also had to endure occasional snobbery not only from aristocrats but from yeomen, too. Given the right circumstances, then, even "respectable" poor whites might be tempted to throw off the harness of social restraints and seize the main chance.[14]

One class of Southerners that remains to be discussed presents special difficulties, for in a basic sense it was not a class at all. Women in the Old South were, of course, quite aware of their distinct and subordinate role in society, but they did not manifest a feminine consciousness that transcended race or social class.[15]

An especially powerful paternalist bond tied women to men (speaking from here on of white women only), a bond far more telling than that which tied, say, yeomen to aristocrats. Because Southern culture strongly discouraged female autonomy and made it hard for women to secure economic independence, nearly all women had to cleave to a man. Wholly dependent on his patronage, they were correspondingly obedient to his authority; moreover, they were loyal. Slaves too were wholly dependent on the patronage of a superior and were correspondingly obedient, but they were not loyal. The difference is that slaves were relegated to an inferior caste and profited little from the social order, whereas women shared their patron's class status and profited much.[16]

To say that Southern women were dependent, obedient, and loyal is not to say that they were ciphers, their personalities but mirrors of their patron's wishes and their identities completely subsumed in his. There were spheres beyond the paternal bond in which women played important roles and gained fulfillment, dignity, and even a measure of power. Within the household, for example, they took responsibility for child rearing, moral guidance, and domestic manufacturing. Within the rural community they could achieve a kind of independent status; that is, one who proved herself a good neighbor and a good Christian could win respectability even if her father was a drunkard and her husband a thief.

Furthermore, although legally subordinated to men and denied a role in public life, antebellum Southern women did not generally see themselves as victims. In the household, the despotic patriarchy of an earlier age had mostly given way to the loving, companionate Victorian family. (This is not to say that husbands did not rule the roost, merely that wives and children were indulged now more than before.) And in Southern culture at large, women enjoyed exalted ideological status, glorified, even sanctified, as nurturers of the family and guardians of virtue.[17]

Sharing as they did most of the rewards and burdens of their patron's rank, women fused their identity in the hierarchical world with his. In all matters where social class counted (that is, outside the strictly familial and communal spheres), women thought and acted less as women than as poor whites, yeomen, or aristocrats.

. . .

If his journey was hurried and his gaze casual, a traveler in the South before the late 1850s might have concluded that it was a land of remarkable complacency. After all, there was little evidence of class conflict, no apparent unrest among the white or black masses, no labor violence, no bread riots, scarcely a voice raised in alarm over the state of society (unless it was the voice of a country preacher battling Satan). But a more attentive observer might have sensed that all was not well. Though hardly a ripple disturbed the surface, currents of anxiety roiled the depths of antebellum Southern society.

One source of anxiety was economic change. To Northerners, caught up in a dizzying economic revolution, the South seemed an immutable land that time forgot; but in fact the South was undergoing an economic revolution of its own—slower-paced than the North's, less dramatic and far-reaching, but still disquieting. Westward expansion, the spread of cotton culture, and the development of steamships, turnpikes, and railroads were drawing more and more Southerners into the market economy. Though self-sufficiency remained the rule in Southern communities, a growing number of farmers and tradesmen staked at least part of their prosperity on the whims of a distant, impersonal, unpredictable market. Beholding this transformation, many Southerners grew uneasy.[18]

Even more ominous than the market revolution was the intensifying sectional conflict over slavery. Beginning about 1820 with the Missouri controversy, and especially after 1848 with the Mexican cession and other issues, national politics simmered in an atmosphere of rising heat. Much of the heat was generated by the abolitionist crusade, which, although endorsed by only a small minority of Northerners, was seen by Southerners as a grave threat to their way of life. But many Southerners also perceived a mortal threat in the attempts of a much larger body of Northerners simply to halt slavery's further spread. With the outbreak of violence over slavery in Kansas in the 1850s and the concurrent rise of the Republican Party, which sought to bar slavery from the territories, many Southerners were moved to ponder the South's future.

Forebodings of powerlessness and dependency engendered by the market revolution fostered malaise in the South, along with a feeling that forceful remedies might be called for. The sectional conflict focused the Southern mind on a particularly drastic remedy: secession. Yet secession would probably never have come to pass without the influence of a third factor: a growing conviction that Northern society and Southern society were diverging radically.

Southerners had long believed that they and Northerners were heirs of two distinct cultural traditions, embodied in the images of the gracious Cavalier and the practical Yankee. But with the antebellum transformation of the North that legend was elaborated. What emerged was a grossly distorted picture of the North, and a considerably romanticized picture of the South, that most Southerners accepted as gospel.[19]

When Southerners looked north they saw a society that was in many ways the antithesis of their own. In the South, paternalism and communalism bound society into a harmonious whole; Northerners, on the other hand, seemed to be driven by selfishness, rivalry, corruption, and mammon worship. Southern society was ordered hierarchically, according to God's plan; but the North was afflicted with a leveling egalitarianism that suppressed society's best elements and encouraged the worst to run riot. At the heart of Southern society was a community of noble, independent yeomen; the North was cursed with a rabble of vicious, propertyless proletarians. Benevolent Southern masters pampered their black servants; ruthless Northern bosses reduced their workers to miserable "wage slaves." The South was a land of serenity where Christian devotion and respect for tradition prevailed; the North seethed with worldly passions, preposterous "isms," and madcap schemes of reform.[20]

By the late 1850s many Southerners had moved so close to the precipice that only a couple of good shoves were needed to push them over the brink into radicalism and secession. Those shoves came in 1859 and 1860 with John Brown's raid and the election of a Republican, Abraham Lincoln, to the presidency.

The raid on Harpers Ferry, Virginia, proved to the satisfaction of most Southerners that Northern abolitionists had abandoned their war of words in favor of direct, armed assault on the institution of slavery. It seemed clear now that the South could never be safe in a Union that allowed abolitionism to flourish. Lincoln's election had both substantive and symbolic import. As president, Lincoln would have ample power to interfere with slavery in the territories, even without the consent of Congress or the Supreme Court. And the fact that he had been elected without the electoral votes of a single Southern state was an affront to Southern honor, for it suggested that the South was now politically irrelevant.

These two events portended more than just abolitionist aggression and Republican hegemony. They thrust to the fore certain worrisome matters that the South was loath to acknowledge, threats not external but internal. Though Southerners loudly affirmed how much they distrusted the Yankees, they only reluctantly admitted how much they distrusted each other.

Many Southerners—especially aristocrats gazing down on society from the top—understood that loyalty to the Southern social order was directly proportional to the benefits received from it. Aristocrats thus had some misgivings about the yeomen, while yeomen and aristocrats alike had substantial misgivings about the poor whites. As long as the South was free from outside interference, there seemed no great danger of unrest. But Lincoln's election raised the prospect that Republicans would, by means of patronage, begin to build a constituency in the South. Would nonslaveholders, particularly the poor, be drawn by the Republicans' siren call? Many Southerners pondered that question and shuddered.[21]

The scariest phantasm haunting the Southern mind was not, however, a poor white Republican but a rebellious black slave. After all, as every

Southerner realized, blacks had the least to lose and the most to gain from the overthrow of the Southern regime. In public, whites boasted that not one slave in Virginia had risen up at John Brown's beckoning; but in private, they worried that the next John Brown would ignite a revolution.[22]

There was a curious personal twist to white racial anxieties. Those who owned slaves (about one white family out of four in the South as a whole) did not as a rule fear their own: it was everyone else's they were really nervous about. Masters generally saw themselves as benign paternalists and believed (wrongly, for the most part) that their bondsmen and bondswomen were grateful, satisfied, and loyal. But when they looked beyond their own farms or plantations, slaveholders could not be so sanguine. By 1860, they along with other Southern whites lived in mortal terror of an abolitionist-led slave revolt.[23]

Vivid portents of Yankee domination and domestic unrest, a firm conviction that the cultures of North and South had taken separate paths, and a vague unease about the distant future brought forth a radical majority in the Lower South that took seven states out of the Union in the weeks after Lincoln's election. The Upper South held back from the precipice, however. Then in April 1861 came the third and final shove: the attack on Fort Sumter and Lincoln's subsequent call for troops to suppress the rebellion. Forced now to choose sides in a war, four states of the Upper South seceded and joined with the Lower South to defend the Southern way of life.[24]

Under the banner of the Confederate States of America, those eleven states girded themselves for battle against the North. Across most of the Confederacy public enthusiasm burst forth with great ardor. Patriotic rallies, parades, and martial gasconade were the order of the day. Aristocrats, yeomen, and poor whites alike hailed the Stars and Bars, pledged fealty to the Southern nation, and vowed to whip the Yankees.[25]

This apparent unity was, for the most part, real. Southerners of all classes had generally seen the events of the preceding years from a common perspective. One did not have to be a slaveowner or a Southern rights fanatic to conclude that the South was menaced by abolitionists and Republicans. Even the most conservative Southerners—those who stood fast after Lincoln's election, who deplored secession and clung to the hope of sectional compromise—were, in many cases, thoroughly radicalized by the North's decision for war.[26]

As loud and harmonious as the patriotic chorus of the Confederacy was, however, it could not drown out the protests of the otherwise-minded. Even as Southerners toasted their new nation and joined hands to defend it, they had to confront the fact that they were not a wholly united people.

Unionism in the Confederate South was a complex phenomenon, not easily defined or explained. Unionists ran the gamut from passive to active, from those who simply remained convinced that secession was wrong to those who actually took up arms against the Confederacy. Whatever the extent of their dissension, Southern Unionists were branded as pariahs. All wars generate a crisis atmosphere that stirs calls for unanimity, but secessionists in 1861 believed that they were fighting for their very survival; dissent was wholly intolerable, a lethal danger. They therefore turned on their Unionist neighbors with great fury, bringing to bear all the community's means of coercion, including public humiliation, shunning, and outright violence. Where Unionism was strong, Confederate civil and military authorities cracked down, too. The majority of Unionists were soon cowed and silenced; many of those who refused to bow down had to flee north for their lives.[27]

As the secessionists persecuted political dissenters, they also moved against blacks. The departure of many white men for the army sparked renewed concerns about slaves (and about the relatively few free blacks). Amid widespread rumors of plots and uprisings, every Confederate state strengthened its slave code, tightening restrictions on blacks and requiring county officials to beef up slave patrols. In many districts the patrols were reinforced by hastily organized "committees of public safety."[28]

Looming behind all these anxious precautions was the nightmarish specter of an armed horde of Yankees marching south. The outbreak of war ended Southern hopes for peaceful secession and made military invasion a certainty. Watching the North mobilize aggressively in the weeks after Fort Sumter, Southerners concluded that Republican demagogues had whipped the Northern masses into a frenzy. Northerners were now united, as a Southern newspaper editor put it, "in one common purpose, and that purpose is *war to the knife.*"[29]

Drawing on their preconceived notions about the North, some Southerners conjured up a frightening prospect. As men without honor, spawned by the North's depraved society, the invading Yankees would most certainly be savages. They would refuse to wage war as gentlemen: they would pillage, destroy, and rape. Moreover, as minions of the diabolical Republican administration they would ally with the Southern Unionists, stir up the poor whites, and incite the blacks to mutiny and butchery.[30]

With such forebodings Southerners braced for invasion in 1861. For all their bluster about a short war and certain victory, none really felt secure. Nervously they stood watch at the borders, and nervously they stood watch at home.

[1]

Citizens and Soldiers

The First Invasions and Early Occupation Policy

Three weeks after the war began, a worried citizen of northern Virginia warned the state military commander about "the condition of things on this exposed frontier." Yankee troops were already massing on the border, he claimed, "not regular and disciplined soldiers, but fanatics and lawless ruffians ready for every outrage and violence." At about the same time, four other northern Virginians raised the alarm. "If devastation and plunder are to form a part of the system of this war, this is certainly an inviting field for it," they wrote. "This was selected as the theater of John Brown's raid, and . . . these Northern troops will be apt to follow [Brown's] footsteps."[1]

Indeed, tocsins clanged all along the Potomac's south shore in those first weeks of war, for northern Virginia was the North's likeliest target. But elsewhere, too, Southerners apprehended imminent danger. Tennesseans and Arkansans, like Virginians, lived on the Confederacy's northern frontier; they were safe only as long as the North hesitated to send armies through the border states of Kentucky and Missouri. Residents of the Atlantic and Gulf coasts were defenseless against amphibious invasion. People along the Mississippi knew that the river was a highway to their doorsteps.

The fears that gripped the South in the wake of Fort Sumter convulsed the most threatened regions, and the closer the prospect of actual invasion loomed the more frenzied was the public agitation. Repeatedly the specter of the predatory Yankee soldier was invoked. A group of tidewater Virginians, beseeching the Confederate War Department for protection, pointed to their region's wealth of resources, "all of which, as well as the lives and liberties of our people generally, and the honor of our women, is exposed to the marauding depredations of the enemy." A resident of Virginia's isolated eastern shore likewise pleaded for Confederate troops: "Being at war, as we are, with an unrelenting and profligate enemy, the women and children of every locality ought to be assured of some protection."[2]

For every admonition about the enemy at the gates, moreover, there was another about the enemy within. "[T]he slave population is becoming restless and discontented," warned the tidewater Virginians in their letter to the War Department. A woman in the same region begged Virginia's governor to exempt her son from militia duty; he was one of the few white men left in the neighborhood, she explained, and without him "I would be exposed to the treachery of the blacks, and the cruelty of an invading foe." Citizens of Loudoun County in northern Virginia asked for Confederate troops not only to protect their rich harvest of corn and wheat, but also to overawe the county's numerous Unionists. A coastal North Carolinian reported that the most patriotic men in his region had volunteered and gone to the front, leaving "a majority . . . unsound and unreliable in case of an attack by the enemy." In tidewater Virginia, a Confederate officer urged quick action to "prevent the possibility of the disaffected element from gaining the ascendency"—an element he identified with poor whites "who have refused to volunteer, and who would undoubtedly join the enemy at the first opportunity."[3]

Civil and military authorities in the threatened regions took action. Along the Gulf coast, for example, the alarm was sounded after Union warships and troopships began gathering offshore in December 1861. The following March, at the request of Louisiana's governor, the Confederacy declared martial law in New Orleans and surrounding parishes. All white males over the age of sixteen were required to register with the provost marshal, and those claiming Confederate citizenship had to take an oath of allegiance; all persons not in sympathy with the Confederacy were to leave "without delay"; citizens were encouraged to report suspected subversives. Fearful of spies, the mayor of New Orleans banned street masking, and Mardi Gras that year was an unusually quiet affair.[4]

On the Gulf coast, and at other points of danger, authorities tightened the screws on the black and white underclass. Restrictions on slaves and free blacks were redoubled, patrols were strengthened, and some slave-owners removed their bondsmen and bondswomen to safer regions. In southeastern Virginia a Confederate officer worried that fishermen along the James River, many of them free blacks, might serve as guides for the Federal army; "I shall order these free negroes to be arrested," he decided, ". . . and the fishing skiffs to be destroyed—those of low white men as well as those of the negroes. Some of the whites are as dangerous as the negroes." In Pensacola, where martial law was in force, the commanding officer took note of "certain hungry, worthless people, white as well as colored, who frequent Pensacola and vicinity and who have no observable occupation. . . . [T]hey are warned to leave or the consequences must be on their own heads. The gallows is erected at Pensacola and will be in constant use."[5]

In most of the endangered areas the Confederate army was stretched too thin to repel an invasion in force. Citizens and civil officials therefore took steps to strengthen the militia and recruit local home defense units. In northern Mississippi, for instance, residents organized "independent scouts" and "military home guard" companies whose purpose was "to annoy the enemy" and "not only to watch, to pursue & to [gather] information but to waylay & strike." In northern Arkansas's White County, local men banded together informally in 1862 "to fight any enemy that came into the County."[6]

There were some who scoffed at such precautions, insisting that the Yankee threat was still remote. But their complacency evaporated the moment the Northern armies actually appeared. The approach of the enemy in force ended all doubts about the imminence of danger and evoked the South's worst fears. "A reckless and unprincipled tyrant has invaded your soil," Confederate general P. G. T. Beauregard told the people of northern Virginia as a Union army moved south from Washington in June 1861. "Abraham Lincoln . . . has thrown his abolition hosts among you. . . . All rules of civilized warfare are abandoned, and they proclaim by their acts, if not on their banners, that their war-cry is 'Beauty and booty.' "[7]

A few weeks later Beauregard and his army met the enemy forces at Manassas and sent them fleeing back to Washington. The reprieve was a brief one, however. By the following spring much of northern Virginia was in Union hands, along with substantial territory elsewhere in the Confederacy, including parts of southeastern Virginia and all of the eastern shore; points along the coasts of North Carolina, South Carolina, and Florida; southeastern Louisiana along the Mississippi River, including New Orleans and Baton Rouge; middle and western Tennessee, including Nashville and Memphis; and sections of Arkansas, northern Mississippi, and northern Alabama. In some cases Union military occupation followed a climactic battle or maneuver that sent the Rebel army reeling in retreat. Often, especially in the case of coastal incursions, there was simply no substantial Confederate force to oppose the enemy.

Shock, confusion, panic: thus did eyewitnesses describe the scene in every invaded region as word spread that the Yankees were coming and could not be stopped. "There is great Panic in town," a South Carolinian reported after the Federals landed at nearby Hilton Head in November 1861, "—particularly among the women." "[E]very one is almost wild with excitement," wrote a Louisianan upriver from New Orleans just after the city fell; "oh what dreadful news it is." As Union troops entered Virginia's Shenandoah Valley in early 1862, Kate Sperry in Winchester described the townspeople as "all crazy—perfectly frantic."[8]

The turmoil in the invaded districts was often aggravated by uncertainty about the enemy's exact location and intentions. With communications disrupted and facts scarce, rumors flourished. "[H]undreds of reports verry contradictory," middle Tennessean Nimrod Porter noted in his journal as the Yankees approached in February 1862; "The awful state of affairs, and the greate uncertainty of events, & the suspense is truly almost too much for me to beare."[9]

The most chaotic scenes were enacted in the cities, for the strategic importance of the cities invited enemy attack and the concentration of people magnified the general hysteria. Nashville, for example, was thrown into utter panic in February 1862 after Fort Donelson fell and the Confederate army began retreating south. News that the Yankees were coming arrived on a Sunday as the citizens were at church. "The congregations . . .

were dismissed," Nashvillian Louisa Pearl reported, "& people were seen hurrying to & fro like crazy people not knowing what to do." By nightfall the post office and the newspapers had shut down, and the governor, the state legislators, and the public archives were on a train headed out of town. Over the next few days stores and markets closed, and groceries, coal, and firewood grew scarce. Paper money became worthless and banks were emptied of specie by frantic depositors. Unable to carry off all the commissary and quartermaster stores, Confederate troops threw open government warehouses to the public, and unruly crowds of citizens gathered to help themselves.[10]

New Orleans witnessed similar scenes two months later as a Federal fleet steamed up the Mississippi River toward the city. Terror seized the populace, businesses and schools closed, military and civil officials left in haste. Mobs broke into the public warehouses, carried off food, and burned or dumped into the river all they could not take. Another mob entered a government munitions factory and seized guns and ammunition.[11]

When Confederate troops prepared to pull out, citizens who earlier had welcomed their presence now found reason to deplore it. In such cities as Nashville and New Orleans military authorities grew desperate in their effort to remove war materiel. Feverishly they rounded up and put to work every man and boy they could lay hands on and seized every horse, mule, carriage, wagon, boat, and railroad car they found. Worse yet was the outright destruction of public and private property. Because everything of use to the enemy had to be removed or demolished, Confederate armies in retreat left a trail of ruin. The citizens of New Orleans watched in dismay as thirteen thousand bales of cotton went up in flames along the levee; nearby in the water drifted the burning remains of boats that could not be taken away. Upriver at Baton Rouge the cotton was drenched with the city's whiskey supply before being set to the torch. Nashvillians lost two fine bridges across the Cumberland River; the people of Fredericksburg, Virginia, lost three across the Rappahannock. In and around Jacksonville, Florida, Confederate soldiers laid waste to sawmills, warehouses, factories, and a railroad station. Most galling of all was the frequent pillaging and wanton vandalism by retreating troops. In Nashville the last remaining soldiers made themselves so obnoxious by drinking and looting that at least one resident was ready to welcome the enemy. "I do hope the Northern army will come & take possession soon," Louisa

Pearl wrote, "or we shall all be in danger. I fear [the Confederates] may take it into their heads to burn us out when they get ready to go."[12]

Many citizens in the invaded areas decided not to await the enemy's arrival, but instead to flee. Some began packing and moving out at the first alarm; as the Yankees neared, roads grew clogged with refugees in wagons and carriages or on foot. Steamboats and railroad cars were likewise jammed with frightened men, women, and children carrying bundles of belongings. Witnesses often vividly described the scene. A South Carolinian in Beaufort in November 1861 "found the people under intense excitement, the mass of whom were making preparations to go to some place of safety on the main-land. . . . I found that the steamer was almost filled with the various and voluminous properties of the citizens, who were eagerly taking advantage of any and every method to get their things away." Middle Tennessean Nimrod Porter breathlessly recounted the "greate excitement" in his community in February 1862: "people leaving every where for the south. . . . [O]ure state bank in Columbia packing up for a run off with all the money[.] Thousands people come from Nashville to Columbia a perfect stampead."[13]

The likeliest persons to flee were leading secessionists, high-ranking Confederate officials, and former Federal officeholders. Such men—be they politicians, judges, civil servants, or other public figures—were generally convinced that their fate at the hands of the enemy would be at least a dungeon cell and possibly a noose. Furthermore, the most zealous and outspoken Confederate loyalists in any community frequently became refugees, too, even if they were people of no particular prominence, either from fear of reprisals or from an especially intense abhorrence of Yankee rule.[14]

Aristocrats were also among those most likely to forsake their homes, for several reasons. First of all, they tended to be among the Confederacy's most fervent champions. And, too, many held conspicuous public positions. Moreover, they had much to lose materially if the invaders turned out to be as rapacious as they were reputed to be. Although fleeing meant abandoning real property, it meant saving a good deal of personal property—especially slaves, but also other valuable, movable possessions such as currency, bonds, jewelry, silverware, and furniture. Furthermore, the aristocrats' wealth, professional skills, and wide social contacts eased the disruptions of refugee life: planters could obtain land and equipment in the interior and return to farming; professional men could procure a house and office and resume business. In fact, many aristocrats in the exposed regions made plans for evacuation and purchased or rented homes in the interior well before any Yankees appeared.[15]

For every Southerner who fled, however, there were many more who decided to stay and face the enemy. One factor in their decision was the hardship and uncertainty of refugee life. Even for those with plentiful resources and good health, the prospect of taking to the road and beginning a new life was daunting. Another factor was the desire to protect property that could not be removed. This was especially common among the yeomen, who had few or no slaves and little other movable property of any great value but who owned farms or shops on which they depended for their living. For most such people, and many wealthier ones as well, fear of losing home and livelihood prevailed over fear of the enemy.[16]

Among many who stayed there was a strong suspicion that the Yankees were not really as beastly as they were cracked up to be, or, at least, that they could be dealt with if one could muster the courage to confront them. One explanation for this is that a good number of Southerners had enough personal acquaintance with Northerners to discredit the most exaggerated stereotypes; and, too, since the beginning of the war the Northern government had repeatedly denied any radical or punitive aims. To what extent Southerners may thus have been comforted about the invaders is hard to gauge. But the fact is that many chose not to flee who certainly would have been among the first to go if they really believed every story about the enemy. Many merchants, for example, remained with their wares and many county and municipal officials remained with their records in spite of the Yankees' alleged penchant for sacking and burning. Substantial numbers of planters remained at home with their slaves despite reports that the Yankees were coming to finish the work John Brown had begun.[17]

Especially noteworthy is the fact that women in great numbers declined to flee despite rumors that the Northern soldiers intended to rape their way through the South. Older women, in particular, often manifested no terror of the enemy and seemed confident that they could come to terms with them. In some families, mothers remained at home while daughters were sent into the interior. In many cases husbands and older sons fled, leaving wives and mothers to protect the home, in the belief that the Federals would not dare to mistreat women. It appears, in fact, that on the whole women were *less* likely than men to become refugees, suggesting that the often-invoked image of the Yankee as rapist was more a propaganda device than a genuine article of popular faith.[18]

Just how many Southerners left the invaded regions is hard to judge. The frequent reports of towns and communities wholly or nearly abandoned must be evaluated with care. In many cases rural folk left home only to seek refuge in the woods nearby, while townspeople often fled just a few miles into the countryside where they were taken in by friends or relatives; many of these fugitives returned home within a few days or weeks, having decided to face the enemy rather than remain in hiding.[19]

In most invaded areas only a small minority of the inhabitants fled for good. In St. Augustine, Florida, it appears that about one-fifth of the population left. In Nashville, perhaps a thousand persons departed, leaving at least sixteen thousand in the city.[20]

There is no doubt, however, that in a few sections many or most of the inhabitants left and stayed away for the duration of the war. This was particularly evident in the plantation districts along the South Carolina and Georgia coast, whose population consisted mostly of very wealthy planter families and their slaves. In some of those districts, depopulation was nearly complete; often no one remained to greet the invaders save a few very old and very young slaves left behind by their masters.[21]

The flight of thousands of Southerners before the Northern onslaught had important consequences for those who stayed. The communities that would endure Union occupation were in certain respects already shaken, weakened, or transfigured before the first blue-clad regiment marched in. In a matter of days or even hours, ranking civil and military figures and the most passionate secessionists—the head and heart of Confederate nationalism and Rebel defiance—had mostly disappeared; they left behind, in many localities, a jubilant contingent of long-suffering Unionists and a larger body of citizens stunned and disheartened by Confederate withdrawal and outraged by the behavior of the retreating troops. Also gone were many aristocrats, and with them much of the pride and self-assurance that bolstered the South's ruling class; yeomen and poor whites who remained at home no doubt observed with some interest the unseemly panic among the elite families that fled and the nervous uncertainty among those that stayed. Likewise, slaves scrutinized their masters' anxious faces and perhaps sensed that, whatever the Yankees might do, white authority was in some way already compromised. Patriarchy, too, was compromised, as women watched their menfolk flee and prepared to confront the enemy alone.

For those citizens who chose to remain at home there was another decision to be faced: to fight or not to fight when the Northern army appeared. Militia companies existed, at least on paper, in all the invaded regions, and in some communities men and boys had formed unofficial or quasi-official home defense units at the first sign of enemy threat. But would these local troops stand and give battle after the Confederate army pulled out? And even if they would, should they?

Some believed that a show of strength by the local militia or home defense company might at least keep smaller enemy detachments at bay. Some even thought that organized partisan warfare could significantly disrupt larger enemy forces. In some invaded regions, therefore, the cry went out to take up arms. The governor of Tennessee called out the militia when his state was invaded and Confederate military resistance collapsed. In southeastern Louisiana, Confederate general Mansfield Lovell urged the residents to form partisan bands when he was forced to withdraw his regular forces upriver.[22]

Almost without exception, such efforts to rally citizen forces failed. Although a few individuals grabbed their guns and headed into the woods determined to fight a guerrilla war, the citizenry as a whole declined to resist invasion by force of arms. In Louisiana, one resident reported that the attempt to organize a partisan unit in his parish "has all ended in smoke." The story was the same in other places. "Where is the boasted chivalry of North Ala[bama]," a Tuscumbia man asked sarcastically in April 1862. The citizens, he said, had earlier vowed that "each one of them would shoulder his *shot gun* and meet the invaders and fight until death for every inch of the soil of Alabama. . . . Now what spectacle presents itself today. When the Northern soldiers landed at Decatur, every one [of the citizens] . . . took to their heels and have concealed themselves."[23]

There were at least three reasons why organized resistance did not materialize when the Yankee army first appeared. For one thing, the wholesale flight of high-ranking officials and other prominent figures undoubtedly deprived some communities of the necessary leadership cadre. Second, the sense of betrayal, abandonment, and disillusionment occasioned by the retreat of the Rebel army may have sapped the public's will to fight. And third, there was the matter of perspective. To someone at a safe distance from the enemy, armed civilian resistance might seem a noble and worthwhile effort; but up close, face-to-face with huge invading forces and the awesome reality of Federal power, it more often seemed futile and potentially disastrous. In McMinnville, Tennessee, the citizens dutifully assembled in March 1862 in response to the governor's militia proclamation, only to decide "that no organization could go on here, now, as we are all under Lincoln rule, and his army is so near us." The mayor of Jacksonville, Florida, having duly considered the pros and cons of resistance as the enemy approached, publicly advised his constituents to submit peacefully. So did the magistrates of Pasquotank County, North Carolina. In southeastern Louisiana, General Lovell's proposed partisan corps aroused frantic opposition. "*[C]itizens earnestly entreated, that the corps should not be raised* there," Lovell reported, "unless I could send a large body of troops to protect them from the additional outrages to which they would be subject from the Yankees, for having raised such a Corps. . . . When I urged that the bridges over the railroad be destroyed, a parish delegation entreated that it be not done, as it would bring down upon them Yankee vengeance."[24]

Though inclined to yield without a fight to Federal occupation, most citizens in the invaded regions remained resolutely determined to subjugate the enemies in their midst. In the last days and hours before the Northerners arrived—indeed, sometimes even as Union warships or troops came into view—citizens and local authorities moved to head off trouble by redoubling the crackdown on blacks, Unionists, and poor whites.

Only a few citizens actually detected any restiveness among blacks as the Union army neared, but all agreed that precautions were in order. "I am afraid of the lawless Yankee soldiers," confessed Betty Maury of Fredericksburg after Federal forces appeared across the Rappahannock in April 1862, "but that is nothing [next] to my fear of the negroes if they should rise against us." Racial anxieties were likewise heightened on the North Carolina coast when Northern forces entered Albemarle Sound in February 1862: the magistrates of Pasquotank County, having resolved to submit to the invaders, nevertheless called up the local militia—not to do battle, but to patrol the county. Shortly after the fall of New Orleans, officials of St. Charles Parish, just upriver from the city, called a special meeting on the slave problem; they not only strengthened the existing patrol system but also created a "River Police" to watch the river night and day "and to arrest all negroes passing up or down in skiffs or otherwise."[25]

Some Unionists were brutally mistreated on the eve of their deliverance, even though they, like the blacks, carefully concealed their emotions as the Federals approached. The night before Union forces occupied Hertford County, North Carolina, on Albemarle Sound, vigilantes there rounded up several Unionists and carried them off at gunpoint. In Jacksonville, Florida, Unionists heard rumors that the retreating Rebel troops meant to kill them and destroy their property. The troops proved to be rather restrained, but an armed mob of secessionist citizens wreaked horrible vengeance on the Unionists, looting and torching their homes and stores, murdering three, and sending the rest fleeing in terror. As this occurred, Union gunboats were just a few miles down the St. Johns River; they arrived in Jacksonville the next morning.[26]

Unlike blacks and Unionists, poor whites sometimes grew obstreperous in the confusion attending the Confederate army's withdrawal. When they did, authorities and "respectable" citizens reacted quickly and harshly. In Nashville, poor whites rioted while carrying off abandoned government supplies. Confederate cavalry was called in to disperse them, and when the cavalry proved inadequate the mayor summoned a fire engine to hose down the mob. When the troops pulled out, the mayor recruited a citizen police force to keep order. In New Orleans, whose huge white underclass had long bedeviled the authorities, the Confederate retreat triggered widespread rioting and looting. The city police were overpowered and the mayor had to call on a local defense unit, the European Brigade, for help. Order was restored only after considerable head cracking and mass arrests. In the interim before the Federal occupation force arrived, the mayor assumed emergency powers and reinforced the police and the European Brigade with a hastily organized citizen constabulary. As calm returned to the city, the editor of the *Daily Picayune* congratulated officials on their efforts to "restrain the rougher elements of our population" under conditions "which have loosened the bands of authority and the habits of obedience. . . . Extraordinary efforts are called for among the reflecting and order loving portion of the community to repress manifestations of disorder, maintain peace and defend the rights of property."[27]

When the last Rebel soldiers and refugees had departed, when order had been secured and the remaining citizens had retired to their homes or gone into hiding, a strange stillness descended on the invaded districts. "The city seems deserted," wrote Louisa Pearl of Nashville in the final hours before the advent of the Yankees, "—it seems like . . . a big empty house." Betty Maury described the scene in Fredericksburg as the Union army took position just across the river: "Every thing is so quiet, the stores have been closed for the last three days, and the streets are deserted except by negroes."[28]

The emotions of those awaiting the invaders ranged from muted joy to cautious optimism to fearful uncertainty, with the last predominating. "The Yankees are in our Parish," Louisianan Mittie Bond wrote in her diary; "My husband and his brother . . . have fled for their lives—are exiles from home. God only knows what the consequence will be. We are looking for the Yankees every moment—such suspense, such agony of mind." As a Union fleet anchored just beyond the levee, a New Orleans man confessed that "we are all in confusion" and worried that the occupiers would be unable "to organise matters to avoid starvation, bloodshed & general trouble amongst the lower classes." Another Louisianan, planter Isaac Erwin, prophesied that his community would be "devastated by sword and Fire[.] A Kind Providence alone can protect us." In middle Tennessee, preacher Jesse Cox learned that the enemy was very near: "will the Lord save us," he pleaded, "from such an unreasonable foe."[29]

Many such appeals went heavenward as the Union forces approached, many earnest prayers that the Lord, Who for His own inscrutable reasons had delivered some of His people into the hands of the foe, would at least preserve them from the foe's worst passions. Other prayers went up, too, though fewer and quieter, prayers that the coming of the Northmen would bring a new dispensation. Which supplicants would the Lord favor? The answer was at hand, for the sound of distant drums and marching feet was growing louder.

. . .

The Northern soldiers who invaded the South in 1861 and the first months of 1862 carried with them a set of sectional stereotypes and preconceptions hardly less distorted than those embraced by Southerners. They also brought along a clear sense of mission, but it was far from the radical, malevolent design that many Southerners imagined.

Like the people of the South, those of the North had come to believe that the American nation comprised two increasingly divergent cultures. Most Northerners insisted that their own society—progressive, democratic, egalitarian, and free—was the legitimate heir of American ideals, whereas Southern society—stagnant, aristocratic, hierarchical, and unfree—was a bastard child, a feudal atavism. Atop Southern society, as most Northerners saw it, there sat a haughty and brutal slaveowning elite, "lords of the lash" who ruled in their own interest over the downtrodden slaves and degraded poor whites (few Northerners conceded that anything like a respectable middle class existed below the Mason-Dixon line). Not content to tyrannize their own benighted region, some of these aristocrats had colluded in a "Slave Power conspiracy" to seize control of the national government and thus dominate the North. But having failed in that aim, they had duped many of the poor whites into supporting secession and then led the South out of the Union.[30]

To a great many Northerners, secession was intolerable. The Founding Fathers had warned that republics were peculiarly susceptible to demagoguery, corruption, anarchy, and despotism, and secession seemed the very embodiment of those evils. Furthermore, many in the North were deeply committed to the belief that the American experiment in democracy was of world-historical import; secession was a rejection of democracy which, if successful, would discredit republican government and dishearten the friends of liberty around the globe. Finally, the firing on Fort Sumter galvanized Northerners no less than Southerners and persuaded even those who had been inclined to let the seceding states go in peace that the South was now waging a war of aggression that threatened the very survival of the republic.[31]

From the highest levels of government down to the common citizen, Northern war aims at the outbreak of the conflict were thoroughly conservative. Most Northerners desired only to depose the revolutionary clique of "slavocrats" and ambitious politicians who had engineered secession and to reestablish the supremacy of the national government throughout the South. Few Northerners sought the overthrow of slavery, for although most considered the institution morally corrupting and economically stifling and wanted to halt its spread, they deemed blacks unfit for freedom in a republic. Moreover, Federal policymakers hesitated to take any action regarding slavery that might alienate Southern Unionists, especially those in the border states still in the Union.[32]

The U.S. Congress affirmed these narrow goals in the Crittenden Resolution of July 1861, passed with hardly a dissenting vote, which declared "that this war is not waged, on our part, in any spirit of oppression, nor for any purpose of conquest or subjugation, nor purpose of overthrowing or interfering with the rights or established institutions of these States, but to defend and maintain the supremacy of the Constitution and to preserve the Union, . . . as soon as these objects are accomplished the war ought to cease." These last twelve words reflected the fear that a prolonged war might rage out of control, burst its bonds, and devour the very ideals and institutions it was meant to preserve. Abraham Lincoln himself worried that an extended conflict would "degenerate into a violent and remorseless revolutionary struggle." Nevertheless, most Northerners anticipated a quick victory, for they were convinced that the Confederacy lacked moral strength, that it was a house built on sand.[33]

The belief that secession was a conspiracy by an elite cabal dictated a twofold policy: stern measures against the Rebel leaders, liberation and conciliation for the mass of Southern whites. Northerners assumed that a large proportion of the Confederacy's citizens were loyal Unionists subjugated and silenced by the Rebel despots; most of the rest were simply ignorant pawns manipulated by secessionist rabble-rousers. The Unionists must be freed from tyranny and protected by Federal bayonets; the others must be enlightened and coaxed back into the arms of the Union. Punishing or terrorizing the Southern people or tampering with their peculiar way of life would, most Northerners believed, merely play into the hands of the Slave Power.[34]

With such notions and intentions Northerners rallied to the cause and enlisted by the hundreds of thousands in the first year of the war. As the great armies of the republic formed ranks and moved southward in 1861 and early 1862, commanders repeatedly lectured their soldiers on the war's goals and the need to win back the Southern citizens led astray by false prophets. General Don Carlos Buell reminded the Army of the Ohio: "We are in arms, not for the purpose of invading the rights of our fellow-countrymen anywhere, but to maintain the integrity of the Union and protect the Constitution." General Henry W. Halleck informed his troops that the people of the South "have been told that we come to oppress and plunder. By our acts we will undeceive them." General William T. Sherman warned his men that misconduct "attaches itself to the cause, and prevents that respect with which it should be our aim to impress our enemies now, who must become our friends before peace can be hoped for." Above all, military authorities wished to allay Southerners' fears on the sensitive subject of slavery, hoping thereby to woo them more readily back to the Union. "[T]hey have got it into their heads that we want to steal and emancipate their negroes," said General John A. Dix as he readied a force to invade Virginia's eastern shore in November 1861; ". . . by giving them the strongest assurances of kind treatment and protection . . . they may be gained over without bloodshed."[35]

Such pronouncements from army headquarters were not generally motivated by any suspicion that the soldiers had renounced conciliation in principle, but rather from an understanding of the natural bumptiousness and rowdiness of raw troops on campaign. Subordinate officers in the field likewise knew the inclinations of citizen-soldiers and therefore reiterated the standing orders as they led their columns into Dixie. Colonel John W. Geary of the Twenty-eighth Pennsylvania Infantry halted his regiment after crossing the Potomac and reaching the outskirts of Lovettsville, Virginia, and there, according to one soldier, "made a few remarks, admonishing us to act as Gentlemen and not as the Seceshionist[s] termed us, Brutes, Robbers &c."[36]

As Colonel Geary's final words echoed across the northern Virginia countryside, the men of the Twenty-eighth shouldered their muskets and started toward Lovettsville with flags flying and the regimental band playing. In the town, as in hundreds of other towns and villages abandoned by the Confederacy during the first year of the war, men and women listened, watched, and waited.

• • •

For some Southerners, one glimpse of the enemy was enough to confirm prevailing beliefs about Yankee character. Kate Sperry watched Union troops enter Winchester in March 1862 and declared that she "never saw as many faces where evil predominated—a kind of sinister expression— horrible to look at." A little later she characterized the occupiers as "the meanest set of *poor white trash* I ever beheld." When the Federals captured Tuscumbia, Alabama, in April 1862, one resident described the scene succinctly and contemptuously: "Town swarming with low dutch & Irish."[37]

Whatever their appearance, the Northerners' behavior on arrival almost always belied the gloomiest predictions. The horde of vandals and cutthroats many Southerners had expected generally turned out to be a rather reserved and well-disciplined body of soldiers. In fact, the first experience of occupation, at least for residents of cities and larger towns, was often an official ceremony in which the invaders marched in to the accompaniment of martial music, accepted the formal surrender of the town, raised the Stars and Stripes, proclaimed their authority, and announced their intentions. Such rituals, though humiliating to proud Confederate citizens, at least indicated that anarchy was not at hand, and that the Yankees would observe certain proprieties in due and ancient form.[38]

The official proclamations of the military authorities were reassuring. "[W]e have come amongst you with no feelings of personal animosity," declared General Thomas W. Sherman when his troops landed at Port Royal, South Carolina, in November 1861, "no desire to harm your citizens, destroy your property, or interfere with any of your lawful rights or your social and local institutions." General Dix assured the residents of Virginia's eastern shore that his soldiers "go among you as friends. . . . They will invade no rights of person or property; on the contrary, your laws, your institutions, your usages will be scrupulously respected." After taking Roanoke Island, North Carolina, General Ambrose E. Burnside informed the citizens that his sole purpose was "to assert the authority of the United States, and thus to close with you the desolating war brought upon your State by comparatively a few bad men in your midst. . . . They impose upon your credulity by telling you of wicked and even diabolical intentions on our part; of our desire to destroy your freedom, demolish your property, liberate your slaves, injure your women, and such like enormities, all of which, we assure you, is not only ridiculous, but utterly and willfully false."[39]

At the same time, however, the occupiers made it clear that they had come to stamp out rebellion and would brook no defiance of Federal authority. Active resistance would not be tolerated, nor would citizens be permitted to give aid and comfort to the armed enemies of the United

States; furthermore, all persecution of Unionists must cease. Stern warnings on these matters went forth from military headquarters hand in hand with the propitiatory appeals. The army authorities were also committed to apprehending the secessionist ringleaders, but that was a moot point, for the top Rebel leaders had fled. The occupiers therefore contented themselves with seizing the departed secessionists' homes, along with public buildings and other facilities abandoned by the Rebel government and army.[40]

Having thus asserted their authority and staked out the limits of their tolerance, the Federal army officials set out earnestly to win over the errant Southern people. Most eschewed mass arrests and mandatory loyalty oaths in favor of a "rosewater" policy of leniency and suasion; and they provided emergency rations and fuel to needy citizens and encouraged the quick resumption of agriculture, business, and local government. (In all this they were aided by the military governors whom President Lincoln appointed in 1862 for the occupied parts of Tennessee, Louisiana, Arkansas, and North Carolina, with orders to rally Union sentiment and initiate the reestablishment of loyal state governments.) The protection of private property was a matter of special concern. Some appropriation of property was unavoidable, for the armies were occasionally strapped for provisions and had to feed themselves off the land; they sometimes had to requisition horses, wagons, lumber, and tools when their own materiel ran short. But the high command insisted that this be done sparingly, legally, and with full compensation to owners. Subordinate commanders were ordered to do their requisitioning strictly by the book.[41]

Pillaging and vandalism by men in the ranks were persistent problems, as with all armies in all ages, but Northern commanders had anticipated those difficulties and took pains to curb them. In western Tennessee, for example, planter John H. Bills noted that the newly arrived Federals had "professed much good will to citizens & a determination not to despoil any property. . . . Most of the houses in town are guarded. All [citizens] that apply get guards." Scenes such as that witnessed by Betty Maury in Fredericksburg in May 1862—two soldiers lashed to a tree in front of the courthouse, beneath a sign reading "For entering private houses with out orders"—became common in the occupied regions and served not only to warn the troops but also to demonstrate the authorities' sincerity to the citizens.[42]

In their first face-to-face encounters with the invaders, many Southerners found them exceedingly conciliatory. The day St. Augustine was occupied a naval officer met with the town fathers "to calm any apprehension of harsh treatment that might exist in their minds" and then called on local ministers to ask them "to reassure their people and to confide in our kind intentions toward them." A Union army officer recounted his meeting with three women at a Virginia farmhouse in the spring of 1862: "They were almost beside themselves with fear, telling us they had heard such dreadful tales of the Yankee soldiers, and that they went to bed every night, expecting to have their throats cut and house burned down before morning. We quieted their fears . . . and soon talked them into a better state of mind." In the Shenandoah Valley, Lieutenant Colonel Alvin Voris of the Sixty-seventh Ohio reported that he was endeavoring "to make all I come in contact with feel as if we were not conquerors, that we did not feel exultant, . . . that we had no desire to play the tyrant."[43]

Again and again, Southerners remarked the astonishing fact that the Northern invaders could be well behaved, reasonable, obliging, even affable. Betty Maury was "much struck with the superior discipline of these Yankee soldiers over ours. I have not seen a drunken man since they have been here." A North Carolinian whose farm was visited by a squad of Northern soldiers reported that "they committed no depredations, except stealing a duck. . . . They were disposed to prowl about the yard & examine the premises, but at my representing to them the impropriety, they desisted"; on departing, the soldiers all shook hands with the farm owner and his young son. A woman in Columbia, Tennessee, wrote that she had met all the ranking Federal officers and "some of them I liked. Genl Buell was as nice a gentleman as I ever met he treated the people well."[44]

Not all Southerners were thus impressed by their initial encounters with the Northerners, however, for not all Northerners were so eager to please. Some appeared hostile, vengeful, or simply unruly. A Shenandoah Valley woman angrily described the first visit of the enemy to her plantation: "Some of these gallant Federal soldiers did not hesitate to use the most profane language in our presence, nor did their officers make the least attempt to restrain them. They searched the house from garret to cellars. . . . They threatened to burn the premises." But even those Southerners who suffered at the hands of undisciplined or vindictive Union troops often interpreted the experience ambivalently, sensing in the Yankees' behavior a degree of restraint. Roxa Cole of Ripley, Mississippi, told how the enemy descended on her town in 1862, "rob[b]ing our corn cribs . . ., ruining our gardens and fields, stealing horses"; and yet, she concluded, the town was lucky, for the soldiers did not pillage smokehouses or pantries, steal silver or jewelry, or arrest anyone "as we expected they would." Even where the Yankees were at their worst, they rarely went beyond vituperation and plundering: physical violence against peaceful citizens was almost unheard of.[45]

Not only did the invaders seem more or less well behaved, but they often appeared positively indulgent, tolerantly disregarding the citizens' sometimes provocative behavior. For example, when an Alabama woman boldly waved a Rebel flag and hurrahed for the Confederacy as Federal cavalry rode by, the troopers simply saluted and kept on riding. In Baton Rouge, a Presbyterian minister who noticed several Union officers among his Sunday congregation "did not allow their presence to keep me from offering up our prayers in behalf of our Confederacy" and indeed "went farther than usual"; nevertheless, the officers seemed to enjoy the service and complimented the minister afterward.[46]

Thus, the first encounters with the enemy were in certain respects a gratifying surprise to the citizens. The Yankees inflicted little destruction and almost no personal violence, and to that extent confounded earlier prophecies. But they might yet unleash racial chaos. Anxiously the citizens sought signs that would ease their fears about the fate of slavery.

The slaves themselves gave some troubling indications. For one thing, many made no effort to hide their jubilation when the Federal army appeared. When New Bern, North Carolina, was captured in March 1862, one witness described the town's blacks as "wild with excitement and delight." A Union officer leading his men through middle Tennessee at the same time wrote that "at every plantation negroes came flocking to the roadside to see us. They are the only friends we find. . . . [They] welcome us with extravagant manifestations of joy. They keep time to the [band] music with feet and hands and hurrah 'fur de ole flag and de Union.'" Moreover, blacks began sneaking away from home and hanging around the Union army camps wherever they could get away with it; some ran off to the camps with no intention of returning home. Others perpetrated more subtle acts of disloyalty to their masters. After a squad of soldiers went to Betty Maury's house and seized weapons, Maury discovered that one of her servants had tipped off the military authorities; the incident occurred only a few days after the Federals arrived in Fredericksburg, but already Maury had decided that her slaves were "getting very insolent and unbearable."[47]

There were, on the other hand, certain hopeful signs from the invaders. Both in word and deed, most of the occupation authorities gave evidence of a determination to safeguard slavery. General Dix's proclamation to the people of the Virginia eastern shore announced that "special directions have been given not to interfere with the conditions of any persons held to domestic service; . . . commanders of regiments and corps have been instructed not to permit any such persons to come within their lines." True to Dix's word, the subordinate commander who led the eastern shore invasion force routinely returned runaways to their masters; in one instance involving a slave who had repeatedly run off to the army camps, the commander ordered the man whipped in the presence of other black fugitives.[48]

Not all Federal officers were so accommodating. Although most considered blacks a nuisance and were glad to bar them from camp, some welcomed them as laborers; even those who turned blacks away did not always trouble to return them to their masters. But with the exception of cases falling under the first Confiscation Act (enacted by the U.S. Congress in August 1861 to prevent the return of runaway slaves who had been employed in the Rebel cause), Union officers did not as a rule interfere with masters' attempts to reclaim fugitives or in any other way challenge the masters' authority over their slaves. Occasionally soldiers in the ranks encouraged blacks to run off, out of mischief or vengeance or from antislavery principles, but such acts were not officially sanctioned. The Federal army was in no sense an active agent of emancipation during the first year of war. (In two instances where Union commanders exceeded their authority and declared slaves in their departments free— General John C. Frémont in 1861 and General David Hunter in 1862— President Lincoln promptly overruled them.)[49]

Most slaveowners and other Southern whites in the invaded regions therefore breathed a qualified sigh of relief. Thanks to the passive if not always active cooperation of the army, masters retained the power of compulsion over their slaves. The Yankee enlisted men would bear watching,

Southerners decided, but the officers appeared generally conservative and reliable. Moreover, the slaves themselves had confuted the direst predictions of whites: nowhere did Union invasion trigger the bloody servile uprising that many had feared; nowhere, in fact, did slaves react violently at all. The blacks did show a disturbing enthusiasm for the Yankees, but there were signs that it might soon wane as the slaves realized that the bluecoats were no abolitionists. Not long after the Federals entered Murfreesboro, Tennessee, for example, young Alice Ready wrote in her diary that "Papa is some what uneasy about one of his negro men, who was seen this evening in the [army] Camp," but the next day's diary entry reported: "Our negro returned this afternoon—he went into the Camp with a confederate coat on—they called him a secesh negro and put him to hard work . . . he gave them the slip and came home . . . says he will never leave his master again."[50]

Nevertheless, Southern whites could not rest easily as long as the enemy remained. The interposition of Federal military power had abruptly overturned the customary structure of authority. All authority was now exercised by the sufferance of the occupiers. Masters realized, perhaps with a certain sense of irony, that they were now wholly dependent on the Union army to sustain the institution of slavery. Thus far, through the spring of 1862, the Yankees seemed mostly agreeable; but who could foretell what changes the future might bring, and who could take for granted that which was contingent on the enemy's whim?

Furthermore, even if most masters still cherished the belief that their own slaves were loyal, they were growing increasingly doubtful of others and fearful of the corrosive effects of continued occupation. Joshua Moore of northern Alabama worried that blacks lingering around the army camps "will become demoralized and it will be a wonder if they do not commence the commission of crimes of the deepest dye. I apprehend great danger. . . . [O]ur negroes so far have kept at work, but if other negroes become demoralized they will corrupt others." Planter James Willcox in the Virginia tidewater reported that several slaves from neighboring plantations had run off. "None of my servants have left me yet," he added, "but I am looking out daily for them to do so. . . . [T]he worst has not [yet] come, God only knows what is to become of the country."[51]

Most Southerners in the invaded regions would readily have agreed with Willcox that God alone knew their fate. They searched anxiously for signs of His intentions, but the signs they saw were often obscure or contradictory. It seemed apparent that He had chosen the Northern army as the primary instrument of His will. All eyes, therefore, were on the invaders as the days of occupation lengthened into weeks and months.

. . .

As Southerners scrutinized the enemy they were in turn being scrutinized. Like travelers in a foreign land, the Northern soldiers who marched into the South in 1861 and early 1862 gazed with fascination at exotic sights. The guidebooks they carried—that is to say, their preconceptions about Southern society and the origins of secession—were in many ways mistaken or exaggerated, but they were authoritative and persuasive and thus shaped the Northerners' interpretation of all they saw.

Many Union soldiers who took part in those early invasions found confirmation of their belief that the Confederacy was a hollow shell that would quickly crumble. Despite a few stunning Confederate military victories, notably in Virginia, Federal forces had seized considerable Rebel territory by the spring of 1862, often with little or no opposition.

It was not just the impotence of the Confederate army that impressed many Northerners; it was also the apparent submissiveness, or at least innocuousness, of the Southern citizenry. Among the first sights that many Union soldiers saw in the invaded regions were white flags hung from houses or public buildings. Often the first Southern citizens they met were timorous municipal officials coming forth with hat in hand to surrender their town, offer assurances of the inhabitants' peacefulness, and plead for mercy. Moreover, the civilian population as a whole seemed unthreatening: the white people seen were mostly women, children, and old men, many of them obviously frightened, peeking furtively from windows; the blacks were friendly, some exuberantly so. There was no armed and organized civilian resistance as the army marched in: no local militia company standing firm to block the Federal advance, no partisan unit firing from ambush. Scattered, small-scale guerrilla attacks did begin to crop up in a few areas by the spring of 1862, notably in Tennessee and northern Alabama where the Federals had penetrated deeply into the Confederacy. But most of the invaded districts remained quiet, and the Yankees saw little or no evidence that the populace as a whole was actively resisting occupation.[52]

What Northern soldiers did see in Dixie was the alien and backward culture they had envisioned. "The people the army found in Virginia," wrote a newspaperman who covered the Peninsula campaign of 1862, "seemed to be an entirely different race from that living in the North,— one which had degenerated in intellect, energy, and every thing which makes up the character of true manhood. . . . [T]he habits of all were such as to astonish sober, steady-going Northerners." An army officer in western Tennessee agreed: "They are all lazy, and do not want to work dow[n] here. If it was not for their negroes they would starve to death." Moreover, he observed, the wealthy reside "in large ellegant Houses, have plenty [of] fine furniture, and live well, are ve[ry] aristocratic. But the poor are the most misserable looking thing[s] you ever saw, a great deal worse off than the negroes, ragged, and dirty, and they live in little Misserable Huts, on Corn Bread, and Pork." Many other Northerners were likewise struck by the class disparities they saw: "The poor whites are as poor as rot, and the rich are very rich," wrote an officer in middle Tennessee. "There is no substantial well-to-do middle class here." Lieutenant Colonel Voris in the Shenandoah Valley found that "the popular mind is not educated here. . . . The great mass of the people are not intelligent. A few men of wealth and influence do the reading and thinking for them."[53]

Such observations certainly reinforced the contempt many Northerners felt toward the South, but they also reinforced the belief that the Southern plain folk were oppressed and misled and ripe for reeducation. "I am laboring industriously to undeceive the people," a Federal officer in Arkansas reported; ". . . A few weeks of work here will make this region safe for the Union forever." Indeed, some Northerners saw evidence even as they arrived that the spellbound masses were coming to their senses. On occupying Roanoke Island General Burnside heard local farmers and fishermen complain of mistreatment by the Rebel government and noted that they "seem to be delighted at the arrival of our troops." A naval officer on the Arkansas shore of the Mississippi River observed that the poor people there had chafed under Rebel dominion and now desired only "that the former state of things may return."[54]

Even more striking and gratifying was the outpouring of Unionist sentiment that greeted the Northern soldiers in some of the invaded regions. An officer who led his troops into Loudoun County, Virginia, in March

1862 reported that "a general expression of loyalty has transpired . . . and joyous manifestations of fealty to the old Government have greeted us." A naval officer who led a squadron of gunboats up the Tennessee River in February 1862 noted that hundreds of citizens "shouted their welcome, and hailed their national flag with an enthusiasm there was no mistaking. . . . Tears flowed freely down the cheeks of men as well as of women." Similar scenes were enacted in parts of Arkansas, northern Alabama, and eastern Florida and North Carolina. Where such demonstrations failed to materialize, the Federals surmised that Unionists were silenced by (as one Northerner put it) "fear of Southern power, persecution, and future retribution" and only needed assurance that Federal occupation would be permanent.[55]

The military authorities were encouraged by these signs of loyalty to the Union and disaffection toward the Confederacy, but at the same time they had to face the fact that most citizens in the invaded regions remained resolute and unrepentant Rebels. The formidable power of the Federal army may have awed secessionists into nonresistance, but it had not won their hearts and minds. On entering Nashville General Buell saw "no violent demonstrations" but found that "the mass of the people appear to look upon us as invaders." Likewise, the people of Yorktown, Virginia, "assumed a sullen air," as one soldier reported, "and were not inclined to enter into friendly relations with what they were pleased to term the invaders of their homes." Lieutenant Colonel Voris in the Shenandoah Valley wrote that "the tenor of society here is hostile to us. *I may say hatefully so.*"[56]

Such animosity neither surprised nor discouraged the occupiers. They had not, after all, expected a warm welcome in the South, for they presumed that most citizens were still under the demagogues' spell. But as long as the citizens eschewed armed resistance and active aid to the Rebel government, most occupation authorities favored a policy of restraint and indulgence. Secessionist utterances, passive resistance, and enmity toward the Federal army they regarded as little more than annoyances that time and patience would dispose of.

Indeed, some of them saw signs even in the first weeks of occupation that the conciliatory approach might soon bear fruit. "I find considerable secession proclivity here," wrote a Union officer in Leesburg, Virginia, just after the town was captured in March 1862, "but we have made an impression upon [the citizens] by a respect for property and proper exhibition of decorum, which they have been educated to suppose was foreign to us." The post commander in Lebanon, Tennessee, reported in April 1862 that "the [conciliatory] policy adopted and pursued by me is working to the reclamation of many misguided men." At the same time, the provost marshal in Fayetteville, Tennessee, affirmed that "a great change is going on in the minds of the people" and that "mild yet firm measures in the course of two or three months will bring the people back to their allegiance."[57]

As these optimistic voices spoke in the spring of 1862, however, events were challenging the assumptions underlying the conciliatory policy. As spring gave way to summer and fall, more and more Northerners became convinced that rose water would never douse the fires of rebellion. Before another spring arrived the war would be transfigured, and the citizens of the occupied South would confront a new and terrifying reality.

[2]

Rebels and Conquerors

Civilian Resistance and the

Transformation of Northern

War Aims

"I am a greater rebel than ever before. . . . I cannot feel yet . . . that God has forsaken us. I do not believe it, he will yet smile upon [us]." These words, written by Alice Ready of Murfreesboro, Tennessee, a few days after Union troops arrived in March 1862, echoed the sentiments of many a citizen in the occupied South. Though enemy invasion dealt a staggering psychological blow, Confederate morale did not abruptly collapse and die. It endured and by so doing radically altered the course of occupation and, indeed, of the entire war.[1]

Confederate morale persisted in the occupied South, first, because it was deeply rooted. Outside of certain highland regions, the great majority of citizens believed in the Rebel cause. Although Confederate loyalty tended to be less devout on the lower end of the social scale, it is fair to say that it cut across class lines. Moreover, it transcended gender, for women as a whole were no less committed to the Southern cause than men. Indeed, some deplored their restricted role. "I . . . cry out in agony almost that I am not a man, so that I might fight," Alice Ready declared. "How I should love to fight and even die for my Country—our glorious beautiful south—what a privilege I should esteem it, but am denied it because I am a woman."[2]

Even the stoutest loyalty will wither if it is not nourished by faith in the ultimate success of the cause. What sustained Confederate morale in the occupied South was the belief, or at least the hope, that the Northern invaders would eventually be driven out by a resurgent Rebel army. The anger and disillusionment provoked by the unseemly Confederate retreat faded quickly under enemy occupation; citizens now prayed for redemption and cheered every rumor of a counteroffensive. Until their liberators arrived, the people were determined to uphold the faith. A Union soldier in Middleburg, Virginia, in early 1862 described the residents as "Secesh to the *back bone*. They say the Southern people will never give up, untill everything is entirely sacrificed." In Athens, Alabama, Mary Fielding spurned the notion of surrender: "I wouldn't do it while there's a [Confederate] soldier left in the south. As I told one of [the Federal soldiers] this evening 'maybe when all the men are killed you'll have the glory of conquering the women & children but we won't give up before.' "[3]

By the spring of 1862, however, some Southerners in the occupied regions were undergoing a crisis of faith. Confederate forces everywhere were in retreat. Union armies were marching into the heart of the Confederacy and to the gates of the Rebel capital. The prospect of redemption grew dimmer and dimmer. Mary Fielding spoke with her uncle on May 5 and found him "completely down in the Slough of Despond; thinks we . . . are completely whipped & ought to give up & go back in the Union." Visiting her cousin a few days later, Fielding found her "entirely subdued, ready to do anything they say, for peace."[4]

The late spring, summer, and early fall of 1862 witnessed a spectacular series of military reversals. Federal forces were driven back from Richmond and expelled from most of northern Virginia, and a Confederate army crossed the Potomac into Maryland; in the west, a Confederate offensive liberated northern Alabama and the southern portion of middle Tennessee. Although the North eventually recaptured the lost territory, the moral impact of the Rebel resurgence was enormous. The spectacle of enemy occupation forces frantically packing up and pulling out, of Rebel troops returning in triumph amid the cheers of the populace, renewed the hope of redemption in all the occupied regions and revitalized Confederate morale. A man in one of the occupied towns of the North Carolina coast smugly informed a Union officer in September 1862 that "the idea of overrunning the South was now exploded, . . . it could never be done . . . our people never would submit to their government."[5]

Union military occupation was profoundly repugnant to secessionist Southerners. This truth might seem self-evident, but it is worth examining. The citizens' bitter hostility toward the invaders—manifested even when the Yankees were at their most conciliatory—is incomprehensible if enemy occupation is seen merely as the negation of the secessionists' political goals. The fact is that invasion and occupation shook the Southern psyche to its foundations.

Three themes or images recur repeatedly in the accounts of citizens in the occupied South: violation, pollution, and degradation. Having defined Northern culture as an alien "other" even before the war, and having confirmed that sense of separateness through the act of secession, Southerners regarded Union soldiers as outsiders, intruders, foreign invaders violating the sovereignty of the Confederate nation. "The Yankee Gunboats pass up and down our dear river displaying the hated flag of the Union," wrote a Mississippi woman; ". . . it does make me so mad . . . to think of the invaders being on *our* river unmolested." Two Virginia women got into an angry debate with a Federal officer: "Well what makes you hate us so," he finally asked them in exasperation. "Because," one replied, "you are trespassing on us." This sense of transgression was most acutely felt at the personal level, when Northern soldiers violated the sanctity of the home to search for contraband or to plunder. "[H]ow awful we felt when the wretches were prying into every sacred thing in the house," wrote a Georgia woman, "even into father's papers and relics of the dead. . . . If I live a thousand years I shall never forget the enemies of our country."[6]

The Northern soldiers were not merely invaders: they were also advance agents of a corrupt and corrupting civilization. Many Southerners had endorsed secession as an act of purification, a withdrawal from the materialism, licentiousness, and disorder that supposedly infected the North. In their eyes, invasion and occupation threatened to pollute the South, to contaminate it irreversibly. Just two months after the Union army captured Fredericksburg, Betty Maury remarked disgustedly that "the town is intensely Yankee and looks as though it never had been any thing else. Yankee ice carts go about selling Yankee ice. Yankee newsboys cry Yankee papers along the streets. Yankee citizens and Yankee Dutchmen have opened all the stores on Maine Street. Some of them have brought their families and look as if they . . . intended to stay here until they died."[7]

Worst of all, enemy occupation was deeply degrading, particularly for Southern men, for it violated devoutly held principles of personal honor and republican independence. Subjection to military rule was the apotheosis of the dreaded loss of liberty that made men dependent and servile; such men were without honor—they were slaves. Over and over, proud Southerners spoke of the humiliation of occupation, of the forced submission to arbitrary authority, the debasing sense of impotence, the mortifying subservience to inferiors. "[O]ne is subject to petty tyranny in a military [government]," complained western Tennessee planter Robert H. Cartmell, "can go nowhere without a pass, have no controul of any species of property, there is not a moment but it is liable to be appropriated. . . . The annoyances are innumerable." Planter Colin Clarke wrote to his son about "our wretched condition here" in occupied Virginia: "We are all *worse* than *paupers*, . . . with rude and vulgar masters. . . . *Good God*!! Who could have dreamed of this. . . . Imagine the most *desolate*, *destitute*, & *degrading* condition in which your parents & friends & county can be placed & your imagination will not equal the reality." In a later letter Clarke described himself as "sick and nauseated with the slavish life of humiliation I am leading here."[8]

It is no exaggeration to say that many citizens in the occupied South ranked honor above all else. After living under Federal rule for several months, a North Carolina man vowed that "I have not in word or act compromised my character, dignity, honor, cause or state nor will I at any cost." Robert Cartmell declared that "property may go to the dogs or elsewhere before I will do any thing my conscience will not approve of or calculated to throw a stigma on my children. *Honor* before property & *death* preferable to disgrace."[9]

Though unable to halt the violation and pollution of their land, citizens found ways to counter the degradation of enemy occupation and thus preserve their honor. Many did so by flaunting their Confederate patriotism and their loathing of the invaders. Encouraged by the occupiers' indulgent rosewater policy, citizens waged a campaign of provocative acts and defiant words. They cheered for Jefferson Davis, they sang "The Bonnie Blue Flag," they ostentatiously avoided walking under Union banners, they held their noses when passing Federal soldiers on the street. The spunkiest seemed to relish meeting the invaders face-to-face and loosing a barrage of secessionism and insult. In Virginia, a farm woman who was approached by a Union naval officer desiring to buy some eggs "commenced a violent tirade against the United States and the Yankees," as the officer recounted, "and stated that if she was overflowing with provisions and a Yankee ship was starving she would not sell them a dollar's worth; that she and her husband were secessionists and she gloried in it." Another Virginia woman refused to play the piano when asked to do so by Union soldiers who had entered her home; when one of the soldiers sat down and began to play it himself, the woman grabbed a hatchet and chopped the strings, declaring: "That's my piano, and it shall not give you a moment's pleasure."[10]

Women, in fact, comprised the vanguard in this campaign of verbal defiance. There were limits to the occupiers' tolerance, even under the rosewater policy, and the citizens soon learned just how far they could go. It quickly became apparent that the Federals applied a sliding scale: the less threatening they deemed the perpetrator, the more leniently they responded. Victorian ideals and the masculine culture of the military encouraged the assumption that women were harmless; thus, Southern women assertive enough to take on the invaders encountered few deterrents and were often humored, even goaded, by amused soldiers. Virginia French of Tennessee, for example, first met the enemy in June 1862, when a squad came to her house demanding food. "[T]hey were the roughest kind of men," she wrote in her diary, "and I did not know how to address them. I . . . feared I would not say the right thing so I forced myself to silence." Their subsequent decorum emboldened her, however, and "while they were eating . . . I generally gave them a 'piece of my mind.' . . . They did not seem to get angry—acknowledged that I was telling the truth—and thanked me for their dinner!" A Union infantry sergeant in Tennessee laughingly recounted how a young woman approached him and his comrades, "called us all Yankees & [said] that we were the meanest men on the face of the green earth. She said . . . that if it were in her power she would kill us every one right there"—whereupon one of the men offered her a gun, which she declined.[11]

Even when the military authorities took action against outspoken females, it rarely amounted to more than a paternalistic scolding. Two young Alabama women were arrested for waving Rebel flags and were taken before a Federal general, to whom they proudly declared their secessionist sympathies; but the general merely lectured them and then released them, saying "Women, go home and behave yourselves." In Nashville, twenty-year-old Laura Carter was arrested for spitting on Union soldiers and was brought before military governor Andrew Johnson. "Oh, you musn't mind these little rebels," Johnson told the arresting officer. "There is no harm in Laura. . . . Let her go."[12]

Children and old men likewise discovered that the Federals did not take their hostility seriously and would permit them great latitude. When a soldier offered Betty Maury's daughter some candy, the girl replied, "No . . . Yankee candy would choke me"; the soldier, Maury noted, "seemed much amused." Seventy-year-old Jesse Cox of Tennessee regularly tongue-lashed Federal soldiers with impunity; on one occasion when a foraging party visited his farm, Cox "talked very plain to the officers I told them they were all rogues and that God would punish them."[13]

Young and middle-aged men, on the other hand, were less often granted such indulgence. Able-bodied secessionist men, even when unarmed, seemed threatening to the Federals; therefore, in ways both official and unofficial, the occupiers curtailed masculine assertiveness. The most flagrant cases often provoked arrest and imprisonment, even where conciliation was the rule. More common perhaps were responses like that witnessed by Mary Fielding: "Link Thach was drinking Sunday evening & 'hurrahed' for Jeff Davis, The Southern Confederacy, &c while the soldiers were on dress parade," she wrote; "as soon as they were dismissed they ran after him & beat, kicked & knocked him about considerably."[14]

Thus, men became more circumspect; women grew bolder. "The women are almost universally bitter Secesh and spit it out with venom," wrote Lieutenant Colonel Alvin Voris in the Shenandoah Valley; "the men are mostly so, but are more descreet and keep their sentiments to themselves." Indeed, few Northerners recorded their impressions of the Southern people without mentioning the virulence of the women. A naval officer in St. Augustine found "much violent and pestilent feeling among the women." A soldier stationed in middle Tennessee wrote that "everyone I meet are secessionist . . . the *women* have denounced me most bitterly."[15]

Secessionist Southerners unwilling to confront and revile the enemy could still affirm their honor and patriotism through noncooperation or passive resistance. Many resolved to shun the Federals, to avoid any sort of compromise with them, to separate themselves from Yankee pollution, to spurn the offer of conciliation. Such resolutions were, for the most part, rather easily kept during the first year or so of the war, when the rosewater policy prevailed, for the Federals' practice was to encourage and persuade rather than demand. There were exceptions, however. Some military authorities, reasoning that a little judiciously applied force was the best kind of persuasion, singled out influential citizens—aristocrats, county and municipal officials, ministers, and especially newspaper editors—and tried to compel them to cooperate in one way or another and thereby set an example for the masses.[16]

Such coercion posed an agonizing dilemma: just how far could a man give in to threats and still preserve his honor and not betray the Confederate cause? A few capitulated outright. Some ministers, for instance, quietly dropped the customary prayer for the Confederate president and in other ways toned down their Sunday sermons; a number of newspaper editors purged their columns of secessionist sentiment. Others compromised. Episcopal clergyman Henry Lay, who was arrested and jailed in May 1862 along with several other leading men of Huntsville, Alabama, argued back and forth with Union general Ormsby Mitchel over the precise terms of a public letter condemning guerrilla warfare that Mitchel insisted they sign; after nearly two weeks of confinement and debate, Lay and the others persuaded themselves that they could sign the document in good conscience and were released. More often the occupiers' demands met a firm refusal. Most of the citizens targeted for coercion rejected cooperation or compromise and accepted the consequences.[17]

The Federals encountered the stoutest resistance when it came to loyalty oaths. Oaths were deeply revered in nineteenth-century America, not least in the South, where the cult of honor made a virtual fetish of them. During the great crisis of American nationalism from 1861 to 1865, oaths assumed especially profound public and personal meaning. In the occupied South Federal authorities had the task of bringing Southerners back to their allegiance to the Union, and they regarded the oath of loyalty as the sacred emblem of such conversion. But their early attempts to pressure leading citizens into taking the oath rarely succeeded. Those subjected to such pressure often echoed the sentiments of a Tennessee justice of the peace who vowed that he would "have his neck streached as long as a clothes line" before he would thus repudiate the Rebel cause. When the occupation authorities in Murfreesboro, Tennessee, ordered all the town's merchants, doctors, lawyers, and other professional men to take the oath or do no business, thirty of thirty-seven closed up shop. Nashville city officials almost unanimously rejected the oath demanded of them in March 1862, whereupon military governor Johnson dismissed from office the mayor and twenty-one councilmen and aldermen. In addition, Johnson imprisoned seven Nashville clergymen, a college professor, and the superintendent of the state insane asylum for refusing the oath.[18]

Civilian morale and resistance in the occupied regions were not just matters of private faith and individual conscience; they were also communal. In the South, ethics, conscience, honor, dignity, virtue, and self-esteem were in many respects inseparable from community. One's consciousness of right and wrong and one's evaluation of one's own worth were not only an inner light but also a reflected one that originated in communal consensus. Southerners acted always with the awareness that the community was watching and judging. Thus, when the citizens of the occupied South pondered the proper course of conduct, they looked outward as well as inward. Lawyer and politician Thomas M. Jones of Giles County, Tennessee, for example, adamantly refused to take the oath despite the threat of punishment; if he submitted to the enemy, he said, he "would be degraded in the estimation of the Community."[19]

Southern communities under Federal occupation brought to bear (so far as they were able) all their traditional sanctions, their informal methods of support, cohesion, and compulsion, in order to sustain Confederate morale and bolster resistance. These included, on the one hand, neighborly encouragement and solace and mutual aid. When James Matthews of Maury County, Tennessee, was arrested and held in an army guardhouse, friends visited him daily to keep up his spirits. Federal foraging parties passing through the countryside sometimes came up empty-handed because rural folk would spread the alarm from house to house and neighborhood to neighborhood, enabling the farmers to hide their provisions and stock.[20]

While with one hand communities encouraged and succored, with the other they chastised and intimidated, disciplining the wayward and cautioning the unreliable by means of rumor, gossip, shaming, shunning, and the threat of violence. A North Carolina man suspected of complicity with the enemy complained that "the country is rife with vile lies & slanders about me, I have been most grossly slandered." In Huntsville, Alabama, some women who visited captured Confederate soldiers in a Federal hospital were shocked to learn that two had taken the oath. "[We] Expressed our mortification and disappointment," one of the women wrote, ". . . and exhorted the others never to do likewise." A Federal officer in northern Virginia reported that some citizens were refusing to take the oath "from fear of their neighbors, who, they say, would persecute them."[21]

As time went on, a growing number of citizens dared to go beyond verbal defiance and noncooperation to take up active resistance. In the first days and weeks under Federal rule in any invaded district, active resistance was almost nil. Disheartened by Confederate retreat, abandoned by many of their leaders, faced with overwhelming Federal power, uncertain of the enemy's intentions and capabilities, and fearful of the worst, citizens were in no mood to defy the occupiers' stern warnings against resisting Federal authority and aiding the armed enemies of the United States. "We intend to be as quiet as we can," wrote a Mississippi woman the day Northern troops arrived in her community, "and not give them any cause for ill treatment." But as they grew accustomed to the routine of occupation, gained an understanding of Yankee temperament and tolerances, and learned the army's weaknesses and limitations, some citizens—including many women—found opportunities to strike covertly at the invaders.[22]

Smuggling was one of the most widespread forms of active resistance. During the war a considerable amount of contraband materiel—medicines, uniforms, and so forth—found its way from the occupied regions into the beleaguered Confederacy despite the Federals' determined efforts to enforce a blockade. The goods were transported by citizens, working on their own or with organized smuggling rings, in boats, in false-bottomed wagons, even in the voluminous skirts of women. Another common act of resistance in the occupied South was harboring Confederate scouts or soldiers separated from their commands. Some of the boldest citizens spied on the Federal army and passed information to the Confederacy.[23]

For Southerners and Northerners alike, however, the ultimate incarnation of civilian resistance was not the smuggler or the spy, but the guerrilla. Nearly every section of the South held by Union forces eventually became a theater of guerrilla warfare. The perpetrators were armed and mounted men in civilian clothes operating in groups of no more than a few dozen (usually much fewer) who seemingly appeared from nowhere to carry out their attacks and then vanished into the countryside. They tore up railroad tracks, burned bridges, cut telegraph wires, fired on river steamers, and ambushed foraging and scouting detachments. At first little more than an occasional annoyance to the occupiers, guerrilla attacks eventually posed a grave threat to Federal control of some of the most strategic regions, including northern Virginia and middle Tennessee.[24]

The origins of guerrilla warfare in the occupied South are obscured by the dearth of firsthand accounts by guerrillas themselves, but a few general conclusions can be hazarded. Clearly, guerrillaism was a masculine phenomenon representing, at least in part, the defense of personal honor against the degrading tyranny of Federal rule. Ennoblement through violence was an article of faith among Southern males. Their ritual violence took many forms, including conventional warfare and dueling, but in the occupied South guerrillaism was the only feasible violent answer to Yankee insult. Certainly, too, guerrillaism was seen by many as the only direct response to the violation and pollution of their homes and communities. Verbal defiance, passive resistance, smuggling, and spying preserved honor and aided the cause, to be sure, but true redemption for self and community meant killing Yankees.[25]

Like the other forms of active resistance, guerrillaism was slow to appear. At the moment of invasion, citizens overwhelmingly rejected as futile the idea of resisting the enemy by force of arms. Only as the days passed and the nature of occupation became clearer did they discover that the enemy was in some ways vulnerable and that armed resistance was not necessarily suicidal—the Federals were, after all, trying to hold vast territories and could not be present in strength everywhere at once. Then, too, although guerrilla bands were spontaneous, informal, loosely structured entities, they could not spring up overnight like mushrooms. They coalesced only gradually, as word spread through the rural neighborhoods and men gathered furtively to assess their chances, reconnoiter the enemy, and plan a course of action.

A third factor delaying the emergence of guerrilla warfare was the scarcity of manpower. Able-bodied men—especially the more youthful, vigorous sort best suited for war—were in short supply in the occupied South. Most had joined the Confederate army or had fled when the Northern forces invaded. As the war continued, however, some of those men drifted back home, particularly Rebel soldiers who had deserted, become separated from their units, or been discharged. Evidence suggests that these returnees—especially army deserters—strongly reinforced the guerrilla movement in every occupied region.[26]

Finally, guerrillaism reflected the broader state of civilian morale and was hindered through the spring of 1862 by doubts about the Confederacy's ability to survive. But with the great Rebel military victories of the late spring, summer, and fall, guerrilla activity exploded. "[G]uerrilla bands are being organized in almost every direction," a Union officer in middle Tennessee reported on July 30. "They are now becoming very troublesome."[27]

It is important to distinguish guerrillas from the other armed and mounted bands that bedeviled the occupiers. Throughout the war Confederate cavalry forces—those under Nathan Bedford Forrest and John Hunt Morgan being the most prominent—raided behind Union lines, capturing isolated garrisons and generally wreaking havoc. Though sometimes mistaken for guerrillas by the Federals, these were in fact regular military units that were under Confederate control and returned to Confederate lines when their mission was completed. Furthermore, in some regions the Confederacy commissioned "partisan rangers"—notably in northern Virginia under the command of John S. Mosby—to operate behind Union lines. Although the occupiers refused to draw any distinction between these forces and guerrillas (partisan rangers were generally residents of the region where they operated, and some doffed their uniforms and returned home between raids), the rangers were enrolled soldiers formally organized along military lines and more or less responsive to Confederate authority.[28]

Guerrillas, on the other hand, were not soldiers, but citizens; they were not an arm of the Confederacy, but of the community. Though they saw themselves in a general way as part of the Confederate war effort, their war was really a personal and communal one. They rarely traveled far from their home county and were unresponsive to Confederate authority. They fought when and where they chose.

Guerrillaism epitomized the communal nature of resistance in the occupied South. Guerrillas embodied the rural community's will, mirrored its constituency, drew strength from its solidarity. Available evidence suggests that guerrilla bands included members of every social class—and often included boys and middle-aged men as well as those in the prime of youth. The typical guerrilla was not a footloose adventurer but a longtime resident of the community with a network of friends and kinfolk willing to offer support, shelter, and protection. Although many guerrillas stayed with their gangs more or less permanently, camping out in woods and hollows between raids, others regularly went home and carried on their customary vocation. Either way, guerrilla bands were embedded in the community, inseparable from it. They visited rural families and picked up neighborhood gossip along with information about the enemy, they secured provisions and equipment from local farmers and merchants, they had their horses shod by the village blacksmith and their rifles repaired by the village gunsmith. In one Tennessee community guerrillas held a public auction of booty taken from the Yankees; in another they hosted a dance.[29]

By the latter part of 1862 guerrillaism was a potent force in the occupied South. In many districts the Federals found it exceedingly dangerous to venture out from their fortified posts except in large, heavily armed parties. "The countryside seems to have degenerated into bushwhackers," a Union officer wrote from Arkansas. "It is hardly safe to go out of our lines a mile." After losing numerous men to guerrilla ambushes in northern Virginia, the cavalry commander of the Army of the Potomac forbade his troopers to travel the countryside except on urgent business. "[E]very grove," he warned, "[is] a lurking place for guerrilla bands."[30]

What these Federal officers saw when they peered beyond their picket lines was a discouraging, sinister, lethal landscape—a very different prospect from that which greeted the invaders during the war's first year. The persistence of Confederate morale and the emergence of civilian resistance had transformed the occupied South in the Northerners' eyes. This land was not what it had seemed. A new reckoning was in order.

. . .

Eighteen sixty-two was the turning point. When that year opened, the great majority of Northerners still hoped and believed that their government would soon vanquish the Confederate armies, win the misguided citizens of the South back to their old allegiance, and restore the Union as it was. But when that year closed, a large and growing number had concluded that the war would be long and arduous, that the Southern people were obdurate Rebels who must be subjugated, and that the South must be revolutionized.

The Confederate military triumphs of 1862 demonstrated not only the strength and prowess of the Rebel armies, but also the unity and resolve of the government and people that stood behind those armies. The notion that an elite cabal kept itself in power by tyrannizing and manipulating the Confederate citizenry grew increasingly untenable. A speaker told a New York audience in 1862 that the idea of a "divided, bewildered South" must now be abandoned: "She is in earnest, every man, and she is as unanimous as the Colonies were in the Revolution."[31]

The lessons of battle were confirmed by the lessons of occupation. The vast legions of Southern Unionists who were supposed to come forth to aid their liberators and reconstruct the Southern polity failed to materialize. Moreover, the belief that conciliation would enlighten and convert the secessionist masses crumbled in the face of continuing civilian resistance. "I have done my utmost to conciliate the people," General Ormsby Mitchel wrote from northern Alabama in 1862, ". . . but the genuine rebels will not listen to reason." Testifying before a congressional committee that summer, General Lew Wallace declared that the conciliatory approach "conciliates no secessionist. The secessionist whose property is protected by our troops is a secessionist still. . . . [He] laughs at [our] clemency." General Abner Doubleday's testimony also affirmed that the rosewater policy did not work, "Not in the slightest degree. . . . [O]ne of [the secessionist citizens] said to me that we might guard every atom of their property, and still they would hate us just the same."[32]

It was not simply that the Southern people could no longer be considered potential friends; more and more, they were proving to be mortal enemies. The extent of active resistance, especially guerrillaism, was appalling to the Yankees. They had, of course, come south prepared for a political contest in the occupied regions, but few had foreseen that occupation would provoke a bloody war within a war. Union soldiers were now dying far behind the front lines at the hands of Southern civilians; untold numbers of others were dying at the front because of aid given the Confederate army by citizens of the occupied regions. As the toll mounted, the distinction between enemy soldiers and hostile civilians appeared less and less meaningful. Increasingly, Federal authorities spoke of subduing the Southern citizens in the same way they spoke of defeating the Rebel army. "We must whip them," General Doubleday told Congress; "that is the only thing for us to do." Union general-in-chief Henry W. Halleck affirmed in March 1863 that "the character of the war has very much changed within the last year. There is now no possible hope of reconciliation with the rebels. . . . There can be no peace but that which is forced by the sword. We must conquer the rebels or be conquered by them."[33]

Of all the Union commanders, none more cogently articulated—or more dramatically realized—the evolving "hard" policy than William T. Sherman, prophet of modern warfare. Sherman, it may be recalled, had originally endorsed conciliation, cautioning his troops in early 1862 against mistreating Southern civilians, "who must become our friends before peace can be hoped for." But subsequent events convinced him that propitiation was futile. Compulsion, he decided, not persuasion, must be the cornerstone of Federal policy in the occupied South.[34]

At the heart of Sherman's revised version of Northern war aims was a conception of war opposed to the traditional, narrowly circumscribed approach exemplified by Union general George B. McClellan. Sherman had little use for the "rules of war" and the gentlemanly sparring matches that they encouraged. War was in effect a renunciation of rules, he insisted; it was "simply power unrestrained by constitution or compact." Victory was all that mattered: "[I]n war we have a perfect right to produce results in our own way, and should not scruple too much at the means, provided they are effectual."[35]

Furthermore, said Sherman, the peculiar nature of the American Civil War demanded a rethinking of the role of the civilian. In the Old World, he explained, "wars are between kings or rulers, through hired armies, and not between people. [The people] remain, as it were, neutral. . . .

Therefore the rule was and is, that wars are confined to the armies and should not visit the homes of families or private interests. . . . [But] [t]he war which now prevails in our land is essentially a war of races." In such a war neutrality was impossible, the distinction between passive and active resistance a fiction: "all who do not aid [us] are enemies, and we will not account to them for our acts." Moreover, distinguishing between enemy soldiers and civilians was overscrupulous: "We are not only fighting hostile armies, but a hostile people, and must make old and young, rich and poor, feel the hard hand of war." Victory would come only when the Southern people no longer had the means or the will to resist, Sherman concluded, and that would be achieved not through conciliation but through coercion, destruction, and killing. The North's proper course toward Southern civilians was "not [to] coax them or meet them half way, but make them . . . sick of war."[36]

As heartless as some of his pronouncements sounded, in reality Sherman was remarkably free of malice toward the Southern people. He urged a warfare of terror not out of vindictiveness, but simply to win the war as quickly as possible. But many other Northerners were drawn to the hard policy by their deepening hatred of Southerners. As the army casualty lists lengthened, no Northern community was left untouched. The death or maiming of tens—eventually hundreds—of thousands of Northern men inevitably stirred cries for revenge. Simple victory and the restoration of the Union would no longer suffice; there must be retribution. But against whom? The events of 1862 had exploded at least one tenet of the "Slave Power conspiracy" thesis: it now seemed clear that the Southern people as a whole were not befuddled and innocent but willful and guilty. All must be punished.[37]

Hatred and the thirst for vengeance grew especially fierce among Union soldiers in the South, for they saw with their own eyes the carnage of war and regularly came face-to-face with hostile, unrepentant Rebel citizens. "[T]he more I see of these rebels the more I hate them," wrote an artillery officer in the Shenandoah Valley. "[T]hey are so infernal impudent in the[ir] treason that it is enough to make one mad. They come and ask a guard to protect their pigs and fowl &c and yet insult the very guard who watches over them."[38]

Even more infuriating was the citizens' active complicity with the Confederacy, their deceit and treachery. "Clothed in the peaceful garb of the citizen," one Union officer complained, "they enter our camps and pass through our lines, and the citizen's dress is generally but the disguise of a spy." Above all, the burgeoning guerrilla violence in the countryside convinced many Union soldiers that they were at war with a deadly, merciless foe who must be repaid in kind.[39]

The implacable and increasingly lethal hostility of the Southern people pushed many Northerners toward still another conclusion: Southern society as it existed was simply incompatible with American nationhood. Even if vanquished in war, the South would remain a menace to the Union unless Southern society was fundamentally reformed. Aristocratic ascendancy, poor white degradation, black enslavement—all the atavistic elements of Southern life that shaped the egregious Southern character— all must be swept away so that the South could be reconstructed in the image of the North. Only then could America fulfill its sacred destiny.[40]

With this decision the transformation of Union war aims was complete. In 1861 the Northern government and people had sent forth an army to defeat the Slave Power, win over the Southern people, and restore the Union as it was. But these conservative goals rested on assumptions belied by the subsequent course of events, and they were gradually abandoned. The radical goals that replaced them were, it must be noted, never embraced unanimously in the North: many members of the public, the government, and even the army held firmly to the original war aims. But by the latter part of 1862, and increasingly thereafter as the conflict accelerated toward its bloody apogee, the momentum of the war encouraged harsh means to radical ends. The occupiers now had a very different mission: not to conciliate, but to conquer and avenge; not to protect, but to seize and destroy; not to restore, but to prepare the way for a new South, and a new nation.

• • •

The triumph of the hard policy manifested itself in many ways, none more conspicuous than the treatment of private property. Under the rosewater policy, Federal commanders had scrupulously protected Southerners' property in an effort to gain their allegiance. When that effort failed, the commanders reconsidered.

Military necessity was now the paramount consideration, for the North's immediate aims were to destroy the Rebel armies and subjugate the Rebel populace. This meant, first of all, that the Federal forces could abandon the cumbersome policy of trying to supply themselves wholly from the North so as to avoid levying on Southern civilians and instead use the South as a major source of sustenance, taking food and forage, livestock and equipment, in whatever amounts were needed. Leading the way was Major General John Pope, commander of a Union army in Virginia, who in July 1862 announced: "Hereafter, as far as practicable, the troops of this command will subsist upon the country in which their operations are carried on." Pope's decree was endorsed by his superiors, and living off the land soon became official army policy. And, of course, there would be no more indemnifying of secessionists for seized property.[41]

The logic of military necessity led even further: supplies must not only be appropriated for the Union army, but also denied to the Confederate army. Anything of military use that might find its way to the Rebels must be destroyed if it could not be carried away. Thus, in occupied areas near the Confederate lines or in danger of recapture, and in areas raided by the Union army but not held, the Federals often pursued a scorched-earth policy. For example, General Frank Blair Jr., who led a raiding expedition up the Yazoo River in Mississippi in 1863, reported that "we found supplies and forage sufficient to supply Joe Johnston's [Confederate] army for a month. . . . I used all that we could and destroyed the rest. . . . Joe Johnston will [now] find very little for his army in [that] country." Moreover, after President Lincoln issued the Emancipation Proclamation on January 1, 1863, slaves were regularly confiscated just like any other Confederate resource. "I brought [back] with me an army of negroes," General Blair boasted, "nearly equal to the number of men in my command."[42]

The South's key resource, however, was the fighting spirit of its people. Sherman and other commanders insisted that that moral asset must be destroyed along with the Confederacy's war materiel. This they proposed to do by hitting Southerners where it hurt—by not only killing Rebel soldiers, but also blighting the South and impoverishing its citizens. Thus, Sherman and his disciples justified seizing secessionist property even when it strengthened the Federal army not a whit, and they endorsed destruction even when it deprived the Rebel army of nothing— as long as the Southern people were thereby made "sick of war." "General Sherman is perfectly right," said one of his staff officers, "—the only possible way to end this unhappy and dreadful conflict . . . is to make it *terrible beyond endurance*. . . . [I]t is neither barbarous nor useless but just and indispensable to utterly destroy everything, no matter whose, or what, or whom, that does or can uphold, sustain or encourage this gigantic crime [of secession]."[43]

Men in the ranks agreed that destruction was strategically justified, but many also came to rationalize it as an act of righteous vengeance. "[I]t does us good to distroy the greesey belleys property," wrote Elias Brady, a Union soldier in Tennessee. "[W]hen some of the boys gets holt of any property of any kind belon[g]ing to the rebels they distroy it as fast as they can and then say dam him he was the coss of bringing us here." And, though still officially proscribed and not infrequently punished, the soldiers' pillaging and vandalism were increasingly ignored by the authorities. "[O]ur company officers," said Brady, "do not care how mutch we confiscate."[44]

Many of the communities that fell into Union hands after mid-1862 witnessed terrifying scenes of havoc when the troops entered—in striking contrast to the generally decorous, orderly invasions of the war's first year. "They broke open every store in town," reported a northern Mississippi woman after the Federals appeared in the fall of 1862, ". . . ruining and destroying what they did not take off. . . . They robbed the meat-house[s] and pantries, some families were left without a mouthful to eat. They took all the corn and fodder, took every horse worth the taking, shot down our cows and hogs wherever they found them, leaving them to rot. . . . They completely gutted houses that had been left by families too timid to stay." Union soldiers' accounts corroborate such reports. "We burnt every thing," wrote an Iowa infantryman about an expedition into Mississippi in 1863, "& took all the Horses Mules & Niggars that we came acrost. . . . At Jackson we had a fine old time. The soldiers was allowed to take whatever they wanted . . . their was but little left in Jackson when we come a way."[45]

It was Sherman's campaign through Georgia and the Carolinas in late 1864 and 1865 that best epitomized the North's ruthless war against Southern property. From Atlanta to Savannah, according to the general's own report, his troops cut a swath sixty miles wide, wrecking railroads and stripping the countryside of provisions, livestock, and slaves. Sherman estimated the value of the lost property at $100 million, of which the army used or carried off about one-fifth; the rest, he said, was "simple waste and destruction." And, yes, he acknowledged with a wink, his soldiers had been "a little loose in foraging, they 'did some things they ought not to have done,' yet, on the whole, they have supplied the wants of the army with as little violence as could be expected."[46]

The fact is that the soldiers' destructive urge was only feebly restrained on the march to the sea, and it was wholly unleashed thereafter, when the army moved northward. "We have given South Carolina a terrible scourging," one of Sherman's officers wrote in March 1865, as the army prepared to move on to North Carolina. "We have destroyed all factories, cotton mills, gins, presses and cotton; burnt one city, the capital, and most of the villages on our route as well as most of the barns, outbuildings and dwelling houses, and every house that escaped fire has been pillaged. . . . There was a recklessness by the soldiery in South Carolina that they never exhibited before and a sort of general 'don't care' on the part of the officers."[47]

Few other invaded regions of the South suffered such sudden, sweeping devastation as South Carolina, but all were eventually ravaged by the ungloved iron fist of the Northern army. In the meantime, the hard policy was being implemented on another front as well. While with one hand the invaders seized or demolished the Southern property they had once vowed to protect, with the other they set about subduing the Southern people they had once sought to befriend.

. . .

Union military commanders in the South claimed broad authority, and they exercised that authority with few official restraints. Constitutionally minded Northerners debated the precise legal status of the seceded states—whether they comprised a belligerent foreign power or an insurrectionary district—but few soldiers bothered themselves with the niceties of that controversy. Under the accepted rules of war, any place occupied by a hostile army was, ipso facto, under martial law. The ranking military officer assumed supreme (though not absolute) power in such localities and was obliged to keep order; the civilian inhabitants owed temporary allegiance to the occupying power and were forbidden to resist by force. That was all the legal justification most commanders needed or cared to know about.[48]

Except for its brief sojourn in Mexico in the 1840s, the United States army had had no experience with military rule in enemy territory before the Civil War. Thus, commanders in the occupied South had few regulations or precedents to go by and had to improvise policy. Eventually the army high command codified a body of rules for occupation (General Order 100, published in 1863), but it was simply a set of general guidelines drawn mostly from the law of nations and military custom. From the beginning of the war to the end, the high command granted wide latitude to commanders in the field, few of whom felt much constrained by anything other than their own understanding of the rules of war, the broad aims of the Federal government, the demands of military necessity, and the dictates of conscience.[49]

Armed with the powers of martial law, and more or less free to govern as they saw fit, almost all occupation authorities eventually renounced conciliation and cracked down hard on secessionists. Among their first targets were expressions of Rebel sentiment and insults aimed at Federal soldiers, which had been regarded rather indulgently under the rosewater policy. "[W]hoever shall utter one word against the Government of the United States," decreed the Washington, North Carolina, provost marshal in August 1862, "will be at once arrested and closely confined." An Arkansas man was sentenced to six months at hard labor in 1864 after a witness testified that he had declared "he was a rebel and would be as long as the red blood run warm in his veins." A man in Vicksburg, Mississippi, went to jail for saying that he "wished to God [Nathan Bedford] For[r]est would come and kill every Yank" in town; another suffered the same fate for inviting a Union officer to "Kiss his Mule."[50]

Influential secessionists were singled out, particularly ministers. Some had been silenced even during the rosewater period, but now the occupation authorities began systematically muzzling them. In the western Tennessee town of La Grange, the provost marshal forbade minister John Waddel to hold services and then justified his action in a fiery letter: "You have hitherto used all the means in your power to aid this wicked Rebellion. . . . Instead of being an Humble follower of our Saviour . . . You have stirred up Dissensions . . . and urged Vile Treason toward the best Government that God ever created on Earth." After Sherman's army captured Marietta, Georgia, in 1864, the post commander refused to let the town's only remaining minister preach or even leave his house, calling him "too unsound," an "ultra Secessionist."[51]

Newspaper editors had been ordered to expunge Rebel sentiment from their columns or cease publication even when the conciliatory policy prevailed, for the Federals held newspapers responsible in great measure for whipping up secessionist fervor. Those editors who agreed to the Yankees' terms and continued publishing under their watchful eye found themselves subjected to ever greater scrutiny as the occupiers' attitude hardened. A newspaper purged of overt secessionism was no longer enough: it must also avoid any criticism, however indirect, of the Federal government or the occupation authorities. Thus, when the *Memphis Avalanche* implied that the citizens' rights had suffered under Union rule, the city provost marshal called the article "exceedingly objectionable," denounced the newspaper as "incendiary and treasonable," and ordered its suspension; it was allowed to resume publication after the author of the article resigned. When Sherman captured Savannah, he permitted two newspapers to continue publishing but warned that their editors would "be held to the strictest accountability, and will be punished severely in person and property for any libelous publications, mischievous matter, premature news, exaggerated statements or any comments whatever upon the acts of the constituted authorities."[52]

While commanders and provost marshals were issuing their orders, soldiers in the field were informally serving notice that they too would no longer tolerate Rebel insolence. "One woman was so drunk and abusive the other day," wrote a soldier on picket duty outside Memphis, "that the officer of the guard tied her to a tree till she got sober." A northern Mississippi woman stood by quietly while a party of Northern troops ransacked her house but then, according to a neighbor's account, "Just as they were leaving she remarked to the Major that they had treated them very unkindly and ungenerously in taking all they had. The Maj[or] replied 'Madam not another word or I will call my men back and show you what they can do.'" Such threats were quite serious: coercion and retaliation became progressively harsh as the war went on. A Union soldier marching through the North Carolina countryside in 1865 recorded that when one of the inhabitants directed some insulting remarks at the troops, "his house was burned down before his eyes."[53]

Besides clamping down on seditious or offensive speech, the occupiers imposed an array of other measures to control the civilian population and to curb smuggling, spying, and guerrillaism—measures so stringent and extensive that they created what can only be termed a police state. Military authorities subjected citizens to arbitrary search, seizure, and arrest; they enforced strict curfews; they required passes for anyone entering or leaving an occupied town or traveling to, from, or through the Union-held regions; and they required permits to buy or sell goods (including food), to practice certain trades, and to engage in any number of other activities. In Athens, Alabama, any citizen found on the streets after nine o'clock at night was subject to arrest. On Virginia's eastern shore, the provost marshal forbade any citizen to own or operate a boat without obtaining a permit and posting bond. Nor were these the severest examples. When Sherman's forces occupied Marietta, they flatly prohibited all travel, trade, or communication between the town and the surrounding countryside. As one resident explained, the Federals were troubled by guerrilla attacks and apprehensive about "spies and unfriendly Citizens"; all the inhabitants, he added, were "suspected & rigidly watched."[54]

Just how much the people of the occupied South were suspected and watched might have surprised even those most wary of the Yankees. In every occupied region, local commandants and provost marshals were instructed to gather intelligence—not just on Rebel military forces, but also on the civilian population. As General James B. McPherson told a subordinate in Mississippi, "make yourself familiar with the character and sentiments of the people in your jurisdiction."[55]

Many occupation officials carried out such orders energetically and meticulously. Authorities in Falmouth, Virginia, aware of the townspeople's "illicit communication with the enemy" and convinced that "strict surveillance is necessary," compiled a register of all inhabitants, noting age, sex, and occupation. A provost marshal in another part of Virginia drew up a list of every secessionist in his district, briefly characterizing each: "Very violent; has refused to take the oath"; "A treacherous rebel, an unprincipled hypocrite; will do anything for money." The Jacksonville, Florida, provost marshal kept a similar file on hundreds of citizens: "Union Man, Reliable in his promises . . . Rebel in feelings & actions, has slaves beyond lines . . . Suspicious character . . . Secessionist at heart, not reliable, gambler, believed to sell whiskey . . . No account in no way . . . Eccentric, dont think much of either Cause . . . Non compos mentis . . . No love for the Union, He is here to avoid [Confederate] conscript[ion] . . . Has brothers in Rebel Army, upright and honest . . .

Union, *Not Briliant* . . . Not sound, of no character, *watch* . . . Very lazy Union man."[56]

To get such information, and to ferret out crime and subversion, occupation authorities not only interrogated citizens and sent out uniformed scouts, but also employed spies, secret agents, professional detectives, and paid informants. The provost marshal at Hilton Head, South Carolina, had three detectives on the payroll in 1864. The Norfolk, Virginia, post commander put some of his soldiers into civilian clothes and ordered them to hang around the docks at night to apprehend Rebel mail carriers, smugglers, and citizens who helped Federal soldiers desert. The Little Rock authorities hired a detective to pass himself off as a Rebel spy and report the names of citizens who aided him. Army officials in New Orleans called in the famed detective Allan Pinkerton to organize an extensive "Secret Service" for military intelligence gathering and for "detecting resident traitors, sympathizers and spies, contraband traders and frauds upon the Govt." In Nashville the army maintained a large secret police force that posted agents in hotel lobbies and railroad depots and even infiltrated private social gatherings.[57]

Silencing and thwarting the secessionists was not enough, however: the occupiers were also determined to make them acknowledge defeat, formally renounce the Confederate cause, and swear loyalty to the Union. Thus, the authorities set about extracting oaths of allegiance—not just from the men of prominence they had sometimes targeted even in the conciliatory period, but also from the plain folk, who had proved to be Rebels of a deeper dye than the Federals had at first believed. Such oaths must of course be voluntary to be meaningful and binding, so the Federals could not simply clap the citizens in irons or hold guns to their heads and then demand the oath. But they could, and did, make it hard in other ways on recalcitrant Rebels. In many districts, for example, the occupiers decreed that the passes and permits required for travel, trade, and work would be denied to those who refused the oath.[58]

The most effective tactic was the threat of expulsion. By 1865 Federal authorities in nearly every occupied region had laid down the law: take the oath or pack up and go to Confederate-held territory. (In many districts, citizens who chose the oath were required to post bond for good behavior, whereas those who chose exile forfeited their property.) This rule would not only remove and punish some of the most troublesome inhabitants and ensure a more tractable civilian population, the Federals reasoned, but also reduce the number of mouths to feed in the occupied areas and throw a corresponding burden on the Confederacy.[59]

Thus did the occupiers forsake conciliation and turn to coercion and reprisal. It is important to understand, however, that as unrelenting as the hard policy was in theory, in practice it was restrained in significant ways. The U.S. Army was certainly capable of waging a war of extermination, as the Indian campaigns of the nineteenth century demonstrated, but the conquest of the Confederacy did not degenerate into such wanton massacre. Even at their fiercest, the Northern invaders maintained a clear distinction between humane and inhumane war making. Though they came to hate the Southern people and sought to subjugate and punish them, and were increasingly willing to restrict their freedom and confiscate their possessions and even starve them into submission, they did not often pursue such tactics to their logical extreme. Moreover, they drew the line at bodily assaults on unarmed civilians: even at the height of the hard policy, violence of that sort remained rare and was never officially sanctioned.

One major factor in the Yankees' restraint was their deep ambivalence toward Southern women, who comprised the majority of citizens in the occupied South. As the war went on, most Federal soldiers discarded their original assumption that the female inhabitants were harmless. Not only did women make themselves obnoxious with their brazen secessionism—one Union officer called them "intense bitter & unbearable"—but they also spied, smuggled, and aided guerrillas while hypocritically demanding the traditional indulgence accorded the "weaker sex." Furthermore, insisted the Federals, even those secessionist women who did not actively resist were guilty of aiding the enemy by encouraging the fighting spirit of their menfolk. "The women of the South [have] kept the war alive," one soldier declared, "—and it is only by making them suffer that we can subdue the men."[60]

Yet most Northern soldiers could never bring themselves to wholly defeminize the women of the South. As dangerous as such women might be, they remained, in the Yankees' eyes, women. Thus the Federals often found themselves torn by conflicting impulses: on the one hand to punish and coerce hostile women as military necessity demanded, on the other hand to indulge and protect them as the Victorian ethos encouraged.[61]

This ambivalence was manifested in many ways. In some cases the soldiers went ahead and applied the sternest restrictions and penalties to women while at the same time expressing regret or offering excuses never deemed necessary in the case of a man. On the march from Atlanta to the sea, one of Sherman's officers justified the destruction as "inevitable & necessary to end the war" but confessed that he felt "sorry . . . for the women here & their anxiety & terror. . . . As to the men, I am not sorry for them." Having approved sanctions against an outspoken secessionist woman, Provost Marshal J. W. Strong on Virginia's eastern shore felt obliged to send her a note assuring her that "none respect a true and virturous woman more than myself, but when wom[e]n act in a disloyal manner so as to subject themselves to arrest, they not only loose there clame to the privalege of there sect but are liable to the punishment the crime deserves."[62]

Often the Federals mitigated penalties against women or applied a kind of indirect coercion. Provost Marshal Strong ordered one woman confined to her room incommunicado until she apologized for her "insolent conduct" toward him, though such conduct by a man would certainly have earned him a jail term, with or without an apology. On a raid in Tennessee, Union troops were subjected to a secessionist tirade by a Mrs. McMillan and her daughter, whereupon (according to a neighbor's report) "the Feds marched off old Mr. McMillan with them—just on account of his wife and daughter's tongues." An Arkansas woman refused to release her hold on a blanket that some Federal soldiers were trying to steal until one of the soldiers pulled out a pistol and pointed it at her husband.[63]

When it came to active resistance, differences between the treatment of men and of women narrowed. The occupiers prescribed the most rigorous punishments for aiding the enemy. They did not, it is true, invoke the death penalty against women, as they sometimes did against men in the most serious cases. But in judging those offenses deemed less than capital, they often granted women no special consideration. Thus, Maria Tabb, of Portsmouth, Virginia, convicted in April 1863 of trying to smuggle letters and money to the Rebels, was sentenced to forfeiture of her house and imprisonment for the duration of the war. The military commission that tried her ignored her plea to "be as lenient as possible. All I did was to oblige others. My husband is in North Carolina, a blacksmith, & I have three small children. . . . This is my first offence."[64]

The harshest retribution was reserved for men and women who waged or abetted guerrilla war. Aside from defeating the Rebel armies and maintaining order and security in the garrisoned posts, the most critical task assigned to Union forces in the South was quashing the guerrillas, whose shadow warfare not only jeopardized Union victory but also haunted every Northern soldier with the threat of sudden death at the hands of unseen assassins.

The occupiers' earliest counterguerrilla tactic—one they pursued throughout the war with little success—was thoroughly conventional: that is, sending out regular military forces to find and destroy guerrilla bands. District and post commanders behind the front lines were allotted infantry or cavalry units for that purpose, while field commanders at the front often sent their own troops on guerrilla-hunting expeditions. The problem was, of course, that guerrillas almost never obliged their enemies by confronting them openly and fighting pitched battles. Occasionally a scouting detachment might stumble over a guerrilla band; but generally the guerrillas laid low when they were being hunted (having the advantage of a network of local informants), and the Federals had to content themselves with making a show of strength, searching homes for weapons, and seizing horses in neighborhoods where guerrillas were active.[65]

The occupiers had more success when they dispatched their forces not blindly, on random patrols, but on specific missions guided by hard intelligence. Here the use of detectives, secret agents, and informants proved valuable. The Memphis provost marshal sent an agent through the countryside to pick up information on guerrillas while posing as a Confederate soldier separated from his unit. Men of the Eighty-third Illinois Infantry, stationed in Clarksville, Tennessee, also disguised themselves as Confederates and roamed the rural districts pumping the citizens for news about guerrilla bands. And throughout the occupied South, Federal authorities relied on tips passed furtively by blacks and Unionists. With such information Northern troops were occasionally able to surprise guerrillas in their hidden lairs, or thwart their planned attacks, or at least identify and arrest the citizens who harbored them.[66]

Union soldiers were not inclined, nor encouraged by their superiors, to take guerrillas alive. General Order 100 stated that guerrillas, "if captured, are not entitled to the privileges of prisoners of war, but shall be treated summarily as highway robbers or pirates." Occupation authorities were more explicit: "[S]hoot [them] on the spot," ordered General Grenville Dodge in Mississippi in 1863. "I don't want any prisoners of that kind."[67]

A number of guerrillas were nevertheless arrested and brought in as captives. Some were then granted formal trial by military commission, but others were held as hostages or were executed summarily and publicly as an example to the citizens. The Union commandant in northwestern Arkansas ordered that any time the telegraph line in that district was cut, one guerrilla prisoner in Federal hands "shall have withdrawn from him that mercy which induced the holding of him as a prisoner, and he shall be hung at the post where the wire is cut; and as many bushwhackers shall be hung as there are places where the wire is cut." An officer in Tennessee reported the capture of several guerrillas in 1864, one of whom "I had shot in Lawrenceburg, and made the citizens bury the body."[68]

The army was never able to capture or kill enough guerrillas to put an end to guerrillaism. They were simply too elusive, their potential hiding places too plentiful, their allies too vigilant. It was not that the occupiers failed to understand the nature of their enemy; most, in fact, recognized the truth early on. Plagued by guerrilla attacks in northern Alabama in the spring of 1862, General Ormsby Mitchel dutifully sent his cavalry in pursuit but remarked: "I doubt the capture of prisoners, as I believe that most of [the guerrillas] are to-day citizens at home superintending their cotton planting." When a telegraph wire was cut in Tennessee that summer, a Federal telegrapher explained that "the secesh attend their farms in the day-time and go bushwhacking at night."[69]

Nor were the Federals under any delusions about the extent to which the guerrilla bands were sustained by the rural populace. Indeed, it was this understanding that gave them the weapon that eventually broke the back of the guerrilla movement in some of the occupied regions. "[P]eople of the neighborhood . . . harbor and feed these lawless men," said General Nathaniel P. Banks while campaigning in Louisiana in 1863, " . . . and it is by punishing them that this detestable practice will be stopped."[70]

Many other Union commanders had already reached the same conclusion, having come to understand the communal nature of guerrillaism. Guerrillas were not freebooters; they were constituents of the local community and thus subject to its will. If the guerrillas themselves could not be caught, if the particular citizens who sheltered and provisioned them could not be identified and punished, it mattered not: the community as a whole supported guerrillaism and could, if it chose, withdraw that support and put an end to it. Thus, the Federals reasoned, sanctions could rightfully be applied to an entire community, regardless of the technical guilt or innocence of individuals.[71]

It became a standard practice to levy cash assessments on all secessionist families in any neighborhood where a guerrilla attack occurred. Leading the way once again was the relentless General Pope in Virginia. He established the rule (among other harsh antiguerrilla measures that won him notoriety in the summer of 1862) that local citizens must pay for damages done by guerrillas to railroads, wagons, and telegraph lines. Many other commanders eventually followed Pope's example, ordering especially heavy penalties in cases where Union soldiers had been killed. When an army surgeon was shot to death in Robertson County, Tennessee, for instance, the district commandant raised a fund of $5,000 for the victim's family by assessing local residents. When five soldiers were killed by guerrillas in Lincoln County, Tennessee, Federal authorities ordered the secessionist members of the community to come up with $30,000, to be contributed in proportion to their wealth.[72]

At least as common as cash assessment was the outright destruction of secessionist property. "Yesterday you fired into our transports," proclaimed a Union officer to the citizens along the Arkansas River in 1863. "To-day I have burned one of your mansions. If you repeat your useless but assassin-like attacks I will devastate this entire country." When one of General Philip Sheridan's staff officers was shot down from ambush in the Shenandoah Valley in 1864, Sheridan ordered every house within a radius of five miles destroyed. Not long afterward, in a section of Virginia described by one officer as a "hot-bed of lawless bands," Union cavalry was sent in with orders to seize or destroy all food supplies, livestock, barns, and mills.[73]

Often the occupiers chose to strike at communities that sanctioned guerrillaism by warring not against property, but against persons. Retaliatory expulsion was common. While in western Tennessee in late 1862, General William T. Sherman ordered that ten local families be banished to Confederate territory for every Federal river vessel fired on by guerrillas. A short time later, in northern Mississippi, General Ulysses S. Grant decreed that the same fate would befall ten families for each guerrilla raid on the Memphis and Charleston Railroad.[74]

The Federals also resorted to hostage taking. When guerrillas kidnapped a Unionist in Sumner County, Tennessee, the post commander at Gallatin arrested five persons, including the wife of one of the suspected perpetrators, and held them as security for the abducted man's safe return. When one of his staff officers died at the hands of guerrillas in Louisiana, General Banks rounded up a hundred men in the vicinity and threatened to hold them until the killers surrendered or were delivered up by the community. In the wake of guerrilla attacks on a Virginia railroad, the Federals seized numerous citizens living along the track and forced a contingent to ride on each train.[75]

Where every other tactic had failed, the occupiers contemplated using the most drastic of all. If the guerrillas could not be flushed from hiding, and if the community could not be persuaded to suppress them, then the community itself must be uprooted and swept away. "I know of no way to exterminate [guerrillaism]," General Philip Sheridan decided in the Shenandoah Valley, "except to burn out the whole country and let the people go North or South." A frustrated officer who had been chasing guerrillas in another part of Virginia concurred: "Every man and horse must be sent within the [picket] lines, every house destroyed, every tree girdled and set on fire, before we can [achieve] security. . . . Attila, King of the Huns, adopted the only method that can exterminate these citizen soldiers. . . . I can clear this country with fire and sword, and no mortal can do it any other way."[76]

Fire and sword were indeed the fate of a number of Southern communities as the occupiers unleashed their full fury against the guerrillas and their allies. After a Mississippi River steamer was attacked and almost captured by guerrillas in September 1862 while docking at Randolph, Tennessee, General Sherman sent a regiment there with orders to destroy the village; afterward he reported that "the regiment has returned and Randolph is gone." Five months later General Stephen Hurlbut dispatched several companies to Hopefield, Arkansas, a place he regarded as "a mere shelter for guerrillas." The troops gave the people of Hopefield one hour to remove possessions from their homes, then burned down the entire town. Similar expeditions wiped out two villages in Louisiana and one in middle Tennessee.[77]

It was northern Virginia, however, that witnessed the most ambitious undertaking: the virtual obliteration of an entire district. Having tried and failed for years to halt guerrilla attacks on the strategic Manassas Gap Railroad, which stretched some seventy-five miles from Manassas Junction to the Shenandoah Valley, Federal authorities took the final step in the fall of 1864. Army chief of staff Henry W. Halleck himself gave the order to General Daniel McCallum: burn down every house within five miles of the railroad unless needed by the army or owned by known Unionists, arrest and imprison every man suspected of aiding guerrillas, send all other inhabitants north or south as they choose. "Forage, animals, and grain will be taken for the use of the United States. All timber and brush within musketry fire of the road will be cut down and destroyed. Printed notices will be circulated and posted that any citizens found within five miles of the road hereafter will be considered as robbers and bushwhackers."[78]

Stretches of uninhabited wasteland became a common sight in the occupied South as the war went on. They were the most conspicuous sign that the war had become a fierce and transforming struggle hardly conceivable in 1861. Beholding their ravaged land and the enemy legions that ruled over it, the people of the occupied South were forced to reconsider the matter of resistance. How to answer the invaders' demand that they renounce their cause or be beggared and brought to their knees or driven from their homes? As Northern rule became increasingly Draconian, that question loomed ever larger.

• • •

As the hard policy bore down on them, the people of the occupied regions reassessed the enemy. At no point had they abandoned their conviction that the Yankees were invaders who polluted the South and abased its citizens, but while the rosewater policy reigned they had tempered their original judgments about Northern character and intentions. Just as civilian resistance transformed Southerners in the Federals' eyes, however, so the hard policy reshaped—or, more accurately, restored to its original form, with certain elaborations—the citizens' conception of the Northern enemy.

On every hand Southerners saw proof that the Yankees were without honor—unprincipled, vulgar, degenerate. "All sense of shame and decency seems to have deserted them," a Virginia woman wrote, "and they stalk abroad and take everything before our eyes, cursing and swearing in the most Godless manner." Tennessee planter Robert Cartmell denounced the occupiers' gratuitous and blasphemous "waste & destruction"; they had stooped to plundering cemeteries, he claimed, and had even "used [churches] as Privies and bibles & hym books as waste papers."[79]

Southerners denounced the hard policy as barbarous and unconscionable—a crime against humanity. "This is the first war on this continent," Alabamian Joshua Moore declared, "that has on the Federal side degenerated into individual robbery and a war upon private citizens." Indeed, many believed that the Yankees were guilty of villainy of world-historical proportions. "We have been robbed and personally maltreated to an extent unparalleled," two Arkansas citizens affirmed; "at any rate not exceeded in all Christian history."[80]

Such ferocity seemed so disproportionate to the Northerners' declared war aims that Southerners began to suspect darker motives. "They have . . . burned my houses, meat & bread," one planter wrote bitterly, "stole and carried of[f] my stock indeed robbed me of all I had to support my family and now say they do so for the Union. . . . I can but think they desire possession of our lands indeed all our property and to reduce us to want." Many citizens worried that the enemy would stop at nothing less than annihilation. "They . . . are striving to exterminate us by slow degrees," a Virginia woman insisted. "They are like the cat with a mouse." Another Virginian feared the enemy had grown so vengeful that the South could anticipate "the hoisting of the *black flag*, unless Christendom interposes to save us."[81]

The soldiers who waged such warfare were not just vicious: they were demons, they were savages, they were beasts. These three images of the enemy cropped up repeatedly in the statements of citizens of the occupied South. "[T]he most horrible set of creatures I ever saw," a Virginian testified after Northern troops raided her farm. "There was one terrible wretch with the face of a fiend incarnate. . . . Certainly there was never such an army of demons collected before, outside of the infernal regions." Roxa Cole described a raid on her northern Mississippi town in which soldiers "came down upon us in the 'dead of night,' surrounding every house, creeping stealthily around and peeping in at the windows. I could but think of the stories of the early settlers and their Indian foes." Virginia French wrote of her home being "so over-run with Yankees that I felt as one feels in some horrible drama when fancy pictures hundreds of wild beasts all around you, and you almost at their mercy."[82]

Such imagery was not merely rhetorical. It signified something deeper: the dehumanization of the enemy. In the minds of a growing number of Southerners, the invaders had forfeited their claim to humanity. The links that bound even mortal enemies into a civilized community with certain standards of mutual respect had been shattered. The Northern soldier who ravaged the South and terrorized its people was not a worthy foe, not a brother in Christ, not even a fellow human being. "Of the hundreds who were here," wrote a Virginian after a raid on her plantation in 1864, "there might be three or four who might be termed gentlemen—if they had not been Yankees. About as many more [were] *men*—all the rest were brutes and demons in human shape." Preacher Jesse Cox, of Tennessee, who devoutly anticipated the fulfillment of biblical prophecy, believed that the Northern army might be "anti christ, the Beast that [is to] assend from the botomless pits."[83]

Dehumanization alone can explain the extraordinarily bitter enmity and cold, even cruel, callousness manifested toward the Federals by some Southerners—among them many women who had been schooled from infancy to be gentle, compassionate, and merciful. "[I]f I were a man I would never take a [Union soldier] prisoner," a Virginian declared. "I would consider it my duty to rid the world of all such monsters. God can have mercy on them if he chooses." Virginia French reported that when Rebel troops temporarily retook McMinnville, Tennessee, the women of the town demanded that the troops summarily execute the captured Federal provost marshal, whom they despised (the soldiers refused). A Fredericksburg woman wrote of her experience when Union forces held the town: "My only amusement was watching them bury their dead. I got quite fond of looking at [the corpses]." Cordelia Scales of Mississippi told how the Federals set up a field hospital in her home after a battle and brought in a number of wounded soldiers: "I did feel so happy," she wrote, "when I looked on the suffering & heard the groans of those blue devils."[84]

Even as their loathing of the enemy intensified under the hard policy, Southerners found it more dangerous to resist, whether by verbal defiance, noncooperation, aiding the Confederacy, or guerrillaism. Thus, they were forced to contrive new strategies to reconcile the demands of honor, patriotism, and self-preservation.

Some decided to flee Federal rule and rejoin the Confederacy. In some cases this was a matter of simple survival: families whose livelihood had been wiped out by the occupiers' trade restrictions or by their looting and destruction of farms and shops sometimes had no choice but to head for Confederate lines. More often, though, it was a matter of principle, especially where the Federals required the oath. West Tennessean John Waddel chose exile over the oath demanded of him in December 1862: "If I take the oath," he explained, "I shall be forever disgraced according to my view of duty & principle." When Federal authorities in Memphis delivered the ultimatum that year, many residents of the city packed up and left, as did over a hundred Nashvillians in 1863 and several hundred citizens of New Orleans in 1864.[85]

The great majority of Southerners stayed on, however, and endeavored to get along under Federal rule. Most eventually concluded that it was wisest to placate the enemy and to avoid the kind of angry confrontation many had relished in earlier days. "This is the way we get on," is how an Arkansas man explained his family's meek compliance with the frequent demands of Federal soldiers for food. "With an assumed cheerfulness to save ourselves from plunder and insult, we give away the bread for which our poor children must in a short time cry." Forced to stand by helplessly while foragers loaded their wagon from his stores of corn, R. B. Creecy of North Carolina regarded the matter with resignation: "Such things are hard to bear," he sighed, "but can not be resisted." In August 1862, just two months after she had told off a party of Federal soldiers who had come looking for dinner, Virginia French fed another such party but this time held her tongue. Like other Southerners, she now loosed her venom only in private. "I abominate the very sight of the miserable wretches," she fumed in her diary later that day, "—they are so brutal looking—so impertinent—and so insufferable."[86]

Small acts of open defiance were still possible, but they had to be carefully calibrated so as not to provoke retaliation. Elderly or disabled men could sometimes take advantage of the Yankees' lingering qualms about rough treatment of citizens who appeared harmless. A Virginia man ran off a gang of pillagers "by threatening to break the head of one of them with my crutch if he did not behave himself." Seventy-three-year-old Tennessean Nimrod Porter deterred a band of soldiers intent on stealing chickens by making it clear that they would have to fight him to get what they wanted. Indeed, some men protected themselves by deliberating projecting an image of innocuousness. Robert Mecklin of Arkansas did so whenever Federal troops came by: "I am quiet and submissive," he explained, "take no interest in what is going on, and am looked upon by them as a harmless, inoffensive old dotard."[87]

Women, too, sought to capitalize on the Yankees' ambivalence toward them. A common strategy was to strike a pose of utter feminine helplessness (complete with tears and anguished pleading in some cases) and then try to shame the Federals into abandoning their designs. "I'm all alone," a Fredericksburg woman replied when soldiers asked to use her house as a hospital. "I hope you have more honor than to come and disturb defenseless, unprotected women." Virginian Amanda Chappelear confronted a group of soldiers who were leading her horse away and, though she "was in a rage with the vile beings," she choked back her anger and chided them gently, reminding them that no true gentleman would steal a lady's horse.[88]

Other feminine survival strategies included coquetry and flattery, feigned stupidity or innocence, and (in the manner of Nimrod Porter) maneuvering the Yankees into a situation where they would have to use physical force to get what they wanted. "[I] Have condescended to chat a little with our sentinels," wrote an aristocratic young woman of Williamsburg, Virginia, after two soldiers were posted outside her home. They were "rather hard cases," she said, but she and her family were anxious to win them over "by a little attention—so completely do we feel at their mercy." Marching through Mississippi in 1863, the men of the Thirty-ninth Ohio Infantry came upon a woman who professed never to have seen a Union soldier before: "What, are you-all Yankees?," she exclaimed. "Why I thought they were covered with hair, like wild men. Why, you-uns look just like our men." In 1864, in another part of Mississippi, Federal soldiers looted the home of Elizabeth and Sarah Beach, taking almost everything; the women managed to save their stored dresses by sitting down on them and vowing not to relinquish them without a fight.[89]

Another strategy, adopted by men and women alike and refined by some to an art, was lying or dissembling. R. B. Creecy deceived a detachment of Northern troops who came by his farm and questioned him and his father about "our political sentiments—were we *Union* men &c, to which we replied that we were for *peace*—with the mental reservation myself as to the *kind of peace* I was for." In fact, many citizens employed such subterfuges not only with enemy soldiers but with all strangers, for it was no secret that the Federals sent out spies. As one Tennessean remarked, "the Detectives are out here constantly dressed in citizens clothing, and we do not know who we are talking to."[90]

Guerrilla activity, in particular, was screened by a curtain of lies and evasions. "It is very difficult to gather any reliable information from the white people," a Union officer complained after returning from a fruitless guerrilla-hunting expedition in North Carolina. "There are so many contradictory statements." An officer on a sweep through western Tennessee was told by white residents that there were no guerrillas in the vicinity, only to learn from blacks that bands as large as twenty strong were passing by every day. Where the presence of guerrillas was undeniable, citizens solemnly assured the Federals that their community frowned on the guerrillas but had no control over them.[91]

Submitting passively to the enemy's demands, dickering or currying favor with them, lying, and dissembling all deeply troubled the honor-obsessed people of the South. Most rationalized such behavior by pointing out that they had no alternative short of starvation, prison, or exile. To be thus compelled to compromise one's principles was, they insisted, no dishonor. Tennessean John Waddel, for example, gave in to an insistent officer who wanted his house as a headquarters, "and now," he lamented, "my house is just filled up with Federals. . . . It is however no mortification to me as I was *forced* to submit." Roxa Cole concluded that "perhaps one is not to be blamed" for yielding to "a cruel tyranical government," for "self-preservation is the first law of nature."[92]

Such excuses could not satisfy those proud Southerners who maintained that honor must not be compromised even under the threat of death. Such men and women may have devised a subtler rationale for violating their principles. The concept of honor presumed the existence of some sort of legitimate authority (law or community, for instance) that recognized and validated and upheld honor as a system of values, an authority to which all owed obeisance and all could appeal. But the Yankees—who were not men of honor, not even human beings according to some—had imposed their own alien and illegitimate authority on the people of the occupied South. Honor simply had no place within that sphere of authority. Southerners were still obliged to act honorably among themselves, on this reasoning, but they owed the enemy no such due and would not be disgraced by bowing to the necessities imposed by Federal rule.[93]

Such logic was invoked especially when Southerners confronted the question of the oath. As the war went on, more and more citizens reluctantly yielded to Federal pressure and took an oath of loyalty to the United States. But a great many who took it did so with no intention of respecting it and thereafter violated it without compunction. Though oath breaking was regarded as sacrilege within the circle of honor, those who violated the Federal oath generally felt no shame and were not condemned by their peers, for in the eyes of the community the invaders' regime lacked legitimacy. The oath "[is] often lightly esteemed, or entirely disregarded," a Union provost marshal observed, "by disloyal persons who are deemed honorable and otherwise trustworthy." Southerners themselves admitted as much in private. "I got out of prison by taking oath and giving bond," Tennessean James Matthews noted in his journal, but "in heart I am far, very far from being a yankee." Harrison Tunstall of Arkansas wrote his brother that "we are having a hard time of it here with the Feds. . . . [T]hey order the citizens up to Batesville about every two weeks to take new oaths . . . but the more they make us take the oath the stronger we grow in Confederate faith."[94]

Indeed, Confederate faith stubbornly endured throughout the occupied South. Though they were compelled to kneel in the presence of the conquerors, citizens kept the faith alive around their hearths and in their hearts. "I have never been 'whipped,' " Mississippian John Burruss told a kinsman in 1864. "I have known but one feeling for years—no submission." The persistence of Confederate morale was in fact quite evident to the occupiers themselves, despite the citizens' dissembling and prevaricating. "There is very little Union feeling in Memphis," observed a Federal soldier in June 1863, a year after the city's capture. "Nothing but the bayonet keeps it loyal."[95]

That the Rebel spirit was so resilient in the occupied South is remarkable, considering its inherent limitations. After all, it was wholly deprived of the institutional buttresses—the Rebel press, pulpit, and public rituals—that bolstered morale behind Confederate lines. Moreover, its vitality was weakened by the departure of many of the most uncompromising and outspoken secessionists, who fled as refugees when the Federals arrived or were banished later.[96]

On the other hand, there was a powerful compensating factor that stiffened Confederate morale and resistance in the occupied South. This was the hard policy itself, which was (at least in the short run) egregiously counterproductive. Even under the conciliatory policy, the citizens had stoutly resisted, for the mere fact of enemy occupation seemed to defile the South and degrade its people. Small wonder, then, that when the occupiers took up their new agenda of devastation, subjugation, and revolution, the citizens' determination to resist only grew more fierce and desperate. Moreover, the invaders' intensifying hatred and lust for vengeance was matched by the citizens' own. Every Federal reprisal reinforced Southerners' belief that their Northern adversaries were brutal savages whose outrages must be avenged.

In other words, as Harrison Tunstall had suggested to his brother, the harder the invaders tried to snuff out the flame, the brighter it burned. Tunstall went on to explain: "[B]efore [the Yankees] come every body was so tired of the war that they would have almost submitted to Lincoln to get peace but far from that is the case now[.] [A]s soon as this crop is made and gathered there will be a general turnout of the people of this section to defend their and their childrens rights against negro equality." Tunstall's sentiments were seconded by many other citizens. Edward Carter Turner of Virginia believed that the rosewater policy might, in the long run, have encouraged the people of the South to come to terms with the North, but "under the present exasperated state of feeling, & burning for revenge for insults and injuries received, it would be next to impossible." Another Virginian declared that the Yankees must "be made to pay the penalty of all these outrages; sooner or later the day of visitation will come, & [they will] not escape the punishment they so justly deserve— retribution full & equivilant must be demanded for all the wrongs & injustices inflicted upon us."[97]

The cornerstone of Confederate morale, however, was the persisting faith in eventual military victory. Though this faith was tested severely as the war turned against the South, it could not be extinguished as long as the Confederacy kept armies in the field capable of challenging the enemy. "[W]e are full of hope," said a middle Tennessean in May 1864, after more than two years of occupation; "We are expecting a great deal from [Robert E.] Lee." Even in the war's darkest days the citizens' faith was now and again rewarded and renewed by a sudden Confederate counter-offensive or a daring cavalry raid that liberated, if only for a few hours or days, the long-suffering citizens of some occupied town or region.[98]

The tenacity of Confederate morale, the grim determination to thwart the invaders' coercive and revolutionary designs, the hunger for vengeance, and the dehumanization of the enemy soldier all found their fullest expression in guerrilla warfare. Even as guerrillaism was quelled by Union reprisals in some districts, it burgeoned in others, fueled by the citizens' growing wrath or by encouraging news from the front. And, increasingly, the guerrillas' war became a war of vicious cruelty and bloodlust. Late in 1863, near the village of Mulberry, Tennessee, guerrillas captured five Federal foragers whom they mounted on horses and led into the woods; hours later the guerrillas finally halted, built a fire, tied their prisoners' hands, lined them up, and then shot them down in cold blood. In Virginia, a man recounted a conversation he had with one member of a guerrilla band that had captured and later murdered eight Federal scouts: "he said [they] took them out and shot them. . . . He said the scouts plead[ed] for mercy. I asked him how he could shoot men who begged for mercy. He said . . . like damned dogs."[99]

Thus did the people of the occupied South accept the enemy's challenge and gird themselves for Armageddon. But that was not the only challenge they confronted. Even as it spawned a mortal struggle between Southern citizens and Northern invaders, occupation unleashed long-restrained forces within Southern society itself. More immediately, it posed the dilemma of simply how to survive.

[3]

....

Three Worlds

*The Garrisoned Towns,
the Confederate Frontier,
and No-Man's-Land*

....

      Union occupation had not only a temporal dimension, evidenced in the transformation of Federal war aims and policy over time, but also a spatial dimension, a distinctive geography. Wherever the Northerners invaded they imposed a new pattern on the South's social and economic landscape.

    That pattern was simply a function of the distance between a given Southerner's home and the nearest Union army post. When the Federal army captured a piece of Confederate territory, it did not scatter its occupation forces throughout, but instead concentrated them in a few fortified posts, almost always in towns of some strategic importance. From these posts would regularly go forth patrols, foraging detachments, and guerrilla-hunting expeditions that traversed the surrounding countryside, and occasionally raiding parties that roamed farther afield, beyond the acknowledged limits of Federal control and into regions where Confederate authority persisted.

Thus, Union occupation created in effect not one occupied South but three: the garrisoned towns, whose citizens lived constantly in the presence, and under the thumb, of the Northern army; the Confederate frontier, which the Federals penetrated only sporadically, its citizens at all other times being in the Confederacy's grasp; and no-man's-land, the zone surrounding the garrisoned towns, which was beyond the pale of Confederate authority and endured frequent Yankee visitations, but did not experience the constant presence of a Federal force (see Figure 1).

These three spheres might well be considered different worlds, so starkly did they delineate distinctive experiences within the occupied South. Of course, citizens could and did pass from one sphere to another—often without even leaving their homes, for in the ebb and flow of military campaigns some captured districts were at one time or another temporarily relinquished by the Union army, and what was a garrisoned town or no-man's-land one day might be Confederate frontier the next. However fluid, the three worlds of the occupied South were sharply defined in many respects, not least in the manner in which the inhabitants and their institutions struggled to survive.

. . .

No fewer than a hundred Southern towns were occupied and garrisoned as Federal army posts at one time or another during the war. Among them were a number of the region's major cities, including New Orleans (the South's largest), Memphis, Nashville, Norfolk, Portsmouth, Alexandria, and, late in the war, Savannah, Charleston, and Wilmington.

Dependent as they were on commerce and, to a lesser extent, industry, these towns were hard hit economically by the advent of the Union army. Shackled by military rule, cut off from their customary sources and markets by the Federal land and sea blockades, and in some cases crippled by the seizure or destruction of their property, the merchants and industrialists and artisans of the captured towns saw their trade fall off precipitously or vanish altogether. The declining prosperity of these classes in turn touched those who provided labor and services for them, from draymen and dockworkers and shop hands to clerks and lawyers. Many people were thrown out of work, especially unskilled laborers, who found themselves competing for scarce jobs with the newly freed blacks who flooded into the towns.[1]

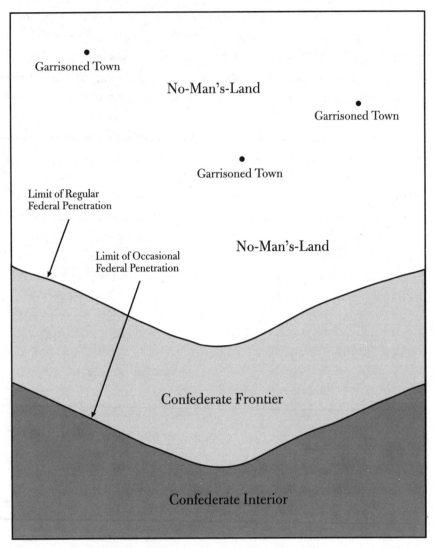

Garrisoned Town

No-Man's-Land

Garrisoned Town

Garrisoned Town

Limit of Regular
Federal Penetration

Limit of Occasional
Federal Penetration

No-Man's-Land

Confederate Frontier

Confederate Interior

FIGURE 1. *Schematic Representation of the Occupied South*

The unemployment problem was only partly relieved by the new work opportunities that came in the Federal army's wake. The services of certain artisans—blacksmiths, shoemakers, coopers, and so forth—were much in demand by the army, particularly in such cities as Nashville and Alexandria, which became major Union military depots and production centers. Among the professional classes, clerks and doctors had skills that the Union army could use. Unskilled citizens, male and female, could sometimes find employment, too, as day laborers, cooks, or laundresses.

Moreover, the presence of thousands of well-paid but in certain respects deprived soldiers provided opportunities for numberless hucksters and prostitutes, who peddled their wares—milk, butter, pies, cakes, liquor, and sex—wherever the soldiers congregated. Prostitution, in particular, was (to judge from Union soldiers' accounts) a significant element of the local economy in some of the garrisoned towns. One soldier in Nashville wrote of being billeted "in an abandoned part of town given up most entirely to prostitutes and there is hundreds of them. . . . [I]t seems as though there was nothing else here for they monopolise every thing, all the public hacks and drivers, the front seats at all places of amusement. . . . U.S. officers are there principle maintaners."[2]

The army's voracious demand for goods and services did not provide work for every citizen who needed it. For one thing, many Southerners refused to do any sort of business with the hated enemy unless extreme necessity compelled it. Moreover, those who bowed to that necessity and sought jobs or business with the army (which usually meant taking the oath) found themselves competing with people whom the Federals often favored. Not only were there plenty of blacks in the towns to provide unskilled and some skilled labor, but there were also droves of Northern civilians who had followed the army south to seek their fortune. Among them were tradespeople and entrepreneurs of every sort, from grocers, dry goods dealers, army sutlers, and cotton speculators to carpenters, wagon makers, dentists, daguerrotypists, entertainers, gamblers, and, of course, prostitutes.[3]

Besides throwing citizens out of work, Federal occupation diminished the supply of food, fuel, clothing, medicine, and other basic commodities available to townspeople. Trade regulation was one of the most complicated and controversial aspects of military occupation. Contradictory orders and policies emanated from Washington, the army and the Treasury Department argued over jurisdiction, and each local commandant had his own ideas about the matter. Every garrisoned town was subjected to a bewildering and frequently revised array of regulations. The point of it all was, of course, to strangle and starve the Confederacy. Federal authorities knew that contraband goods were smuggled from the occupied regions to Rebel-held territory. They therefore sought to restrict the supply of such goods and to scrutinize their disposition. This meant not only regulating imports of civilian supplies from the North (which were already limited to some extent because they competed with military supplies for cargo space), but also regulating the importation of goods into the towns from the surrounding countryside, because anything exchanged for such goods might find its way to the Confederacy. Although these regulations were often weakly enforced, their overall effect was to curtail the supply of provisions available to Southern civilians in most towns.[4]

Even where supplies were plentiful, the citizens' ability to buy them was hampered by persistent currency problems. In most towns the occupation authorities outlawed the use of bills issued by the Confederacy or by Rebel state governments; even where they did not, such paper depreciated rapidly under Federal rule. Specie continued to circulate, along with local bank notes, but the latter were not always accepted by Northern suppliers, while specie was forbidden to be exchanged for goods from the countryside because it was useful to the Confederacy. Currency shortages normally deflate prices, but along with the Yankees came an infusion of U.S. Treasury notes (greenbacks) that more than offset the local currency shortage. Occupation authorities ruled greenbacks legal tender for all purchases and forbade their discounting, thus rendering them preferable to local paper, but citizens had trouble securing greenbacks unless they did business with the army. The complaint of a Leesburg, Virginia, woman was typical: "You cannot imagine how hard it is to get any thing here," she wrote in 1864; ". . . No money used here but Yankee greenbacks—Virginia money 3 to one in Federal. . . . I have tried to raise money & give good security—but no person has money [to lend]."[5]

The inexorable result of the influx of greenbacks and the scarcity of provisions was skyrocketing inflation. Add to that the problem of unemployment and the shortage of cash among the citizens, and it is not surprising that many towns soon faced the threat of widespread privation. "[T]imes hard and tight," is how a Tennessee woman described conditions in Murfreesboro, "every thing sells high . . . eatables very scarce and price high." In Nashville, where not only food but also firewood and other indispensable supplies became exorbitantly expensive, the *Daily Press* reported that "the laboring classes have been ground to the earth almost, beneath the oppression. Never before were our men of small means so harassed by all-devouring prices for articles necessary to sustain life.... [T]hey have been forced to abandon every luxury, and live on the scantiest rations, with no preparations for a 'rainy day.' " General John A. Dix observed conditions in Norfolk and Portsmouth in 1862 and found that prices were high, unemployed citizens were using up their savings, and some critical items were "not to be had at any price." "The state of things . . . is deplorable," he concluded. "The people are suffering for want of almost all the necessaries of life."[6]

Many townspeople were hard put not only to keep food on their tables, clothes on their backs, and wood in their stoves, but also to maintain a roof over their heads. Nearly every garrisoned town experienced a severe housing shortage. This was in part a consequence of the army's seizure of buildings for military use: although most of those seized were government edifices, factories, stores, offices, schools, churches, and other such structures suitable as barracks or warehouses or hospitals, quite a few private homes were taken for officers' quarters; many were vacant, having been abandoned by refugees, but when necessary the army seized occupied houses and evicted the tenants. More significant was the influx of Northern civilians and freed slaves, which swelled the population of the towns. Memphis, whose prewar population was about 23,000, white and black, had by early 1863 about 35,000, not counting soldiers. Nashville, which had (with its suburbs) around 30,000 residents in 1860, had 75,000 (excluding soldiers) by early 1865. The population explosion in these and other garrisoned towns drove real estate prices and rents skyward and spawned enormous overcrowding.[7]

Federal authorities could not ignore the threat of privation in the towns. A combination of political, humanitarian, and military considerations compelled them to act. While the rosewater policy prevailed, assisting the needy seemed a good way to remind the citizens of the benevolence of the government they had forsaken and thus encourage them to return to their allegiance; failing to help, on the other hand, would presumably discourage latent Unionism. Thus, General Dix's report on Norfolk and Portsmouth in 1862 warned that privation among the citizens was an "infliction . . . not calculated to add to the number of our friends."[8]

At the same time, purely humanitarian motives were at work, and they persisted even after the occupiers abandoned conciliation. However committed to the hard policy, Union soldiers were loath to turn their backs on harmless and helpless Southern civilians facing real destitution.

Of all the citizens of the occupied South, those in the garrisoned towns posed the least threat to the Federal army, for armed resistance there was out of the question. Furthermore, townspeople were the most dependent of Southerners, for, unlike rural folk, they lacked the means to produce any of their necessities. It was one thing for the army to strip the rural areas of bacon and cornmeal and shrug off the protests of farm families, who (the Yankees reasoned) could always raise more corn and hogs and who in any case were probably harboring guerrillas. But it was another thing to take control of a town and then ignore the pleas of the indigent inhabitants, who were entirely in the Federals' power and had nowhere to turn for sustenance but to their captors. "They are helpless women and children," wrote General Egbert Viele in Norfolk, "who are begging daily at my headquarters for food." Sherman himself, avatar of the hard policy, felt obliged "to feed the inhabitants of the conquered country after they have fallen helpless in our power."[9]

In a subtle and unintentional way, however, the citizens of the garrisoned towns did pose a military threat to the occupiers, and that threat provided a third rationale for Federal benevolence. Unrelieved destitution in the towns could very well touch off civil disorder. Military authorities had plenty to do keeping their posts secure against Rebel cavalry raids without having to worry about bread riots, too. "We are, in point of fact, holding here in custody about 20,000 people," General Viele declared in a plea for relaxed trade restrictions. "Food must be allowed to come in or the people will starve. . . . I have always considered that the [main object] to be attained here was perfect tranquillity. This has been secured so far; in order to continue it the steps I have referred to appear to be necessary."[10]

For all these reasons, Federal authorities sooner or later undertook relief efforts in nearly every garrisoned town. Within a week after the capture of Vicksburg in 1863, the army appointed a committee composed of a Federal officer, an army chaplain, and a Vicksburg citizen and ordered them to compile a registry of needy residents and issue provisions. Elsewhere, including Morganza, Louisiana, and Fernandina, Florida, provost marshals regularly doled out rations to anyone who applied. In some of the bigger towns extensive relief programs were set up. Portsmouth's army officials were feeding no fewer than 1,200 residents by September 1863. In Nashville, military governor Johnson arranged railroad transportation to bring in firewood for the needy. In New Orleans the army provided pork, beef, fish, flour, rice, peas, coffee, and soap to tens of thousands of native whites, not to mention large numbers of blacks and Union soldiers' families—all told, nearly a quarter of the city's civilian population. General N. P. Banks, commanding in New Orleans in 1863, remarked that provisioning the city's needy had proved to be "a labor of far greater intensity . . . than the creation of an army and the conduct of campaigns."[11]

Besides offering direct relief to the indigent, Federal authorities sought in a number of other ways to alleviate economic hardships in the garrisoned towns. Some established markets, regulated and protected by the army, to encourage local farmers to bring in their surplus produce. In some towns authorities tried to control inflation (which they generally blamed on greedy speculators rather than the ineluctable laws of supply and demand) by fixing commodity prices and rents. The Vicksburg commandant, claiming that "speculators in staple articles of food have monopolized the supply and are grinding the faces of the poor," promulgated in August 1864 a schedule of maximum prices for flour, pork, bacon, ham, salt, and soap; violators, he warned, risked fines, imprisonment, and confiscation of their stock. A month later the town's provost marshal, declaring that rents "have become extortionate and intolerable," ordered them rolled back to no more than 25 percent above their prewar level.[12]

Relief measures were just one of many tasks that occupation authorities undertook in the garrisoned towns. The complexity of urban life demanded substantial government activity, unlike rural life, and the larger the town the more dependent were its citizens on strictly enforced ordinances, formal institutions, and professional administration. The arrival of the Yankees brought local government to a standstill, and the occupiers had to act immediately to avoid turmoil. This was, understandably enough, one matter in which the populace was usually willing to cooperate with the enemy.[13]

In some towns—including Vicksburg, Fort Smith, Arkansas, and Gallatin and Clarksville, Tennessee—army officials responded by leaving municipal government in abeyance and assuming its duties themselves. These duties included levying and collecting taxes, which the occupation authorities deposited in a special fund and used to defray expenses incurred in administering municipal affairs, just as any town council would do. Into this "post fund" (or "civil fund") went not only the property taxes, fines, and business license fees that customarily supported municipal government, but also special taxes that the Federals imposed in some towns, such as tariffs on locally imported and exported goods. (Here, as in all other aspects of Federal rule in the South, the high command granted local occupation officials a great deal of autonomy.)[14]

Although the post commander (or, in some cases, the military governor) was the ranking authority in a garrisoned town and personally oversaw some municipal matters, the key figure in the day-to-day administration of town affairs (and civilian-related matters in general) was the provost marshal, who was technically not a subordinate of the post commander but of the provost marshal general attached to district or departmental headquarters. In every town the provost marshal's office was a busy place, where a steady stream of orders issued forth and a steady stream of citizens came and went, drawing rations, paying taxes and fees, seeking passes and permits, lodging complaints, and taking the oath.[15]

In many garrisoned towns, including all the big cities, Federal authorities balked at the enormous task of managing every detail of government. They therefore encouraged the revival of civil government and shunted a share of administrative burdens onto the shoulders of local civilian officials. As Sherman explained in January 1864, municipal officers should as far as possible retain the responsibility to "preserve good order and government" and thereby "free the hosts of [army] guards and officers whose time has heretofore been absorbed in civil matters." Other commanders had in fact pursued this policy from the beginning of occupation in many towns, including Nashville, New Orleans, Memphis, Norfolk, Portsmouth, and Murfreesboro (all captured in 1862), and Sherman did so himself when he took Savannah late in 1864. In each of these towns, local government resumed, under Federal aegis, with scarcely a pause.[16]

The apportioning of duties between army and civil officials varied from town to town, but between the two all the critical functions of municipal government were carried out. One of the most important was preserving public health and safety. Here again, as with relief measures, the Federals' motives were both humanitarian and military, for a hazardous urban environment not only endangered the lives and property of citizens but also compromised the security of the post. Fire, for one thing, was an ever-present threat in the wood-built and stove-heated towns of the nineteenth-century South, and thus one of the occupiers' first concerns was to see that the local fire department was manned and equipped and that hydrants were in working order. Army officers or civil officials also took responsibility for street, wharf, and levee repairs and street lighting.[17]

Wartime overcrowding aggravated the danger of fire, the deterioration of streets, and every other urban health and safety problem, particularly that of sanitation and disease control. In an age when systematic waste removal was generally unknown and hordes of animals inhabited the towns, streets and yards were deluged with rubbish, offal, manure, and carcasses. Consequently, in every town the occupation authorities cracked down on citizens who improperly dumped refuse or let animals run at large, and in some towns they undertook major cleanup operations. In New Orleans, General Benjamin F. Butler put a small army of unemployed men to work scouring the streets and markets. (Even the bitterest Yankee haters were forced to admit that the city had never been cleaner.) Later, in Norfolk, which he found even filthier than New Orleans, Butler recruited cleanup crews from among jail inmates and soon had the city livable.[18]

Butler and other commandants also took steps to control the contagious diseases that periodically swept the towns. In a number of places, including Norfolk, Vicksburg, Alexandria, Nashville, and Jacksonville, the army ordered all citizens to be vaccinated against smallpox and generally provided the service free. In towns where smallpox or other diseases had already appeared, the authorities set up quarantine centers. The stern quarantine measures that the army enforced in New Orleans may well have prevented a yellow fever outbreak of the sort that had devastated the city in the 1850s.[19]

Venereal disease spread so widely among prostitutes and soldiers in some towns that the army was forced to act. The most drastic solution was attempted in Nashville, where in July 1863 the provost marshal rounded up all known prostitutes—several hundred in number—and sent them north on trains and steamboats. They were generally turned away wherever they tried to disembark, however, and the provost marshal soon had to countermand the order; by August most of the women were back at work in Nashville. The city's military authorities then tried a novel approach, in effect creating America's first system of legalized prostitution. The women were licensed, ordered to undergo weekly medical inspections by army surgeons, and required to pay a fee that went to support a venereal hospital for women (a similar hospital was set up for soldiers); any prostitute found working without a license and health certificate was subject to arrest. The success of the system (the incidence of venereal disease dropped significantly) inspired similar experiments in other towns, including Memphis, Norfolk, and Portsmouth.[20]

No less important than safeguarding public health was preserving public order. Nineteenth-century Southern towns, at least the larger ones, were often very disorderly places, inadequately policed and rife with crime and rowdiness. (New Orleans, in particular, seemed to many of its citizens to be perpetually on the brink of anarchy.) In many garrisoned towns, the population boom that followed the Union army's arrival triggered a wave of lawlessness that threatened to overwhelm the already hard-pressed forces of order. New Orleans and Nashville were egregious examples, but perhaps the worst was Alexandria: military commandant John P. Slough exaggerated only a little when he described that city's condition upon his arrival in August 1862 as " 'a reign of terror.' . . . The streets were crowded with intoxicated soldiery; murder was of almost hourly occurrence, and disturbances, robbery and rioting were constant. The sidewalks and docks were covered with drunken men, women and children, and quiet citizens were afraid to venture into the streets."[21]

"Quiet citizens" in Alexandria and elsewhere often pleaded with the army for help. The town fathers of Carrollton, Louisiana, petitioned the provost marshal in 1863 for a military guard to act as a night patrol, pointing out that occupation had brought in "many traders, hucksters, and other dealers from different parts of the country . . . for the purpose of trade, and others for the purposes of gain by any means," and that "many depredations have been committed on the property of citizens during the night." The occupiers, for their part, were eager to maintain order in the garrisoned towns, for military as well as humanitarian reasons, and so they willingly provided patrol squads to supplement the local police or simply assumed all police duties themselves. In Memphis and Nashville, army authorities left the civil police force intact and reinforced it as necessary with garrison troops, whereas in Vicksburg, Norfolk, Portsmouth, and New Bern, North Carolina, the provost marshal acted as the town's police chief and employed his provost guards as policemen.[22]

As soon as they began rounding up civilian malefactors, or allowed the civil police force to do so, military authorities faced the question of what to do with them. (Uniformed offenders were dealt with under long-established rules of military justice.) Because martial law prevailed, the occupiers would have been within their rights to dispose of such cases summarily, but they generally preferred a more systematic approach that rendered homage to the American tradition of due process. For lesser offenses—public drunkenness, disorderly conduct, petty theft, and so forth—the usual procedure was an informal trial. In towns where civil authority was functioning these proceedings were sometimes carried out by existing municipal tribunals, such as the recorder's courts of New Orleans and Nashville. In most towns, however, the provost marshal or a specially appointed provost judge held hearings and handed out sentences. Jails and workhouses, supervised by military or civil officers, awaited convicted offenders not fortunate enough to get off with a fine or a scolding.[23]

Serious crimes, including robbery and murder, were generally granted more formal disposition. In some cases this was provided by civilian criminal courts existing by sufferance of the army or revived under a reconstructed state government. But in most towns no such courts were operating, and major criminal cases were therefore tried by military commissions, whose composition and evidentiary and procedural rules paralleled those of courts-martial. (The army had established the precedent of using military commissions to try civilians in occupied enemy territory during the Mexican War.) Citizens accused of military or political offenses, such as smuggling, spying, theft of army property, or violation of the oath, were almost always tried by military commission, even where civilian courts were functioning.[24]

In many towns, the occupiers assumed responsibility for a host of noncriminal judicial matters as well. Because few civilian courts with appropriate civil jurisdiction were operating in the garrisoned towns before the war ended, most citizens had nowhere to turn but to the army to settle legal disputes and certify legal procedures. Though some occupation authorities were indifferent to such matters, deeming them irrelevant to their military mission, most could no more turn their backs on defenseless citizens clamoring for justice than they could helpless citizens demanding food. "The military authorities," said the Huntsville provost marshal in 1864, "are bound . . . to see that justice is done between citizens, in the absence of the Civil Courts. . . . They will not—can not—be indifferent to the perpetration of wrongs—private or public." Consequently, provost marshals and provost judges resolved all sorts of issues that citizens brought before them, particularly debt claims and probate but even domestic disputes as well. "You are hereby notified," Provost Marshal Edward Bigelow told a Thibodaux, Louisiana, man in 1865, "to take such steps to provide for your wife and children as are necessary to make them comfortable. Your wife complains that you do not provide well for the children. . . . Husbands are supposed to take care and provide for their families & children."[25]

In fact, Federal officials extended protection to all sorts of people whom their Victorian ethos identified as helpless and deserving of public guardianship—not only neglected wives and children, but also the "worthy" poor, the sick, and the insane. In most garrisoned towns the army assumed direct control of, or assured the continued civil administration of, the public institutions that cared for society's unfortunates. The provost marshal in New Bern, North Carolina, established a thirty-acre farm (dubbed the "U.S. House of Refuge") on the outskirts of town to house and support widows, orphans, and other indigents. In New Orleans, General Butler granted cash subsidies to the city's charity hospital and various orphanages. Nashville's occupation authorities oversaw not only the county poorhouse but also the Tennessee Hospital for the Insane with its three hundred patients.[26]

Public education provided another example of the Yankees' Victorian social conscience at work. In New Bern, Vicksburg, Jacksonville, Norfolk, and elsewhere occupation authorities oversaw the establishment of free schools for the children of the town; these schools were supported by the post fund or by Northern humanitarian agencies, which also provided many of the teachers. Where free schools were already in place the Federals generally undertook to maintain them, notably in New Orleans. That city boasted the South's largest and finest municipal school system (forty-four schools, including a normal), and the occupiers saw to it that it continued operating throughout the war—though to make sure that the classrooms would no longer serve as "nurseries of treason" they brought in Northern textbooks and required teachers to take the oath.[27]

In fact, the state of education remained, on the whole, remarkably healthy in the garrisoned towns, even where public schools were not operating. Private schools, which were still the most common form of education in the South in that era, were mostly resuscitated soon after the Union army arrived, and new ones sprang up as the war went on. To be sure, the economic problems of occupation plagued these schools and in some cases shut them down: financially strapped parents were hard put to scrape up tuition, and textbooks and other school materials were in short supply. Moreover, the Federal army seized some school buildings for military use. But overall, education in the garrisoned towns continued, thanks to the Federals' policy of benign neglect. As long as they were satisfied that the schools were not nurturing disloyalty, the occupiers were quite happy to let them go about their business and thus enlighten the presumably benighted children of the South.[28]

The same circumstances allowed most urban churches to survive Union occupation. The Victorian ethos accorded deep respect to organized religion, and thus the Yankees' natural inclination was not to interfere with the Southern churches. At the same time, the occupiers were convinced that Southern religious leaders were dangerous agents of secessionism, and so they cracked down hard on Rebel preachers. Those churches whose ministers remained openly defiant often suffered the full wrath of the Federals. When the Reverend David Pise, rector of St. Peter's Episcopal Church in Columbia, Tennessee, adamantly resisted the post commander's order to offer a regular Sunday prayer for the U.S. president, the Federals locked the church building and forbade further services; it remained closed from December 1863 until June 1865.[29]

Pise was an exception, however: most ministers in the garrisoned towns eventually came to terms with the enemy and preserved their churches by obeying the letter, if not always the spirit, of the occupiers' demands. (In New Orleans, when General Banks ordered that a recent presidential proclamation be read at all Sunday services, the priest of St. Mary's Italian Catholic Church read it in English, which was unintelligible to most of his congregation; a priest in another part of the city read it as his parishioners were filing out the door after services ended.) Once assured that a given church was rendering the proper obeisance and devoting itself to a "pure" gospel purged of Rebel propaganda, the Federal authorities were content to let it pursue its spiritual mission.[30]

Wartime economic hardships touched the urban churches just as they did the schools. Collection plates often came back distressingly bare, and belt tightening was the rule in most churches. Even more disruptive was the Federal army's confiscation of church buildings for military use. When Sherman's forces captured Rome, Georgia, they turned the Presbyterian church into a warehouse for rations, the Baptist and Episcopal churches into hospitals, and the Methodist church into an ammunition dump. Army authorities in Nashville, too, had possession of most of the city's church edifices at one time or another. Many displaced congregations found alternate accommodations, especially when other churches extended the hand of Christian fellowship. The First Baptist Church of Nashville held Sunday services in a theater and Wednesday evening services in a Christian church building obligingly offered by its pastor. In Norfolk, the faithful of Christ Episcopal Church generously took in the brethren of St. Paul's Episcopal, dispossessed in 1863, and the two churches in effect merged for the duration of the war. Thus, although nearly all of the urban churches were crippled to some extent, and some were wholly disrupted for shorter or longer periods, most survived to carry on their work.[31]

Churches, schools, and the other institutions that undergirded urban life survived, ironically enough, because they were sheltered from the worst storms of war by the Federal army. Union cannons and muskets maintained safety and order in the garrisoned towns and thus preserved something akin to normality there, even as the surrounding countryside was engulfed by violence and disorder. Of course, Southerners in the towns would have vehemently denied that life under Union occupation was in any sense "normal," for it was plagued by economic problems and convulsed by political and social conflict. But in fact the structure of daily life remained in certain respects remarkably intact in most towns, though its features were altered. Thus, although prices were high and permits were required, a woman could still walk to the market and buy food for her family or obtain charity if she was penniless. She could still get redress when her neighbors got too rowdy or her husband spent his wages in a saloon, even though the policeman or judge who heard her complaint might wear a blue army uniform. And she could still send her children off to school each morning and shepherd them to church on Sunday, though the teacher and the preacher might be muzzled by a loyalty oath.[32]

Such continuity was, to be sure, not the case in all garrisoned towns. Some of the smaller ones were simply swallowed up by Union occupation. Rome, Georgia, an important military base during the Atlanta campaign, was held by an entire division of Sherman's troops, who dug fortifications all around town, seized most of the churches, stores, and public edifices, and dismantled the citizens' outbuildings, fences, and abandoned homes in order to build barracks; "the town," one citizen lamented, "is being gradually destroyed." Fredericksburg, Virginia, having survived a rather benign occupation in the spring and summer of 1862 and a second brief but destructive occupation during the battle there late that year, was overwhelmed by a third when the Army of the Potomac undertook its great spring offensive of 1864 and the town was deluged by tens of thousands of wounded soldiers and medical personnel. "The city is a vast hospital," one witness wrote; "churches, public buildings, private dwellings, stores, chambers, attics, basements, all full. There are thousands [of wounded] upon the sidewalk." Decatur, Alabama, situated in an exposed position on the south side of the Tennessee River, was turned into a huge fortress, all of its buildings taken by the army, many torn down to make way for rifle pits or artillery emplacements; every citizen in the town and for a mile around it was sent away.[33]

Most of the garrisoned towns, however, especially the big cities, throbbed with life. "I walked down King Street this evening," wrote Alexandria resident James Ward in 1862, "and found it as crowded as Chestnut Street, Philadelphia, the stores and public houses all brilliantly lighted, places of amusement open, &c." New Orleans, healthier and better governed than ever before, hummed with activity and confirmed its reputation as the mecca of Southern hedonism; its famed theaters, restaurants, barrooms, and bordellos brimmed with pleasure seekers, Southern and Northern, civilian and military. Even Vicksburg boasted a well-attended theater, a busy racetrack, and a baseball club and early in 1865 hosted S. B. Howe's Great European Circus; meanwhile, in little Beaufort, North Carolina, a billiard parlor-cum-bowling alley opened next door to the provost marshal's office. In Clarksville, Tennessee, ladies and gentlemen climbed aboard Captain Carroll's pleasure boat, which featured a dance band and offered excursions on the Cumberland River, even as bands of another sort roamed the nearby countryside wreaking bloody vengeance on the occupiers.[34]

Thus did the garrisoned towns embrace curious dualities: islands of order in a sea of violence, they saw ironfisted military despotism hand in hand with Yankee benevolence, bitter popular hostility alongside abject public dependence, and institutional continuity amid political and social upheaval. But beyond the picket lines and fortifications that shielded the towns there were other worlds.

. . .

Far from the garrisoned towns, beyond the limits of the districts that the Union army was able to hold and regularly patrol, lay the Confederate frontier. Though not within the grasp of the occupiers, the Confederate frontier was within their reach. Periodically, Federal raiding parties would sweep through the frontier regions on missions of seizure and destruction.

Though these visitations were irregular and relatively infrequent—frontier communities often went untouched for months at a time—they could be ruinous. In November 1862, for instance, some months after occupying Plymouth, North Carolina, the Federals mounted an expedition from there up the Roanoke River into Martin County, where they sacked the town of Williamston, burned five houses, killed all the cattle, hogs, and poultry in and around the town, and carried off every mule, horse, wagon, and buggy they could find, as well as every slave who cared to go; Cushing Hassell, who owned a store in town and a farm nearby, both of which were stripped, estimated his loss at ten thousand dollars. Three months later Union troops returned to Williamston for more mischief. After Rome, Georgia, fell to Sherman in the spring of 1864, that post became a base for raids into northeastern Alabama. Sarah Espy, whose Cherokee County farm was hit in June and again in October, lost five hundred bushels of corn, a hundred of oats, two hundred pounds of flour, over two hundred of bacon, much fencing, and nearly all of her livestock. "There is not a living thing on the place," she wrote after the October raid, "except a few chickens. God help us, for we have almost nothing. . . . My beautiful farm is in ruins. . . . We had hogs enough for two years, but they are gone, and [our] corn too, . . . and desolation all around."[35]

Though the typical frontier community was in Union hands only a few days or weeks during the course of a year, being at all other times under

Confederate control, the vulnerability of the frontier made life there a very different experience, in many respects, from that in the secure Confederate interior. For one thing, fear was a part of everyday existence on the frontier, for no matter how infrequently the enemy actually appeared the threat of a raid was ever-present. "We never feel safe," a Mississippian wrote, "as there is nothing to keep the Yankees from us."[36]

Every report that enemy troops were coming, whether true or false, temporarily disrupted the whole community: farmers halted work and scurried about to hide their livestock, merchants locked up their stores, magistrates adjourned court, schoolteachers dismissed class, circuit-riding preachers headed for home, housewives abandoned their chores and rushed to hide their silver. Moreover, the persistent threat of seizure or destruction of their property discouraged some frontier inhabitants from producing or stockpiling food and other necessities. "The people think that this part of Ala[bama] will be run over [by the enemy]," a man reported from the south side of the Tennessee River in the spring of 1864, "and [therefore think] it is useless to cultivate the lands." Early in 1863 citizens of De Soto County, Mississippi, on the state's exposed and often-raided northern border, pleaded with their governor "for aid in this our time of need. It is utterly impossible for us to plant and cultivate a crop this spring unless we have some guarantee of being protected."[37]

Protection, however, was rarely forthcoming from the hard-pressed Rebel authorities. To provide every threatened district with Confederate troops or state militia sufficient to repel a raiding party of any substantial size was simply impossible, given the Confederacy's limited manpower. Confederate and state military commanders did post small cavalry detachments along the frontier to keep an eye on the Federals, enforce government authority, and gather provisions. These troops, who were generally useless against enemy raids and often poorly officered and ill-disciplined, were as much a nuisance as a boon to the inhabitants. A Louisiana woman wrote her daughter that "the yankies has not ben up here sinse you left home but our [own] men has done a great deal of damage to the country they are stealing horses every day . . . nearly every body has to gard there lots at night to keep the solgers from stealing there mules." Sarah Espy told of cavalrymen who came by her farm, fed themselves and their horses, "and left without paying a cent. . . . They are a contemptable set and are dreaded almost as much as the yankees."[38]

One other affliction that distinguished the Confederate frontier from the interior was a severe labor shortage due to the loss of slaves. Federal raiders routinely carried them off in droves. Some slaves, moreover, did not wait for deliverance but instead fled toward the Union-held regions; many successfully escaped despite the distance and the risk of recapture by citizens or Rebel cavalry. In Charles City County, Virginia, at least half of the black population had absconded or been taken away by March 1863, according to one resident's estimate, including 70 percent of the able-bodied men. Such losses spurred many slaveowners on the frontier to send their remaining blacks into the interior, a policy often encouraged and sometimes mandated by Confederate authorities. Consequently, many acres of farmland in the frontier regions lay idle.[39]

The fallowing of land due to labor shortages and uncertainty, the disruption of work by Yankee alarms, and the loss of provisions and livestock to both armies inevitably added up to want and suffering. Most frontier districts were unable to produce enough food. "The country is ruined," wrote Roxa Cole of Tippah County, northern Mississippi, in 1864. "I do not know how the people are to live, there has been already much suffering during the year past, for bread meat and salt, there will be much more this year I fear." Later that year citizens of neighboring Tishomingo County petitioned the Confederate Congress for relief from taxes, telling of Federal raids and Rebel impressment that had left the inhabitants in "so destitute a condition, that not more than one family in twenty [have] the means of subsistence. . . . [U]nless some relief can be had, *starvation* and *ruin* must ensue."[40]

In desperation, many inhabitants of the frontier areas resorted to trading with the enemy. This could be arduous and risky, for it generally meant hauling goods (most often cotton, which was still abundant in many districts and which Northern traders were eager to get) long distances into Union-held territory while avoiding Confederate troops, whose orders were to prevent trade with the Yankees. But for many citizens there was no alternative. "[N]early every man & woman . . . has trafficked with the enemy," a militia officer reported from northern Mississippi in September 1863. "The scarcity of salt & meat is the alleged excuse for this illicit trade."[41]

Citizens all across the Confederacy railed against their government's onerous restrictions and demands, but such protests were especially vehement in the hard-hit frontier regions. Confederate and state authorities were never absent for long there. Though every Yankee alarm sent Rebel cavalrymen, tax collectors, impressment officers, and conscription agents fleeing for safety, no sooner was the panic over than the soldiers and officials were back at work. Their activities provoked bitter complaints and anxious appeals: the Confederate and state governments were inundated with petitions, like that of the Tishomingo citizens, recounting the travails of the frontier inhabitants and begging for exemption from taxes or impressment. The authorities also heard many a plaintive plea from individuals such as Mary Tribble, of Spotsylvania County, Virginia, who beseeched Governor William Smith in 1864 to exempt her husband from conscription: "I have seven little children entireley dependent on his labur for support[.] if he is taken away wee will surtainley suffer a great deal[.] the yankeys has taken evry thing we had twice[.] the last Sheringdon [Sheridan] raiders toock evry mouth full we had to eat . . . if he bee taken away we will have know body to save what little crop we have mad[e]."[42]

Even as they cursed the agents of the Rebel government, however, the frontier inhabitants had reason to be grateful for their presence. As people elsewhere in the invaded regions of the South were coming to understand, outside the garrisoned towns the only alternative to Rebel authority was anarchy. Persisting Confederate and state authority on the frontier preserved a more or less orderly environment there, in which the formal and informal institutions that undergirded society could carry on. Local government, for example, generally continued to function in the frontier counties despite the disruptive alarms and raids. Even in northern Mississippi's Tippah County, one of the most often-raided frontier sections, the county commissioners omitted only two of their monthly sessions between December 1863 and the end of the war, despite the fact that the county seat was frequently in Union hands and the courthouse had been burned down.[43]

With state authority and county government intact, many frontier districts were able to maintain local militia or home guard companies. Though weakened by the dearth of able-bodied white men that affected all sections of the Confederacy, these companies could provide a measure of security for their communities by acting as slave patrols, checking or at least slowing the stream of black runaways, and, as scouts, watching for the Yankees and sending word of their approach so that the citizens could take precautions. Though they almost always scattered or simply declined to muster when the enemy arrived, in rare instances—when confronting only a very small raiding party—the militiamen or home guardsmen would stand firm with their muskets and shotguns and trade lead with the invaders. The citizens of King and Queen County, Virginia, for example, fed up with the enemy's "horse thieving & negro stealing expedition[s]," as planter Benjamin Fleet put it, organized a home guard in 1863 that patrolled the county and occasionally skirmished with Federal detachments. "[W]e mean to let the villians see," Fleet declared, "that they will not be permitted hereafter to pillage & burn without at least some show of resistance on our parts."[44]

The persistence of local government and state authority on the frontier meant also that organized relief efforts were possible there. Every Confederate state enacted laws requiring counties to provide for needy families of soldiers and authorizing local officials to levy taxes for that purpose; many states undertook to procure and distribute critical supplies that could not be produced locally, such as cotton cards, medicines, and salt. These relief measures were particularly important to the suffering frontier districts; often they were the only thing standing between the citizens and utter destitution. Moreover, some states, including Virginia, Georgia, and Alabama, passed special appropriations for the needy in counties ravaged by the enemy.[45]

The burden of implementing state relief measures fell on local governments, and those on the frontier often had to make extraordinary efforts to fulfill their duty: raising funds for relief was one thing, but actually purchasing and distributing provisions was quite another. The commissioners of Tippah County, Mississippi, found it impossible to buy victuals at "reasonable and just prices" in the county and had to resort to various expedients, including authorizing the sheriff to impress what was needed, levying a tax-in-kind on farm produce, and finally sending an agent south to buy corn in the interior and haul it back to Tippah. Marshall County, Alabama, likewise dispatched a corn agent to the southern part of the state who carried a proclamation from the governor urging the citizens there to donate corn or at least sell it "at *peace* prices" for the benefit of the northern Alabamians who "have had to suffer from the enemy." The magistrates of Hertford County, North Carolina, acknowledged early in 1865 that they could not "obtain supplies for those committed to [our] care. . . . We have laid taxes & collected them, but money cannot buy within our reach the articles required." They therefore took a drastic step, ordering that the relief funds be invested in cotton that would be hauled across the Chowan River into Union-held territory and there traded for bread and meat.[46]

Churches, too, were faithful to their trust and endeavored earnestly to carry on. The brethren of Hephzibah Baptist Church of East Feliciana Parish, Louisiana, assembled for worship regularly throughout the war, with but one exception: in October 1864, according to the church records, "a protracted meeting [was planned] but a yankee raid to Clinton and Woodville at the time prevented [it]—the whole community being in a state of excitement." Some churches endured harsher trials: Luray Baptist of Page County, Virginia, was frequently disturbed by raids and rumors of raids: "No preaching to day," read one entry in the church minutes, "the pastor not Being present, owing to the excitement from the invading Federal army having occupied the Valley." As a rule, though, the fellowship of the faithful survived the hazards of the Confederate frontier.[47]

Like local government, churches helped alleviate the hardships of frontier life. To the best of their ability, congregations provided for the less fortunate among them. The members of Mount Tabor Baptist Church of Hertford County, North Carolina, established a poor fund and appointed a committee to see to the wants of the neediest brethren. Along with sustenance for the body, the churches offered sustenance for the spirit. Not long after the second devastating raid on her farm, Sarah Espy went to Sunday meeting and was heartened by the minister's sermon: "His text [was] 'Trust in the Lord and do good, that thy days may be long in the land and verily, thou shalt be fed' which he applied to our present situation."[48]

The country church was part of a broader rural community that likewise survived the disruptions of frontier life and sustained many a family in its hour of need. Sarah Espy and her dependents struggled through the bleak winter of 1864–65 with the help of neighbors who gave her some hogs. "[W]e have lost nearly everything," she said, "but we have been fortunate in having good friends." Robert Mecklin of Washington County, Arkansas, recorded in August 1863 that "I needed my oxen to do some hauling, important to be done before the Feds should make another raid upon us. But my neighbors needed them more." So he loaned them to a woman who wanted to put in a turnip patch and then to another neighbor who had a wheat crop to be gathered. A few weeks later Mecklin noted that there was "no doctor in the county, and very little medicine," but that his daughter "has a little and has been dividing it with our neighbors; all of them have had sickness in their families and she has been to see them."[49]

Persisting rural communalism and institutional continuity on the Confederate frontier meant that life there retained many familiar features. Certainly there was privation and sometimes real suffering; certainly there was pervasive anxiety and daily tribulation and periodic panic. But between Yankee alarms life went on: farm families rose with the sun and went about their chores as village blacksmiths fired up their forges, people gathered at country stores and churches and courthouses, boys and girls toiled at their lessons in log schoolhouses, neighbors and kinfolk visited and shared. Sometimes the war could seem far away, as it must have appeared to the widower Thomas Batchelor of Point Coupee Parish, Louisiana, when he took a new wife in 1864 and his friends converged on his home for the traditional raucous wedding night serenade: "a splendid shiveree," Batchelor wrote, "of all the unearthly noises you never heard in your life[,] it frighten[ed] the dogs off the place[,] the cows bellowed[,] the horses & mules were frightened . . . it soon passed of[f] pleasantly an[d] agreeable."[50]

The war was never out of mind for long, however. Two weeks later Batchelor complained that "we are in a great deal of trouble at present on acct. of our enemy who makes frequent raids up our way. . . . [N]egroes completely demorilized since the last raid." Then he heard rumors that the Yankees "intend to desolate the country of every thing so that no one can live in it. . . . [I]f these things should take place I want to get out of the country[.] I can not live here it is no place for a quiet peaceable old man with a helpless family."[51]

Batchelor and other inhabitants of the frontier often looked wistfully toward the Confederate interior, envying the relative security and abundance there and cursing the fate that put their own communities within the Union army's reach. But when they gazed the other way and contemplated the lot of those who lived every day in the hands of the enemy, they thanked God for His mercy.

. . .

Surrounding the garrisoned towns and stretching all the way to the Confederate frontier was no-man's-land. The Northern occupiers claimed this territory as their own, and so it was, in a strictly military sense: Union forces regularly patrolled it, could project their power at will anywhere within it, and were able to exclude Confederate power and authority from it (aside from the occasional Rebel cavalry raid). By that reckoning, the citizens there were—and they considered themselves to be—in enemy hands.

At the same time it was unpacified territory, seething with hostility and guerrilla violence: Federal authority prevailed only when and where Union troops were actually present, and it extended no farther than the range of their muskets and carbines. Because Union troops could not be everywhere at once in the vastness of no-man's-land, but did pose a sufficient threat to keep Rebel military forces and government agents away, the citizens there—unlike those in the garrisoned towns or on the Confederate frontier—lived most of their days in a kind of vacuum of authority, a twilight zone neither Union nor Confederate.[52]

Though they did not experience the continuous presence of a Federal military force, as did the people of the garrisoned towns, the inhabitants of no-man's-land saw far more of the enemy than did the people of the Confederate frontier. All the disruption and loss and agony that the frontier suffered because of occasional Yankee alarms and raids were multiplied many times over in no-man's-land. Robert Mecklin, whose frontier community became no-man's-land when the Federal army captured and garrisoned nearby Fayetteville, Arkansas, in September 1863, was horrified by the ensuing wave of Yankee rapine and violence. "Theft, plunder, arson, murder and every other crime of the black catalogue have lost their former startling significance of horror by their daily occurrence amongst us," he declared (with some exaggeration) in November. "Thus we live, not knowing when we lie down at night [if] we will be let alone till morning."[53]

Foraging squads regularly set out from the army posts and swept the countryside, along with scouting patrols and other detachments whose men and horses were always hungry. Thus, few residents of no-man's-land went for long without a visit from soldiers who demanded cornmeal, salt pork, hogs, cattle, chickens, hay, fodder, and any other edibles. Citizens unlucky enough to live close to a post were hit the hardest. "50 waggons came to day to get forrage, and evry thing else in the neighborhood," wrote Jesse Cox, who had a farm near Franklin, Tennessee, "and such a scene I never witnessed and I pray God I never may [again]." But soon the soldiers were back: "the yankies hear for something to day," read another of Cox's diary entries, ". . . every day 2 or 3 times in the day and never pay anything." Belle Meade plantation, just outside Nashville, also endured almost daily requisitions and pillaging. By September 1862, according to the plantation mistress, troops had seized hundreds of wagon loads of grain and hay and all the stored vegetables. "There is not a fowl left on the place," she added. "And now, at this moment while I am writing a sweet potato patch of about 4 acres of potatoes not one fourth grown are being dug by at least fifty soldiers. . . . At the same time there are thirty-seven wagons standing on the pike getting ready to load up with the small amount of hay and oats left on the place."[54]

Another crippling blow to the inhabitants of no-man's-land was the loss of work animals. "Every mounted regiment that goes through the country takes what it pleases of stock," a Union officer reported from Tennessee. "[T]here are many large farms without one serviceable work beast on the place." The loss of so many horses, mules, and oxen, and the scarcity of feed for those that remained, drastically curtailed agriculture in no-man's-land. "The geese and cranes going north reminds me that spring is approaching," Robert Mecklin noted early in 1864, "and that it is time to be preparing grounds and fences for a crop. But when this is done we have no teams to plow our grounds, and if we had the teams no forage for them."[55]

No less devastating to the farmers was the loss of fencing, which allowed wild as well as domesticated animals to roam freely through fields and feed on growing crops. Fence rails were among the first things to go when troops came by, for they made excellent firewood. In those sections of no-man's-land where large bodies of soldiers frequently passed, especially areas abutting the garrisoned towns, fencing virtually disappeared. "There is not I suppose a wooden fence within 20 miles of this place," a Union soldier wrote from his post in the Shenandoah Valley. "[T]his place looks like one general common."[56]

Furthermore, in no-man's-land, to a far greater extent than on the Confederate frontier, agriculture was debilitated by the loss of slaves. The absence of Confederate authority and the proximity of the Federal posts made it relatively easy for slaves to escape. "Farming operations are at a stand-still about here," wrote a resident of Montgomery County, Tennessee, early in 1864. "So much of the labor of the county has been lost that it will be impossible for the planters to make anything like their usual crops." A Union soldier in Thibodaux, Louisiana, observed that "there is a good many thousand acres of sugar cane that will rot on the ground this season for the want of hands to gather it. The negroes concluded that they had worked for nothing long enough."[57]

Even those farmers who were able to plant a crop could not be certain that they would retain sufficient human and animal labor to cultivate and harvest it, or sufficient fencing to protect it as it grew; nor could they count on the Yankees leaving them much after it was gathered and processed and stored. Tennessee planter John H. Bills spoke for many: "We are in the midst of trouble, no one knows what to do, whet[h]er to try to plant. . . . Negroes not inclined to work, our mules being stolen, horses poor & broken down for want of fodder. No protection from the soldiery & no prospect of an end to this desolation war." In the face of such uncertainty—which was much deeper and more dismaying than that which pervaded the Confederate frontier—many farmers in no-man's-land scaled down their planting to a bare minimum and abandoned once-prolific fields.[58]

Trade as well as agriculture was severely disrupted in no-man's-land. Considerable hardship resulted from the Federal land and water blockades, which interdicted supply lines from the Confederate interior. This was a key distinction between no-man's-land and the Confederate frontier, for the frontier inhabitants could, except when Federal raids intervened, freely export goods to markets in the interior (if they were lucky enough to have a surplus to trade) and freely import whatever supplies were available. But no-man's-land was sealed off by the occupiers.[59]

Smuggling did allow a trickle of goods to move both ways between no-man's-land and the Confederate interior by way of the frontier, but it was dangerous and difficult. Virginian Colin Clarke, for example, got small shipments of produce from his tidewater plantation to Richmond by employing smugglers who used wagons and canoes, traveled back roads and creeks to avoid Union patrols, and kept half the goods as their fee. Clarke's son in Richmond would sell the remaining half, buy supplies, and send them back to Clarke the same way. "[S]ee at what risk & expense we have to send even that little to market," Clarke complained, "& what is left [on the plantation] is at the mercy of a hellish crew of yankees."[60]

Trading with the enemy was easier but was limited by Federal regulations. Though many military commanders encouraged rural people to bring in their produce to sell in the garrisoned towns, they were very strict about what the sellers took away in return, for fear that it would find its way to the Confederacy or to guerrillas. So were the Treasury Department agents who oversaw the cotton trade. Some commanders simply forbade any citizen living in a district where smugglers or guerrillas were especially active to take any supplies home. Some of those citizens resorted to illegal trading with persons who had access to Northern markets, but that was just as risky as trading with the Confederacy.[61]

More frustrating than Federal trade regulations was the simple fact that the people of no-man's-land had so little to trade. The farmer whose fields lay mostly fallow and unfenced, whose barn and smokehouse had been cleaned out by Northern foragers, whose wife was dipping into the last barrel of cornmeal and carefully guarding her last few hens, was hardly in a position to trade even if he had free access to market. Citizens who did not farm were more helpless. Even those with a cash reserve were no better off, unless it was in specie or good bank notes, for Confederate currency was generally worthless in the garrisoned towns. And, unlike citizens in the towns, those in no-man's-land had little or no opportunity to earn greenbacks by working for the Yankees.[62]

Nor did residents of no-man's-land have much hope of begging rations from the Northern forces. The occupiers undertook relief efforts in the garrisoned towns because they recognized that townspeople could not produce their own food, and could not in most cases directly aid the Confederacy, but could threaten the security of the post if they got desperately hungry. The occupiers took just the opposite view of the citizens of the surrounding countryside, however. On occasion Federal officers, touched by the plight of poor country people who came to the post pleading for help, would issue them rations. But official policy was that indigent citizens living in hostile districts should not be provisioned, unless they were Unionists, but instead "should be sent South to feed upon the enemy." Indeed, some Union soldiers insisted that the hungrier the country people got, the sooner resistance would end.[63]

Denied outside sources of subsistence, the people of no-man's-land turned desperately to one another. Those who had something were implored to share with those who had nothing. When word spread through William King's northern Georgia community that King had a small, hand-operated corn grinder, neighbors came from all around to borrow it, for no mill was operating and some people had been reduced to using a mortar and pestle; others came who had no corn, and King generously gave what he could. So did Robert Mecklin in Arkansas: "We still have a little to eat ourselves," he wrote in the winter of 1864, "and have to divide that little with those who are worse off than we are."[64]

Communal sharing was hindered, however, by a phenomenon peculiar to no-man's-land and one that ultimately had profound consequences. This was the restriction of mobility. It was due in part to the extreme scarcity of horses, mules, oxen, and wagons, the deterioration of roads, and the destruction of bridges and boats. These problems, which prevailed nearly everywhere in no-man's-land, made it difficult for people to travel beyond their immediate neighborhood, especially if they had goods to haul.[65]

Even more constraining was the citizens' terror of the enemy. The people of no-man's-land lived in fear—an unremitting sense of anxiety far more unsettling than that which plagued the Confederate frontier, for in no-man's-land the enemy was never far away. A woman in Jackson, Tennessee, which Union forces garrisoned for a time but subsequently abandoned, contrasted life in a garrisoned town—where the occupiers sought to preserve order and a certain quotidian regularity—with life in no-man's-land. Now, she said, "we are constantly having raids, which are more to be feared than a standing army. . . . We are in constant suspense and anxiety."[66]

Traveling about multiplied one's chances of encountering malicious Union soldiers. Especially frightening were unofficered detachments and bands of stragglers, who frequently harassed or robbed people they met on the road. Moreover, citizens dreaded the possibility that troops might come by their home while they were away: pillagers could sometimes be deterred by a strong-willed man or woman standing in the doorway, whereas an unoccupied home was an invitation to unrestrained looting and vandalism. "[T]he accounts from the country[side] are terrible," a Rome, Georgia, resident reported in 1864, "no safety for any thing [the people] have. . . . [T]here are gangs of high way men [i.e., Federal soldiers] taking all they can find in some sections compelling the people to stand guard over their property to retain any thing[.] [T]hey steal negroes, Horses & rob [people,] no Traveling is safe." William King's community was just as dangerous: after a friend of his was robbed on the road by Yankee stragglers, King observed that "there is but little safety in moving about now." Over the next few weeks he reported more highway robberies and numerous attempts by stragglers to plunder his farm, which he managed to thwart only by constant vigilance.[67]

Consequently, the inhabitants of no-man's-land generally stayed home as much as possible, venturing out only on the most urgent errands. When Jesse Cox of Williamson County, Tennessee, paid a call on a sick neighbor in June 1863, he noted in his diary that it was "the first time I have been outside of my farm in three months." William King longed to visit kinfolk and friends in an adjoining county but decided against it because there was "such a multitude of depredators roving over the country"; even his slaves stuck close to home because they could not "move about safely." In fact, King was reluctant to set foot off his farm even for a moment: "to leave the House unprotected will secure its destruction."[68]

Mobility was the lifeblood of the rural community. Without that vital circulation, without the ability to meet freely and often with one's neighbors and kin, rural communalism and institutions could not survive. Neighborly sharing and succor, barter and gossip, and all the other informal customs of mutuality that sustained rural life depended on unrestricted social intercourse. Schools could be conducted only where teachers and pupils knew the roads were safe to travel. Country churches could carry on only so long as congregations could gather on Sundays, preachers could ride their circuits, and elders could meet to administer church business and judge and punish the sins of the flock.[69]

The churches were especially hard hit by the restriction of mobility in no-man's-land; most simply ceased to exist for the duration of the war. "[W]e continued to meet untell some time in the year 1862," wrote the secretary of Christian Chapel Church of Christ in Tennessee after the war, "[but] owing to the Troubled condition of the Country the members thought best for their personal safety and well being to absent them selves untell more favorable oppertunity should offer and [there] was no regular meeting untell some time in the year 1865 when the members that survived be gun again to come to gether from their respective homes." Likewise, the secretary of Ebenezer Baptist in northern Virginia noted in the summer of 1865 that "the Church has not met together for up[w]ards of three years and the cause thereof was the ware in thes United States."[70]

Local government in no-man's-land suffered the same fate as the churches. County magistrates, sheriffs, constables, and relief agents stayed fearfully at home like everyone else. The commissioners of West Feliciana Parish, Louisiana, managed to convene for only three of their monthly meetings in the three years between the Federal invasion of the state and the end of the war; they held no meetings at all after September 1863, until the summer of 1865. The magistrates of Loudoun County, Virginia, were even less successful: "owing to the continuance of the war," the county court clerk noted in 1865, "no Court was held in this County from February, 1862, until July, 1865." In some instances, where Union forces garrisoned the county seat, county government was revived under their aegis. But even where this was so, the hazardous conditions of the countryside discouraged civil officials from traveling about and made rural citizens reluctant to journey to the courthouse, so that in reality the county government did not extend beyond the limits of town.[71]

The disruption of county government in no-man's-land deprived the citizens there of the one local institution capable of extensive relief measures—an institution that proved critically important on the Confederate frontier. A Virginia man, W. A. Little, described the condition of Stafford County, one of the worst-hit sections of no-man's-land, in the winter of 1864: "[T]here are many destitute families . . . actually suffering for food. . . . They have had no session of the County Court for two years past, no overseers of the poor, no provision for the families of soldiers or persons in destitute condition. The Justices of the Peace take no action in the matter."[72]

Clearly, however, it would have made no difference even if county government had survived in no-man's-land, and even if the churches had remained sufficiently intact to carry out their own informal relief efforts like churches on the Confederate frontier—simply because in no-man's-land there was little or nothing left to be distributed to the needy, and outside sources of supply were cut off. W. A. Little recognized as much, even as he bewailed the county's inaction: "I have done individually what I could," he said, ". . . But I have been literally beggared by the wanton destruction of all that I possessed by the Yankees, & our people are generally without means to do more than maintain their own families." Another Virginian, Edward Carter Turner of Fauquier County, made a similar point: "One-half of the people of this truly unfortunate country have been robbed to destitution," he wrote, "& the other half have nothing to spare for their relief."[73]

In every part of no-man's-land citizens endured grievous privation; in the most ravaged areas, especially northern Virginia and middle Tennessee, they faced famine. "Many of us are now in want of and will actually starve for Bread unless we can get some help," another Stafford County man reported in 1864. "[T]he yankeys took from us our stock, corn, &c . . . and [we] are now suffering. . . . [M]any of us cant stand it more than a week or 2 longer." That year a Federal officer described parts of middle Tennessee as "bordering upon famine. . . . [E]ven those [people] formerly wealthy are utterly reduced, and many of the poorer are now actually starving."[74]

Witnesses were struck not only by the intense suffering in no-man's-land, but also by the awful devastation and the eerie lifelessness. "The first acre of Tennessee soil betrayed the ruthless track of war," wrote a Northern newspaper correspondent who traveled south to Nashville late in 1862. "Fallow fields were spread out before the vision. . . . Fences had been absorbed in camp-fires; the click of the old mill wheel had ceased; broken windows and shattered frames stared from deserted homesteads. . . . Ravage and desolation everywhere. There were no little children gamboling on cabin thresholds. Hardly a dog barked." Edward Carter Turner described the strange scene that presented itself when he ventured out from his plantation two days after Christmas in 1862: "I am riding all day & scarcely meet a single individual on the road. The country is almost deserted. On former and happier times Christmas week was a time of general hilarity. . . . At present there is scarcely to be seen a sign of human life, much less of human enjoyment. . . . A solemn silence reigns on all the surrounding ruin."[75]

The "solemn silence" of no-man's-land contrasted starkly with the communal and institutional continuity of the Confederate frontier and the vibrant bustle of the garrisoned towns, the one sustained by persistent Confederate authority and the other by the sheltering power of the Union army. Now and again, however, the silence was shattered—not only by the sound of conflict between citizens and Yankee invaders, but also by the clamor of desperate struggles being waged among the people of the occupied South themselves.

[4]

. . . .

Deliverance and Disillusion

The Ordeal of the Unionists

. . . .

"Rejoice with me," exclaimed Maggie Lindsley of Nashville soon after the capture of the city in 1862. "The glorious star spangled banner of the United States is again floating above us. . . . I am wild, crazy almost with delight." Indeed, it was the sight of the flag, even more than the ranks of blue-uniformed soldiers, that thrilled the Unionists of the South. "The Stars & Stripes now float over our city," Memphian Lewis Norvell wrote exultantly in June 1862, "and never will I under any circumstances live under any other flag again." A Federal officer in northern Alabama told of a woman who came into camp not long after her husband's death at the hands of secessionists: "the main thing she came for she said, was to see the old Flag. Some of our boys brought her a Flag—she took it and geathered it up in her hands and kissed it while the tears rolled down her cheek."[1]

The ardor with which Southern Unionists greeted the sight of Old Glory bespoke how deeply they had suffered under Rebel rule. In nearly all parts of the Confederacy after the outbreak of war, Unionists had been cowed into silence and submission by threats or outright violence. Those whose true sentiments were known to their neighbors often endured continuing harassment—even if they obediently rendered unto the Confederate Caesar—until the moment Union troops arrived.[2]

Long muzzled and shackled and terrorized, Unionists hailed the Northern invaders as liberators even as the secessionist majority bemoaned its own enslavement. "I thank God and the union army that I am once more permitted to Express and write my feelings freely," Lewis Norvell declared. "I have prayed for the approach of the union army more fervently than I have ever done for the salvation of my own soul— My prayer[s] have at last been answered and now Treason gives way to Justice and truth." Norvell was one of many Unionists who saw in the coming of the Yankees the answer to their prayers. The righteous were now delivered from evil, it seemed, and would surely have their reward.[3]

. . .

The wellsprings of Unionism were many, but three were especially important. One might be described as cultural: a small but significant proportion of Southern Unionists were Northern-born immigrants, some of whom still identified strongly with the North, others of whom regarded themselves as good Southerners but took a more detached and skeptical view of Southern rights agitation than did their Southern-born neighbors. One of the latter sort was Henry Barker, of Gallatin, Tennessee, who had emigrated from Connecticut in 1838. "I am as much for the South as [the secessionists] are," Barker wrote in 1862, "I am for her *best good* a thousand times more than they are, but I am for 'One Government'—the 'Government of Washington.' . . . I am for the Constitution of the 'United States' as it was & is." The Confederate South was in the grip of hysteria, he believed: "Madness now rules—Men are demented."[4]

A second, and more significant, source of Unionism was political. Before the war many conservative Southerners, especially Whigs, had viewed secessionism as nothing more than demagoguery, and some held to that belief even after Fort Sumter. They saw secession as a plot hatched by ambitious and unprincipled rabble-rousers and carried out against the best interests of the bewildered masses who, as one Tennessee Unionist wrote, were mostly "union men at heart" but were "coaxed and browbeat by their devlish aggressive leaders"—a view shared by the Northern public early in the war.[5]

The third source was social. Some yeomen and poor whites, mainly in the Southern highlands where planter influence was limited, saw the Confederacy as a slaveholders' regime, an engine of aristocratic self-aggrandizement fueled by the sweat and blood of the plain folk. It was such people as these that a Union general encountered while leading an expedition through the eastern highlands of middle Tennessee early in 1863: they "rushed into the road and joined our column," he reported, "expressing the greatest delight at our coming, and at beholding again what they emphatically called 'our flag.' . . . These people were generally illiterate and somewhat timid, and did not seem to understand much about the present troubles, except that their more wealthy and better-informed neighbors insisted upon the poor people taking up arms to oppose the Government that they had been taught to love, and which had never oppressed them, . . . for the defense, as they were told, of a species of property with the possession of which they had never been burdened."[6]

However varied the roots of their faith, Unionists liberated by the Yankee army shared certain objectives, assumptions, hopes, and fears. One objective was to cooperate with the Federal authorities in the speedy restoration of loyal state governments. In many towns Unionists convened public meetings soon after the Federals arrived, in which they proclaimed their fealty to the Union and urged that the business of reconstruction get under way. In Jacksonville, for example, about a hundred Unionists met at the courthouse just eight days after Union troops took possession of the town in March 1862. The resolution they drew up repudiated the Rebel government, denounced "the terrors of unrestrained popular and military despotism" inflicted on Southern Unionists, and called on all other loyal Floridians to help them erect a new state government.[7]

Implicit in the Unionists' calls for political reconstruction was the assumption that they themselves would, and should, play the predominant role. They conceded the necessity for Federal military help and protection, of course, but believed that military authority should withdraw from the political arena as civil authority revived under Unionist control. They insisted, too, on a narrow definition of the "Unionists" who would be included in the reconstruction process, fearing that the Federal authorities might bring in outsiders or might be overly generous in enfranchising secessionists who claimed a change of heart. A Memphis Unionist advised Tennessee military governor Andrew Johnson that "*All important appointments Should be given to old Citizens in preference to Strangers. . . . Nothing is more discouraging to a people than to have Strangers rule over them.*" Another Tennessee Unionist cautioned Johnson to "take a firm and decided policy and not allow too much of the Leaven of disunionism to steal in on you under the profession of coming to their senses—[be] especially careful not to place them in positions of trusts until well tried."[8]

The matter of Federal protection was also much on the minds of Unionists. It soon became apparent that such protection could not be taken for granted, at least not in the countryside. Because Union troops were not always close enough to deter secessionists and guarantee the safety of Unionists in no-man's-land and on the Confederate frontier, Unionists there all remained fearful of secessionist reprisals, and most continued to avoid open expressions of loyalty.[9]

Unionists in the garrisoned towns, on the other hand, were at all times protected by Union bayonets. In the towns they flaunted their loyalty and publicly celebrated their liberation. Memphis Unionists organized a great parade in November 1862, featuring a float adorned with the Goddess of Liberty and thirty-four attendants representing the states; when the procession reached the New Memphis Theater, General Sherman himself addressed the crowd. When Shelbyville, Tennessee, was retaken by the Union army early in July 1863 (having been back in Confederate hands for nearly a year following its first occupation by the Federals), the town's Unionists warmly greeted the Yankees with Union flags waving and then held a grand Fourth of July celebration.[10]

Yet the experience of Shelbyville exemplified a disturbing truth: towns captured by the Federals could also be abandoned by them. Unionists who openly declared their sympathies after the Union army came were haunted by the fear that the army might later pull out and leave them at the mercy of the secessionists. Many of those who openly cooperated with the occupiers feared for their lives if the Yankees should withdraw.[11]

The Unionist dilemma was poignantly illustrated in Jacksonville. Unionists there, it will be recalled, had suffered murderous and destructive violence at the hands of secessionists as Federal troops neared the town in March 1862. When their liberators arrived, the Unionists welcomed them with open arms and then convened publicly to urge the reconstruction of state government. Uncertain about the occupiers' intentions, however, they sought assurance that the town would be held permanently; a friendly visit from the departmental commander in mid-March and the arrival of reinforcements for the garrison on March 25 seemed to bode well. But in the meantime, a new departmental commander was appointed. He reassessed troop dispositions and concluded that holding Jacksonville was strategically pointless. His order to evacuate the town arrived on April 6; the post commander broke the news to the Unionists the next day. "This intelligence," one of them wrote, "fell on our ears like a death knell." Several hundred Unionists thereupon frantically packed up their belongings, left their homes, and boarded Union transports along with the departing garrison troops. A Northern newspaper correspondent watched them "hurrying down to the wharf, each carrying some article too precious to forsake"; it was, he said, a "melancholy scene." As the boats took them away to safety, the Unionists saw Confederate troops march into the town.[12]

Unionists in all the garrisoned towns recognized that only a thin blue line stood between them and Rebel vengeance. Thus, no less anxiously than their secessionist neighbors, they watched the occupiers for signs of their intentions. As they did, the occupiers were looking back, considering the role that the Unionists would play in the salvation of the Union.

. . .

Many a Yankee soldier was deeply touched by the passionate demonstrations of loyalty that materialized in some of the regions invaded early in the war. The shouts of joy the troops heard as they marched in, and the tears of gratitude they saw, were persuasive evidence that the North had been right to believe that the Southern Unionists were many and could be counted on to rally 'round the flag and help restore the Union as it had been.

Optimism pervaded the early reports of Federal officers in the occupied areas. General Buell wrote from Nashville soon after its capture to advise President Lincoln "to reconstruct the machinery of the [state] Government out of material here, of which an abundance can be found that is truly loyal, though for some time overpowered and silenced." Colonel Rush Hawkins, stationed at Hatteras Inlet, North Carolina, in 1861, told of being visited by a delegation of thirty local men who assured him of their loyalty and informed him that "secret Union meetings" had been held in all the counties bordering Pamlico Sound. If those counties were occupied, the delegation said, the citizens there would "vote themselves back into the Union and take up arms to defend themselves if necessary." Hawkins was enthusiastic: "Could this be done now," he opined, "I have no doubt that one-third of the State of North Carolina would be back in the Union within two weeks."[13]

The occupiers recognized, however, that reconstruction would never succeed until Unionists were wholly freed from the fear of secessionist reprisals. Indeed, they believed that such fear accounted for the dearth of open Unionism that characterized many invaded areas. Protecting the Unionists was therefore a key element of Federal reconstruction policy.[14]

The suffering of the Unionists in Rebel hands evoked deep sympathy from the occupiers and reinforced their determination to protect those they liberated from further persecution. "I have never felt so glad to be a soldier as I have since I came into these mountains where we could do so much good to the poor down trodden [Union] people," Colonel Hans Heg wrote from northern Alabama. "There are hundreds here that have laid in hollow log[s] and caves for months hiding themselves [from the Rebels]."[15]

For humanitarian as well as political reasons, therefore, the occupation authorities were determined to stop the harassment of Unionists. When General Neal Dow led his troops into a Mississippi town in 1862, he called together some of the leading citizens and, according to one of his soldiers, "made them a speech. He told them that if anybody was injured or insulted on account of union sentiments, he should exact the fullest satisfaction." An officer who led a force into northeastern Arkansas in 1863 informed the citizens bluntly that "the rule for the future is, that where a Union man cannot live in peace a secessionist shall not live at all."[16]

When warnings were ignored the occupiers retaliated harshly. Angered by "outrages and depredations" against Unionists in Wilson County, Tennessee, army authorities laid down the law in 1863: harassment of a Unionist by anyone who had taken the oath would be treated as a violation of the oath; harassment by anyone who had not taken the oath would be punished by confiscation of his property and expulsion beyond the Federal lines; Unionists whose property was destroyed would be indemnified by assessments on local secessionists; where a Unionist was killed, hostages would be taken. Such measures, or even more Draconian ones, became the rule everywhere in the occupied South. In Georgia, General Sherman decreed that if a Unionist was murdered a secessionist would be chosen by lot to die: "In aggravated cases retaliation will be extended as high as five for one."[17]

Only in the garrisoned towns, however, could the Northern army fully ensure the safety of Unionists. As the war went on and secessionist harassment and violence continued in no-man's-land and on the Confederate frontier, the towns became havens for Unionists. Refugees became a familiar sight at every post, trudging in from the countryside singly or in families, or disembarking from rescue boats, tearfully recounting tales of Rebel oppression and pleading for sanctuary. The occupiers, for their part, willingly took these supplicants in and cared for them. At many posts they established refugee camps and levied on secessionists to maintain them.[18]

The occupiers not only fed and sheltered Unionists in the garrisoned towns but also elevated them to positions of power. In New Orleans, army authorities appointed Unionists to administer the public school system and gave cash subsidies to a Unionist newspaper, the *Times*. In Nashville, authorities discharged the secessionist superintendent of the state insane asylum and replaced him with a Unionist. They also intervened in a struggle between the Unionist and secessionist members of Nashville's Second Presbyterian Church. The secessionists had seized control of the church and ousted the Unionist pastor when Tennessee seceded. After the Northern army captured the city, the Unionists appealed to the post commander and, with an escort of Federal troops, entered the church and forced the secessionists to turn over the keys, records, and funds. The Unionists retained control of the church, by order of the post commander, through the end of the war and beyond.[19]

Sufficiently protected and empowered, the Unionists would presumably provide a solid foundation on which to reconstruct the Southern state governments. Federal authorities, especially President Lincoln, were anxious that political reconstruction go hand in hand with the military conquest of the Confederacy. A quick restoration of government would, Lincoln believed, help keep the war from degenerating into the sort of "violent and remorseless revolutionary struggle" that he dreaded. If the Republican Party could be institutionalized in the South at the same time, so much the better. But Lincoln's primary aim early in the war was to rally Southern Unionists—who, he was certain, were a majority in every state except South Carolina—regardless of party, and with their help to restore the Union as it had been. He ignored the debates over the precise constitutional status of the seceded states and instead acted on the simple assumption that the loyal citizens comprised the state. And he adroitly warded off congressional attempts to dominate reconstruction policy and to the end of the war retained control himself.[20]

His approach was never rigid, but flexible. He began in 1861 by recognizing as the legitimate government of Virginia a Unionist body in the northwestern mountains under Francis H. Pierpont that had sprung up in protest against the state's secession. In 1862, as Federal armies penetrated the Confederacy, Lincoln appointed military governors for Tennessee, Louisiana, Arkansas, and North Carolina; the primary duty of these governors, who held military rank but functioned outside the army's chain of command, was to oversee civil affairs, organize the Unionists, and get the reconstruction process under way. Finally, in December 1863, Lincoln issued a proclamation outlining a general plan of reconstruction: when a number of citizens in any state equal to 10 percent of the 1860 voting population had taken an oath of future loyalty to the Union, they would be entitled to draw up a new state constitution; the government they created would be recognized by Lincoln and could apply to Congress for seating of its representatives.[21]

In these three stages of presidential policy can be traced the North's gradual disillusionment with Southern Unionism. Lincoln had hoped that the spontaneous appearance of a Unionist government in Virginia would be replicated in every Confederate state, and that reconstruction would therefore be a simple process of recognizing and supporting those governments. But no broad-based restoration movements materialized outside Virginia, and thus Lincoln resorted to the appointment of military governors to prod Unionists elsewhere into action. Yet by late 1863 no loyal state government other than Virginia's existed in the occupied South, so Lincoln was forced to devise a plan that reflected a far more modest view of the strength of Southern Unionism than he had originally held.

What had gone wrong? The subject of wartime reconstruction is complex and no two states had identical experiences, but a few generalizations can be offered. First and foremost, Northerners had in the beginning grossly overestimated the number of Southern Unionists. This was in part a consequence of their assumption that secession was not a popular political movement but an aristocratic plot. But it was also a consequence of the outpouring of Unionist sentiment that greeted the Union army in some of the first regions invaded. Those regions, however, which included northwestern Virginia, coastal North Carolina, Florida's north-eastern port towns, the Tennessee River valley in Tennessee, and the mountains of Arkansas, were untypical of the South as a whole. The false confidence that these early encounters generated eventually faded as Union forces entered other regions and met anything but a warm welcome. At least one Union general subsequently argued that a whole new military as well as political strategy was called for: "Our great error has been in occupying too many positions," John A. Dix wrote in 1863. "There was an excuse for scattering our forces while there was reason to believe that the people of the South would rally around them as nucleus for the restoration of the Union. This hope is now gone."[22]

Even where Unionists were relatively numerous the Federal army often found it impossible to provide sufficient security to allow meaningful political activity. In most parts of the occupied South, Unionists outside the garrisoned towns could openly assemble or vote only at the risk of their lives. Until the countryside was pacified, Federal authorities could enlist the full political support of only those Unionists in or very near the garrisoned towns, who, though their numbers were swelled by refugees from the countryside, were a small minority of the South's Unionists. By the same token, even where Unionist governments were created, they were generally unable to extend their authority beyond the town limits.[23]

Finally, the Yankees eventually learned to their regret that loyalty to the Union, however fervent, did not necessarily translate into support for the North's increasingly radical war aims. With every step that the Federal authorities moved away from their original conservative policy—especially with regard to slavery—they saw a diminution of Unionist enthusiasm. From the perspective that most Northerners had adopted by the latter part of the war, conservative Southern Unionists were hardly better allies than outright Rebels. Federal authorities therefore began to turn their backs on Unionists who declined to endorse wholeheartedly the administration's war policy.[24]

In one state after another President Lincoln encountered disappointment. After West Virginia gained statehood in 1863, the Pierpont administration moved to Alexandria and continued to act as Virginia's legitimate government, but its authority never extended beyond Alexandria, the eastern shore, Norfolk, Portsmouth, and a few other garrisoned towns; even in those places it had the support of a mere handful of citizens. North Carolina's military governor, native Tar Heel and conservative Unionist Edward Stanly, found far less Unionism in that state than was anticipated, made little progress toward reconstruction, and finally resigned in January 1863 in protest against the Emancipation Proclamation. Lincoln appointed no successor and made no further attempt to reconstruct the state. The president was also dissatisfied with the progress of restoration in Arkansas and recalled that state's military governor in 1863. Later in the war Unionists did convene a state constitutional convention in Little Rock and subsequently held elections and organized a state government, but the proceedings were so irregular and so lacking in popular participation that Congress refused to seat the congressional representatives. In states where Federal military penetration was slight—Florida, South Carolina, Georgia, Alabama, Mississippi, and Texas—Lincoln made no real effort at all to create Unionist governments.[25]

Tennessee and Louisiana seemed to offer the most fertile fields for political reconstruction, but even there the administration encountered formidable obstacles. In Nashville military governor Andrew Johnson was handicapped by the dearth of Unionism in the lowland sections of western and middle Tennessee, by persistent guerrillaism and frequent Confederate military raids throughout the state, and by the stubborn opposition of conservative Unionists. Only in 1865 did a state constitutional convention finally assemble and create a new state government. But in order to get the sort of government he and Lincoln wanted, Johnson threw his support to the radical Unionists and thoroughly alienated the conservatives, many of whom simply withdrew from political activity. Even with the participation of predominantly Unionist eastern Tennessee, the state barely met Lincoln's 10 percent quota.[26]

Louisiana exceeded that quota, but only by virtue of the Union army's possession of New Orleans, which contained a substantial portion of the state's white population and had a strong Unionist contingent. By 1864 occupied Louisiana had a new constitution and a functioning reconstructed government recognized by President Lincoln. But the state's Unionists, who included urban workingmen, Whiggish sugar planters, Northern-born businessmen, foreign-born liberals, and a host of other diverse interests, were riven by factionalism. The civil government that came to power under Governor Michael Hahn represented a moderate

Unionist faction that had triumphed over both radicals and conservatives with the assistance of General N. P. Banks, the ranking Federal commander in New Orleans. Hahn's government remained dependent on, and dominated by, the army, and it had little authority or popular support outside New Orleans.[27]

If Northerners were ultimately disappointed with Southern Unionism, many Southern Unionists were no less disappointed in the North. For one thing, they were bitterly frustrated by the army's failure to protect them outside the garrisoned towns. A group of western Tennesseans petitioned Governor Johnson early in 1865 from Kentucky, where they had fled for safety: "The Loyal men [in western Tennessee] feel greatly discouraged. . . . [They] are anxious to hold an election, and flattered themselves that thier country would be rid of the [Rebel] deserters and gurrellas before this. [But] it would be madness for them to attempt it in the present condition of things." A Federal officer in middle Tennessee acknowledged the army's failure: "Union men with their families are compelled to flee for their lives. . . . It is a disgrace to our Government that Union men cant live at home when their homes are 50 or 60 miles inside the lines of the Union Army."[28]

Many Unionists were disillusioned, too, by their treatment at the hands of Union soldiers. Though official orders sought to protect Unionists from abuse and pillaging and uncompensated requisitions, troops in the field did not always discriminate carefully. "Many good loyal people have been shamefully treated by our army," reported an officer in Arkansas; the Unionists, he said, "have nearly all been robbed of everything they had by the troops of this command, and are now left destitute." A Virginia citizen recounted the tragedy of Robert Scott, a Fauquier County Unionist, who was killed by a renegade band of Union army deserters in the spring of 1862: "His death caused infinite consternation in the community . . . and did more to destroy the remaining Union feeling existing in that section of Virginia than any other event of the war that had occurred up to that time."[29]

As occupation continued, many Unionists lost their enthusiasm not only for the Union army but also for political reconstruction. Some foresaw danger in the revival of state courts while the war was still going on. "Many Citizens here owe debts North, and have debts due them South," a Memphis Unionist explained. "Now if the Civil Courts were organized here, a merchant at New York Could Collect his debt from a Memphis

Merchant but a Memphis Merchant Could not Collect a debt against a man in Mississippi for the reason that he could not reach him." Another Tennessean worried that the courts would become "a means of terrible oppression to the people," because creditors would use them to enforce claims against debtors, most of whom were hard-pressed by the economic dislocations of occupation: "what would be the financial condition of the people of this county, in thirty days [if the courts were restored]? *Ruined!* Every poor man, and man of moderate means, would be sold out of house and home."[30]

Even more disturbing to the Unionists was the prospect of a reconstructed state government that they themselves did not control. Lincoln's lenient reconstruction proclamation of December 1863 alarmed a good many Unionists because it enfranchised any man who took a simple oath of future loyalty. Though many professed to believe in the innate Unionism of the Southern masses, most Unionists distrusted erstwhile secessionists who embraced Unionism after the Northern army arrived; it galled them to see such Johnnies-come-lately equated with those who had been steadfastly loyal from the beginning. They took a dim view, too, of the outsiders who had come in the Federal army's wake and now sought a role in reconstruction. One of Andrew Johnson's correspondents described the situation in Memphis from the viewpoint of the native, "original" Unionists:

> [T]here are a few, (not many) *Reliable loyal* men (citizens) in Memphis,—They are mostly men who have been driven from the interior Counties of West Te[nnessee]. . . . There are many there, *professing* loyalty, who have gone thither from other states since the Federal occupation of the City; a few of whom are doubtless sincere, Reliable, Gentlemen,—but—they are mostly—hangers on,—place hunters [or] speculators—mere gamblers—in Search of mammon. . . . There is another class there composed of former citizens who were *active traitors* while the Rebels held sway but who now *profess* to be the only Reliably loyal men in the country and . . . these men have generally succeeded by some means in controling Federal officers in the dispensation of the favors and privileges of the Government.[31]

Where reconstructed state governments were operating, Unionists were frequently exasperated by conflicts of authority with the army and by the military's disregard for civil officials. In Virginia, for example, officers of the Pierpont government waged a running battle with the army. "I regret to inform you," said Mayor William Brooks of Norfolk to Governor Pierpont, "that our civil government is much weakened by the interference of the military, and I think unless a change can be made we shall cease to be a government." The city provost marshal, complained the mayor, said "I must respect his name in every way whenever I saw it attached to a paper, no matter what its requirements were." Another Norfolk man told Pierpont that the district commandant "seems not to entertain a very high respect for the restored government of Virginia, and judging from his conduct, is disposed to embarrass its operation, if not crush it out."[32]

More than anything else, however, it was the North's growing radicalism that alienated many Unionists. For some, such as Margaret Nourse of Fauquier County, Virginia, disenchantment came with Congress's enactment of the second Confiscation Act of 1862, which threatened all the people of the Confederacy, rich and poor alike, with harsh retaliation and forfeiture of their property. Nourse, an earnest but not vindictive Unionist, was deeply shaken. "[O]ur government has become so ruthless," she wrote, "that it would crush all the poor people without a thought of regret. Is there no pity for them at the North[?]" For many other Unionists, emancipation was the final straw. One was Emerson Etheridge, of western Tennessee, a former U.S. congressman. When offered a federal judgeship by President Lincoln, Etheridge turned it down in protest against the Emancipation Proclamation, which he regarded as "treachery to the Union men of the South."[33]

Disillusioned by the course that occupation had taken since they first sighted the Stars and Stripes and cried for joy, many Unionists came to feel like citizens without a country. They were the true patriots, they insisted; they alone held steadily to their faith in the old Union while the South degenerated into reaction and hysteria and the North swerved toward tyranny and revolution. Their disappointment was aggravated by their realization that the coming of the Yankees had not fully broken the power of the secessionist majority, and that the struggle against the Rebels must go on.

. . .

Secessionists were certain that God, truth, justice, logic, and history were all on their side. The arguments for leaving the Union and warring against the North were to them so compelling as to defy contradiction; Unionism, as a principle, seemed inexplicable. They therefore concluded that Unionists could not be honorable men and women with virtuous motives. Indeed, unless they were simply stupid or insane, Unionists must be villains, self-seekers, white trash—no other explanation made sense. "You talk of the Union sentiment!," wrote an anonymous "Wife of a Southern Planter" to General Butler soon after the capture of New Orleans. "*You* are *welcomed* by natures *congenial* to your own. The *basest* and *most degraded* of our sex. And by the *lowest* class of foreigners, whose souls are in their pockets. . . . Some *few* others also, who desire City offices, and would take the oath to *Beelzebub* if it would further their base selfishness." A secessionist in occupied North Carolina wrote to a friend to assure her "that the people [here] are *true*," and that those few who had gone over to the enemy were "the offscouring of the people & foreigners, people who can neither read or write & who never had a decent suit of clothes . . . poor ignorant wretches."[34]

The contempt that the secessionists felt was, however, laced with fear. How vengeful the Unionists might become with the power of the Union army behind them was anyone's guess. "I fear these lawless unprincipled Buffalos," confessed a North Carolina woman, using the epithet that Tar Heel secessionists bestowed on Unionists who allied with the Federal army; "they are worse than the Yankees & under even less restraint." A Union officer in western Tennessee reported that secessionists there were convinced that Unionists were about to "rise in arms to get up a counter-revolution." But Unionists were a threat even if they did not take up arms, for secessionists knew, or suspected, that they acted as informants. A Portsmouth man noted in his diary that Federal troops had entered the home of a friend looking for weapons and contraband mail. "This search," he concluded, "was no doubt prompted by so called Union Parties."[35]

Secessionists in the occupied South were no more reconciled to Unionist liberation than they were to Northern military rule. Just as they resisted the Federal occupiers by every means at hand, so they struggled against the Unionists with whatever weapons they possessed. In the garrisoned towns secessionists could not physically abuse or publicly threaten Unionists, but they could sometimes intimidate them subtly, especially by playing on their fear that the Federals might at some point pull out and leave them at the mercy of the Rebels. Nashville Unionist Hugh Thompson told how he was accosted by some secessionist acquaintances soon after the city fell and was asked menacingly how he liked the Yankees. When he replied that he liked them just fine, he was told, "very well old fellow we will jerk you off the ground when they go away from here." "[T]his sort of thing," said Thompson, "keeps the union people afraid to talk."[36]

In the towns secessionists got a good deal of satisfaction from reviling Unionists to their faces. Though the occupation authorities eventually cracked down on such behavior, just as they did the secessionists' public cursing of Union soldiers, they frequently tolerated it while the rosewater policy prevailed, as long as no threats were made. A Unionist woman in Clarksville, Tennessee, spoke of "the earnest vindictiveness, the deep . . . bitterness of hate" that secessionists manifested: "Sorely have I been denounced . . . and . . . dubbed as a 'Lincoln Spy.' " A Memphis "Union Lady" wrote the editor of the *Union Appeal* in 1862 to ask, "Why is it that the families of Union men are insulted by the secession rabble that yet infest the city? Why are the wives of the cowardly Secessionists allowed to bawl at the loyal citizen, 'Yankee,' 'Traitor,' 'Coward.' "[37]

Even where secessionists could not get away with such invective, they could still retaliate against Unionists by shunning them. Any man or woman who stepped forward when the Yankees came and publicly announced for the Union risked social isolation. In Nashville, soon after it fell, three members of the First Baptist Church declared their Union sympathies and accepted political appointments from military governor Johnson. The other members of the church were, according to the pastor, "immeasurably mortified" and thereafter avoided the three men and their families "as if they had been infected with leprosy."[38]

Shunning, cursing, and vague threats of future retribution were but frail weapons against a resolute Unionist. Though they might intimidate a few individuals, secessionists in the garrisoned towns could not overawe the Unionists as a class. The secessionists were fundamentally impotent and the Unionists fundamentally invulnerable, thanks to the constant presence of Federal troops.

Circumstances were very different on the Confederate frontier. There, except during the Federals' periodic raids, Rebel authority held sway and Unionists were generally defenseless. Confederate civil and military officials had a more or less free hand to subjugate the Unionists and guard against subversion. Governor John Letcher of Virginia ordered county magistrates in the frontier districts to organize vigilance committees to watch for "strangers or suspicious characters" traveling toward the Union lines, and to arrest them if they appeared to be communicating with the enemy. After the fall of New Orleans, Governor Thomas O. Moore of Louisiana activated the militia organizations in the state's frontier parishes and ordered them to "arrest . . . each and every individual who gives aid and assistance and comfort to the enemy or against whom good grounds of suspicion exist." Soon after, he sent in a force of state "partisan rangers" to reinforce the local militia.[39]

Rangers, militia, Confederate troops, conscription and impressment agents, and informal bands of citizens ruthlessly persecuted known or suspected Unionists on the frontier. The Quaker brethren of Hopewell Meeting in the Shenandoah Valley, for instance, were repeatedly victimized whenever the Confederate army controlled their contested region. "Property was constantly in jeopardy," they stated after the war, ". . . from the depredations of independent bands of rebel soldiers who . . . regarded those who did not sympathise with them in their treasonable efforts to destroy the Government, as their lawful prey." In one northern Alabama community a citizens' outfit known as Graves's Company took upon itself the duty of hunting down Confederate deserters and hounding Unionists. A Unionist woman whose husband hid from Confederate conscription reported that members of the company, including one Cowan, had vowed that "they would come to my house and if they did not find [my husband], they would not leave until they had burned our place up. Mr. Cowan [said] he was going to kill my husband." Later, she reported, Cowan confronted her and threatened to "Bushwack us all, and [said] he would kill as long as he could pull [a] trigger, 'So help him God.'"[40]

Vicious harassment of that sort sent thousands of avowed or suspected Unionists on the Confederate frontier fleeing to the Federal lines and served as a warning to those whose sentiments were still secret. A few of the latter chose to flee, too, but most were held back by the knowledge that they would not only be abandoning their property to the Rebels, but also severing themselves, perhaps forever, from their communities—for people who went to the enemy were branded as pariahs. A northern

Mississippian reported in 1863 that two men who earlier had disappeared from the neighborhood were reported to have turned up at a Federal post in Tennessee, "So it seems they have literally gone to the Yankees. Their future fame is undesirable: for they now rank as 'tories.'" The elders of Cool Springs Baptist Church in Gates County, North Carolina, ordered in 1864 that "bro[ther] John L Smith and sister Emma Smith his wife be excluded from the fellowship of this church for leaveing their country and seeking yankee protection."[41]

The power of the secessionists on the Confederate frontier was not in every case unlimited. In a few districts where Federal raids were frequent, secessionists were restrained by fear of reprisals. "Our Southern friends beseech me not to interfere with the Union men," a Confederate officer wrote from western Tennessee while that region was still in Confederate hands, "since [the Unionists] will be certain to report them, and thereby bring down . . . retaliation on the part of the Federal troops. . . . I have therefore determined not to arrest any Union sympathizers unless known to be aiding and abetting the enemy." On the whole, however, the balance of power on the Confederate frontier weighed heavily on the side of the secessionists, and Unionists defied them at their peril.[42]

The balance was closer to equilibrium in no-man's-land. Though secessionists were a majority in nearly every section of no-man's-land, and in most cases a very large majority, the absence of Confederate authority and the proximity of the Federal posts diminished their power and strengthened the Unionists. The result was a degree of desperation on the part of the secessionists and a degree of defiance on the part of the Unionists that fueled one another and ultimately exploded into savage fratricide.

Most secessionists in no-man's-land were cautious about harassing their Unionist neighbors because Federal troops were never far away, but some of the more reckless did not hesitate to make open threats when Union forces were not in the immediate vicinity. Secessionists grew especially bold when Confederate cavalry made their occasional forays into no-man's-land; they would often point out Unionists and urge the Rebel troops to punish them. Kate Sperry in Virginia recounted the fate of a "strong Union" man named Dooley, who had "been a detective for the Yankees" and "caused all the [secessionists'] houses to be searched . . . and did everything he could against the citizens" when Federal troops were present. In January 1864, when no troops were on hand, Dooley made the mistake of showing up in public "expecting the Yankees to come up in force," whereupon a detachment of Confederate scouts, tipped off by secessionist citizens, nabbed him and carried him off.[43]

It was the guerrilla, however, not the Rebel cavalry raider, who was the true avenging arm of the secessionists in no-man's-land. Adept at eluding the occupiers, guerrillas were not afraid to persecute Unionists, and they did so regularly and often brutally. A western Tennessee Unionist described a visitation by guerrillas who seized his horse, saddle, and shotgun "and threatened to blow my brains out. . . . They threatened to take me over the River and try me for my life." In middle Tennessee, a woman testified about a local guerrilla gang whose leader "came to my house and said in a great rage that he was after my son because he had been with the God Damned Yankees. . . . [H]e swore he would kill my son . . . if he could find him."[44]

When guerrillas warred against Northern soldiers they were fighting to defend their community against invaders, but when they attacked Unionists they were fighting an enemy within. This was civil war in its most basic sense, a struggle of neighbor against neighbor, for guerrillas and Unionists were both deeply rooted in their community. Guerrillas knew of Unionists from local gossip or personal knowledge; frequently, in fact, they were longtime acquaintances of their Unionist victims. Alfred Wilson of Maury County, Tennessee, was at the home of his friends the Literals one night in the summer of 1863 when a gang of guerrillas burst into the house. Wilson recognized them all as neighborhood men and knew them by name; the guerrillas knew their victims well, too. "They said they were going to kill [Mr.] Literal because he was a union man and had reported [secessionists' concealed] horses to the federals," Wilson later testified. "They were very abusive and threatened to kill [all the Literals] and burn their house and gave them until the next day to get out of the house and leave the neighborhood."[45]

These last words, and a good deal of other evidence, suggest that in attacking Unionists the guerrillas were seeking basically to purge their communities, to expel an undesirable and dangerous element. Many of their actions were intended to make it impossible for even the most defiant Unionist to remain in the neighborhood. For example, guerrillas frequently not only threatened to, but actually did, burn down their victim's house. They also stole or destroyed livestock, food, and even clothing.[46]

As ruthless as such reprisals were, they appear rather restrained when contrasted with the murderous, no-holds-barred warfare that the guerrillas waged against the Northern invaders. Why the guerrillas did not simply slaughter all the Unionists is an interesting question. The answer may be that, although secessionists despised and feared their Unionist neighbors, they did not as a rule dehumanize them as they did the Yankee enemy—at least not Unionist women and children, who comprised a large majority of the Unionists who remained in no-man's-land.

Guerrillas regularly threatened Unionist women and children in the most menacing terms but almost never assaulted them physically. Mildred Heardy of Giles County, Tennessee, recounted a revealing episode that occurred in 1864, when she was visited by a band of six guerrillas led by one Powhatan Hardiman, who demanded to know if it was true that her husband had taken up with the Yankees and "told me to come out as he was going to burn up my damned old 'shebang.' I left the house with my children. They set fire to the beds and throwed everything topsy-turvy and ransacked the whole house. [Hardiman] said he ought to burn the house with the whole family in it." But Hardiman did not harm Heardy or her children. He did, though, commit one act of bodily violence before he left: he "drew a pistol," Heardy testified, "and struck my father-in-law over the head."[47]

As this incident suggests, Unionist men were not immune from guerrilla violence as women and children were. Guerrillas were, in fact, quite ready to use lethal force against Unionist men. When a woman defied them by remaining in the community despite warnings, guerrillas would do no more than destroy her house and her subsistence and thus uproot her from the community. But when a man defied them, the guerrillas did not hesitate to kill. As the internecine struggle continued in no-man's-land, those Unionist men who refused to flee to the garrisoned towns dug in their heels and prepared to fight to the death. The guerrillas responded in kind.[48]

By the latter part of the war, in many sections of no-man's-land, guerrillas had declared a war of no quarter against Unionist men. From the eastern highlands of middle Tennessee came a report that "numerous bands of desperate men . . . have made there appearance in the Country & [are committing] depredations & th[r]eathnings & murders of loyal citisens. . . . No Loyal man feels it comfortable or safe to remain. . . .

[D]esperate roving parties, taking courage from the abscence of Federal Troops—come forth at noon day to persue . . . their work of murder & robbery." In western Tennessee, according to a Union officer's report, guerrillas kidnapped five Unionist men and "brutally murdered them in cold blood." In one of those cases the guerrillas demanded ransom money from the victim's wife after they had taken him off; when she paid, they "cursed and abused her; said they had her money and would kill the damned old tory beside." And so they did: three days later he was found dead and mutilated near his home. Northwestern Arkansas also witnessed widespread guerrilla violence and many killings: "not a single loyal man is safe for a moment outside of garrisoned towns," a Fort Smith newspaper reported. "[U]nless the proper and necessary steps are speedily taken, the Union men in the country will be exterminated or driven from their homes."[49]

Even as the guerrilla onslaught began, however, Union men in many sections were taking steps to avert extermination or exile. Emboldened by the prospect of Northern aid, they resolved to defy the will of the secessionist majority, defend their homes, and answer violence with violence.

. . .

The coming of the Yankees unleashed a host of long-suppressed forces in Southern society. Among them was the hunger of many Unionists for vengeance. Liberation and the restoration of the old Union were enough to satisfy some, but others yearned for retribution. "I long to see the day," wrote one Tennessean, "when . . . Traitors [will be] hung."[50]

Some Unionists, in their righteous wrath, took immediate revenge on their Rebel neighbors. In Alexandria, for example, no sooner had the Federal army occupied the city in 1861 than Unionists began pointing out the homes of secessionist refugees, which the army then promptly seized. When Federal forces invaded central Arkansas in 1863, a delegation of Unionists from Pine Bluff went to meet them and escort them to their town. On arriving in Pine Bluff, the troops proceeded to ransack the homes of Rebel sympathizers; as one resident noted, "They knew every ones name & where they lived."[51]

Unionists also avenged themselves by aiding the Federal army and undermining the Confederacy. They served as guides for Union troops, passed word of Confederate military movements and guerrilla activity, identified citizens who harbored guerrillas, and helped men who had deserted from the Rebel army or were avoiding Confederate conscription, often at great risk to their own safety.[52]

The most embittered Unionists demanded an eye for an eye. One was a man named Harris who lived in Madison County, Alabama. In the spring of 1863, when that area was under Confederate control, Harris's neighbor Bradford Hambrick had repeatedly threatened him, declaring that Harris "would have to leave the country. That he couldn't stay in it. That a man of his politics couldn't live there." Eventually Hambrick shot and wounded Harris and drove him into hiding. When the Yankees came that summer, the tables turned: Harris announced his intention to kill Hambrick and then "get some of the Union soldiers and take everything out of [Hambrick's] house and burn the whole place up. . . . He has been a big fellow for a long time, but now is my time to bring him down."[53]

Many Unionists took violent revenge on the Rebels by formally enlisting with the Rebels' foes. A Northern officer on the coast of North Carolina early in 1862 wrote that many of the citizens there were "deep and bitter in their denunciations of the secession heresy, and promised a regiment, if called upon, to aid in the restoration of the flag." Indeed, such men were called upon, in North Carolina and throughout the occupied South, and in considerable numbers they were enrolled in the Union army. In Decatur, Alabama, for instance, an officer reported in July 1862 that men were coming in to the lines "begging me to give them protection and a chance to defend the flag of our country." He signed up 40 volunteers there, then led a raiding party into the hill country south of Decatur and came back with 150 more.[54]

All told, over 100,000 white men from the seceded states served in the Federal army during the war. Tennessee contributed more than any other state (some 42,000), but Virginia, Arkansas, Louisiana, North Carolina, and Alabama accounted for substantial numbers. Some of these enlistees joined outfits from Union states, but the great majority signed up with units that bore their own state's name and were officered by fellow citizens of the state; in many cases these Southern Unionist units were not attached to a Federal field army but were instead employed as occupation forces. In middle Tennessee, former Whig congressman William B. Stokes, who had withdrawn from public life when his state seceded, accepted a U.S. army commission in 1862 and then recruited an entire regiment. To the end of the war, the men of the First Middle Tennessee Cavalry served as scouts, guerrilla hunters, and avenging angels in their homeland.[55]

Some Unionists warred against the Confederacy without donning a Federal uniform. In certain sections of the Confederate frontier, where Unionism was particularly strong, Unionists banded together and dared to wage guerrilla war against the Rebels. Operating much like the secessionist guerrillas who roamed no-man's-land, these men (dubbed "jayhawkers" in some regions) harassed secessionist citizens and bedeviled the Confederate army. Sarah Espy's community in northern Alabama, for example, was terrorized by a band of vengeful Unionists. Between the visitations of these jayhawkers and the raids of the Yankees, Espy lamented, "it seems there is no safety anywhere."[56]

It was in no-man's-land, however, that Unionists most fully gratified their lust for vengeance. In northern Virginia a Federal officer learned of a group of local Unionist men who "have suffered very much from Guerrillas, and have now determined to act in self defence. Seven of them attacked a band of nearly twice their number last night and though armed only with shot guns, they succeeded in wounding three and driving the whole party from the neighborhood, capturing one." Noting that "the same disposition to defend their homes is evinced in other localities," the officer recommended that Unionists be provided with arms. If this could be done, he said, "I have no doubt that the country in this vicinity would soon be cleared of Guerrillas."[57]

Federal authorities elsewhere, too, saw evidence that Unionists were eager to defend themselves and to wrest no-man's-land from the enemy. "The constant cry from them to me is, 'Send us arms . . . and we will drive the secessionists out,' " reported an officer in Tennessee. Unionists in Washington County, North Carolina, organized a self-defense unit just eight days after Federal troops arrived in May 1862, even before it was certain that the county would be permanently occupied. When Sherman's troops entered the town of Jasper, in the northern Georgia mountains, hundreds of Unionists came in from the countryside to greet them and then raised a force for local defense on the spot.[58]

Impressed by the Unionists' zeal and by the evident military advantages, Federal authorities set about formally enrolling and equipping

Unionist home guard companies in many sections of no-man's-land. Two were on duty in Bedford County, Tennessee, as early as June 1862, and a number of others mustered elsewhere in the state by the fall of that year. By late 1863 companies were organized in several Arkansas and Virginia counties as well. One based in the village of Accotink, Virginia, was especially active, picketing the roads leading into the community, watching for guerrillas, rounding up Confederate stragglers, and keeping on eye on the secessionist inhabitants. The local provost marshal reported that that district was "now more secure than it has been for a long time."[59]

The primary mission of the home guards was to make their communities safe for Unionists. The most effective way to do that was not simply to guard against guerrilla raids and defend their homes when attacked, but to take the offensive, to seek out and destroy the guerrillas. In many sections of no-man's-land the home guards went about that task with deadly determination and efficacy. "[T]hey are killing many of the worst men in this part of the State," a Union officer reported from the eastern highlands of middle Tennessee in 1864, "& will soon drive all the Guerrillas out. They are passing through the Country in small parties killing (they take none) all the robbers & Scoundrels, I am convinced of their usefulness." In northwestern Arkansas a special force of Unionist "Rangers" was recruited; mounted and heavily armed, they were the shock troops of the home guard. "Captain Turner's company of Rangers are doing good work, ferreting out and killing bushwhackers," a Fort Smith newspaper reported in 1864. "They are on the move all the time. . . . They are in earnest, and not only know how to hunt, fight and whip bushwhackers, but know how to treat them when they *happen* to take prisoners."[60]

No prisoners, no quarter: the remorseless war of guardsman versus guerrilla, neighbor against neighbor, added another dimension to the violence that deluged no-man's-land after the Yankees arrived. Beholding that bloody strife, Unionists came to understand that the advent of the Union army was not the answer to all their prayers, not a sign of final deliverance but merely a herald of continuing struggle. They were not alone, for certain others in the occupied South who had watched the arrival of the Yankees with a sense of hope were also discovering how powerful still were the forces of reaction.

A drayman poses with his ox and cart in occupied Mississippi as a Federal officer looks on. Southerners who decided to stay and face the invading enemy were often agreeably surprised to find that the military authorities were conciliatory and intended to let them carry on their lives as normally as possible. (Chicago Historical Society)

Northern troops prepare to cross the Potomac River into Virginia in 1861. The early invasions of the South were marked by orderly behavior on the part of Federal soldiers, who were convinced that Southern secessionists were simply deluded and could be brought to their senses if treated well. (*Harper's Weekly*)

South Carolina civilians and Confederate troops flee a Union coastal invasion. Fearing that the Yankee invaders would be vengeful and rapacious, some Southerners in threatened regions gathered their movable property—including slaves—and headed for safety in the Confederate interior. (*Frank Leslie's Illustrated History of the Civil War*)

Federal workmen in Tennessee repair railroad tracks damaged by guerrillas.
Continuing civilian resistance in the occupied South, especially the bloody guerrilla
warfare, helped persuade Federal authorities to abandon the conciliatory policy.
(Library of Congress)

Union troops in northern Georgia, 1864. By the latter part of the war Federal soldiers were only too glad to help carry out the new punitive policy toward Southern civilians. The men shown here would soon be following their commander, William T. Sherman, on a devastating march through Georgia and the Carolinas. (Library of Congress)

A bustling marketplace in occupied Norfolk, Virginia. In the garrisoned towns life went on much as usual, even after the "hard" policy was instituted. Citizens and soldiers in the towns eventually worked out a satisfactory if not necessarily congenial modus vivendi. (Massachusetts Commandery Military Order of the Loyal Legion and U.S. Army Military History Institute)

The provost marshal's office in a garrisoned Southern town. The provost marshal was responsible for all matters relating to civilians in the occupied areas, including the issuing of passes, trade permits, and emergency rations. (National Archives)

Federal troops forage at a Virginia farmhouse. Citizens living outside the garrisoned towns felt the full brunt of the hard policy; hungry Union soldiers often stripped farms of provisions and sometimes pillaged homes. (*Frank Leslie's Illustrated History of the Civil War*)

Alabama Unionists joyfully greet Federal gunboats on the Tennessee River in 1862. The Unionists of the South hailed the arrival of the Yankee army but often became disillusioned with their liberators as the war went on. (*Harper's Weekly*)

Blacks at a Federal army camp in Virginia, 1862. Slaves in the occupied regions deserted their masters in great numbers and headed for the Union army posts, even before the army's policy was officially antislavery. (Massachusetts Commandery Military Order of the Loyal Legion and U.S. Army Military History Institute)

Aristocratic ladies beseech Union troops for provisions. Enemy occupation was a humbling experience for the South's aristocrats, who found themselves stripped of their wealth and power and often dependent on Federal handouts. (Bettmann Archive)

A refugee family of the yeoman class arrives at a Union post. Large numbers of Southern "plain folk" went to the garrisoned towns as the war progressed, either to escape danger and starvation in the rural areas or to seek new opportunities. (Library of Congress)

Southern women pose outside a farmhouse in occupied Virginia. The majority of citizens in the occupied regions were women, for many men had fled the Northern invaders or were away in the Confederate army. (Library of Congress)

A Union soldier executed by the army for attempted rape in Virginia, 1864. Sexual molestation of Southern women by Federal troops was actually rare; army authorities condemned and rigorously punished such behavior. (Massachusetts Commandery Military Order of the Loyal Legion and U.S. Army Military History Institute)

A wrecked bridge in the Virginia countryside, 1864. Destruction and danger in the rural sections of the occupied South created a no-man's-land where community life disintegrated. (Library of Congress)

Bandits accost a wayfarer on a country road in the occupied South, 1864. By the latter part of the war banditry was common in the anarchic rural districts surrounding the garrisoned towns. (*Harper's Weekly*)

[5]

· ·

To the Red Sea

The Struggle against
Black Freedom

· ·

Joshua Moore of Alabama had a revelation in the spring
of 1862. Despite the assurances of Northern politicians and generals,
Moore realized that the coming of the Yankees meant the end of slavery.
He had seen what happened when Federal troops passed through Tuscumbia in April. They were an ill-disciplined and malicious lot, untypical
of the Union soldiers who marched into the South in that early period of
the war. "They acted very badly while in town," Moore wrote later that
month, "breaking open houses, cellars, etc. taking what they pleased."
Furthermore, he reported, "they have completely demoralized the negroes . . . large numbers have run away. . . . They made the ignorant
blacks believe they had come to free them. . . . The negroes were delighted with them and since they left enough can be seen to convince
anyone that the Federal army, the negroes and white Southern people
cannot inhabit the same country. . . . [F]rom the very nature of the contest, so sure as the war continues it is the death blow to negro slavery."[1]

Moore had glimpsed the future, and in the succeeding months the
truth of his prophecy became more and more apparent. As Union sol-

149

diers came to understand that conquering the Confederacy would be a long and grueling task, many repudiated the official conservatism of their government and agreed that slavery must be destroyed. "There is a mighty revolution a going on in the minds of men [in the army] on the niger question," an Illinois soldier wrote in July 1862. Among those men were several whom a North Carolina citizen spoke with in September. "They contended that if it was necessary to put down the rebellion that slavery would be abolished," the appalled Tar Heel reported, "that they could & would take every negro out of the country where they went, & would likely stir up a servile war, that every means must be adopted to put down this rebellion."[2]

By the latter part of 1862 Federal soldiers across the occupied South, officers and men alike, were routinely welcoming runaway slaves (dubbed "contrabands") into the army camps and turning a deaf ear to the pleas of fugitive-hunting masters. A number of motives were at work, besides the preeminent one of weakening the Confederacy. Some soldiers were converted to abolitionism after viewing the horrors of slavery at first hand; others saw emancipation as the first step toward transforming the backward South. Many sought to punish secessionist slaveholders, whereas for some it was just a practical matter of securing labor to do the army's dirty work. Whatever the motive, one by one the soldiers of the Union army declared war on slavery. Though most were content for the time being merely to protect contrabands from reenslavement, some began encouraging slaves to abscond or simply rounding them up and taking them away willy-nilly. "Now what do you think of your husband," an officer in Tennessee teasingly asked his wife after telling her of his slave- and livestock-gathering expeditions, "degenerating from a conservative young Democrat to a horse stealer and 'nigger thief.' . . . Yes, while in the field I am an abolitionist."[3]

Official government policy lagged a step behind the soldiers in the field, and several steps behind the contrabands, but caught up by the end of 1862. The second Confiscation Act, passed by Congress on July 17, allowed the government to seize secessionists' slave property and prohibited military men from surrendering fugitive slaves to any claimant. The Militia Act of the same date permitted the army to use blacks, and an executive order promulgated a few days later authorized the seizure of private property in the South, including slaves, for military purposes.

Furthermore, these edicts permitted blacks entering Union lines to be employed as more than just trench diggers, cooks, and teamsters: before the summer was out, the army was recruiting black soldiers. Both the Confiscation and Militia Acts broached the matter of emancipation, too, though hesitantly and awkwardly. The Militia Act freed any black man who served in the army, as well as his family, if owned by a secessionist. The Confiscation Act declared free all slaves seized from disloyal masters but gave Federal courts the ultimate responsibility of deciding the status of individual slaves.

Meanwhile, President Lincoln was moving toward a policy of general emancipation. Early on he had resisted attempts to convert the conflict into a crusade against slavery (though he hoped to persuade the South to accede to a plan of gradual, compensated emancipation). But several factors pushed him from conservatism toward revolution. Northern abolitionists exerted increasing political and moral influence after the South resorted to secession and war. In Congress, radical Republicans likewise spoke with a more authoritative voice as the war dragged on and the Rebels proved to be strong and defiant. Too, European opinion loomed more important as the war continued, and it was certain that emancipation would boost the North's image abroad. Moreover, the realization that Southern Unionists were not the potent force that they had first seemed made Lincoln less reluctant to alienate them with radical measures. But mostly the president was moved by the plain fact that slavery was already beginning to crumble in the South, thanks to the actions of Union troops and especially of the slaves themselves, and that by encouraging and speeding that disintegration the North could strengthen itself and eviscerate the Confederacy.

Lincoln's Emancipation Proclamation of January 1, 1863, declared free all slaves in the Confederate states (except Tennessee, six occupied counties in tidewater Virginia, and thirteen occupied parishes in Louisiana, where citizens had taken steps toward reconstruction sufficient to redeem them in the president's eyes). The proclamation cut through the equivocations of the July congressional acts by making no distinction between the slaves of loyal and disloyal owners, nor between those who came into Union lines or served in the army and those who did not; and by requiring no judicial decree of freedom. Though it could not, of course, immediately free any slaves in the vast majority of Confederate territory, the proclamation was more than just a gesture, for it firmly committed the army to a policy of outright emancipation in many of the areas then under occupation—and all those that would fall into Union hands in the future—and served notice to all soldiers in the field, including the dwindling number of conservatives, that liberating slaves was now their sworn duty.[4]

Officers and men thereafter carried out that duty with a vengeance. The army's revised policy toward blacks, as one Union officer described it, was to "keep all we get, and get all we can." As the war went on, the geographic exemptions in the proclamation proved increasingly meaningless. From the standpoint of army policy, Tennessee and the exempted districts in Virginia and Louisiana became indistinguishable from occupied Alabama or Georgia or Arkansas. Late in 1863 a Union officer in Nashville, questioned about the status of slavery in Tennessee, unhesitatingly announced its demise: "Slavery is dead," he declared; "that is the first thing. That is what we all begin with here, who know the state of affairs."[5]

The army acted not only as the annihilator of slavery but also as the midwife of the free labor system. As early as 1862, military authorities in Louisiana began supervising the hiring out of blacks to white employers under wage contracts. By 1864 such programs were in place in all occupied regions. The "contraband camps" that the army established at various places to shelter black refugees served also as labor depots where whites could apply for workers and army officials could oversee the terms of contracts. Many of the employers were Northern civilians who were leasing abandoned plantations under Treasury Department regulations; in some cases the government itself took over abandoned estates, appointed an overseer, and hired black workers. In Louisiana alone, the army-supervised contract labor program eventually encompassed 50,000 black workers on 1,500 estates.[6]

The army's vision of the place of the freed blacks in the South's emerging reconstructed society was, however, a narrow one. The contract labor system discouraged black autonomy and instead sought to keep blacks in a semidependent condition under white control. The orders governing labor on Virginia's eastern shore, for example, required all blacks to enter into contracts and warned them that "insolence, insubordination or improper conduct" were contract violations punishable by the army. Union soldiers themselves, from generals down to privates, almost unanimously rejected the idea that blacks deserved to be treated as fully equal citizens, and most harbored deep suspicions about the innate character of blacks. General Sherman, for one, though quite ready to liberate slaves in order to hurt the Confederacy, considered it his duty also "to restrain the violence and passion of the [freed] negroes."[7]

Thus the Union army decreed an end to black bondage but staked out certain limits to black liberty. Meanwhile, the people of the occupied South, white and black alike, were struggling to impose their own notions about slavery, freedom, and equality.

• • •

The fortress of slavery shook and crumbled as the Northern army bombarded it from without, but it might well have withstood the assault had the slaves themselves not undermined it from within. Even in the early days of Federal occupation, when conservatism reigned in the Union ranks, slaves sensed that the coming of the Yankees might offer deliverance from bondage. Cautiously at first, but with increasing boldness as the mood of the invaders shifted, blacks in the occupied South chipped away at the foundation stones of the peculiar institution.

Running off to the army camps was the first and most obvious sign that many slaves were ready and willing to subvert the institution. Slipping away in the night as their masters slept, these early fugitives presented themselves at the army picket posts and hoped for the best. Many were turned away, others were reclaimed by their owners, but enough found refuge to encourage others to do the same, and before long the trickle of fugitives became a stream and then a flood. A Louisiana plantation owner wrote in July 1862 that "there has been a perfect stampede of the negroes on some places in this vicinity"; one of his neighbors had lost ten in a single night. Planter Colin Clarke witnessed a similar exodus in the Virginia tidewater region that summer: "Negros are constantly going off," he said, "& I doubt if 100 will be left [in the county] by the winter, if the enemy remain at York."[8]

Many blacks stayed on with their masters, however—some out of loyalty but most out of fear of the hazards of flight or uncertainty about life in the contraband camps and army labor battalions. Yet those who stayed were able in many cases (depending on how much their master's authority was weakened by the imposition of Northern power) to challenge the institution of slavery and enlarge their own sphere of autonomy. Many became openly insubordinate and "disloyal." They informed on masters who had hidden provisions or contraband goods from the Federals, they evaded work and defied orders, and they "talked back" to whites. In September 1862 a Louisiana planter found his slaves "in a state of insurection. . . . [S]ome of them would not work at all, & others wanted wages." A Tennessean reported "General insurbordination amongst our slave population" that summer; by November he had decided that the "worthlessness & insolence" of the blacks had become "most unbearable."[9]

Once Union policy became firmly emancipationist, most blacks who could do so cast off all their chains. A provost marshal in Louisiana was struck in June 1863 by "the change that has taken place. . . . The negroes [now have] altogether different feelings from those of former times . . . a spirit of independance—a feeling they are no longer slaves. . . . They will not endure the same treatment, the same customs and rules, the same language, that they have heretofore quietly submitted to." One who exemplified the new sense of freedom was a black Louisianan named Samvill, who in early 1865 was challenged by a white man named Dwyer over his right to work a certain plot of land. Samvill's reply, according to a witness, was "that no white man could stop his ploughing it. . . . [He said] that it was not rebel times now. . . . [H]e would plough any spot of land on the place that he chose; he said he dared Mr. Dwyer to come and tell him that he should not plough there."[10]

In many districts invaded by the Union army after the Emancipation Proclamation, slavery did not so much dissolve as explode. "The arrival of the advance [scouts] of the Yankees alone turned the negroes crazy," a Louisiana planter reported in May 1863. "They became utterly demoralized at once and everything like subordination and restraint was at an end." Overseer Alfred Quine of Mississippi witnessed a similar scene the same month. Work continued more or less normally on Quine's plantation, despite reports of the enemy's approach, until May 25. "All hands went to work," he wrote in his journal that day, "and worked up to 12 oclock and [then] the yankees came and set the Negros all Free and the work all stoped." The next day he reported "Negros all Free no work dun"; on May 27, "Negros doing nothing . . . Saulsbery Daniel Little John and Henry with waggon & oxen went with the yankees"; on June 1,

"Negros all riding about and doing nothing"; on June 4, "Some of the Negros went to workeing out corn as ther own"; on June 5, "Negros All frolican"; and on June 6, "holiday all the time now with the Negros."[11]

A few blacks resorted to violence, or the threat of it, in pursuit of their own freedom or that of loved ones. In Prince William County, Virginia, a fugitive slave returned to the home of his former master, a man named Harrison, accompanied by a squad of Federal cavalrymen. The black man angrily demanded the release of his wife and child, who were still in bondage, and "flourished his sword over Harrison & told him he now had power & intended to use it." In January 1863, at a plantation in Jefferson Parish, Louisiana, a number of blacks armed themselves, refused to work, and demanded that their owner formally emancipate them. When he refused they shot at him and drove him into his house, where he remained for some time a virtual prisoner.[12]

The vast majority of blacks, however, chose nonviolent means to escape bondage and broaden their freedom. And in large numbers they were drawn to the garrisoned towns, which seemed to offer the best hope of real independence from white control. The disapproving editor of the *Alexandria Gazette* noted as early as September 1862 that the city was "filled with 'contrabands'" who were showing disturbing signs of insubordination: "They have not yet quite lost, in all cases, their habits of respect and obedience—but many of them are entirely different, and for the worse, from what they were before they became 'contrabands.'"[13]

Most who made the trek to town preferred, rather than going to the army's contraband camps and awaiting mandatory contract labor, to crowd into black shantytowns and hire themselves out around town. These shantytowns, despite their miserable living conditions, fostered a sense of liberation and community vividly manifested in the black demonstrations and parades that became common in the towns as the war went on. On January 1, 1863, for example, blacks in Norfolk staged a "Jubilee procession," as one observer described it, in which some five thousand people marched bearing banners and flags. On March 20, 1865, Nashville's black population celebrated in like fashion the formal abolition of slavery by state constitutional amendment. "The procession was composed of both sexes and all ages," wrote a Union officer who watched it, "on foot and riding in carriages, hacks and vehicles of all kinds[.] Two fine Brass Bands were with them[.] Business and labor generally was suspended among the colored people and the principle thorough-fares of the City were *black with Darkies* dressed in their best *go to meetin' clothes*. . . . The Darkies here seem to think 'De year ob Jubilee am cum' and I expect they are about right in regard to the matter."[14]

The "year of jubilee" did indeed come, but not everywhere at once. The progress of emancipation in the occupied South depended not only on how much the Union army was prepared to concede to the black quest for freedom, but also on how successfully whites were able to thwart it.

. . .

Southern whites contemplated the prospect of emancipation with horror. For many, all the other perils and tribulations of military occupation seemed trivial by comparison. A Union officer in Tennessee in 1862 described how the Rebel citizens chafed under his harsh treatment, which included arbitrary arrests and imprisonment, but he noted with interest that "their greatest trouble is their negroes. They seem to be more anxious about the safety of them, than anything els[e]." A Virginia woman reported that year that slaves in her neighborhood were "running away every night & when I go to bed, I expect to find some of ours gone. *Dreadful*, DREADFUL times."[15]

As the drift of Federal policy became clear, whites desperately rearticulated familiar arguments about the justness and necessity of the peculiar institution. Property rights were a crucial element of the proslavery apologia. "[N]egroes . . . are the private property of their masters & [runaways] ought to be returned," declared Tennessean John Waddel in November 1862; the Federal army, he insisted, was guilty of a "great crime in stealing these negroes." Another Tennessean, who had tried to reclaim a fugitive but was arrested by Federal troops "for dareing to take my own negroe home," indignantly reminded Governor Johnson that "[I am] as much entitled to the controll & injoyment of [my slaves] as you or I am to our Horses & Cattle & Houses."[16]

The most compelling arguments for slavery, however, took as their premise the supposed nature of blacks themselves. Two images of blacks coexisted in the white mind. One depicted them as bestial, naturally "idle and vicious," as a Virginia man put it. Slavery was imperative, in this view, for the well-being of the South. Without white control, blacks would be a burden and a threat to society, an unproductive and dangerous underclass.[17]

The other face of the black, as whites saw it, was the face of a child. Blacks were simple creatures incapable of caring for themselves, whites insisted; they needed maternal nurturance and paternal guidance from the master race. Thus, slavery was imperative for the well-being of the blacks themselves. A corollary to this belief affirmed that the slave system was benevolent in practice as well as theory and that, aside from a few malcontents, blacks were satisfied to live their lives in servitude to their kind masters. "[L]et the negroes be," a Louisiana woman advised the Yankees, "they are far happier in their present state, than they will be in *their so called free one.*"[18]

As proof of these assertions, slaveholders in the occupied South flaunted every evidence of their own paternalism and their slaves' loyalty. "Just come from a negro funeral," a Tennessean smugly recorded in her diary in April 1862, "—a [white] parson by the name of Willis preached & one by the name of Miles had service at the grave—O Yankee what would you say to that." On the first day of 1863 another Tennessee woman noted that "this is the day in which Abraham Lincolns emancipation proclamation . . . is to be carried out. . . . The day so long looked for by the North in which the 'poor oppressed race' would rush to their northern bretheren has dawned upon us, and yet we have witnessed no insurrections no massacres, but all moving quietly along." Her own slaves, she maintained, "seem perfectly contented."[19]

Whites nevertheless were confronted every day by seemingly contrary evidence: slaves were disappearing from home in considerable numbers. But most whites declined to interpret the black exodus as a refutation of their cherished beliefs; instead, they explained it away within the confines of their proslavery ideology. They claimed, first of all, that Union troops were forcibly dragging away unwilling blacks. (Although this was true in a number of instances, it was far less common than whites wanted to believe.) And when there was no denying that blacks were leaving of their own free will, whites ascribed it to their childishness. The blacks— ignorant, credulous, trusting—were simply "deluded" (a favorite expression of whites); they were "induced" to leave their masters by outside agitators who held out the promise of a life of abandon and played on the blacks' puerile "love of change." Sooner or later, whites insisted, the runaways would come to their senses and realize that true happiness was to be found back on the old plantation.[20]

When fugitives did in fact return home, as some did, masters trumpeted the reappearance of the prodigal children as a vindication of slavery and of their own faith. And they gloated over every report of black dissatisfaction with the occupiers. A Louisiana woman recounted stories of harsh conditions in the army labor battalions and remarked wryly: "That is *sweet* freedom. I'll tell you a yankee is a *hard master*, and the negroes are heartily tired of them. . . . Ours say they got *nuff* of the Yankees."[21]

As more slaves sought freedom and abandoned their customary deference, whites began to emphasize the counterimage of the black, the ugly and threatening countenance that had long haunted them. Now, unruly blacks were not wayward children, but "ingrates," traitors, or beasts. As the image of the black was transfigured, the confidence many masters retained in their own slaves gave way to suspicion. "I don't trust the negroes now," declared Kate Carney of Murfreesboro, Tennessee, after four months of occupation. "They have too much of the yankees about them, to suit me."[22]

Lurking in the shadows of every white Southerner's mind was the figure of a murderous black insurrectionist, a specter as old as the South but now grown more palpable and frightening than ever as white power withered and blacks grew obstreperous. "[T]he slaves seduced from their homes have flocked in[to] town," a Portsmouth citizen wrote near the end of 1862, "idle impudent and thievish dreaming of freedom by first of January, and liable to be led to acts of disorder and violence by rabid Abolitionists. Lord in mercy protect and deliver us." A Louisianan expressed fears of "A Servile outbreak" on Emancipation day: "My mind revolts at the idea of the bloodshed and incendiarism that would ensue." Women, especially, lived in dread of a black uprising, for the slave-rebel that whites envisaged was not only bloodthirsty and destructive but also brutishly lustful.[23]

Black soldiers—runaway slave men clothed in Yankee uniforms, armed with Yankee muskets, and sent forth to do battle against their former masters—were the white South's racial anxieties incarnate. "Heard of another army coming with a Regement of negroes," wrote Alabama diarist Sarah Espy in 1864. "May the Lord forbid for negroes have no mercy.

Passed a sleepless night." A Virginia man claimed that white Southerners were being "handed over to the tender mercies of brutal negroes, who under the cover of legitimate warfare are to murder the unarmed and defenceless, fire our dwellings, and ravish our women."[24]

Few whites actually suffered violence at the hands of blacks, but as slavery came apart many had to suffer what seemed even worse: assaults on their honor. Submitting to the "insolence" of an "inferior" race was humiliating to the proud people of the white South, even more so than bowing to Northern military rule. "[T]he country presents a horrible specticle," said Tennessean Robert Cartmell, "lazy negroes impudent and saucy struting about. . . . To one born and raised in the South & accustomed to keeping the Sons of Ham in their proper place, the impudence of these negroes is hard to endure." Virginian Colin Clarke spoke the sentiments of many a white in the occupied South: "I feel so degraded," he wrote, "whilst in the power of the Yankees violence & the negros insolence."[25]

Whites responded to the "degrading" assertiveness of the blacks in precisely the same way they responded to the degrading military rule of the enemy: by resisting it in every way they could. "[T]here is one thing that I never will submit to," a Savannah woman declared soon after the Union army entered the city and liberated all the slaves, "[the idea] that the negro is our equal. He belongs to an inferior race." A Federal officer in Louisiana in 1863 observed that "planters and overseers do not sufficiently appreciate or regard the change that has taken place" in race relations. The blacks' newfound sense of liberation, he said, "is, in many cases, either entirely ignored, or not sufficiently respected, by those who have charge of them on the plantations, and the consequence is trouble."[26]

Underlying white resistance was not only horror at the thought of black equality, but also hope—the hope that slavery itself could be preserved. Just as the dogged persistence of the Confederate armies sustained the faith that Northern military rule might some day be overthrown, so it preserved the belief that the peculiar institution might be resurrected. The Federal officer who declared in late 1863 that "Slavery is dead" in Tennessee added that "the bulk of the [white] people here are not yet exactly satisfied that the slaves are to be free. . . . [T]here is a lingering hope that by some hocus-pocus things will get back to the old state." A North Carolina overseer, whose slaves had been told by Federal troops in early 1863 that they were free, urged the blacks to stay on the plantation and made concessions to keep them there, secretly hoping that "if peace should come they might be saved."[27]

Many Northerners in the occupied South, seeing black men and women break their shackles and set forth to realize their freedom, were reminded of the children of Israel who fled servitude in Egypt. One of them, a Yankee schoolmarm in Tennessee, carried the metaphor further as she observed the determined efforts of whites to keep the blacks in bondage: "I think the I[s]raelites are about passing through the Red sea," she wrote in 1863, "& Pharaoh is still following on."[28]

Southern whites did not, of course, identify with the obstinate Pharaoh who led his legions to destruction; nor did they concede to the blacks' exodus the righteousness of the Israelites'. They saw themselves, rather, as embattled guardians of civilization, fighting to save the South from chaos and ruin at the hands of unleashed savages. The struggle would be arduous, they knew, but it must be won.

• • •

Whites faced their greatest challenge in the garrisoned towns, for there Yankee ascendancy was incontrovertible and blacks were at their most independent and assertive. But as long as the army acquiesced, which it did in the early part of the war, masters retained the power of compulsion over their slaves. In the big cities servitude had long been regulated formally by municipal government, and when government was revived under Federal authority, so too were the municipal slave codes. During the first months of occupation in Nashville, for instance, hardly a day passed that some slave was not hauled into the recorder's court and sentenced to one or two dozen lashes at the city whipping post for disobeying his or her master.[29]

The contrabands who flocked into the towns from the countryside posed a special problem, however. As slaves without masters, they were something of a legal anomaly and in certain respects were beyond the reach of municipal authority. Whites complained incessantly about the contraband problem. The Nashville board of aldermen declared in November 1862 that the city was "literally overrun with stragglers . . . [who have no] means of subsistence, and are strolling about over the city by day and night, while our citizens are clamoring loudly for protection from their depradations." The presence of these disorderly blacks would, whites feared, "demoralize" those still under white control. As the editor of the *Nashville Dispatch* reminded his readers, "It is a well known fact that one bad negro will corrupt many [good ones]."[30]

As whites watched and worried, they became convinced that the "bad apples" had indeed spread their insidious rot, for slaves as well as contrabands began defying white authority. With municipal government proving increasingly inadequate to the task, whites tried informal methods to bring the blacks to heel. Some thought that a determined display of white solidarity might work. In Fredericksburg, as Betty Maury related, an elderly doctor had given in to his slaves' demands and agreed to begin paying them wages, "but the gentlemen of the town held a meeting and wrote him a letter of remonstrance telling him that he was establishing a most dangerous precedent, that he was . . . a traitor to his state. So the old man refused to hire them." Other whites resorted to violence. A Portsmouth man assaulted a black girl in August 1862, cutting her head severely. When questioned by the provost marshal, he insisted that "he was simply asserting his rights, as a white man."[31]

In their desperation, whites also beseeched the occupiers for help. The army was generally willing to help control the contraband population, simply to preserve order in the towns, but as Federal policy turned toward emancipation military authorities were less willing to side with masters against their slaves. Early in 1863, for example, a Nashville slaveowner called on the army to retrieve a slave who had left her and taken up residence elsewhere in town, but an officer informed her that he would not "lend his services to fugitive-slave catchers." Moreover, the army began to protect blacks from physical abuse and other gross mistreatment. In Portsmouth a teenage boy who slapped his family's female servant for "impudence" in January 1863 was jailed by the provost marshal after the woman complained; when the boy's mother protested, she too was locked up.[32]

Day by day, white authority over blacks in the garrisoned towns slipped away. One slaveowner's depiction of the situation in Jackson, Tennessee, in August 1862, reflected the growing exasperation and sense of powerlessness that whites in the towns experienced: "Negroes have every thing in their own hands and they know it, surrounded and protected as they are by Federal soldiers. As many as see proper can walk off

& there is *no remedy*. We have to submit to any and every thing." White townspeople also suffered repeated affronts to their dignity. A citizen of New Bern, North Carolina, claimed: "It is nothing unusual for the negroes to curse their masters & mistresses in passing along the streets. They are allowed to do so [by the Yankees]."[33]

Whites ultimately failed to stifle black freedom in the garrisoned towns. Reduced to impotence by the continuous presence of Federal military power, they stood by helplessly while the army and the blacks decided the fate of slavery and the terms of emancipation. But outside the towns the balance of power among the three contestants was quite different, and the struggles that emerged had their own distinctive contours.

• • •

White rule on the Confederate frontier was threatened by the proximity of Union-held territory. Though the trek could be long and very risky, many slaves escaped to the Federal lines. Many others went off with, or were taken off by, the Union raiding parties that intermittently swept through the frontier districts; in the wake of the enemy's visitations, even those slaves who did not depart often grew unruly. These dangers prompted some masters to send their remaining slaves—or at least the young, able-bodied ones most likely to be lost or to cause trouble—to safe locations in the Confederate interior.[34]

On the other hand, white rule on the frontier was safeguarded by the persistence of Confederate authority, local government, and rural communalism. Because Rebel law and order prevailed during the long stretches between Federal raids, the white community continued to wield formidable power over blacks.[35]

Slaves trying to flee to Union lines from the frontier were frequently recaptured. Many frontier counties maintained slave patrols to police the black population and nab fugitives. In some counties home guard or militia companies picketed the roads and river crossings leading to the enemy lines, and many a black was caught in their net. Furthermore, Confederate troops on the frontier had standing orders to apprehend escapees and did so frequently. Often slaveowners themselves retrieved their runaways, after enlisting the help of neighbors and setting out with shotguns and bloodhounds.[36]

Every black fugitive dragged back in chains stood as a warning to those who still labored under their master's watchful eye. Whites noted with satisfaction the deterrent effect of a few recaptures. A North Carolinian reported in 1863 that the twenty men of the Duplin County patrol "have been of *great* service in preventing escapes of Slaves. . . . [T]hey have been 'the ounce of preventitive in place of the pound of Cure[.]' We are here not far distant from the Yankee lines. . . . [But] Since the organization of this Company, there has been *no* attempt of escapes by the Slaves *but one*, (save in the Raid in July)."[37]

Slaves who went off with Union troops were usually lost for good, but the disruption spawned by raids could be quickly suppressed. As soon as the troops moved on, whites cracked down on the fractious slaves who remained. John H. Ransdell of Rapides Parish, Louisiana, told what happened when a large Federal force swept through his community in the spring of 1863. While the Yankees were present the blacks "had a perfect jubilee," abandoning their work, visiting other slaves on neighboring farms, stealing livestock, and looting the home of one absent planter. Whites stayed fearfully indoors while the slaves ran riot, but when the Yankees left they reemerged, furious at the blacks. "Confound them," exclaimed Ransdell, "they deserve to be half starved and to be worked nearly to death for the way they have acted." Two days later he reported: "Things are just now beginning to work right—the negroes hated awfully to go to work again. . . . [M]ost of those left were whipped and matters are getting on better now." Whipping was the fate of the lucky ones: "Several have been shot," Ransdell noted, "and probably more will have to be."[38]

Lethal violence against blacks became common on the frontier, as whites grew nervous about the fate of slavery. In 1862 citizens on the Georgia coast pleaded with Confederate authorities to let them deal summarily with slaves caught fleeing to the enemy. Mere whippings "will not abate the evil," they insisted; what was needed to deter potential runaways were "a few executions . . . by hanging or shooting." As the war went on, more citizens on the frontier were ready to inflict the ultimate punishment, with or without legal authority. Four blacks were hanged in Florida in 1864 after whites discovered their plot to lead a mass escape to the Federal post at Fernandina. When a band of blacks was spotted the same year escaping by boat down a Virginia river, whites turned out with shotguns and rifles and ambushed the fugitives from the river bank, shooting down men and women alike. And, increasingly, the apprehensive white community was willing to tolerate brutal violence against blacks for even minor offenses. When a northern Mississippi master named J. F. Tankersley shot and mortally wounded his female slave for insolent behavior in 1864, his church took up the matter. In less troubled times Tankersley would certainly have been expelled for such an offense, but now the church elders excused him "in view of the peculiar state of things in the country, & the demoralized condition of the servants, requiring the most absolute & rigid discipline."[39]

In a few sections of the frontier—districts that lay close to the Federal lines and where Confederate authority was unusually weak—masters were forced to relax discipline rather than tighten it. Slaves there could readily go to the Yankees, and they did so whenever they calculated that their situation would thereby be improved. "[T]he facilities which are given to negroes to escape from their masters . . . makes the enslavement of the negro a voluntary matter altogether," declared the magistrates of Rockingham County, Virginia, in September 1863. "A negro can leave home at six o'clock in the evening, and before the same time the next morning he can be with the enemy." In such communities white authority over blacks was tenuous. The impressment of slave laborers by the Confederate government, for example, was virtually impossible, for every requisition triggered a black stampede to freedom. Slaveowners in those districts begged the Rebel authorities to forgo impressment attempts, and they compromised with their own slaves. "You have no idea of the condition of things within hearing of the Cannon," a Mississippi planter wrote to a kinsman in the interior. "I do not more than heretofore tolerate insolence in any shape, but idleness, half work . . . has to be winked at."[40]

In most of the frontier areas, however, masters made no such concessions to their bondsmen and bondswomen. Their hand remained firm and their word remained law; the institution of slavery persisted despite the heavy blows struck against it by black fugitives and Federal raiders.

The experience of Cushing B. Hassell of Martin County, North Carolina—a farmer, merchant, Primitive Baptist preacher, and owner of fourteen slaves—is illustrative. Hassell's community, which was a good distance inland from the Federal garrisons on the coast, was raided ten times between 1862 and 1865. Many local slaves, including one of his own, went off with the Union troops; others, two of his men among them, escaped to the Federal lines between raids; and a number of others were moved or sold into the interior by worried masters. But the rest stayed on, toiling away under the peculiar amalgam of cruelty and paternalism that was slavery.

As Hassell rode his preaching circuit through the county, he ministered to the black faithful as well as the white. In August 1863, during the "lay-by" season when rural folk traditionally relaxed, he and his slaves went to a friend's plantation where the overseer was giving a dinner for all the blacks. "[T]he affair passed off quietly," Hassell reported, "& apparently very satisfactory to the negroes." Early in 1865 Hassell was forced to sell his woman Harriet, who had grown unmanageable. "She was a great strumpet," he explained, "lazy & impudent & whipping did not reform her in the least." But he insisted that selling her into the interior was in her best interest, "better for her than to send her to the Yankees." Hassell's ten remaining slaves did not follow the example of Harriet or the runaways. As late as May 1865, they were still working dutifully in the fields alongside their master and his sons.[41]

Until the Confederacy breathed its last, slavery survived in the frontier districts. Cushing Hassell and his brethren of the master class lost many of their bondsmen and bondswomen, it is true, but they were able for the most part to impose their will on those who remained. The occasional Yankee raid might knock the whip from their hand, but they quickly retrieved it when the enemy marched on. As long as they wielded it, they could postpone the year of jubilee.

• • •

In the matter of race relations, as in other respects, no-man's-land was bitterly contested terrain. White control there was weakened, and black autonomy strengthened, by the proximity of Federal posts and by the absence of Confederate authority and local political and communal institutions—entities that undergirded white control on the Confederate frontier. On the other hand, the Union army could not exercise in no-man's-land the unremitting and invincible power in behalf of black emancipation that it exercised in the garrisoned towns, though it was certainly a more potent force in no-man's-land than on the Confederate frontier. With none of the three contenders able to attain clear supremacy, no-man's-land became a theater of fluid conflict where each side saw advances and retreats, victories and defeats.

In many sections of no-man's-land, especially those nearest to garrisoned towns, slaves could leave virtually at will and masters were powerless to recapture them. Many whites therefore resorted to strategies or compromises to keep their black laborers at home. Some spread horror stories about the treatment blacks could expect at the hands of the enemy. Masters in western Florida warned their slaves that "the Yankees would work [them] in yokes" if they ran off to the Federal post at Pensacola. Others coaxed their blacks to stay by easing up on discipline or appealing to their good sense. "I would advise you to look closely after those [slaves] who are still at home," Tennessee planter William Lewis advised his son-in-law in March 1863, "and direct your overseers to abstain, as far as possible, from giving them any excuse for leaving you." He had managed to persuade his own slaves, he said, "that the very best thing they can do for themselves is to remain quietly at home and attend to their work, and wait until it is known what disposition is to be made of the negroes generally." Two months later Lewis sent a trusted slave man to his son-in-law's plantation so "that he might see and talk with your negroes. I think his advice to them may have a good effect upon them."[42]

Where they thought they could get away with it, masters did not hesitate to use force. One Tennessee slaveowner lured back a runaway slave in 1863 by kidnapping her child and holding it hostage in his home; when she returned to reclaim the child, the master locked her up and cruelly beat her. The overseer of a North Carolina plantation reported in September 1862 that "I had a dificulty withe old Pompey . . . heay broke and run [so] I shot him withe my pistol." Some masters even dared to spirit their slaves away to the Confederate interior, chaining them up, loading them in wagons, and slipping them past Federal patrols like so much smuggled contraband.[43]

Whites battling to preserve slavery in no-man's-land found an ally in the guerrilla bands. As they waged their clandestine war against Yankees and Unionists, guerrillas also struck at blacks who sought freedom. One band lurked in the Virginia countryside near the Dismal Swamp canal and tried to nab fugitives headed for the Federal post at Portsmouth. Guerrillas in Montgomery County, Tennessee, acted as a virtual slave patrol, according to one black resident; because of their activity, he said, "the colored people were afraid to pass around much at night." In Maury County, Tennessee, Nimrod Porter noted that guerrillas had recaptured a number of runaway slaves, and thus "some of the rest have taken a scare."[44]

No amount of assistance from the guerrillas, however, could keep slavery intact in no-man's-land. The visitations of the Federal troops were too frequent, their posts too accessible, for masters to retain absolute power over their slaves for long. Compromise and cajolery were signs that slavery was in extremis: every concession granted to keep blacks at home, every appeal to argument instead of the whip, marked the further ebbing of the life force of the peculiar institution. As power slipped from the hands of the slaveowners, blacks renounced their habitual servility. Though most stayed on with their masters, with increasing boldness they let it be known that doing so was the volitional act of a free man or woman. "[T]heir voluntary presence on the plantations excites in them a feeling of independance," grumbled a Louisiana planter, "which they are ready to exhibit on all occasions, either by neglecting their duties, or treating [their owners] with insolence."[45]

Whites bewailed their loss of mastery. "[N]egro property is worse than useless," a Tennessee woman wrote in 1863, "for they do no work unless they choose & the owners dare not correct them else off they go and report [it to the Yankees]." John H. Bills, of Tennessee, who up to early 1863 had had little trouble on his plantation, noted later that year that "many of my servants have run away & most of them left had as well be gone—they being totally demoralized & ungovernable." By October things were "in a wretched condition. Negroes not in mutiny but in a wretched state of idleness & we have not the power to control them."[46]

Sooner or later, most masters in no-man's-land who retained any hope of making a crop had to capitulate to the demands of the blacks and the occupiers and begin paying wages or shares. The transition from master to employer was a bitter pill for whites habituated to command. "I have at last paid off all the Negroes," wrote a planter in the Natchez area early in 1864, "& a more unpleasant, disgusting business I never have attended to. . . . They tried very hard to make their own terms & wished to exact a great many things." An indignant Louisiana planter characterized negotiations with his laborers as a "tug of war." Eventually he settled on terms "very distasteful to me, but I could do no better. Every body else in the neighborhood has agreed to pay the same and mine would listen to nothing else."[47]

Whites learned, however, that as long as they acceded to basic demands regarding the treatment of blacks, they could often count on the Union army to help control those who grew unruly or assertive. "I send you under guard seven negroes from Madame Brand's plantation," a Union infantry officer told the provost marshal of Ascension Parish, Louisiana, in 1864. "They have been quarrelling with the old lady and she wants them to leave the plantation. They refused to leave and I have thought best to take them off from the place." Later that year the provost marshal asked another officer in the parish, "in case of any disturbance with the negroes," to send troops "to quell it & force obedience from the negroes."[48]

On the other hand, the army was often willing to intervene in behalf of the blacks when whites went too far. Provost marshals would step in when whites tried to defraud their black laborers, or hold them against their will, or inflict corporal punishment. On more than one occasion in Nimrod Porter's community, for example, white men were arrested and jailed for whipping their black workers. In Lafourche Parish, Louisiana, a provost marshal justified the action he took after a black complained about a local overseer: "If my course resulted in the removal of Mr Fielder from the plantation it was truly a God send to the Free Labor System. He was a man actuated to[o] much by passion and with to[o] little respect or sympathy for the colored men. He may have been a good overseer under the old system but under the new to[o] passionate and unconsiderate."[49]

The army's ability to enforce a free labor system and to prevent abuse of blacks was less than absolute. No-man's-land was vast, and the army could not be omnipresent. Though most whites there were constrained by fear of Northern retaliation, they did not feel as powerless as those in the garrisoned towns. There was, moreover, one class of whites in no-man's-land who regarded themselves as altogether beyond the reach of Federal authority.

Guerrillas could not halt the dissolution of slavery, but they could, and did, curb black liberty. In many sections of no-man's-land they launched a campaign of terror against the newly freed blacks. They targeted, in particular, those employed by the army, those living in contraband camps, and those working on government-licensed plantations. Nimrod Porter noted in May 1864 that guerrillas had ambushed an army labor gang in his neighborhood, shooting two blacks and creating "great excitement & running amongst the [others]"; for days thereafter the blacks dared not return to work. A plantation lessee in Ascension Parish, Louisiana, reported that guerrillas had attacked his place, "stealing everything they could lay hands on and frightening the negroes so that they will not go to their work." A band of guerrillas raided another leased plantation in Mississippi in June 1864, taking horses and mules and forcing off at gunpoint six blacks employed there. Witnesses testified that the six were never seen again.[50]

Guerrilla terror reached a horrifying climax in March 1865 on the South Carolina coast near the post of Beaufort. The planters there had all fled to the interior, and many of their former slaves were operating abandoned plantations on their own. According to a Northerner who interviewed some of the blacks later that year, a band of guerrillas attacked Lucknone plantation on March 15 and "shot the colered men of the Plantation as they came out of their doors," killing several and sending the rest fleeing into the nearby swamps. "The Dead Boddies Laid in the Negro Houses Street untill the Beasts and Birds Mutilated them and were afterward Buried at Night Just where they Lay in the Street, By those who concealed themselves in the Swamps for several Days Fearing to come Out." The guerrillas then proceeded to hit other plantations, seizing one black man whose body was eventually found "Laying beside the Road badly Mutilated." On the seventeenth they struck again at another place, burning all the buildings and vowing that "they would yet catch the Men [who had escaped] and kill them[,] using the most Brutal expressions to the Women [who remained]." Moving on to yet another plantation, the guerrillas "Shot and Killed Nearly all the Men they found . . . these Boddies Lay unburied up to the Month of July . . . [when] Some of the Neiboring Plantations Men Went out and Buried the Bones and Skulls of These Men About Ten or Twelve in Number."[51]

What had taken shape in no-man's-land by the latter part of the war was something that hovered between the black freedom prevailing in the garrisoned towns and the black bondage that endured on the Confederate frontier. To whites throughout the occupied South, the lesson was plain: the more violence they were able to inflict on blacks, the more thorough was their racial mastery. It was a lesson they had seen confirmed countless times in the past and would see confirmed again and again in the years to come.

[6]

························

The Other Jubilee

*Plain Folk, Aristocrats,
and the Challenge to the
Old Order*

························

In September 1862 planter John Pool and a number of
other prominent citizens of Bertie County, North Carolina, met in Wind-
sor, the county seat, to discuss matters of common concern. Bertie
County was on the Confederate frontier, within reach of the Federal forces
at Plymouth. There were no Confederate troops in the area, the Yankees
had raided the county several times, Union gunboats had been seen on
the nearby Roanoke and Chowan Rivers, and some slaves had escaped to
the Federal lines. Pool and the others mulled over these troubling facts
and came to some conclusions. Three days later Pool sent a report of the
meeting to Governor Zebulon Vance.

"Several months spent in this state of constant danger and anxiety has
enabled the thinking men of this county to see what [is] necessary to be
done more clearly, perhaps, than can be seen by those at a distance," Pool
told the governor. The proximity of the Federal post and the county's
vulnerability to raids, he said, posed great dangers. The threat of further

slave losses would inevitably force masters to remove themselves and their remaining slaves to the interior. "If the slave-holders, being men of means, flee upon the approach of danger and leave the poorer classes . . . exposed not only to the enemy but to the gangs of runaway slaves, it will produce a state of things and of feeling much to be dreaded. Is it not the duty of the influential slave-holder to remain and to exert himself to preserve social order and to prevent an entire disruption of society?" The only solution, Pool insisted, was to station a military force in the county strong enough to deter slave desertions and fend off Federal raids.[1]

There was still another danger, however. Slaves were not the only ones running off to the Union army. "[T]he attempted execution of [the military conscription] law has driven many [men] of not very reliable character to the enemy at Plymouth," Pool pointed out, "and many more of little better character are in readiness to repair to Plymouth or to the gunboats if its further execution is attempted." There were not enough dependable men left in the community "for efficient police duty." Unless the county was exempted from conscription, the disaffected poor whites, taking advantage of the proximity of the enemy, would become wholly ungovernable. "The substantial men of the county," Pool concluded, "dread to see the others made their enemy."

Such fears plagued people of substance throughout the occupied South, for the coming of the Yankees generated shock waves that threatened to unsettle class relations as thoroughly as they unsettled political and racial relations. Aristocrats and plain folk—like secessionists and Unionists, masters and slaves—found themselves in a radically altered environment with new relations of power, new perils, and new possibilities.

. . .

The Northern occupiers did not remain aloof from the evolving class struggle any more than they did the political and racial struggles. Having found in the South the backward, undemocratic society that their preconceptions had prepared them to find, and having concluded that the continued existence of such a society on American soil would perpetually threaten the Union, the invaders were determined to transform the South, to remake it in the North's image. "The more we learn of the despicable social condition of the South," wrote a Union soldier in North Carolina in

1863, "the stronger appears the need of the purification which, in the Providence of God, comes of the fire and the sword."[2]

Ridding the South of the blight of slavery was the first step toward purification, but several other tasks remained. One was to suffuse the South with Northern ideals and practices. "We have not only to conquer the South," declared the Indiana reformer Lyman Abbott in 1864, "—we have also to convert it. We have not only to occupy it by bayonets and bullets,—but also by ideas and institutions." Foremost among the rejuvenating elixirs prescribed by Northerners was Yankee enterprise, a stiff dose of which was needed in the "lazy" South. "I couldn't help thinking of Mrs. Stowe's epithet," wrote a Union army surgeon after getting his first good look at the Southern people, "—*shiftless*. That is just the word. They are the most *shiftless* set that I ever saw." But Northerners acknowledged that the task would be formidable. "It will be no easy matter to awaken aspirations in the minds of [the Southern masses]," wrote a Boston newspaper correspondent in Tennessee in 1862. "They have been so long inert, so long taught to believe that labor is degrading, that rapid progress of Southern society cannot be expected immediately, unless emigration infuses a new vitality into the community."[3]

Indeed, the idea of colonizing the South with industrious Yankees appealed to many Northerners. "The very soil," one soldier remarked, "seems to pray for an infusion of Northern blood and Yankee ingenuity." Immigrants from north of the Mason-Dixon line would spread the gospel of hard work and free labor that had made their country great. New England abolitionist Eli Thayer, who had joined a similar crusade in Kansas in the 1850s, proposed in 1862 to lead a force of several thousand armed Northern settlers into Florida, where they would establish free labor farms, "crowd out slavery," and begin the "economic reconstruction" of the South. Thayer's plan came to naught, but many of the men who traveled south individually to lease abandoned plantations had more in mind than just a fast dollar: they saw themselves as pioneers bringing civilization—in the form of free labor and up-to-date methods of husbandry—to the wilderness. Other Northerners called for similar efforts to invigorate Southern commerce and industry.[4]

The South needed more than just free labor and Yankee enterprise, however. It also needed what one Northerner termed "*moral reconstruction . . .* some radical change in the thoughts, convictions, sentiments and characteristics of the people . . . a change which shall make them, at heart, a better race, and thus fit them to appreciate free institutions and a higher civilization." But the work of moral reconstruction could not proceed until the hermetic, reactionary South was opened up, exposed to new ideas. Northern books must be placed in the hands of the Southern people, Northern-born editors must set the South's newspaper presses humming and proclaim the good news of progress, Northern men of God must carry the true gospel of Christ throughout Dixie.[5]

Northerners heeded these calls. In New Orleans, Memphis, New Bern, and many other places, Northern editors (some of them army officers) established newspapers or, with the cooperation of military authorities, took control of existing secessionist papers. Yankee ministers, missionaries, and colporteurs also flocked to the garrisoned towns. In a number of cases obliging commandants deposed Rebel preachers and turned their church buildings over to the newcomers. In New Orleans a group of army chaplains formed the Union Ministerial Association, dedicated to the moral cleansing of that sin-ridden city, and persuaded the military commander to close the saloons, billiard parlors, theaters, and racetracks on Sundays.[6]

Whereas some Northerners were content to let moral suasion by itself transform the heathen South, others argued for a direct assault on the structure of Southern society. The campaign against slavery was one part of that assault, but only one. The North must also march against the Southern aristocracy, that relic of the feudal past, a class that supposedly monopolized wealth and power, tyrannized slaves and poor whites alike, and had broken up the Union for its own nefarious purposes.

Nothing that Northerners saw in the occupied South caused them to modify their long-standing beliefs about the aristocracy. One Northerner in Nashville observed that until the Union army arrived, "the leading families had had things all their own way." Northerners also noted the fervent secessionism and bitter hostility of nearly every aristocrat they met. A soldier in Virginia offered this maxim: "Find a well-dressed lady, and you find one whose hatred [of Yankees] will end only with death."[7]

Aristocratic hegemony must be destroyed, many Northerners agreed. One of Sherman's officers denounced the "selfishness of the so-called 'chivalry,' whose energy and audacity have been [the rebellion's] motive power. . . . [N]othing can secure the safety of the nation short of blotting out their influence, and if necessary their existence, as a class. . . . [They have] from the first lorded it over the South, and would put their foot upon all our necks if they could." An officer in Tennessee put it more succinctly: "the bad rich men," he said, "must feel our power."[8]

While Congress debated the propriety of a systematic program to depose the Southern aristocracy, occupation officials and commanders in the field took matters into their own hands. Many singled out aristocrats for punishment or coercion. In Tennessee, military governor Johnson (who, though a Southerner himself, shared the Northerners' desire to humble the South's elites) arrested a number of the state's most prominent planters, jurists, and politicians and jailed them, in some cases for months, until they took the oath. In Louisiana, General Nathaniel P. Banks ordered "that the leading families who have been strongly identified with secession" must take the oath or go to Rebel territory. A Union general in Tennessee urged that all aristocrats be expelled from the occupied regions, even those who took the oath and posted bond for good behavior: "If they are sent away," he reasoned, "their presence and their influence are gone." Many commanders also targeted the property of aristocrats for seizure or destruction. One who favored that policy was a Union cavalry officer in northern Virginia, who remarked that "the planters . . . are nearly all secesh, and a little bleeding would reduce their fever a little and do them good."[9]

With the closed South opened up, slavery eradicated, and the aristocracy brought low, one mission remained: to elevate the degraded white masses. Faced with overwhelming evidence that secessionism and resistance cut across class lines, Northerners had abandoned their original assumption that the Southern plain folk had been tricked or bullied into supporting the rebellion, and they no longer expected the plain folk as a whole to rally spontaneously around the Stars and Stripes as the Unionists and blacks did. But they continued to believe that the mass of Southern whites was a benighted, destitute class ground under the heel of the aristocracy.

Rare was the Yankee who recorded his observations of Southern society during the war without mentioning the degradation of the poor whites. (Most Northerners continued to lump all nonelite Southerners into an undifferentiated mass, which they labeled poor whites.) A Union officer in Falmouth, Virginia, wrote that there were only two families of quality in the town: "As for the rest of the inhabitants, they are what is called poor whites, and are very poor indeed, both mentally and physically." A soldier in northern Georgia noted the crude log homes of the common folk and their "primitive style" of life: "The people as a general thing avoid neatness, are ignorant and shabbily clad." Having spent some time among the people of southeastern Virginia, Lieutenant Colonel Alvin Voris concluded: "Poor white folks, mules, niggers, horned cattle and worn out horses occupy the same glorious level. . . . Southern Society does very well for the aristocracy but for nobody else."[10]

The plight of the poor whites touched the hearts of many Northerners. "We have had considerable opportunity to see this class of people," wrote one Yankee in St. Augustine, ". . . and to hear the sad stories of their wrongs. They are miserably poor and ignorant and dirty. In many instances needing as much sympathy and help as the fugitive negro." Other Northerners, too, were struck by the similarities between the poor whites and the freed slaves and decided that the whites were as worthy of benevolence as the blacks. "Shall we not succor them," asked the Reverend Joseph P. Thompson, of New York, who addressed a meeting of philanthropists in Washington early in 1865. "Shall we not relieve their miseries, and trust that God will soften their hearts . . . ?"[11]

Education was the key, many Northerners believed. Teaching the poor whites to read and write and think would not only elevate them morally and socially, it would also free their minds from the baneful influence of the aristocracy and thus help ensure the future safety of the Union. "[I]f the masses of the people in the south had been properly educated," wrote a Union soldier in Arkansas, "this rebellion would never have arisen[.] [I]t is on account of the ignorance of the people that ambitious demagogues have been able to work on the superstitious credulity of the masses for the advancement of their own ambitious schemes." Idealistic Northerners, many of them women, packed their bags and headed south to uplift the poor whites with the aid of the three Rs. "The whole North must become one mighty nation of teachers," a New Hampshire woman declared, "*then—DisUnion*—can never exist." If the older generation of poor whites was corrupted beyond redemption, the younger generation might still be reached. "Yes," announced the Reverend Mr. Thompson, "I will take this poor, naked, starving boy, no matter who his father was or where he is, I will take him by the hand; . . . I will teach him to read; . . . I will teach him that he has a country. . . . And I will sow that land of rebellion thick with these regenerated children."[12]

Some Northerners eventually did conclude that, except for the younger generation, the South's poor whites were beyond help and beyond hope. "They are lower than the negro in every respect," one Union officer sneered, "not excepting general intelligence, culture and morality. . . . They are not fit to be kept in the same sty with a well to do farmer's hogs in New England." Even some of the ardent civilians who went south with McGuffey's *Reader* in hand grew disillusioned. "It is impossible to describe the squalor and filth and indolence in which we found most of these 'low down' crackers!," exclaimed a Northern woman after she arrived in Jacksonville. "It is a great shame that our government should be hampered with the support of such a miserable set of vagabonds!" Moreover, some Northerners, particularly occupation authorities concerned with preserving order, viewed poor whites as troublesome and potentially dangerous; they prescribed not enlightenment and uplift but strict control. The security of New Orleans, said General Butler, was threatened by "a violent, strong, and unruly mob, that can only be kept under by fear."[13]

If there was a strain of elitist contempt among Northerners in the occupied South, there was also a strain of real radicalism. Some Yankees were determined to incite the poor whites against the aristocracy. Although for some this was simply a social means to a political end—an attempt to win the poor whites to the Union cause by convincing them that the Confederacy was ruled by a despotic planter oligarchy—for others the ultimate goal was nothing less than social revolution. The first issue of the *New Era*, a newspaper published under Federal aegis in Fort Smith, Arkansas, denounced the Southern aristocracy as "that abominable set of men who . . . [have sought] the total enslavement and the subversion of the rights of the great mass of the laboring white population" and looked forward to the day of deliverance: "[T]he tables are turned now. . . . Emancipation from the thralldom of the selfish, overbearing Aristocracy, so gloriously begun since the re-establishment of the authority of the United States Government, will be carried forward successfully."[14]

And so the Yankees embarked on their righteous social crusade in the South. It remained to be seen how Southerners themselves would respond to the Northern agenda, and to the other dangers and opportunities that surfaced in the roiling wake of the Union army.

. . .

It was not Yankee manifestos, but hunger and hardship, that first tested the commitment of the plain folk to the old order in the occupied South. Before the war, Southern yeomen as a class had rarely known want. Their economic independence and comfortable, if not luxurious, existence were in fact key props of class unity and social order in the antebellum South. Poor whites, propertyless and unskilled, had enjoyed far less comfort and no independence, but they could always rely on paternalistic aristocrats, generous neighbors, or local government to relieve their suffering, as could any yeoman family that happened to fall on hard times.

All this began to change with the coming of the Northern invaders. Yeomen saw their crops seized, their herds decimated, their shops ransacked, their boats burned. Poor whites were thrown out of work as agriculture, industry, and trade declined. (Aristocrats suffered too, of course, but they generally had greater reserves of provisions or valuables to fall back on than the plain folk had.) The poor, in particular, were often left wholly destitute. In June 1863 a Pennsylvania soldier in northern Virginia spoke with a young woman, an overseer's wife, who "gave me such a story of struggles to keep alive, to get enough to keep from starving, as made all the hard times I have ever seen seem like a life of luxury. I did pity her. On such as she, the poor whites of the South, the burden of this war is heaviest."[15]

In no-man's-land at least, the traditional sources of relief dried up. Aristocrats and other neighbors, hard pressed themselves, could offer little to the sufferers, and the country churches were disrupted and county governments defunct. In the garrisoned towns, municipal governments were in many cases revived, but they were generally in no financial condition to offer relief. In both no-man's-land and the garrisoned towns, therefore, the needy did what they had to do: they appealed to the occupiers for help and thereby, tacitly at least, acknowledged the bankruptcy of the old order.[16]

On the Confederate frontier economic disruption was less severe, local government and communal institutions survived, and formal and informal measures of relief generally continued. But there was still enormous privation, and the plain folk endured more than their share. Another challenge to class unity arose on the frontier in the form of discriminatory Confederate and state legislation, particularly laws exempting large slaveholders from the draft or militia duty. "[T]he Law now makes the rich man superiour to the poor," a northern Mississippian complained in 1862, "forcing the poor [to] the [battle]fields, . . . showing to the world that the rich is to[o] good to become food for bullets." Even after such laws were repealed, the fact remained that yeoman and poor white families suffered economically from the conscription or enlistment of husbands and sons far more than did aristocratic families, whose resources of wealth and black labor sustained them.[17]

Everywhere in the occupied South, hardship and want uprooted many of the plain folk. Thousands of men and women—most of them poor whites but some of them yeomen stripped of their livelihood—restlessly roamed the countryside. "Yesterday a man & his wife stopped here & asked for something to eat," wrote Mary Fielding of northern Alabama in the summer of 1862. "They complained bitterly of the hard times; said they were from Giles County [Tennessee] & had *tramped* over three or four counties in search of work but could find none." William King came across a poor white family in his northern Georgia neighborhood in the summer of 1864, a woman with eight children and a husband too sick to work, all so destitute and miserable that King's heart went out to them. They had drifted in from another county and moved into a vacant house, the woman hoping she might find some work washing or sewing to support her family. Other transients followed the Union armies, scavenging in abandoned campsites for scraps of food and clothing.[18]

Increasingly, the displaced plain folk migrated (like the freed blacks) to the garrisoned towns. As the war went on the towns filled with these people, who were, in a sense, refugees-in-reverse, having taken the opposite path from those Southerners who fled to Rebel territory when the Yankees came. By early 1865 an estimated eighty thousand white refugees had come into the Federal lines. Some were Unionists escaping Rebel persecution, others were deserters from the Confederate army; but mostly they were indigent poor whites, dispossessed yeomen, or people of either class who were fed up with the onerous and inequitable demands of the Confederate government. By going to the army posts, these men and women were not proclaiming their conversion to the cause of the Union; they were simply seeking a haven from affliction. William King met one such refugee in Marietta, a man who had been living comfortably on his small farm thirteen miles from town until a gang of Yankee stragglers cleaned him out, forcing him to look for work in the town. A Florida refugee arrived at the Federal post at Pensacola in a small boat in 1862, identifying himself as a day laborer: "I came to Pensacola to find work," he told the provost marshal, "and something to eat." The same year another man traveled to Pensacola from the countryside "for protection"; the Rebel authorities, he said, had "threatened me for keeping my boys from the war." In late 1864, at another post, a Georgia man sought refuge: he had been a railroad engineer, "but since Sherman has destroyed nearly all the railroads in the interior, I thought they might want me to take a musket, so I concluded to leave them."[19]

The Federal policy was generally to accept all such refugees, especially those fleeing Rebel conscription, as long as they were willing to take the oath. At many posts they were housed in special camps or shelters, often at the expense of rich secessionists levied on by the occupation authorities. Even with government support, many refugee camps became scenes of squalid misery, and so Northern humanitarian agencies stepped in to help—notably the American Union Commission, headed by the Reverend Joseph P. Thompson, which provided food, clothing, blankets, and medicine. The refugees were also objects of earnest attention from the Northern teachers and missionaries who came south to uplift the masses. Many of the refugees went to work for the army, but there were never enough jobs for all. When the burden of supporting them became too great, the government sent them to Northern cities where they could find employment.[20]

Some of the refugees were not so much driven to the Federal lines by hunger or political oppression as they were drawn by the prospect of a better life. Among these opportunity seekers were two bound apprentices who turned up at Hatteras Inlet, North Carolina, just three weeks after Union forces landed there in 1861; the young runaways had sailed or rowed over forty miles from Roanoke Island to escape their master, for whom they had labored eight years. The promise of a new dispensation likewise drew North Carolinian William Eddins—a schoolmaster, exempt from conscription—who arrived at the post of Newport late in

1863: "I came in these lines because I became tired of being hemmed in so narrowly in rebeldom," he told the provost marshal. "If I cannot do such here, I wish to go North, to go into business."[21]

Indeed, a good many of the plain folk—especially poor whites—both inside and outside the garrisoned towns began seizing opportunities denied them under the old regime. From their perspective, military occupation was in some ways a liberating experience, for it undermined traditional forms of authority and control and knocked aside many of the formal and informal barriers that the South's stratified society put in the way of ambitious plebeians. For these men and women, as for the slaves, Union invasion heralded the "year of jubilee." In Louisiana, poor whites took advantage of the waning power of the planters by trading with blacks on the plantations, a practice strictly prohibited in the old days. An Alabama man living at the post of Huntsville developed a lucrative trade in army horses—most of them stolen or purchased illegally from Union soldiers—and was heard to remark that "now was the time to make a fortune, if he did not do it now before the war was over he never could."[22]

Above all, many of the poor sought to stake a claim to land. So many homesteads had been abandoned in the occupied South that it seemed almost a new frontier, with good land for the taking. In Pointe Coupee Parish, Louisiana, landless whites settled on rich, parish-owned land along the levee that formerly had been leased to planters. On Amelia Island, Florida, the provost marshal noted that a number of farms belonging to men in the Confederate army "have been farmed by white persons who have taken possession of the place." From Bolivar County, Mississippi, came a report that "refugees from the hills are flocking in & settling all the vacant places." A lucky few of the landless were able to acquire legal title. In Fernandina, Florida, abandoned secessionist property was condemned and auctioned off by Federal tax commissioners, with town lots going for as little as five dollars. A Northern journalist there wrote that "some 'splendid bargains' are [being] made by the white refugees who are on hand."[23]

Opportunism unleashed by the breakdown of traditional authority, restlessness provoked by hunger and resentment, radicalism propounded by the Yankees—these ingredients made up a volatile brew. But if it seemed that the occupied South might be primed for an explosion of popular insurgency, there were at the same time factors at work that continued to bind the plain folk to the old elite.

For one thing, the great majority of poor whites and yeomen in the occupied South—even those who accepted food and shelter from the occupiers—continued to view the Yankees as invaders and to join with the aristocracy in opposing the Northern "violation" and "pollution" of their land. Many of them rode side by side with aristocrats in the guerrilla gangs (which carried out attacks not only against Union soldiers but also against the Northern plantation lessees who colonized the South). They proved utterly impervious to Northern attempts to "regenerate" them and turn them into "proper" middle-class citizens on the Yankee model.[24]

Race, too, remained a powerful cohesive force. Whites of all classes stood shoulder to shoulder against the attempts of blacks to gain liberty. In Isle of Wight County, Virginia, several poor whites, acting on their own initiative, ambushed a party of runaway blacks in 1862, killing one and returning the others to captivity—a deed that one local aristocrat pronounced "commendable." Northerners were frequently amazed at the extent to which racism encouraged the Southern plain folk to identify with the slaveowning elite. One recorded a conversation he had in Mississippi with a woman who had never owned a slave "or ever expected to do so": "We-uns didn't want to fight, no-how," she told him when he broached the subject of secession. "You-uns went and made the war so as to steal our niggers."[25]

If race and culture continued to unite plain folk and aristocrats in the occupied South, there were signs that politics and property might yet drive them apart. As the occupation continued, a small but vocal number of citizens began to echo the Northerners' call for social revolution. Almost to a man, they were Unionists—some of them no doubt being among the minority of plain folk who had always resented aristocratic domination, others perhaps converted to radicalism by their brutal treatment at the hands of the Rebels.

Whatever the source of their discontent, those who could do so in safety began to speak out publicly for the overthrow of the old order. On Virginia's eastern shore, citizen J. G. Potts published an appeal to "Mechanics, Tenants, and Laborers," denouncing the "overbearing small-potatoe aristocracy who have governed you most despotically" and urging his readers "to commence with the fifth task of Hercules, and sweep the Augean stables—sweep [the aristocracy] out root, stump and branch. Now is the time to trample under foot this petty despotism." An editorial in the *Nashville Daily Times and True Union*, a Unionist newspaper, asserted: "The rapacious slaveocracy have seized all the valuable lands and driven the non-slaveholders from nearly all the soil which is worth possessing. . . . Slavery must be destroyed immediately, . . . in order to produce a division of overgrown farms among the farmers of small means." A letter to the editor in the same newspaper reminded readers of how things were before the Yankees came, when "slaveholders possessed and exercised all social powers. A non-slaveholder was nothing but a poor white man, and his wife and daughters were nothing but poor white trash. . . . Oppressed and cruelly wronged fellow-sufferers, shall we longer remain the base slaves of these cold-hearted aristocratic few?"[26]

Where it was dangerous to openly declare such sentiments, the native radicals acted cautiously but nonetheless seditiously. Michael Graham, a secret Unionist who lived on the Confederate frontier in Virginia and spied for the Union army, worked in subtle ways "to increase the dissatisfaction between the rich and poor" in his community; he urged the occupiers to "impress the poor with the idea that the rich are the cause of all their miseries, and divide the wealth of the rich with the poor." It was, he said, "the wealthy aristocrats of the South who caused the war, and they alone ought to suffer."[27]

In some of the garrisoned towns native and Northern radicals joined hands and tried to create a class-based political movement. In Memphis, the *Union Appeal* published a notice of a political rally intended as a protest not only against the secessionists' "unholy rebellion" but also against Southern aristocrats, who "looked upon all labor as disgraceful, and the white laborer as *less* than a negro. . . . Come out, working men, mechanic and laborer; enter your protest against tyranny." In the garrisoned towns of eastern North Carolina, radicals founded Free Labor Associations and enrolled Unionist poor whites and yeomen. At the associations' meetings, according to one witness, the members heard "Free Labor harangue[s], . . . denunciatory of the Slave oligarchy, and exhibiting the benefits which would result to the masses from its overthrow." The leader of the associations, Charles Henry Foster, a New England native who had moved to North Carolina before the war, announced that he "was pledged, and his oath registered in Heaven, to the extirpation of the accursed negro-driving aristocracy."[28]

The appeal of these populist campaigns was limited. Even among Unionists, the committed radicals and their fellow travelers were a small minority, and most poor whites and yeomen had no wish to be associated with Unionism in any form, whether radical or conservative. But if revolutionary speeches and editorials failed to spark a class-conscious political movement among the plain folk, there was nevertheless growing popular hostility toward aristocrats. Though most humble folk in the occupied South continued to identify the Union army as the principal author of their woes, many came to believe that the aristocracy deserved at least part of the blame. A poor white farm laborer in middle Tennessee complained to Andrew Johnson that "there is a Plenty of [rich] men that helpt get up the rebelion & Promised [poor] men that if they would go into the servis there wives & Children should hav a plenty [to eat] that is [now] a Litting them seffer." A man in Memphis who had deserted from the Confederate army and sought sanctuary in the Union lines explained: "I got tired of fighting for a lot of old Rich Planters. . . . Here I was fighting to save their negroes and property and them remaining at home, living in all the luxuries of li[f]e."[29]

Some of the more resentful plain folk got even with their aristocratic neighbors by informing on them. Planter Colin Clarke in Virginia complained that a number of poor whites in his community had deserted from the Rebel army and returned home and were now "in league with the enemy. . . . They have already carried in lists of the names of gentlemen [who are] rabid secessionists." In another part of Virginia a Union officer found "two classes of white people . . . the poor class and the wealthy or aristocratic class. The poor ones are very bitter against the others; charge them with bringing on the war, and are always willing to show where the rich ones have hid their grain, fodder, horses, &c. Many of them tell me it is a great satisfaction to them to see us help ourselves from the rich stores of their neighbors."[30]

Moreover, there were hints that the suffering and the opportunism of the plain folk, especially the poor whites, might ultimately pose a direct threat to people of property. A man living in the northern Virginia countryside reported that the poor were close to starvation while "there are some about here that could spare bread stuff but they wont [except] at high prices"; one citizen he knew had been heard to say that "the suffering females had better raise [up] & take corn by force." An anxious property owner in an area of no-man's-land on the North Carolina coast prayed that the Confederate government would reassert its authority there and then "take some steps to have order preserved" and "have lawless & dollarless men kept in restraint." A number of poor whites, he said, had been stealing fence rails and threatening to seize farms from their owners: "some of those fellows have already said they will cultivate any mans land they please."[31]

Thus it seemed that resentment and hunger and ambition might do what the appeals of radical Yankees and Unionists could not: set the classes at odds and usher in a new order. But questions remained: how would the defenders of the old order answer these challenges? Would they prove impotent, or did they still command the power to preserve the world as it was?

. . .

People of property in the South, especially aristocrats, had always distrusted the poor. Their republican ethos ascribed to holders of property not only the independence necessary for good citizenship, but also superior qualities of character; those without property, it was alleged, were by their very nature venal and without honor. "You know the lower classes of [eastern North Carolina] have always been very degraded," remarked one plantation lady in 1863. "They could always be bought." A Confederate general in southern Louisiana spoke for many of that region's elite when he described the poor whites there as a "miserable, mixed breed, commonly called Dagos or Acadians, in whom there is not the slightest dependence to be placed." Indeed, many Southern property owners, especially members of the upper class, pictured the world in the starkest terms, as an arena of unending conflict between haves and have-nots. As one Tennessee aristocrat put it in 1862, nothing was more important than "a government . . . in which life, liberty & property is secure from the mob."[32]

Aristocrats had successfully restrained the mob in the antebellum years, and when they perceived dangers to the social order in the wake of Lincoln's election, they had headed off trouble by leading the South out of the Union. But invasion and occupation resurrected those dangers, spawned new ones, and confronted the South's ruling class with its greatest crisis.

Standing on the wide verandas of their homes, aristocrats in the occupied South looked about and were deeply troubled by what they saw. For one thing, continuing privation threatened to drive the plain folk to desperation. (Privation was not unique to the occupied South, of course—it was epidemic in the Confederate interior, too—but it was enormously aggravated in the occupied regions by devastation and economic disruption.) The sympathy that aristocrats expressed for the sufferers was often tinged with nervousness. "The poor people will be in a sad plight here," wrote a North Carolina planter whose neighborhood had just been raided by Federal troops, "& I would not be surprised if there should be a good deal of roguery going on."[33]

Another development that worried aristocrats was the breakdown of authority in no-man's-land, which threatened to untether the villainous impulses of poor whites. A resident of tidewater Virginia denounced certain "men of the low class" who had deserted from the Confederate army and now infested his neighborhood: "Some of them," he averred, ". . . expect to live by stealing." Planters in Jefferson Parish, Louisiana, complained that "there are many white Persons and Negros running about in this Parrish . . . without any ostensible means of a livelihood and we are daily Robbed of our goods and chattles." Moreover, the numbers of the "dangerous" sort were swelling: every dispossessed yeoman was an addition to the ranks of the propertyless.[34]

In the garrisoned towns, too, disorderly poor whites made aristocrats and other property holders uneasy. Citizens of Alexandria complained that "there are numbers of persons [in the city] . . . who have no apparent means of support, and whose practices are subversive of law and order." Nashvillians were likewise apprehensive: "Vagabonds, white and black, abound," the editor of the *Nashville Dispatch* warned, "and they need close watching." The danger in the towns was exacerbated by the influx of poor white refugees, whom one Tennessee aristocrat characterized as a "dirty, filthy, thievish set too lazy to work."[35]

Worse yet, it appeared that the Yankees were determined to do exactly what people of substance had long feared they would do: stir up the poor whites, who—dimwitted and devoid of character as they were—would be easily swayed. A North Carolina plantation lady believed that some of the rabble had been enticed into joining the Union army with offers of a share in the spoils of war. She described them as "poor ignorant wretches who cannot resist a fine uniform and the[ir] choice of the horses in the country & liberty to help themselves without check to their rich neighbors belongings."[36]

As lower-class unruliness waxed in the occupied regions, the elite's ability to suppress it waned. Aristocrats had long dominated the South through the exercise of political and economic power and moral authority. But with the coming of the Yankees that power and authority were compromised, especially in the garrisoned towns and no-man's-land.

For one thing, many aristocrats fled the occupied regions when the Federals first appeared or were later banished by them. Furthermore, in garrisoned towns the occupation authorities displaced the political institutions through which aristocrats had wielded power or, if they allowed those institutions to continue, usually deposed aristocratic officeholders, while in no-man's-land political institutions for the most part simply ceased to function. From a political standpoint, the coming of the Union army produced, as one Northerner wrote, "a convulsion, an upheaval," a virtual "earthquake, overturning aristocratic pride, privilege, and power."[37]

The economic emasculation of aristocrats was less abrupt and less complete than their political dethronement, but it was nevertheless telling. Nearly all aristocrats in the occupied regions suffered severe financial losses—not only from military seizures and destruction and the disruption of agriculture and trade, which touched all classes, but also from the loss of slaves and the devaluation of Confederate currency and bonds, which hurt aristocrats especially. "Gloom & despondency [are] on the countenance of all property holders," Tennessee planter John H. Bills reported in the summer of 1862. "Desolation of crops, loss of stock, insurbordination of negroes, runaways & etc. exceed description. No one knows [if] he is worth a cent today." Some were wiped out financially. After repeated Federal raids on his two plantations, a Virginia aristocrat declared that he had "lost nearly every thing I had save my land" and now found himself "poor and needy with a large family dependant on me. . . . I am ruined and undone."[38]

The decline of aristocratic fortunes had significant social consequences. Obviously, the ability of elites to control events through sheer economic might was curtailed. So too was their ability to offer paternal largess to their plebeian neighbors, a custom that, in the past, had worked to forestall popular unrest and to bolster the moral authority of the aristocracy. A Mississippi man whose much-ravaged community was a scene of "great distress among the people" told of a neighboring planter whose "corn-crib, which he has thrown open to the poor with a generous hand, has relieved many suffering families, [but] now that he has given away all that he can possibly spare, I do not know what arrangements the people can make to get their daily bread." The moral authority of aristocrats was weakened, too, when they appealed to the occupiers for relief, as some were eventually forced to do. A Union general on the North Carolina coast reported that he was provisioning not only the poor citizens but also some "who have but lately been in affluent circumstances, but who now have nothing but Confederate notes, city shin-plasters, worthless notes of hand, unproductive real estate, and negroes who refuse to acknowledge any debt of servitude."[39]

The sight of quondam plutocrats lining up for Yankee handouts alongside the wretched rabble was no doubt shocking to many people in the occupied South. So, too, was the sight of elite ladies and gentlemen wielding brooms, hoes, washtubs, and milk pails. The loss of their slaves compelled a great many aristocrats to take on unaccustomed duties. "Some planters have not even one servant left," a Louisiana man wrote in 1863. "[W]ives and daughters have to take the pot and tub, the men, where there are any, take to the field with the plough and hoe." Most found such chores not only laborious, but deeply humiliating. "I cannot see how we are to get through the winter," sighed a Tennessee lady who had lost all but one house servant, "for I do *hate* to work. . . . We are all tired *to death* by seven oclock." Planter Colin Clarke wrote that the loss of slaves in his community had rendered "our situation . . . most degrading & oppressing. Mrs. Deans [a neighbor] hires a free negro woman to wash, she helps to cook, the girls are the *house servants* & chamber maids, & Mrs Deans does all the ironing, & to this *we* [too] shall come, I have *no question*, if the Yankees remain."[40]

Drudgery and beggary were not the only humiliations some aristocrats had to endure. Every day of occupation brought mortifying reminders that their power had been usurped by outsiders and that they could no longer exercise the command they had been born and bred for. Many a proud aristocrat was humbled at the hands of vengeful Yankees or assertive blacks. On the last day of 1862, planter Edward Carter Turner summed up the year's events as the northern Virginia aristocracy had experienced them: "Any lying negro who felt disposed to do so could involve in the most serious difficulties the first men in the land. . . . [E]xcellent & worthy citizens were stripped of property & otherwise shamefully treated [by Federal authorities] upon the testimony of some unprincipled slave." In Tennessee, George A. Washington, one of the South's wealthiest planters, was set upon by a band of Union soldiers at his home and, according to his wife: "For two mortal hours, threats, curses, jeers and taunts . . . were heaped upon him and . . . pistols were snapped in his face and shaken over his head, my prayers and tears were made a scoff and jest, a band of indians could not have taken more devilish delight in tormenting a prisoner." The ultimate humiliation befell William Clopton, described scornfully by the Union officer who arrested him as a "high minded Virginia Gentleman." Clopton was known "as the most cruel Slave Master in this region," the officer reported, and after his arrest a number of his runaway slaves came forward and testified to his brutality. Though Clopton "put on the character of Snivelling Saint" while in custody, the officer decided to administer "Poetical justice." Stripping off Clopton's shirt, he handed a whip to the blacks and watched with satisfaction as four of them "took turns in settling some old scores on their masters back."[41]

Deprived of power, position, and property, many aristocrats, like Clopton, bowed meekly in the presence of the conquerors. "[T]hese people are cowed by the force of the Gov't," declared the Union officer in charge of recruiting black soldiers in Tennessee. "Slaveholders of all classes—[including] . . . the most aristocratic man and the most aristocratic lady—come . . . to talk with me about their slaves, and are the most polite people I ever saw." Some who had been singled out by Federal authorities because of their prominence longed for anonymity. "It is a happy thing these days to be obscure," sighed Elizabeth Harding, of Tennessee, whose husband was under arrest and whose elegant plantation near Nashville was being pillaged almost daily, "and a man's safety now depends on his insignificance; how I envy such quiet and seclusion, as is to be found in the hills and hollows."[42]

The abasement of the aristocracy aggravated the unrest among the plain folk. Old habits of deference to the elite seemed, to some, absurdly out of place in this new world. Why submit to the moral authority of a man who could barely feed his own family, who could not control his slaves, who worked in the fields like a common laborer, who prostrated himself at the feet of the Yankee occupiers?[43]

With their influence withering and disorder spreading, some aristocrats swallowed their pride and called on the occupiers for help. The planters of Jefferson Parish, Louisiana, for example, acknowledging that they had "no available means of suppressing" the outbreak of lower-class thievery in their community, pleaded with the parish provost marshal to form a police patrol. Such appeals were of little avail, however (except in the garrisoned towns). Restlessness and resentment among the lower orders seemed only to grow, fueling in turn the fears of the threatened elite. In 1864 a Mississippi aristocrat described the situation in Yazoo and other counties near the Union lines, which were being inundated by a "filthy, base, disloyal, deserting, stealing, murdering population" that had fled the Confederate interior. "They ought to be hung," he declared. "They pretend to go there to get corn to live on, but their real object is to avoid our army, steal, plunder, and be with the Yankees. I . . . know them to be a base, vile & worthless set who never made a good or honest living. . . . They are all as rotten as Hell." A few weeks later he warned that "this tide is still rolling on, swelling and enlarging." Many of this rabble, he said, have "seized upon [abandoned] places & supplies at will and are exhorting all behind to follow, alledging that they can thus keep out of the army, have plenty to trade with the yankees and ultimately the yankees will reward them with the places they have thus located upon."[44]

Was there even worse in store? Some aristocrats suspected so. As early as February 1862, planter Charles Pettigrew, of Washington County, North Carolina, began carrying a gun. "The low whites are not to be trusted at all," he thought. "They would betray or murder any gentleman." As the months went by, more people of substance in Washington County and across the occupied South watched nervously for signs of insurrection.[45]

. . .

The worst nightmares of the aristocracy did not come to pass. The masses did not rise in murderous fury; no tumbrels or guillotines appeared. But if aristocrats' lives were spared, their property was not. Before the war was over, many sections of the occupied South witnessed open assaults on property by the propertyless. Hunger, resentment, and opportunism were the impulses behind these assaults, but it was the disruption of traditional authority that unleashed those impulses.[46]

Open attacks on property were least common in the garrisoned towns, because the Federals—however much they desired to revolutionize Southern society—could not tolerate disorder in their strategic enclaves. No sooner did they capture a town, in fact, than they cracked down on the unruly poor. For example, when Union troops entered Savannah and found (as they had found in other cities abandoned by the Rebel army) "a lawless mob of low whites and negroes pillaging and setting fire to property," their first order of business was to disperse it. Thereafter, in Savannah and other garrisoned towns, the occupation authorities rigorously policed the underclass and responded promptly when trouble broke out.[47]

Even so, people of property in the towns saw ample evidence that the propertyless would eagerly redistribute wealth if they had the chance. A woman who lived in Rome, Georgia, while it was garrisoned in 1864 listed her family's personal property that was "stolen and taken off, some by the Yankees and a great deal by the poor people and negroes, who are almost as bad as Yankees about stealing. . . . [T]he white women would come in Mother's yard in the broad daytime and steal peaches and apples, and she did not dare say anything to them for fear that they would tell the Yankees some great story on her." In another Georgia town poor whites brazenly hauled away furniture and other belongings from houses abandoned by families who had fled the Northern invasion. In some of the towns that the occupiers were forced to evacuate, plundering broke out as soon as the garrison troops marched away.[48]

On the Confederate frontier the propertied classes could, and did, appeal to Confederate and local authorities to rein in the restive underclass. But the authorities were sometimes powerless to act. For one thing, in some sections of the frontier that lay relatively close to Union lines poor whites sought refuge with the invaders and then used the Federal posts as bases for larcenous raids into the frontier. This was the predicament that John Pool and his aristocratic friends eventually faced in Bertie County, North Carolina. "[D]isorderly white persons have left here & congregated at [the post of] Plymouth," Pool wrote in July 1863. From there, he said, they found it easy to return to the county by river and "commit depredations." He cited one instance in which "pirate bands from Plymouth" robbed a plantation of fifteen thousand dollars' worth of property. A Florida citizen reported in 1864 that a number of poor white families in his community had gone to the Union lines and many others were preparing to go, spurred by a rumor that the Federals were offering provisions, free homesteads, and cash rewards for cattle and slaves driven in from the frontier. "This is their own statement, they are to be colonized from Cape Romain to the Miami River, and are to receive protection from the Yankees"; once safely resettled under Federal aegis, they intended to raid the frontier and "carry all cattle and negroes they can get a hold of to the Yankees."[49]

Even some of the poor who remained on the frontier dared to strike against the propertied, emboldened by the proximity of the Union army. In Cherokee County, Alabama, Sarah Espy reported that as one of her neighbors was threshing wheat, a group of poor white women "came and impressed 70 bush[els] of it. This looks like a bold thing, but we shall hear of more no doubt." John Pool noted that several gangs of draft dodgers were lurking about Bertie County and committing robberies; one party had visited the home of a widow and confined her in her house while they broke into her food stores. "No military force can reach them," Pool explained, "because as soon as they become [alarmed] they will go over to the enemy, either by crossing the Chowan or by signalling some passing gunboat in the Roanoke."[50]

When Union troops passed through on one of their occasional forays into the frontier regions, some poor whites abandoned all restraint. A Louisiana planter returned home after a raid had disrupted his community and "found that my . . . place had been broken up & robed by the disserters—rogues who have long infested the neighborhood—and every thing taken off the place which could be moved." Workers at a gristmill in North Carolina took advantage of a raid to pillage their employer's supplies, stealing bacon and other goods that they concealed when the employer later came looking for them. Some of the workers at the Roswell Manufacturing Company of Georgia ransacked their employer's property when the Yankees passed by in 1864, not only stealing but also committing acts of spiteful vandalism. "They plundered & destroyed to a large [extent]," company officials reported, "tearing down the shelves in the [company] store to burn, breaking glasses and otherwise injuring the [employees'] houses, hauling off Iron and Copper to sell, and putting the [mill] wheel in motion and seriously injuring it by throwing down rocks."[51]

It was in no-man's-land, where anarchy reigned, that the restless poor were least inhibited. The countryside surrounding Plymouth, for example, witnessed repeated assaults on property by propertyless whites, some of whom were enrolled as Unionist home guards or Federal soldiers. "[S]hortly after you left," a correspondent informed Josiah Collins, who had left his large Washington County plantation in charge of an overseer, "the Union men . . . united and bid defiance to ownership of property . . . and went plundering and destroying with impunity in every direction." The estates of Collins and other planters, and even the farms of some of the more prosperous yeomen, were stripped of crops, livestock, equipment, fencing, and furniture. Another friend told Collins of depredations by the Union army but added that families in the neighborhood were guilty, too: "many of the country people have supplied themselves with corn from your plantation & several of [your stolen] horses have not gone far from home." In many cases personal property that was not carried away was maliciously wrecked. A number of poor whites in the Plymouth region squatted defiantly on planters' land and claimed it for themselves—sometimes provoking violent confrontations with blacks who had the same idea.[52]

One of the most dramatic poor white uprisings in no-man's-land took place in the eastern highlands of middle Tennessee, at a place known as Beersheba Springs. Aristocratic families had been vacationing there since the 1850s, staying at the large resort hotel or in private cottages and enjoying the restorative waters. In the summer of 1863 a number of aristocrats, including Virginia French, gathered at Beersheba believing that the area was safe. They were unaware that the local poor whites, whom they condescendingly dubbed the "mountain people," had grown mutinous.[53]

French's diary vividly records the events of that summer. Beginning in June there were reports of lawless bands in the neighborhood (French suspected that they might be renegade Yankees or Confederate deserters), and three times in July robber gangs struck at the resort. On the third occasion French noted her suspicion that "the mountain people assisted too." The next day all doubts disappeared. "Scenes enacted here today beggar description," French wrote:

> Early in the morning the sack of the place began. . . . [T]he mountain people came in crowds and with vehickles of all sorts and carried off everything they could from both hotel and cottages. . . . Gaunt, ill-looking men and slatternly, rough barefooted women stalking and racing to and fro, eager as famished wolves for prey, hauling out furniture—tearing up matting and carpets. . . . A band would rush up and take possession of a cottage—place a guard, drive off every one else, stating that this was theirs.

French saw one woman enter a cottage and carry away Latin, French, and theology books: "The woman, who did not know a letter to save her life, said 'she had some children who were just beginin' to read and she wanted the books for them—she wanted to encourage em!' " At another cottage a group of mountain people "held an orgie the whole night, singing, shouting, and it is believed dancing." " '[T]he masses' had it all their own way on this memorable day," French concluded, "—the aristocrats went down for the nonce." The next day the mountain people returned for more plunder, and they made sporadic raids throughout the summer.[54]

As sensational as such episodes were, the conflict that they evidenced was singularly muted. Of all the struggles that convulsed the occupied South—including those of Rebels versus Yankees, secessionists versus Unionists, and whites versus blacks—the struggle of the propertied versus the propertyless was the most restrained. Dead bodies of insurgent poor whites did not litter the countryside as the bodies of insurgent blacks and Unionists and invading Yankees did.

The reason is probably this: despite their oft-expressed fears, aristocrats came to understand that the unruly plain folk did not fundamentally threaten the social order. The poor and dispossessed overwhelmingly rejected real radicalism and violence against persons. Their vision of the year of jubilee did not embrace revolution; they demanded merely a less inequitable share of sustenance, property, and opportunity than was their customary lot. And only a minority of the underclass made even those limited demands; most just endured their fate in silence and tried to get along the best they could with the little they had.

Perhaps things would have turned out differently if the war had continued beyond the spring of 1865. The further agitation of the plain folk, and the further degradation of the aristocracy, might well have snapped the weakened but still intact bonds of deference and paternalism that united the white South. If so, then Appomattox signaled not the extinction, but indeed the salvation, of the old order.

[7]

· ·

In a Strange Land

Family and Community
in the Maelstrom of War

· ·

In the spring of 1864 a Tennessee woman wrote to a kinsman from her plantation on the Cumberland River below Clarksville. It was the first letter she had sent him since the occupiers arrived more than two years before, and she knew that he would be anxious for news of friends and loved ones in the community. "Many and sad are the changes that have taken place in nearly every family," she lamented. "Father's family have been *sorely* and *repeattedly* tried." The vibrant communal life of earlier times had also fallen victim to military occupation: "I have only been to Clarksville three times in the last two years and visit but little in the neighborhood." As for the town itself, now a Federal army post, "You would scarcely know the place, it is nothing but a dirty hole filled . . . with niggers and Yankees."[1]

All across the South, families and communities—the essential institutions of Southern life—were touched by the war, even where no Northern invaders ever appeared. In the occupied regions, however, they were not just touched but battered. The advent of the enemy host unleashed powerful forces, in the face of which even the sturdiest features of the social landscape bent or disintegrated.

. . .

War and occupation threatened families in several ways. For one thing, the presence of an armed force not fettered by legal or social restraints endangered the sanctity of the home. For another, devastation and disruption undermined the family's economic foundation. And, too, mobilization, hardship, and disorder posed a challenge to husbands and wives as they endeavored to carry out their prescribed duties within their separate spheres.

Men agonized over their dwindling ability to protect and provide for their families. Many labored long hours and took great risks to meet their obligations. But the signs of their failure were everywhere: Yankee pillagers forcing their way into homes as the man of the house stood by impotently, wives and children going about hungry and ill-clad, whole families uprooted by destitution and danger, taking to the road in desperation. Nevertheless, many households were greatly comforted by the steadfast presence and tireless exertions of husbands and fathers. They were the lucky ones, for a larger number of families had to endure the trials of occupation without a male provider.[2]

Every observer in the occupied South was struck by the dearth of men. Many men had left well before the Yankees came, marching away with their regiments to the front, some never to return. Many others had fled when the invaders arrived, leaving wives or mothers to sustain and defend their homes. Others were banished by the occupiers or were killed in the bloody internal warfare that racked the countryside. Whatever the reason, by the latter part of the war most families in the occupied regions were headed by women. In some districts a virtual matriarchy prevailed: the only white males to be found were very old or very young. William King in northern Georgia heard reports from the countryside that "the men are all gone & none left but women, children & old & sick men." Citizens of Culpeper County, Virginia, described the population remaining there by late 1864 as "a feeble residuum of infirm and tottering old men, a small proportion of immature youth, and a large number of helpless women and children." In the same year a northern Mississippian told of "one thickly populated neighborhood, covering an area of some six miles, where there are not men enough left to bury the dead."[3]

Even those men who remained at home sometimes had to forsake their families for days or weeks at a time to hide from danger. For example, when Federal troops raided Cushing Hassell's community in November 1862 and made known their intention to arrest him, Hassell spent a night in the woods; for the next nine days and nights he dodged around the countryside taking refuge with various friends while his wife and children waited for him at home. In northern Mississippi, Roxa Cole observed: "At every alarm of [the enemy's] approach here, the few men that are left here fly to escape their fate." One man of her acquaintance, she said, "has to be gone nearly all the time, and go in a *run* at that, to keep out of the way of the Yankees." Union men were also driven from the bosom of their families by their enemies. "[I]t is so [bad] at present," a Tennessee Unionist reported during an outbreak of guerrilla violence in 1863, "that a truly loyal man dare not stay at home."[4]

Women worried about their ability to fend for themselves, for the ideal of "true womanhood" to which they subscribed portrayed females as frail and dependent, unequipped to survive in the rough-and-tumble world without a male protector. A Tennessee woman made her husband promise to take the oath if threatened with arrest by the occupiers; she hated to see him capitulate to the enemy, she explained, but she could not bear the thought of his "being taken from us & thrown into prison, leaving our children with no one to protect or provide for them except myself." A Louisianan anxiously weighed the options of leaving home with her four small children or remaining under Federal rule: "I am sick with torturing my brain to try and find out what would be the right course to persue," she wrote her absent husband. "If *you* were only here to tell me."[5]

Many women were especially unnerved by the prospect of confronting enemy soldiers while home alone. The thought of Yankee ruffians violating the sanctity of the home was disturbing enough; the thought of their violating a woman's body was terrifying. Women's fear of rape did not diminish, but in fact grew, as occupation continued. During the early invasions, and while the rosewater policy prevailed, many women had discounted the likelihood of molestation by Union soldiers and had dared to defy and even antagonize them. But as Federal policy turned harsher and the soldiers grew less restrained and more vindictive, women became more anxious about their personal safety. Two events in particular—General Butler's notorious "woman order" of 1862, which threatened to treat any New Orleans female who insulted a Union soldier as "a woman of the town plying her avocation," and the Federal government's decision the same year to begin enlisting black troops—persuaded many women in the occupied regions that they were in real danger of rape or other physical abuse. A Mississippi woman watched nervously as Union cavalry rode past her home in the summer of 1863: "They did not come in," she wrote in her diary, "and I hope if they do visit us they will remember that they have mothers, wives & sisters at home and treat us as they would wish them to be by our men." Roxa Cole told how soldiers forced their way into her house with drawn pistols in the middle of the night and ransacked the place: "I should not have suffered so that night," she wrote later, "had I known that mere robbery was all that I had to fear, but I had seen and heard so much of their lawless deeds and worse threats that we knew not what to fear."[6]

Amid all the disruption and danger in the occupied South, women struggled to remain faithful to their ideals—nurturance, moral guidance, domesticity, femininity. An Arkansas woman stayed up six nights to nurse a sick slave man, after journeying to the Federal post at Fayetteville to beg medicine from a Union army surgeon. Where schools and churches were defunct, many women took on the responsibility of teaching their children the three Rs and the word of God. One was Virginia French, of Tennessee, who affirmed that in such troubled times "home seems to me the best place for a quiet woman." French was also determined to uphold the standards of feminine decorum. She expressed outrage, for example, when she learned that five Unionist girls of McMinnville had gone riding unescorted with some of the Northern garrison troops: "what in the name of common sense and common decency, [could] the mothers of those girls . . . be thinking of[?]" Many women, in fact, worried that the demands of war and occupation might defeminize the gentle sex. A Mississippian, proudly declaring that "the times are making strong women," recounted several incidents in which females had boldly stood up to Federal soldiers, yet she hoped that in all such encounters women would "be sure to stop at the right point, & not border on the masculine."[7]

Inevitably, however, the line of demarcation between the separate spheres eroded. With their menfolk absent part or all of the time, most women were forced to assume traditionally masculine duties. Some women had managed farms on their own before the war, but for most it was a new and onerous experience, a heavy load added to their customary burden of running a household. One Northern soldier, mistakenly assuming that what he observed in the South in 1862 was the normal order of things there, commented: "These Tennessian women work harder, I think, than ours do at home. . . . The wives and daughters of the poorer farmers do all the garden work, and much besides that ours hand over to the men. We see . . . white [women] ploughing, harrowing, and hauling grain, with ox teams, to the mill."[8]

A good many women discovered that they could handle their new responsibilities as capably as any man, but many others had to admit some degree of failure. Handicapped by inexperience, by insufficient brawn, and in some cases by self-doubt attributable to the pervasive ideal of true womanhood, women often found their tasks overwhelming and had to call on men for help. Cushing Hassell, one of the few men left in his community, was constantly busy "attending to calls, questions & distresses of the female portion of the citizens"; some were running short of provisions, others needed assistance with business transactions such as selling slaves. William King likewise found himself called on to act as mentor and provider for helpless women in his neighborhood: two came by with their children in August 1864, he noted, "to get advice [about] what they should do." Destitute and hungry, they did not know where to turn, so King fed them and promised to plead their case to the Federal commandant in nearby Marietta. Some women simply threw themselves on the mercy of the occupiers. Among them were three who sought refuge at a Federal post in Virginia late in 1861, "Alleging that they are poor," the provost marshal reported, "without friends or protectors."[9]

Women felt particularly inadequate when trying to manage their slave laborers, traditionally a male responsibility (except where house servants were concerned). As blacks, and especially black men, grew more and more ungovernable, the authority of white mistresses was severely tested. On the Washingtons' plantation in middle Tennessee, elderly Mary Washington and the other women of the family strove mightily but ineffectually to control their remaining slaves in the absence of the planter-patriarch, Mary's son George. One of the women reported in February 1865 that a runaway slave had returned to the plantation a week earlier claiming that he was willing to go back to work, "but [he] has not done a solitary thing. . . . Cousin P has told him that he could not & should not stay here, but he does not regard it any more than if she did not speak to him." A few weeks later Mary confessed that "I do not know what to do with those negro devils they will not work." In desperation she called on a family friend and neighbor, "Captain" Collier, who agreed to stay at the plantation until George returned. "I feel more safe by his being here," Mary wrote; ". . . the negroes I think will not cut up while he remains her[e]." And, indeed, Collier succeeded where the women had failed. "[I]f he was not here I do not know what we would do," declared Mary's fourteen-year-old grandson, ". . . he has spread terror abrod among the Negros." Mary herself acknowledged that "if the Capt was not here as a protector for us we could not remain here with these devils around us[,] they certainly are afraid of him."[10]

Furthermore, to a limited but significant extent women lost control over their own children. With fathers absent, mothers overburdened with chores, and schools and churches and work routines disrupted, children enjoyed an unprecedented degree of autonomy. "The want of proper restraint, home discipline, and improvement of the mind, has had a most pernicious effect" on children, commented an Arkansas newspaper in 1865. Other observers, too, deplored the paucity of supervision and in- doctrination and sensed that the young were growing unruly. The *Nash- ville Dispatch* reported in 1863 that with the city's public schools shut down, many boys and girls were spending their time "in idleness and wickedness." The Portsmouth provost marshal remarked in 1862 that some children there had become so "insolent in their language and ac- tion" that he had been compelled to take the matter up with their parents. A few days later he reported on a gang of young boys in the city "whom I have had a good deal of trouble with"; one had been caught carrying a pistol, another had knifed a black girl during an argument. It may be, too, that the scandalous behavior of the Unionist girls of McMinnville that so upset Virginia French signified not maternal irresponsibility, but the weakening of maternal authority.[11]

Sexual assault by Union soldiers proved to be rare, though the fear of it continued to haunt women throughout the war. In their official dealings with women, the occupiers maintained strict sexual propriety—neither "Beast" Butler nor any other commander ever authorized the physical abuse of women; troops were instructed to behave with decorum. For instance, when picket guards had to search women for contraband, they were not permitted to go further than bonnets and handbags. If there was a strong suspicion that a woman was smuggling items in her clothes, the provost marshal would call in another female to conduct a body search in private. Yet incidents of rape and molestation did occur, perpetrated in nearly every case by deserters, stragglers, or other unsupervised enlisted men who preyed on women they found alone in isolated farmhouses. When the culprits could be brought to justice, the army was merciless, especially if the guilty soldier was black. Twenty-two Union soldiers were executed for raping white women during the war, half of them black.[12]

Many Southern women, even some of those most cowed and submissive in the presence of Yankee pillagers, made it clear that they would take any steps necessary to defend their bodies. "My pistol is loaded," wrote Virginian Charlotte Wright, "but, I trust never to use it, & never will except in self defence." A Tennessee woman stood by passively while soldiers ransacked her house, according to her sister's account, but when one soldier "threatened to search her body for a pistol . . . she told [him] if he dared to touch her she'd lay him so low that he'd never rise again."[13]

Far more common than actual rape was what might be termed symbolic rape. Many Union soldiers who would never have countenanced ravishing women physically nevertheless seemed to enjoy ravishing them psychologically when they found them alone and vulnerable. These symbolic assaults took various forms, usually involving the deliberate and gratuitous violation of a woman's privacy or dignity. For example, soldiers frequently invaded women's private chambers and carried off personal effects of no military or pecuniary value, including underwear and family mementos. Many soldiers taunted women with provocative or obscene language. Some exposed themselves. To these rituals of degradation were added rituals of coercion and submission: often soldiers would enter a woman's kitchen and force her to cook for them.[14]

Women's accounts of these incidents reveal their profound sense of helplessness and humiliation, for in such circumstances there was little they could do but yield and endure. "[T]his has been a dreadful day," wrote Alabamian Sarah Espy after Northern soldiers plundered her bedroom and kitchen and cursed at her. "I cannot describe my feelings when surrounded by men who appeared so much bent on mischief and before whom I and Olivia were as helpless as infants." Roxa Cole also felt powerless and defiled: "It nearly kills me to have to endure the coarse, bullying ruffians stalking into my house, making all sorts of demands with oaths and threats." A Tennessee woman wrote bitterly of her experience when soldiers broke into her house while she was alone and in bed: "I . . . got up & dressed *with one of them standing in the open [bedroom] door. Five* of them then dashed in shaking their fists & pistols in my face, cursing me, & calling me all kinds of names, . . . jumping *into* the beds & tramping all over them . . . wiping their wet muddy feet on my nicest dresses, . . . taking everything they fancied, Bedclothes, wearing apparel, Jewelry, silver."[15]

It took extraordinary courage to face the soldiers' hectoring and provocations with equanimity. One woman who did so was an elderly Arkansan who, as a neighbor recounted, rushed out of her house upon hearing gunfire and found that soldiers had shot one of her hogs. Grabbing a large stick, she prepared to resist:

"You have killed my hog," said she, "but you cannot carry it away." They cursed and threatened her, but she stood her ground and defied them. When they found that she could not be intimidated by threats and ugly words, one of them went into the house and commenced tossing her bedding about and kicking her sheet of wool rolls over the floor, expecting thereby to draw her away from the hog. But finding that she still stood fast with her club, he returned as near as was safe for him, turned his ugly end towards her, pulled down his pants and emptied his bowels of stinking load in her presence. "Now, sir," said she, "You have made a dog of yourself. I am old and not thus to be abashed, for all my life long I have always seen dogs go. . . ." Upon hearing which the fellow quickly rose, buttoned up, and left for his quarters. Sending for help, the old lady finished butchering her hog and salted it away.[16]

Even the strongest and most self-reliant women were in many cases forced to abandon the attempt to maintain their homes independently. Hunger, harassment, and disorder in the countryside drove large numbers of women to the garrisoned towns. But even there, many resisted the abjectly dependent existence they faced in refugee camps and shelters. One observer in 1864 saw a pathetic sight just outside Nashville: two refugee women with nine children between them, camped on the roadside "without shelter, or money, [and only] a scanty supply of provisions and clothing and five of the children sick"; despite their misery they were gamely trying to eke out a living, because "they would rather go into the woods than the 'Refugee House' at Nashville." A woman living in the Nashville shelter about that time begged military governor Johnson to help her find quarters of her own: "get some of y'r acquaintances who has one little room to spare, to rent me one, I care not how small. I know there is work a plenty here to do[.] I can sew neatly. . . . I feel that I can get the work if I can only get a room. I could then soon pay my rent. I do not wish to sit down and depend upon the Goverment to support my family. I am poor but proud."[17]

Sustaining home and family was the supreme challenge confronting women fending for themselves, but even those who faced that challenge most successfully could not rest content until the circle was once again unbroken. Their wartime ordeal did not weaken women's devotion to the patriarchal system that both subjugated and exalted them; if anything, it strengthened it. Indeed, many women willingly abandoned their homes and their independence in order to join their husbands who had fled to the Confederate interior or to the garrisoned towns; many others took great personal risks—defying Rebel conscription agents, guerrillas, or Yankees—to help keep their husbands at home. And throughout the war, even when acting altogether independently, women never forsook the time-honored precepts of loyalty and deference to husbands and fathers.[18]

Thus, of the four essential divisions among the people of the Confederate South—those of politics, race, class, and sex—only the last did not flare into open rupture after the invaders arrived. Even as Unionists, blacks, and poor whites hailed their liberation and cast off their chains, women struggled to preserve the patriarchal world they had known.

· · ·

The bonds of community were severely strained by war and occupation. A host of factors—the flight or banishment or death of many local citizens; the influx of outsiders; the imposition of an alien power unamenable to popular influence; widespread destruction and privation; danger, immobility, and institutional disruption in the countryside—inexorably eroded the individual's sense of being part of a community from which she or he could expect sustenance and justice, and to which she or he owed fealty and obedience.

Everywhere there appeared signs that communal integrity and discipline were withering. "I can see every day people are for them selves and no boddy else," wrote Mary Washington in 1865. "[M]ost of [the] people have turned out to steal and lie[,] not many that care for any one but themselves." In western Tennessee, Robert Cartmell observed that "all, all, are more or less demoralized & do things, [that] a few years ago, they would have scorned the idea of doing." William King condemned "the corrupt people living among us" in his Georgia community. "All the wicked passions of the people," he said, "seem to be left without restrain[t]."[19]

Enmities and jealousies that in earlier times would have been contained or mediated through communal intervention now burst forth in open conflict. Kate Carney of Murfreesboro, Tennessee, ascribed ulterior motives to certain citizens who were informing on fellow townspeople: "private grudges of years standing, are brought to light," she wrote, "& revenge is considered sweet." Mary Washington was appalled by the hostility that surfaced in her community toward her son: "I think he has many enemies and but few friends. . . . [They] would like for us to be striped of every thing and [see] all [of our] things destroyed. . . . [T]hey seem to have nothing to do or think about but him and his business." Sometimes not individuals but the community as a whole became a target of vengeance at the hands of the aggrieved. In Maury County, Tennessee, a woman rushed outdoors upon learning that a squad of Federal soldiers was up to some mischief in her yard; to her astonishment she found one of her neighbors helping the soldiers set fire to her house. "[He] said he had joined them," she later testified, "[and said] that he had been broken up twice, once by the Rebels and once by the Federals, and he was going to have revenge and didnt care who it was off of."[20]

The dissolution of community was virtually complete in many sections of no-man's-land. There—where neither Union nor Confederate nor local authorities could govern, where depopulation left many neighborhoods bereft of heart and soul, where danger and disruption confined citizens to their homes, cutting them off from one another and from churches, schools, and courthouses—the last vestiges of community and order vanished, leaving a great void. "All is anarchy and confusion here," a Mississippian declared, "—everything going to destruction." Robert Cartmell looked around his neighborhood and saw "Every thing at a standstill. . . . No law, no order, *chaos & disorder*."[21]

The most striking consequence of the collapse of communal authority and the untethering of individual volition in no-man's-land was the rise of banditry. Though almost unknown in the antebellum South, banditry became a frightening fact of life during the war in many of the rural areas where chaos reigned. Operating usually in bands of two to six men, though sometimes considerably more, and frequently disguised in Federal uniform, bandits accosted travelers on the highways or preyed on isolated farm families. "Their mode of action is to hide in the bushes when they hear of the approach [of] travellers," reported a Union soldier in Baton Rouge, "and jumping out suddenly presenting a pistol, just as you have read of banditti and highway robbers, they force the occupants of the carriage to give them what they demand. Such is the state of the country outside our [picket] lines." A woman in Independence County, Arkansas, described how a gang posing as Federal soldiers came to her home, claiming to have authority to search for weapons. Once inside, they drew pistols, ransacked the place for valuables, and demanded to know where she had hidden her money: "They tried to frighten me to make me give it up. . . . I gave up the money. The children were crying and wanted me to give it up."[22]

Although many bandits were outsiders—often vagabond Confederate or Union army deserters—most were longtime members of the community, now free of its scrutiny and coercion. Some were teenage boys set loose not only from communal but also familial control. Unquestionably, many bandits were the same citizens who had once ridden with the guerrilla bands. As the occupiers' counterguerrilla measures took their toll, and as the bonds of community dissolved, these men and boys renounced political and communal purpose for sheer self-interest and shifted their attacks from Yankees and Unionists to any defenseless person they could find.[23]

The makeup and modus operandi of the bandit gangs clearly distinguished them from the restless poor whites who also carried out depredations in no-man's-land. For one thing, the bandits were drawn from various segments of the population, not just the lower class. (One member of the gang that robbed the Independence County woman, for example, was later captured and turned out to be a local physician; a Tennessee teenager, apprehended after a year-long career as a bandit in his community, was described by a neighbor as a boy with social standing "as good as any body's . . . he was a member of the Methodist Church," and his widowed mother "is regarded as well off, has a good farm.") For another thing, the bandits' victims were not just those citizens with substantial property, but often the poor and middling sort: "They steal from friend or foe, rich or poor, white or black," said William King, "they steal whatever they can get hold of, such is the demoralization of war." And whereas the insurgent poor whites (many of whom were women) often acted openly and with no overt threat of violence (witness the pillaging of Beersheba Springs) because they assumed their depredations had a certain moral legitimacy, bandits always worked furtively, seized their booty at the point of a gun, had no women in their ranks, and recognized themselves as moral outcasts. One Tennessee victim recalled a revealing incident when bandits came to her home early in 1865. Alone and frightened, she ingratiatingly addressed them as "gentlemen" but was immediately corrected by one of the gang: "don't call us gentlemen," he ordered, "we are robbers."[24]

Bandits were further distinguished from all the other depredators and armed bands that roamed no-man's-land—which included poor whites, emancipated blacks, Federal soldiers, Unionist home guards, Rebel cavalry, partisan rangers, and guerrillas—by their propensity for brutal violence against innocent, unarmed citizens. In Maury County, Tennessee, according to Nimrod Porter's account, "roberies are committed by attacking the house in the dead of the night gitting the doore open & punishing the inmates by partially hanging & choking them until they tell where there moneys & valuables are." In another part of middle Tennessee mounted bandits held up a man on the highway and, angered at finding that he had only four dollars, stripped him to his underwear, put a rope around his neck, and dragged him along the road behind them. A Prairie County, Arkansas, man testified that bandits burst into his home one night, demanded money, and knocked him to the floor. "As I was getting up," he recounted, "[one of the gang] jerked me into the passage, and knocked me down again, and kicked one, two, three times, after I fell. I got up, and protested that I had no money, he then after threatening to kill me, knocked me down with a chair and stomped me, with his heal, and broke three of my ribs."[25]

These victims were actually among the lucky ones, for many suffered even crueler punishment, and many were murdered outright. Nor were women and children spared. In Giles County, Tennessee, two bandits went to the home of Mary and Charles Goodrum around dusk in the winter of 1864, broke down the door, and demanded money; then, as Mary watched in horror, they put a bullet through her little daughter, who survived, and two bullets through her husband, who did not. A year later, in another part of Tennessee, bandits raided the farm of John Gorham (which was occupied at the time only by his slaves), did some plundering, and roughed up a black woman before departing. "[T]he Negroes becoming uneasy [for fear of another such raid,] My Son a Boy about 18 years of age went to the Farm to protect them," Gorham reported. "[T]hey felt Secure but *alas alas* how Mistaken. On the following Monday Night . . . a band came and forced the doors again after Shooting throw the Shelter *Killing* a Negro Woman and wounding my Son badly, he Killing one of them and wounding another[.] [T]heir conduct after then was too horrible to tell, they then Shot My Son Several times and cut his ears off with a knife & otherwise maimed him and left him for dead[.] [T]hey then Shot the Old Negro Woman in the feat and body and Set the House[,] Beads &c on fire."[26]

By the latter part of the war, many sections of no-man's-land—particularly in Tennessee, Georgia, Arkansas, and along the Mississippi River—were deluged by banditry. "The whole country is overrun with Robbers," declared William King in the summer of 1864, "blue coats, gray coats, citizens' coats & no coats." Nimrod Porter's journal paints a similar picture of rural Tennessee: "midnight roberies . . . are the order of the day, in every part of the country committed in every neighbourhood & every day," Porter wrote. "Many house brakings & robing going on all over the country it is truly distressing to hear of so much lementations coming up from all round the country of robing & plundering."[27]

Where anarchy was at its worst, bandit gangs sometimes brazenly raided not just isolated homesteads but whole villages and towns. In the spring of 1864, when the Union garrison at Fayetteville, Tennessee, was temporarily withdrawn, a gang rode into the town, plundered stores and homes, robbed men and women on the street, and then rode away unmolested with their loot. Less than a week after the Federal garrison pulled out of Rome, Georgia, in November 1864, bandits descended on the town at night, robbed a number of people at gunpoint, and killed a city councilman.[28]

As the bandits grew bolder, the inhabitants of no-man's-land retreated even further into fear and isolation, severing the last frayed threads of the ravaged fabric of communalism. "One cannot go any distance without runing great danger of being robed," said Robert Cartmell early in 1865, ". . . bad enough now, may get worse & probably will." Virginia French, still living in her cottage at Beersheba Springs but now more afraid of bandits than of the "mountain people," wrote: "I do not like to leave the house for any length of time. . . . We are environed by dangers on every side and live as it were on the brink of a precipice. Robberies take place every day or two, and we know not when our turn may come. Lawless men roam at large, all about." When a bandit gang terrorized their neighborhood in the summer of 1864, the members of the Washington family literally barricaded themselves in their house, boarding up doors and windows and stockpiling guns and ammunition. "We have everything so concentrated that I think it would take a battery of 12 pounders to capture our citadel," Mary Washington's daughter-in-law announced with a great show of pluck. A few days later, however, she confessed that "I do not think we can live here much longer."[29]

Indeed, many citizens wondered how long they could hold out in the increasingly perilous countryside. Virginia French considered moving back to the garrisoned post at McMinnville, despite her loathing of the occupiers: "Federal rule is I think preferable to 'bushwhacker' rule, and I believe I would feel much safer down in town . . . than here." William King was convinced that only the presence of the garrison at Marietta kept the adjacent rural neighborhoods from being entirely swallowed up by chaos and violence, and he worried that the garrison might pull out, leaving the inhabitants at the mercy of "wicked marauders running over the Land, stealing & destroying everything."[30]

That the citizens could find such comfort in the proximity of the Yankee occupiers suggests how deeply they feared, and how thoroughly they repudiated, the mayhem of the bandits. Many willingly informed on the bandits, applauded their apprehension by Federal authorities, and urged the harshest penalties. A group of Tennesseans pleaded with Andrew Johnson not to mitigate the sentence of a local man convicted of larceny and highway robbery: "it is absolutely necessary—for the Security of persons and property—during this most unhappy State of Our Country—Surrounded as we are by unlimited Thieves and Robbers, all over the land—to make Suitable Examples of Such." Robert Cartmell watched as Union troops marched four captured bandits to their execution: "it is a hard fate," he remarked grimly, "but the people are suffering, bleeding at every pore & the guilty parties ought to suffer."[31]

The bandits in turn struck back savagely at all who sought to thwart them. When a Crittenden County, Arkansas, man named Griffee reported his onetime friend Calvin Boyle to the Federal authorities as a bandit, Boyle told Griffee "you can call me a Rober But you cant report [me] to the yankees and live in this cuntry." Later Boyle and his gang showed up at Griffee's home, led him away to the banks of the Mississippi, shot him dead, and sent his body floating down the river. Early in 1865 in Tennessee, James Coughran was robbed at his home by a local gang headed by a man named Luttrell; the next day Coughran went to nearby Columbia to tell the army authorities. When they learned of this, Luttrell and his men swore revenge. Returning to Coughran's house, they held him at gunpoint while they dragged his wife upstairs and put a bullet through her brain. They then shot Coughran, plundered the house, and rode away.[32]

Such atrocities only fueled the determination of the citizens to end the bandits' reign of terror. Many now called on Federal authorities to wage all-out war on banditry, and some volunteered their services; a few even set out on their own to bring the guilty to justice. Citizens of Weakley County, Tennessee, asked Governor Johnson for permission to organize and arm a company of men "to put down a class [of] Robbers thieves and marauders [who are] banded togeather and [are] going over the country night and day robbing stealing money and horses . . . [and] killing those who attempt to resist them." A Shelbyville citizen informed Johnson that a group of local men had recently gone in pursuit of a gang of highway robbers and had already captured one of them. "The Citizens are becoming aroused," he declared, "and feele a determination to put down bushwhackers & thieves."[33]

Thus began the last and perhaps fiercest of the conflicts that rocked the occupied South, as the forces of order (Rebel citizens and Yankee occupiers, strange allies indeed) set forth to wrest control of no-man's-land from the forces of chaos. In many districts the Federal authorities agreed to provide weapons to trustworthy local men for defense against bandits, and in some areas they authorized the citizens to form companies for patrol duty and neighborhood protection. Many of these companies did not rest content with defensive measures but on their own initiative hunted down the bandit gangs and destroyed them without mercy.[34]

Among the most successful were those organized late in the war in eight middle Tennessee counties. Armed with shotguns and squirrel rifles, and enlisting boys as young as fourteen, these "home-guard" companies (not to be confused with the Unionist home guards organized earlier to combat guerrillas) eagerly went after the bandits, killing or driving out many of them and recovering a good deal of stolen property. By April 1865 banditry was substantially curtailed throughout the region, and in three counties it was altogether eliminated. The people of the region, a Union officer reported, "now feel more freed from apprehension and terror of lawless men than at any time since the beginning of the war." Moreover, in their battle against rural anarchy these middle Tennessee home-guard companies went beyond the suppression of banditry: with the blessing of the occupation authorities, the older guardsmen established in each neighborhood informal courts of justice to which the citizens could appeal to resolve their problems.[35]

Northwestern Arkansas was the scene of the most comprehensive effort to restore order in the void of no-man's-land. There, where turmoil and violence had rendered many neighborhoods virtually uninhabitable and had driven rural people by the thousands into the garrisoned towns, Colonel M. La Rue Harrison of the Union army conceived a bold plan. Organizing the male citizens into home-guard companies seventy to one hundred strong and arming them, he sent them out into the countryside to establish what became known as "post colonies." Each company selected a defensible site with access to sufficient farmland. There the men constructed a stockade or blockhouse, and in it they stockpiled weapons, food, and agricultural supplies. Around this sturdy fort they built shelters for their families, who joined them at the site when all was ready. Each colony was a self-governing community, parceling out the surrounding acres to each family by democratic rules and resolving disputes under the laws of Arkansas. Some of the colonies even boasted a church and a school. By March 1865 sixteen such settlements of armed and vigilant farm families were in existence, sixteen little islands of community rising precariously above a sea of anarchy.[36]

Northwestern Arkansas and middle Tennessee were fortunate exceptions. In most other sections of no-man's-land the forces of chaos held the upper hand as long as the war continued. There, silent homesteads and empty churches and schools and courthouses stood like tombstones marking the resting place of communities awaiting the day of resurrection.

. . .

The travails of family and community in the occupied South dealt a staggering psychological blow. Enemy invasion, danger and disorder, enormous personal and material losses inevitably took an emotional toll. Confronted with swift and profound changes, many citizens felt as if they had been uprooted and cast into an eerily unfamiliar world, a world where the old routines and comforting certainties were absent. "[W]e can make no calculations on the future," a Mississippian wrote, "and need not be surprised at anything a day may bring forth. Truly we are an afflicted people."[37]

Farm folk felt disoriented, cut adrift, when agricultural disruption robbed them of the work that gave structure and purpose to their lives. "I stay at home now all the time," lamented a Louisiana sugar planter, "having very little or nothing to do, but to think over the past, and speculate on the future. . . . Existance is hardly tolerable." Those living at William King's plantation evinced a similar listlessness: "even the poor servants seem depressed in spirits at the disjointed state of affairs," King observed; "what an affliction idleness is."[38]

People in the garrisoned towns saw their familiar world disappear literally overnight. William King visited nearby Marietta the day after the Federal army arrived and found that "every thing looked changed, all strange faces, but few acquaintances to be found"; immediately he decided to return home, "feeling as I was entirely among strangers." The passage of time only confirmed such transformations: the editor of the *Alexandria Gazette* looked around his city after two years of occupation and remarked: "An old Alexandrian who has been absent . . . would be astonished at the changes which the lapse of only two years has brought about. He would see strange names on the signs, strange people on the streets, and feel as if he could hardly recognize the old town."[39]

Touched most deeply were the people of no-man's-land, isolated and afraid. "[H]ow desolate we feel here," sighed a North Carolinian, "so cut off." Colin Clarke in Virginia bemoaned "our helplessness, hopelessness,

& degradation, & what adds to our bitterness of despair, is the total suspension of all intercourse with our friends & relations." Harassed by Federal soldiers at her Georgia farmhouse, Minerva McClatchey wrote that "my feelings of loneliness helplessness & dread cannot be described. . . . [O]h it is so hard to be cut off from those I love and only see strange rough men and hear nothing but cursing swearing and abuse."[40]

Lost in a strange land, the people of the occupied South struggled to find their bearings. Some never succeeded but instead succumbed to what later generations would recognize as severe psychological depression, overwhelmed and incapacitated by the seeming bleakness of life or by an unshakable sense of impending doom. "I really believe I have been deranged or completely unbalanced in mind since under Federal rule," wrote a man who had abandoned his Tennessee home seeking to escape the miseries of occupation. "I could not sleep in Tennessee & it is no better now—startling dreams at night & absent mindedness & reveries by day consume my time. . . . I am at sea without rudder or compass." A Tennessee widow penned a pathetic plea to Andrew Johnson in December 1863: "Great God, Sir to think of the relations friends and propety I once had around me, and now this christmas day sitting here alone[,] no one even to whisper a kind word of consolation[.] I have lost what little mind I had and my little remaining strength is fast giving away. I see nothing before me but beggery and suffering." A few concluded that they could endure such agony no longer. "The feds took evrything Mr Tummons had," a Mississippian reported sadly in 1864, "[so] he cut his throat and killed himself[. He] has left a large family without anything."[41]

Many citizens, however, found a refuge in that strange and hostile land. One was Jesse Cox of Tennessee: "My dependance is entirely upon the Lord," he wrote in 1863, ". . . in this dark and trying hour." For Cox and others, Christian faith gave meaning and hope to a world that seemed devoid of both. "[S]uch distress of Mind I have to in dure here is far beyond any language to discribe," said Louisianan Isaac Erwin, who was plagued by plundering Yankees and unruly blacks. "I have at times been allmost attempted to comit suicide so great was I suffering but my whole trust was placed in a Kind and Mercifull God who alone sustains me in all my Trials." Those who could do so shared their comforting faith with others. Cushing Hassell, still devotedly riding his preaching circuit on the Confederate frontier in eastern North Carolina, met with the Skewarkey congregation in the war's last days and took as his text Hosea 13:9, in which the Lord speaks to His errant people: "O Israel, thou hast destroyed thyself, but in me is thine help."[42]

For those of little faith there was nothing left but hope in man. But the record of human behavior in the occupied South offered little assurance that man could contain the plagues of war that he had loosed. Absent divine intervention there would surely be no remission, but only increasing violence and chaos and suffering, until the war ceased. As their world continued to crumble around them, the people of the occupied regions began to reexamine their understanding of the conflict and to ask themselves if victory was worth the price.

[8]

No River of Fire

War-weariness and the
Collapse of Resistance

At his plantation in Maury County, Tennessee, elderly Nimrod Porter reflected often on the horrors of war and enemy occupation. Middle Tennessee fell early to the Union army, and for years Porter's community was ravaged by destruction and violence. "There is great trouble in the country," he wrote in his journal in the fall of 1864. The Yankees were "stealing horses mules hogs breaking open smoke house[s] stealing meat &c [being] verry insulting & imposing on every body incouraging negroes to steal & do every manner of rascality[.] [N]othing [is] safe no help for our unfortunate condition." In his anguish he imagined how the Northern juggernaut might be miraculously thwarted and the South preserved: "I wish there was a river of fire between the North & South," he said, "that would burn with unquentible fury for ever more & that it could never be passed, to the endless ages of eternity by any living creature."[1]

No river of fire ever materialized, however, and thus the mighty armies of the North continued their campaign to destroy the Rebel nation. As the war went on, Nimrod Porter and many others in the occupied regions pondered the future of their land and people with increasing despair.

. . .

Among the many factors that gradually sapped Confederate morale in the occupied South was the apparent endlessness of the war. Most Southerners had early on abandoned their expectation that the war would be a brief affair, a quick and decisive Rebel triumph, but few anticipated that it would grind on and on, two years, three years, and more, with no end in sight. Although the Confederate army's endurance was heartening to the Rebel citizens, many began to wonder if the military stalemate would ever be broken. Unending war was a dreadful prospect, especially to those in the occupied regions. "Great God when will this cruel war end," asked Tennessean John H. Bills in December 1862. "Is it not enough that a large [enemy] army has been with us now nearly seven months—the crops of the country & stock all gone—slaves demoralized & yet we see no apparent end. I confess myself worn out." Louisianan Isaac Erwin scoffed at the Pollyannas who had been predicting for the last three years that the war would soon be over. Now, he wrote, "all say and agree that this year 1864 will [be] sure to end the war without doubt but I fear it will last mutch longer[,] perhaps some 5 or 10 years." Months later, at year's end, the outlook was no brighter: "I am a broke Man," Erwin lamented, "and no end to the war."[2]

Not only was the war beginning to seem interminable, but it was also ripening into a catastrophe almost beyond reckoning, especially in the occupied regions. Even the gloomiest prophets of 1861 had not foreseen all the horrors that lay ahead. "What dreadful sufferings has been produced by this unnecessary war," declared Nimrod Porter in 1864, "no one living ever will be able to give a full picture of its consequences & distresses." Another Tennessean, Robert Cartmell, tried to put his experience into words but decided that "there is no use talking or writing" about it; moreover, he believed, "none to come hereafter can well appreciate [this war] as it exists. The historian will never do Justice to the subject."[3]

Scourged by an unimaginably destructive and seemingly endless conflict, the people of the occupied South prayed for peace. "Everybody I meet wherever I go," said a Union cavalryman in Tennessee in 1863, "wishe[s] fervently for the end of this war." In Tippah County, Mississippi, a scene of terrible devastation and disruption, the brethren of Academy Baptist Church gathered in November 1864 for the first time in two years. At the conclusion of services, as the church secretary recorded, the members of the congregation considered their plight and "agreed to observe the 16th inst. as a day of fasting and prayre to God that he may put a stop to this unholy war & bless our country once more with peace."[4]

All Americans, of course, Southerners and Northerners alike, earnestly desired an end to their bloody sectional war; the question was, on what terms would peace be restored? Die-hard Confederates were determined not to lay down their arms until they had won their independence, and they were prepared to make the sacrifices that war entailed. But how much sacrifice would ultimately be demanded of the people of the occupied regions? They would pay a dear price indeed for Confederate victory if their land was laid waste and they were reduced to paupers—which many believed would be the inevitable result of continued occupation. "I can see nothing but ruin," prophesied Alabamian Joshua Moore, "total ruin." Sarah Espy of Alabama saw a similarly bleak prospect: "I was never more depressed in my life for it seems that nothing but ruin is before us. . . . O! that we were in some retired place where there was no inducement for the foe to come."[5]

Many others in the occupied South echoed Espy's wish for a haven from the enemy. They gazed longingly toward the Confederate interior, whose inhabitants, though certainly not untouched by hardship, did not have to contend with Yankee invaders and the afflictions that came in their wake. As time passed, the conviction grew among many in the occupied regions that they had endured more than their share of suffering. Envy of those secure in the Confederate interior often turned into resentment. "Those people have not known what inconvenience is, much less loss & trouble, since this war began," fumed a Louisiana man in 1865. Virginian Colin Clarke sputtered with anger when he considered the unfairness of it all: "Good God what a contrast between us, & the people above Ric[hmon]d," he exclaimed. "*We* have lost negros, [and been] obliged to sell our stock, our crops [are] worth nothing even if we could save them & [we are] threatened with the utter loss of every thing. They have all their negros increased in value, fine crops, a high market for them, & [are living] in ease & safety."[6]

In growing numbers, people in the occupied regions reevaluated the costs and benefits of war and decided they must have peace whatever the price. Still plagued by marauding Federal soldiers four months after he pleaded for a sheltering river of fire, Nimrod Porter vowed that he would consent to "live in any kind of government that would stop our troubles. . . . O for a change Some way[.] I feel like agreeing to any thing to stop the war." In a letter to her husband in the Confederate army, a Louisianan confessed: "I want the war ended, if not in one way in another, I am weary and sick at heart. If I could see the end, in one year, or in two years, but year in, and year out, perhaps you may be ashamed of me, but I cannot help it." By late 1864 Robert Cartmell, too, was willing to compromise his secessionist principles: "I want peace on the best terms it can be had & any one living *now* & passing thro' what we have passed thro' would be in favour of the same."[7]

Even among those who were still prepared to bear the costs of victory there were growing doubts about the instrument they had forged to secure that victory. As the war went on, the Confederate government made greater demands on its people. Those in the occupied South who were subject to Confederate authority—that is, the inhabitants of the frontier districts—joined in a rising chorus of protest against conscription, impressment, and taxation that could be heard from one end of Rebeldom to the other. Some Confederate citizens eventually concluded that the entity they had created had become a monster, a tyrannical regime fully as dangerous to their liberties as the one they warred against. A Confederate government agent who visited northern Mississippi early in 1864 found "much demoralization"; certain citizens, he said, were "proclaiming [that] the Southern Confederacy . . . was nothing but a military despotism." Those who suffered most under Confederate rule, especially the plain folk, became in many cases thoroughly disaffected. A Confederate officer stationed in Plymouth, North Carolina, following its recapture after two years of Union occupation, was appalled by the apathy of the masses: "The ignorant classes here seem to think they have only changed masters instead of regaining their freedom."[8]

Resentment toward the Confederacy was especially intense where Rebel authorities tried to clamp down on trading with the enemy, which for some citizens on the frontier had become a matter of survival. A Mississippian told Confederate president Jefferson Davis late in 1863 that such trading was rife along the Mississippi River. In fact, he said, some of the farmers in those districts who earlier had fled their homes to avoid the Yankees had become so fed up with "the extortion and inhospitality" they encountered in the Confederate interior that they had returned to their farms intending to raise cotton to trade with Northerners. Many people in those areas, Davis's correspondent continued, "[now] have more fear of [Confederate authorities] than they have of the Yankees."[9]

Indeed, many in the occupied South began to recognize that the presence of the Union army was in certain ways a blessing; some were eventually moved to express thanks for favors the Federals bestowed. Those who struggled to survive amid the chaos of no-man's-land sometimes found themselves cheering the sight of blue uniforms. When an armed band of blacks began plundering St. Martin Parish, Louisiana, in 1863, the citizens appealed desperately to the commander of the nearest Federal forces and voiced immense relief and gratitude when troops arrived to protect them. "[The citizens] are very well disposed towards our men," an officer reported, "they seem to think they cannot do too much for them. . . . [They] are very desirous that this should be made a permanent Military Post."[10]

It was in the garrisoned towns, however, that the blessings of Union occupation were most appreciated. There, where the Federal army liberally doled out food and medical aid, provided jobs, and preserved order, virtually every citizen was directly or indirectly dependent on the occupiers for sustenance and safety. Under such circumstances even the most ardent Confederate patriot found it hard to dehumanize the enemy and maintain a posture of utter hostility; thus, over time, most townspeople relaxed their antagonism toward the Yankees. The occupiers responded in kind, and before long citizens and soldiers in most garrisoned towns had worked out a comfortable and often even congenial modus vivendi. "I believe the people [here] are getting more reconciled to Federal rule," wrote a soldier stationed in Athens, Alabama, in 1864. "They find themselves and their property protected, and our boys are getting very friendly with them." A Natchez woman recalled that "when the Federals first came I was disposed to think there was not a gentleman among them," but since that time, she admitted, "I have had kindness shown me and politeness most assuredly."[11]

In some towns, where the citizens and the garrison troops were especially well behaved and the commandant and provost marshal were obliging, real harmony prevailed. "We heard tonight the very unpleasant news that the 124th Ill[inois Infantry] are ordered to leave us, and go to New Orleans!," wrote Mahala Roach of Vicksburg in 1865. "I am really sorry, for while we have Federal troops here I would like to have these." In Athens, Alabama, and Edgefield, Tennessee, and a few other towns, citizens formally petitioned the Union army to keep garrison units they had grown to like.[12]

Thrust together in the garrisoned towns, citizens and occupiers inevitably found themselves mixing socially. Northern soldiers attended concerts, plays, and dances along with citizens and became frequent and often welcome visitors in local churches and fraternal lodges. Mahala Roach recorded that she went to church one Sunday and "found two soldiers in my pew, whom I kept there, and *drilled* in the service!" In Beaufort, North Carolina, army and navy officers helped purchase a new furnace for St. Paul's Episcopal Church; before the war ended an army chaplain was serving as rector, to the great satisfaction of soldiers and civilians alike. When Baton Rouge was captured in 1862, St. James Masonic Lodge was threatened with pillaging by Federal troops; however, as the lodge master reported, "Brethren of the [Masonic] order in the ranks of the army restrained those outside our mystic circle." Since then, he added, Yankee Masons had gathered regularly at the lodge: "brethren without regard to rank or position have put aside their weapons at the door and dwelt together in harmony."[13]

Many citizens in the garrisoned towns eventually established personal relationships with Union soldiers. Some families took in officers as boarders, and many others permitted soldiers to call at their homes. Such intimate contact usually broke down any lingering antagonism and often led to real friendships. "There are 3 or 4 officers boarding now with Mrs. Nicolay," wrote a woman in Pine Bluff, Arkansas; "[they are] very kind and obliging. I meet them often at dinner." In Vicksburg, Mahala Roach befriended a number of Union officers and their wives and received them warmly in her home. One of them called on her regularly and even loaned her money when she was in difficult straits: "he is a *gentleman*," she affirmed in her diary, "and has proved himself a *friend*." Once Southerners and Northerners began really talking to one another, they often found common ground. Late in 1862, for example, archsecessionist John

Waddel of LaGrange, Tennessee, reluctantly agreed to the request of two Union army surgeons for supper. But Waddel was pleasantly surprised as the evening went on and he and his guests chatted: "They seemed to be gentlemen," he admitted, "one of them especially, who was a Democrat, was by no means objectionable in his conversation. Both professed to be opposed to Lincoln's [emancipation] proclamation."[14]

As friendships bloomed in the garrisoned towns, so too did romance. Though many Union soldiers claimed to find Southern women disgusting—especially the ignorant, snuff-dipping poor white women they encountered—many others lost their hearts in Dixie. One stationed in Van Buren, Arkansas, was (in the words of a fellow officer) "nearly crazy after the women here." At the same time, the growing familiarity between soldiers and citizens in the towns encouraged Southern belles to take another look at the bestial Yankees, and some decided they liked what they saw after all. "Our officers are getting to be great favorites with the girls down here," remarked a soldier in Murfreesboro, Tennessee. "I am pretty sure many of the young ladies would be right glad to marry some of our gay and handsome looking officers and the *old Ladies* seem to be very willing for their daughters to get on good terms with our boys." In most garrisoned towns it became commonplace for soldiers to call on local girls, and more than a few serious courtships and even marriages ensued.[15]

The amity between citizens and soldiers in the garrisoned towns should not be exaggerated. Many citizens continued to resent or even hate the occupiers even as they maintained a cordial demeanor, and many refused to countenance any sort of socializing. Even the Natchez woman who complimented the garrison troops for their "kindness" and "politeness" was sickened by the idea of mixing with them: "The Yankees come to our church in crowds and are by degrees filling the pews up with their hateful blue coats," she wrote in her diary. "I cannot bear to be nearer than three or four pews. They are such dirty creatures." Moreover, she noted, "Some of the young ladies around Natchez are receiving attention from the Yankees. I think it shows *so* little character." Nevertheless, far more than the other citizens of the occupied South, those in the garrisoned towns saw, and acknowledged, the human face of the enemy.[16]

More damaging to Confederate morale than any other factor was the deteriorating military situation. Rebel patriots in the occupied South pinned their hopes on the Confederate armies. Their resistance to the invaders was predicated on the faith that those armies would ultimately drive back the enemy hosts, liberate the occupied regions, and confirm the South's independence. But as the months went by and relentless Union pressure ground down the Rebel forces, some lost faith. Though the gray-clad divisions dug in defiantly and made the enemy pay dearly for every advance, it appeared less and less likely that they would ever muster the offensive strength to recapture the occupied territories. Some citizens began to doubt even the defensive capability of the Confederate armies, suspecting that sooner or later they would be overwhelmed and the war lost.[17]

Military setbacks had disturbing implications beyond the merely strategic, for they raised questions about God's disposition toward the Confederate cause. Christian Southerners believed that God took a deep interest in their affairs and had a purpose and a plan for them; understanding and obeying His will were sacred obligations of the faithful. At the outbreak of the war and for a good while thereafter few doubted where He stood on the matter: "we *all* believe He is for us," a Mississippian wrote, "and having this faith how *can* we doubt [the ultimate success of the Confederacy] for an instant." Battlefield reverses and civilian hardships were, up to a point, almost always interpreted not as signs of divine disfavor toward the cause but as deserved chastisement for the moral failings of the Confederate people. "He has permitted this dreadful times to punish us for our sins," an Alabamian declared after a devastating Federal raid on her town. "Let us in humility acknowledge Him as our guide & all will be well." Reflecting on the South's situation in the summer of 1863, Cushing Hassell affirmed his continuing faith in a Confederate victory but warned that it would come "by the power of God & in his own way viz. the punishment and humiliation first of the people of the South. Then [will] follow such a deliverance as [will] clearly display the finger of God & cause the nation to give him glory."[18]

The defeats at Gettysburg and especially Vicksburg that summer, however, and further military setbacks and civilian suffering as the war went on, led many to wonder if the Lord truly intended that the Confederacy should prevail. "I sometimes think that He has forsaken us, or almost forgotten us," confessed Mississippian Roxa Cole after the sixtieth Yankee raid on her town, "we have suffered *so* much." By early 1865

Sarah Espy was racked with doubt: "all the news we hear now is bad," she said. "What is to become of us? God alone knows, and it seems he is shutting us up in the hand of the enemy."[19]

Bad news was pretty much the only news by that point, as far as the Rebel citizens of the occupied South were concerned. The last four months of 1864 brought a series of disappointments and calamities—the fall of Atlanta, Lincoln's reelection, Sherman's march to the sea, a failed Confederate offensive in Virginia, and an utterly disastrous campaign to recapture middle Tennessee—that deepened public pessimism. "I hope we may be able to rally yet," wrote Alabamian Mary Fielding at year's end, "but it is the 'dark day' with us now, certain[ly]. I am not naturally desponding and have always been confident of success because of the justness of our cause, but I beg[i]n to think the issue doubtful." More and more citizens decided that "the issue" was no longer even doubtful: "[W]e are whipped," a Savannah man told a Northern newspaper correspondent soon after the city fell in December, "and [we] have got to make the best of it."[20]

Such defeatism was, in fact, widespread in the garrisoned towns even before the disasters of late 1864. Confronted daily with evidence of the immense power of the Federal army, dependent on its beneficence, and mingling cordially with its officers and men, many citizens of those towns resigned themselves to Yankee rule even before the Confederate cause was clearly lost. By the latter part of the war, those townspeople who still prayed for Rebel victory were probably a minority. But the majority who abandoned the Rebel cause did not necessarily embrace the cause of their erstwhile enemies. "The *real* Union sentiment in this city, I fear, is small," observed a Northerner in Savannah in January 1865. "The people look upon the Confederate cause as lost, and therefore come forward and take the oath of allegiance . . . but they still retain their Southern sympathies and have no love for the Union."[21]

Meanwhile, however, Confederate morale persisted in no-man's-land and on the Confederate frontier—weakened though it was by war-weariness, by resentment toward the Rebel government and those who lived safely in the interior, by doubts about the Confederate armies and the will of God, and by the erosion of community. "[The] Rebels still talk of success," reported a Union army spy who scouted through the northern counties of Mississippi in the winter of 1864, "and [they] claim that they never can be conquered." Later that year an Arkansan who journeyed from his home in no-man's-land to the Federal post at Little Rock sneered at the defeatism he found in the town. "[Y]ou people inside the [picket] lines are subdued, or think you are," he told one townsman, "but we outside are not nor never will be."[22]

As the experience of war and occupation tested the citizens' commitment to the Rebel cause, so it tested their commitment to the institution of slavery. Many whites were profoundly shaken by the revelation that slaves hated slavery and resented their masters, for the belief that blacks were content in their bondage was a cornerstone of proslavery ideology. Whites' attempts to explain black defiance and self-emancipation within the confines of that ideology were eventually overwhelmed by reality—at least in the garrisoned towns and no-man's-land, where the bonds of slavery were broken and blacks were free to express their feelings in word and deed.

Disillusionment left some whites bewildered, others saddened, many bitter. Charlotte Wright of Virginia confessed that her slaves' disobedience and eventual departure "was severely felt—the treachery & breaking up of precious ties & old institutions appalled me." A Tennessean set forth the lesson she had learned from her own slaves' "disloyalty": "as to the idea of a *faithful servant, it is all a fiction.* I have seen the favourite & most petted negroes the first to leave in every instance." Colin Clarke watched his own and his neighbors' slaves run off one by one during 1862 and concluded that "sooner or later *every negro* will leave, or those who remain become so insolent as to force us to shoot them. . . . There is not *one negro* in *all the South*, who will remain faithfull *from attachment to their master & mistress*—not one." A year later, having "lost all faith in every negro," Clarke proclaimed his "utter, thorough, & deep disgust with the whole race."[23]

Slaveholders were further traumatized by the discovery that they needed their slaves far more than their slaves needed them. White paternalists had always insisted that slavery benefited blacks more than whites, for the infantile sons and daughters of Ham could surely not survive without nurturance and guidance from the master race. Emancipation confronted slaveowners with the fact of black self-sufficiency and, what was worse, the fact of their own dependency. Charlotte Wright admitted that what troubled her even more than her slaves' disloyalty was her realization that "my time of ease was over, & I must labour for my daily bread." A desperate Tennessean begged Andrew Johnson not to let army agents enlist his two slave men: "these servants of mine," he said, ". . . [are] *absolutely necessary* for my comfort and convenience—if taken away I do not know how I would supply their place—and I would be compelled to break up Housekeeping."[24]

Hurt, angered, and humiliated by their slaves' manifest desire and ability to get along without white direction, many slaveowners in turn repudiated their ungrateful charges. "Let them go," huffed Amanda Chappelear as the slaves on her Virginia plantation grew unruly and began running away, "yes the last one. . . . The very sight of one provokes me." Fellow Virginian Lucy Ambler likewise renounced her faithless servants: "May the Yankeys take every negro and do what they please with them," she prayed, "but may they take them all away." A Louisiana woman wryly announced the "delightful news" that twenty of her slaves had absconded: "Twenty less to feed! twenty less to clothe! & twenty less to bother ourselves about! Happy riddance! may I never again behold the light of their eyes and may more follow in their foot-steps!" Though often such gestures represented nothing more than the sour grapes rationalizing of slaveholders who had lost all control of their bondsmen and bondswomen, sometimes they signified something deeper: the ideological abandonment of slavery and paternalism.[25]

In time, virtually all slaveholders in the garrisoned towns and no-man's-land were forced to acknowledge that they could no longer command a master's due. Hope endured, however—at least among those who still clung to their proslavery ideology—that slavery might eventually be restored. But that hope rested on confidence in the Confederate armies and on certainty about God's endorsement of the Rebel cause; as that confidence and that certainty waned in the latter part of the war, so did hope for slavery's resurrection. "In my own opinion slavery has run its race in Tennessee," wrote a Pulaski man in 1864, "in no contingency is it likely to be revived or profitable, no use then in electioneering around negroes to stay with us."[26]

On the Confederate frontier, where white power and black deference persisted, it was easier for whites to maintain the delusion that slaves wanted and needed bondage, and thus proslavery ideology continued to reign unchallenged; masters there responded to black perfidy not with disillusionment and indignant rejection but with whip and chain. But whites on the frontier were not immune to doubts about the ultimate fate of the Confederacy and consequently of slavery. Nor were they invulnerable to the afflictions of war and occupation. As their hardships multiplied, they and all the other citizens of the occupied South had to confront the question of whether their war to preserve slavery was worth the cost. More than a few answered no. One was Eliza Sivley, of Mississippi, who despite several Federal raids still had all her slaves in 1864: "if it would close this war," she declared, "I would be willing to give them all up."[27]

As the calamitous autumn of 1864 gave way to the bleak winter of 1865, the people of the occupied South—those who had lost the will to resist as well as those who resisted still—turned anxious eyes toward the armies of blue and gray. Spring would usher in yet another season of war, and all prayed that it would be the last.

. . .

And indeed it was the last. No sooner did April arrive than the Union Army of the Potomac launched a great offensive in Virginia. The Confederate capital fell on April 3, and six days later Robert E. Lee surrendered the Army of Northern Virginia. Military resistance elsewhere in the Confederacy collapsed rapidly after that. By May 26 the remaining forces had all laid down their arms.

As news of the surrender of the armies spread, the Confederate frontier districts were gripped by confusion and uncertainty. "People are still ignorant of the terms of the surrender," wrote northern Mississippian Samuel Agnew on May 8. "What will be done with the negroes is still unknown. The negroes themselves evidently think they are free, but they may be too hasty in their conclusions." As late as May 20 Sarah Espy in northern Alabama knew "nothing definite yet about the surrender"; the rumor she heard was that "our Commissioners are still at Washington [negotiating] the terms of the peace."[28]

As the Rebel armies dissolved, civil officials of the Confederacy abandoned their posts and Confederate authority evaporated. State and local authority evaporated, too, as governors, legislators, magistrates, sheriffs, and other officers ceased their duties and awaited the enemy's arrival. Meanwhile, the Union army methodically extended its control, town by town, through the frontier districts and into the Confederate interior. It was slow work, and some of the more remote areas remained in limbo for weeks. Sarah Espy and her neighbors were still in a state of uncertainty in the latter part of June, waiting for Yankee troops to appear and assert Federal authority. "[T]here is no business doing in Centre [the county seat], at all," Espy wrote in her diary on June 21, "nor will [there be], I suppose[,] till the new regulations are set up."[29]

The anarchy in the frontier districts was aggravated by the presence of thousands of footloose Rebel soldiers. Some of these men had formally surrendered and been paroled, others had simply abandoned their units in the last chaotic days of the Confederacy; most were trying to get home, but many were just drifting. All were hungry. Some still had their weapons.[30]

Not surprisingly, many of the frontier districts were soon plagued with trouble. "[W]e . . . are left without law & order," citizens of Itawamba County, Mississippi, reported in June: "Crime is rife in our midst, we are helpless, without any protection either to life or property." In nearby Tippah County, as Samuel Agnew noted in mid-May, "robbing parties are getting bold. . . . Lawlessness seems to be the order of the day." No-man's-land also was deluged with vagabond or returning soldiers, thus compounding the anarchy and violence that had long reigned there.[31]

Freed now from the threat of Rebel military forces, the Union army was able to turn its full attention to restoring order in the countryside. Troops eventually went into every district to suppress hooliganism and banditry; in many areas they also helped organize and arm civilian police forces, which were authorized to arrest disorderly persons and turn them over to the army for trial. On May 24, for example, a Federal officer accompanied by a squad of soldiers arrived in Williamston, North Carolina, and consulted with local citizens, among them Cushing Hassell. On the twenty-ninth Hassell presided over a public meeting that appointed fifty policemen from among the citizens and designated three as officers. Within a few days the force was on duty and business in the community was rapidly returning to normal.[32]

The citizens of Williamston, like those everywhere else in the occupied South during that spring of 1865, cooperated readily with the Union army because they had lost all desire to carry on the struggle for independence. Their hopes had rested on the Confederate armies (or on God's blessing of those armies); surrender meant that the cause was lost, and few disputed the point. "Nothing could be more complete, more absolute, than the conviction of the people here that the 'C.S.A.' is utterly, hopelessly, 'gone up,' " wrote a Union officer in North Carolina on April 15, "and they acquiesce in it"; so much, he added, for "the nonsense about our being 'unable to hold the South after we conquer it.' " A Federal naval officer steamed up the Rappahannock River to Fredericksburg on April 12, just days after Rebel troops evacuated the town, and talked with the mayor and other citizens. All assured him "that the people generally considered that with the surrender of General Lee and his army the rebellion was virtually at an end, and that they were therefore ready to submit quietly."[33]

On every hand there appeared tangible evidence that the citizens had indeed given up the fight. Men and women by the thousands lined up at provost marshals' offices to take the oath of allegiance. One Mississippian was struck by the willingness of even the most rabid secessionists to rejoin the Union. "It is astonishing, & at the same time amusing," he said, "to see how meek & mild all these violent fellows now are"; furthermore, he noted wryly, "All those who were going to leave the country when the Yankees conquered are still here, and have no idea of going." Moreover, encouraged by a policy of amnesty announced by the army, many of the guerrillas who had held out to the last now gave themselves up and were paroled; the rest just quietly holstered their guns and went home.[34]

Where slavery had survived masters now relinquished their grip. Cushing Hassell called together his ten black laborers on May 16 and "told them they had by the military authorities of the United States been set free and they might therefore remain with [me] or go where they pleased"; within a week he and they had agreed on the terms of their employment. Though many whites still held fast to their proslavery beliefs, few denied the fact of emancipation. "I thought, and so expressed myself from the beginning, that the institution of slavery was staked upon the result of the war," a northern Mississippian declared. "We have played and lost, and I for one am willing to surrender the stake."[35]

Standing amid the rubble of their fallen Confederacy, the citizens reflected on the past, present, and future and bared their deepest feelings. Some, especially those in the most devastated regions, greeted the war's end with profound relief. "General Peace will soon be proclaimed through out our land," Isaac Erwin wrote on May 28, "thanks be to a mercifull and Kind Providence." Others spoke bitterly of their disappointment and their abiding hatred of the enemy. "God only knows the deep sorrow, misery & humiliation it has caused me to see my dear, dear country brought into subjection," said Amanda Worthington of Mississippi; "He knoweth too that the spirit is not subdued though the body is forced to yield, for the deep fire of hatred burns as fiercely in my bosom now as it ever did and I feel that I can never forgive [the enemy] the injuries they have done." Many grieved over the war's human and material cost. One was Nimrod Porter, who sadly beheld the "aking hearts" of those who, like himself, had suffered "the loss of there friends & there *All*. We will set down & mourn in Sack Cloathes & ashes for many days, weeks, months, & years to come."[36]

The future they confronted inspired little optimism. Many anticipated cruel vindictiveness from the Yankee conquerors and their Unionist allies, especially in the wake of Lincoln's assassination. Many were apprehensive, too, about the freed blacks: "what is to be done with them[?]," asked Joshua Moore, "—turn them all loose and a white man can't live amongst them. To some extent they must be controlled." All worried about rebuilding their livelihoods and putting food on their tables. "[O]ur sub-[si]stance [is] all gone," a northern Mississippian wrote. "There is much suffering now, & will be more this winter."[37]

Men and women of faith, however, spied a beacon of hope piercing the gloom. "God intends some good to us," affirmed Eliza Smith, of Virginia, as she contemplated the Confederacy's demise. "[N]ever murmur at any dispensation of His providence, . . . [for] 'He does all things well.'" As the apocalyptic spring of 1865 drew to a close, the faithful resigned themselves to His will and searched for signs of His benevolent purpose. Others fixed their gaze on their enemies and friends and prepared to face the new dispensation that man had wrought.[38]

. . . .

Epilogue *Summer 1865*

. . . .

The Southern landscape was verdant by early summer, but the lush foliage could not conceal the raw wounds of war. How long those wounds would take to heal was anyone's guess. Writing from his tidewater Virginia plantation in June, Hill Carter predicted that the fencing destroyed by the armies would take years to replace. In the meantime what cattle and sheep and hogs were left were roaming unrestrained, rendering futile any effort to raise a crop. Unless owners of livestock were required to corral their animals, said Carter, "thousands of acres will be left uncultivated for many years, & our country will become a wilderness."[1]

Nor was that the only baneful legacy of war plaguing the tidewater region as summer began. "There are thousands of dogs all about the country," Carter continued, "which followed the armies to eat up the refuse meat & bread, & they have become wild in some neighbourhoods, & are killing hogs & sheep in every direction." His own flock of fine Southdown sheep, reduced from 120 to 15 by the voracious armies, was now being further ravaged by dogs, though he kept the sheep penned. "The negroes too," he added, "over whom we have no control now, all keep dogs, though they have not bread for their families, and we are overrun with dogs." Carter wanted the authorities to take rigorous measures: "a very heavy tax upon all dogs, & a reward for the killing of every wild dog, & every dog found off his master's premises. . . . The dogs ought to be exterminated."

At summer's end Northerner J. T. Trowbridge visited another part of the Old Dominion, the hard-hit region on the south side of the Rappahannock River. His account, published later, revealed how little the passage of one season had done to repair the damage inflicted by years of war and occupation. In Fredericksburg he found that "scarcely a house in the burnt portions [of the town] had been rebuilt. Many houses were entirely destroyed, and only the solitary chimney-stacks remained. Of others, you saw no vestige but broken brick walls, and foundations overgrown."[2]

Traveling from the town into the countryside, Trowbridge toured the Chancellorsville and Spotsylvania battlefields and saw how desperately the inhabitants were trying to wring a living from the blighted land. At one point he observed a woman and two girls with a pail rummaging through the woods near some abandoned breastworks; at first he thought they were gathering nuts but then realized that they were hunting minié balls to sell for scrap. Elsewhere he noticed shallow pits where, he was told, scavengers had dug up the bones of army horses killed in battle. These they hauled to Fredericksburg to sell to a chemical factory. Trowbridge wondered how many human bones might have been trundled off to the factory as well.

At Spotsylvania Courthouse Trowbridge spoke with the court clerk, who pointed out the destruction of county records by Northern troops and described conditions in the surrounding district. "The county had not one third the number of horses, nor one tenth the amount of stock, it had before the war," Trowbridge learned. "Many families were utterly destitute. They had nothing whatever to live upon until the corn-harvest; and many would have nothing then."

On the other hand, there was much to celebrate that summer in Virginia and everywhere else in the occupied South. With the disbanding of Union field armies, the reduction of garrison forces, the suppression of banditry, and the return of refugees, dormant rural communities sprang back to life. The country roads were soon alive with traffic, as in the old days, and country churches were once again filled with the faithful on Sundays. Business in town and countryside began to revive, too, as the roads became safe to travel and the army relaxed trade restrictions. In Nimrod Porter's community outside Columbia, Tennessee, which had been one of the most anarchic and violence-ridden sections of no-man's-land, things were already returning to normal by June; when the circus came to town that month, many of Porter's neighbors went to see the show. The chaotic northern Alabama countryside likewise saw order restored that summer: Mary Fielding of Athens took a job teaching in Pettusville, a small village some distance from the town. It paid little, she wrote, but "'tis better than doing nothing." Not only had the people of the Pettusville community revived their school, Fielding noted, but they also gathered in August for a camp meeting.[3]

Local government also was restored throughout the occupied regions that summer. The army relinquished control of civil affairs as town and county governments were reorganized under the loyal state governments recognized by Lincoln and the provisional governors appointed by his successor, Andrew Johnson. The political situation was confused, however, and in many cases state authorities had to take unusual steps to get local governments revived in a hurry. Alabama provisional governor Lewis Parsons, for one, ordered on July 20 that until a new state constitution was adopted and elections held, those local officials in office before the Yankees came would simply resume their positions as long as they were willing to take the prescribed oath. Across the state, citizens responded promptly to Parson's proclamation. In the northern Alabama town of Florence, which had been held by Federal forces on and off for years, the town's last elected mayor and aldermen convened, took the oath, and on August 5 notified the governor that they stood ready to take up their duties. "Our Section is very quiet," the mayor added in his message to the governor, "you would be astonished at the improvement in our town in so short a time—we have a large trade here and as many or more inhabitants than we ever had."[4]

Many other observers remarked how quiet the occupied regions now seemed. With the surrender of the guerrillas and the eradication of the bandit gangs, the bloody violence in the countryside quickly ebbed. Indeed, of the five great conflicts that had convulsed the occupied South, it was clear that two had been wholly resolved: the Federal government had stamped out all resistance to its authority, and the forces of order had put to rout the forces of disorder in no-man's-land. But as the summer wore on, it became obvious that the other conflicts—those of politics, race, and class—were not at all resolved but were merely entering a new phase.

Unionists had cheered the Confederacy's demise in the spring, and, putting aside now their misgivings about the Federal occupiers, they looked forward confidently to leading their states back into the Union. But they had not reckoned on the lenient reconstruction policy President Johnson pursued once in office. Johnson's program of amnesty and pardon restored full civil and political rights to almost all former secessionists and allowed them to take part in the reorganization of state and local governments. Unionists were aghast. "I most respectfully beg to know," a Virginian wrote Governor Pierpont in July, "if loyal men who have suffered all manner of persecution . . . are to be ruled by the same men who inflicted these persecutions. . . . Is this the reward of loyalty—was it for this I remained faithful to my country,—was mobbed and cruelly beaten[?]" An army officer in eastern North Carolina observed that the Unionists there "have suffered from their treatment [by secessionists] to an extent beyond reconcilliation and . . . they prefer another war to submitting to the authority of such men."[5]

Unionists, in fact, feared for their safety. A Northern newspaper correspondent who visited Norfolk in July talked with a Unionist there who was worried about the volatile combination of returned Confederate soldiers and "low drinking saloons," both of which were plentiful in the city: "what these men wouldn't do sober they will do when they're drunk," he explained, ". . . and I tell you, sir, Norfolk isn't a very safe place for a Union man unless he's a very mild sort of a Union man. . . . I wouldn't think of walking two blocks at night without my revolver." Many were convinced that the withdrawal of Federal military forces would leave them at the mercy of vengeful ex-Rebels. "You can not comprehend our condition up here," a northern Alabama man told Governor Parsons in early September, ". . . we are now threatened by the secessionists when the soldiers leave. The fire is not all out. The secessionists . . . are just as hostile in feeling as ever, and we do not intend if it can be prevented for the soldiers to be removed, we are in a bad fix."[6]

A good number of Unionists decided that they would not just sit fearfully at home awaiting the onslaught of the resurgent Rebels. They prepared to fight back; some even took the offensive. From Van Buren County, Arkansas, there came a report in June that bands of Unionists were harassing paroled Confederate soldiers; the victims pleaded with the local Federal commandant to disarm these "marauders." In northern

Alabama the same month a gang of Unionists went on a rampage: convinced that even with law and order restored they would never obtain legal redress for the wrongs they had suffered at the hands of secessionists during the war, they shot two of their persecutors to death and burned down a mill belonging to two others in an attempt to drive them out of the neighborhood.[7]

Unionists were not the only inhabitants of the occupied South who were uneasy that summer. Black men and women also eyed the season's developments with growing apprehension. Many Southern whites, encouraged by President Johnson's leniency, made no secret of their determination to consign the freedmen to a fate as close as possible to slavery. On August 1, for instance, the commissioners of East Baton Rouge Parish, Louisiana, revived the antebellum slave patrol system in toto: they appointed patrol captains, authorized them to call up every citizen liable to duty, and ordered them to disarm all blacks and arrest any found off their employer's plantation without a pass. Whites justified such restrictive regulations with old, familiar arguments. "[Blacks] must be controlled in some way or white people cannot live amongst them," explained Alabamian Joshua Moore. "[T]hose who know the negro . . . know that these measures are absolutely necessary for the security in person and property of the whites."[8]

Many whites, moreover, intended to resume their old ways of managing black laborers. An army officer in Louisiana reported that one plantation overseer, a returned Rebel soldier, had on several occasions pulled out a revolver and threatened to shoot his black workers for refusing to obey him; he had also stripped and whipped eight female employees who had incurred his wrath. When called to account, the overseer insisted "that he had a right to do so." Southern whites put on notice the freedmen's few white friends, including sympathetic army officers, Northern humanitarians, and agents of the newly established Federal Freedmen's Bureau. The commissioners of West Baton Rouge Parish, Louisiana, warned in August that "any attempt on the part of emissaries, and missionaries, of whatever political or religious faith to create dissatisfaction and discontent among the colored population . . . will meet . . . the disapproval of this body, . . . [and] all honorable means will be employed to put down such influences and prevent the evil results which would necessarily follow."[9]

At the same time, the freedmen's friends made clear their own determination (as did the freedmen themselves). "[T]he U.S. is in *earnest* in regard to the freedom of the negro," declared an army general in Nashville after reviewing the case of a planter charged with abusing blacks. "To those citizens of Tennessee who are unwilling to recognize the freedom of the negroes, but oppress and brutally punish them with the lash, let me say that they may yet find the lash to be a two edged sword." But many Southern whites ignored such threats. Among them was a recently elected constable in King and Queen County, Virginia, who openly announced that he had "fixed himself to whip every negro who crosses his path, and he intends to make them see Hell."[10]

Before the summer was out it had become apparent that the forces of reaction were resolved to put an end to the other jubilee as well, that of the liberated poor whites. In East Baton Rouge Parish, the newly appointed patrol captains were ordered not only to keep the freedmen in line but also "to arrest all suspicious persons & vagrants, & all persons who have no visible means of support, or who follow no regular ostensible, honest occupation for a living." In Virginia, J. T. Trowbridge listened as the Spotsylvania County court clerk denounced the "shiftless whites" who were being provisioned by the Union army. "[They are] steeped in vice, ignorance, and crime of every description," the clerk asserted, and he urged that the army stop feeding them and let local authorities take charge of them. Furthermore, in those parts of the occupied South where poor whites had seized abandoned lands, the owners—now returned and armed with their amnesty rights—set about to reclaim their property.[11]

There were others, however, who were resolved to bring forth a more egalitarian society in the South. One was the editor of the *Fort Smith New Era*, a radical who carried on the campaign to transform Dixie after the cannons fell silent. In June he warned Southern aristocrats that the triumphant North would make sure that their days as the "exclusive leaders of [Southern] society" were over. You have forfeited your power, he told them, over "the class whom you so disdainfully stigmatize as the 'poor white trash' "; the poor have "forsaken you, and they will be your masters."[12]

If the poor whites themselves had no such revolutionary aims, many did still hope that a better world would rise from the ruins of the Confederacy. Among them was a Virginian named Elijah, whom J. T. Trowbridge hired to guide him around the battlefields. Elijah confessed that he was "right ignorant; can't read the fust letter; never went to school a day"; but he knew enough, he told Trowbridge, to see that "it's the rich that keep this country down. The way it generally is, a few own too much, and the rest own noth'n'." The war's outcome seemed to Elijah to herald a new era: "I reckon thar's go'n' to be a better chance for the poo' man after this. The Union bein' held together was the greatest thing that could have happened for us."[13]

And so the lines were drawn for the struggles of the Reconstruction era. At stake was nothing less than the fate of the South. The central question was this: would the South of the future be merely the Old South redivivus, or would it be a New South, born in the liberating chaos of war and occupation?

Map Appendix

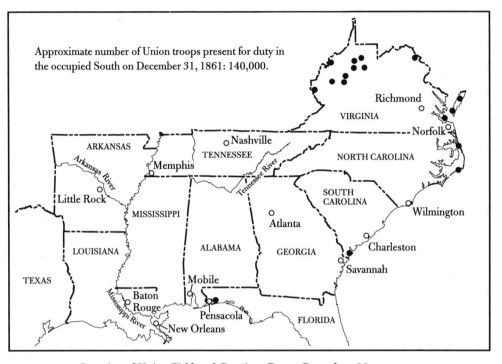

Approximate number of Union troops present for duty in the occupied South on December 31, 1861: 140,000.

Richmond
VIRGINIA
Norfolk
ARKANSAS
Nashville
TENNESSEE
NORTH CAROLINA
Memphis
Tennessee River
Little Rock
Arkansas River
SOUTH CAROLINA
MISSISSIPPI
Atlanta
Wilmington
LOUISIANA
ALABAMA
GEORGIA
Charleston
TEXAS
Mobile
Savannah
Baton Rouge
Pensacola
Mississippi River
New Orleans
FLORIDA

MAP 1. *Location of Union Field and Garrison Forces, December 1861*

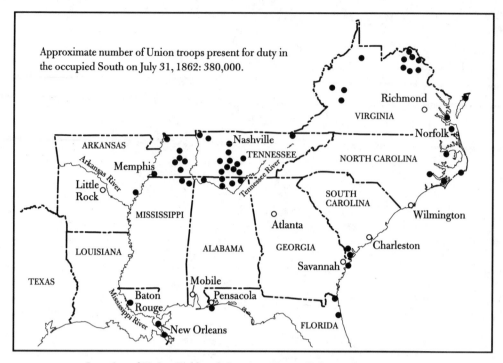

Approximate number of Union troops present for duty in
the occupied South on July 31, 1862: 380,000.

ARKANSAS

Arkansas River

Memphis

Little
Rock

MISSISSIPPI

LOUISIANA

TEXAS

Mississippi River

Baton
Rouge

New Orleans

Nashville

TENNESSEE

Tennessee River

ALABAMA

Mobile

Pensacola

Atlanta

GEORGIA

Savannah

FLORIDA

Richmond

VIRGINIA

NORTH CAROLINA

SOUTH
CAROLINA

Wilmington

Charleston

Norfolk

MAP 2. *Location of Union Field and Garrison Forces, July 1862*

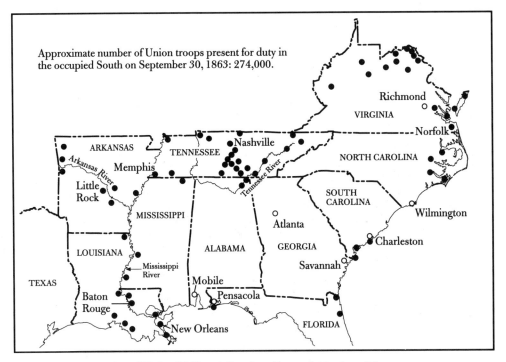

Approximate number of Union troops present for duty in the occupied South on September 30, 1863: 274,000.

MAP 3. *Location of Union Field and Garrison Forces, September 1863*

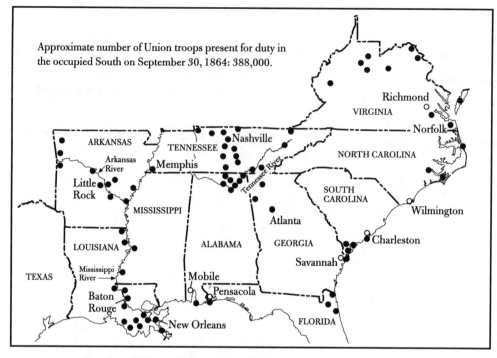

Approximate number of Union troops present for duty in
the occupied South on September 30, 1864: 388,000.

MAP 4. *Location of Union Field and Garrison Forces, September 1864*

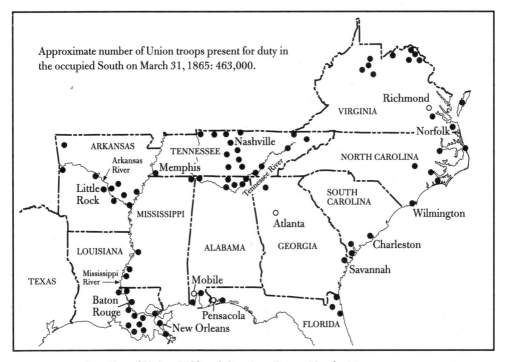

Approximate number of Union troops present for duty in
the occupied South on March 31, 1865: 463,000.

MAP 5. *Location of Union Field and Garrison Forces, March 1865*

Notes

ABBREVIATIONS

ADAH   Alabama Department of Archives and History, Montgomery
AHC   Arkansas History Commission, Little Rock
Duke   William R. Perkins Library, Duke University, Durham
GDAH   Georgia Department of Archives and History, Atlanta
LC   Library of Congress, Washington
LSA   Louisiana State Archives, Baton Rouge
LSU   Hill Memorial Library, Louisiana State University, Baton Rouge
MDAH   Mississippi Department of Archives and History, Jackson
NA   National Archives, Washington
NCDAH   North Carolina Division of Archives and History, Raleigh
OR   U.S. War Department, *The War of the Rebellion: A Compilation of the Official Records of the Union and Confederate Armies. OR* citations take the following form: volume number (part number, where applicable): page number(s). Unless otherwise indicated, all citations are to series 1.
OR Navy U.S. War Department, *Official Records of the Union and Confederate Navies in the War of the Rebellion*
ROJAG   Court Martial Files, Records of the Office of Judge Advocate General, RG 153, National Archives
RUSACC   Records of U.S. Army Continental Commands, RG 393, National Archives
SHC   Southern Historical Collection, University of North Carolina, Chapel Hill
TSLA   Tennessee State Library and Archives, Nashville
UTK   Special Collections, University of Tennessee, Knoxville
VHS   Virginia Historical Society, Richmond
VSL   Virginia State Library, Richmond

PROLOGUE

1. Durham, *Rebellion Revisited*, 16.

2. On racial subordination as the key to Southern distinctiveness see Ulrich B. Phillips, "Central Theme of Southern History." The role of plantation slavery and planter hegemony in retarding the South's economic development is discussed in Genovese, *Political Economy of Slavery*, and Luraghi, "The Civil War and the Modernization of

American Society." Further evidence of aristocratic economic and political hegemony is in Shugg, *Class Struggle in Louisiana*, 95–156; Campbell and Lowe, *Wealth and Power in Antebellum Texas*; Wayne, *Reshaping of Plantation Society*, 1–28; and Escott, *Many Excellent People*, 3–31.

3. On political democratization see Green, "Democracy in the Old South," and Wooster, *People in Power* and *Politicians, Planters, and Plain Folk*. Certain aspects of the South's premodern ideology are analyzed in Genovese, *Political Economy of Slavery*, and Wyatt-Brown, *Southern Honor*.

4. Studies that portray Southern aristocrats as a self-conscious, paternalist elite include Genovese, *Political Economy of Slavery*, and Williamson, *Crucible of Race*, 24–29.

5. Stampp, *Peculiar Institution*, 86–140; Genovese, *Roll, Jordan, Roll*; Levine, *Black Culture*, chap. 1.

6. Bailey, *Class and Tennessee's Confederate Generation*, 59–63, 69–73; Cecil-Fronsman, *Common Whites*, 31–66.

7. Genovese, "Yeomen Farmers in a Slaveholders' Democracy"; Ash, *Middle Tennessee Society Transformed*, 50–51.

8. On racism as a binding force between white classes see Ulrich B. Phillips, "Central Theme of Southern History"; Cash, *Mind of the South*, 68–69, 86–87; Frederickson, *Black Image in the White Mind*; Collins, *White Society in the Antebellum South*, 6–7, 51–66; and Cecil-Fronsman, *Common Whites*, 18–30, 67–82. On republicanism see Thornton, *Politics and Power in a Slave Society*, xviii–xix and passim; Hahn, *Roots of Southern Populism*, 50, 107; J. William Harris, *Plain Folk and Gentry*, 15–22; and Ford, *Origins of Southern Radicalism*, 50–51.

9. Owsley, *Plain Folk of the Old South*, 133–38; Cash, *Mind of the South*, 49–50; Collins, *White Society in the Antebellum South*, 6, 38–40.

10. Potter, *The South and the Sectional Conflict*, 15–16; Thomas, *Confederate Nation*, 9–10; J. William Harris, *Plain Folk and Gentry*, 94–104; Bailey, *Class and Tennessee's Confederate Generation*, 63–64; Collins, *White Society in the Antebellum South*, 8–9, 142–59; Kenzer, *Kinship and Neighborhood*, 6–51; Burton, *In My Father's House*, 57–60.

11. On the contingent nature of yeoman loyalty see Escott, *After Secession*, 99–104.

12. McIlwaine, *Southern Poor-White*, xvii–xxiv; Flynt, *Dixie's Forgotten People*, 1–32; Ash, "Poor Whites in the Occupied South," 41–42. For a contemporary view of the "poor-white trash" through the eyes of a "respectable" Southerner see Hundley, *Social Relations*, 250–83.

13. Buck, "Poor Whites of the Ante-bellum South," 42–48.

14. On the economic status of poor whites see Bolton, *Poor Whites of the Antebellum South*. Class resentment on the part of poor whites is documented in Bailey, *Class and Tennessee's Confederate Generation*, 24–26, 38, 56, 69–70, 72.

15. Fox-Genovese, *Within the Plantation Household*, especially 78–82; Rable, *Civil Wars*, 15–17, 31–37; Friedman, *Enclosed Garden*, xi–xvi.

16. On women's legal and economic inequality and the social pressures pushing women toward domesticity see Fox-Genovese, *Within the Plantation Household*, 193–

98, 202–6; Rable, *Civil Wars*, 8–12, 22–29; Clinton, *Plantation Mistress*; and Lebsock, *Free Women of Petersburg*.

17. Affectionate family relations are documented in Censer, *North Carolina Planters and Their Children*, 20–41. On the idealization of Southern womanhood see Scott, *Southern Lady*.

18. Thornton, *Politics and Power in a Slave Society*, xix–xx and passim; Ford, *Origins of Southern Radicalism*, 336 and passim; Oakes, *Slavery and Freedom*, 111–13, 118–23.

19. William R. Taylor, *Cavalier and Yankee*, 15 and passim; Cash, *Mind of the South*, 61–67; Franklin, *Southern Odyssey*, xv, 203–5, 258–59; Michael C. C. Adams, *Our Masters the Rebels*, 5–10.

20. Eaton, *Waning of the Old South Civilization*, 37–38, 75, 80; Jenkins, *Pro-Slavery Thought in the Old South*, 197, 296–300; McCardell, *Idea of a Southern Nation*, 172–74; J. William Harris, *Plain Folk and Gentry*, 130–31.

21. Roark, *Masters Without Slaves*, 21–22, 64–65; Escott, *After Secession*, 28–33; Michael P. Johnson, *Toward a Patriarchal Republic*, xx, 85–94; J. William Harris, *Plain Folk and Gentry*, 65–93.

22. Channing, *Crisis of Fear*, 38–40, 264–73; Mohr, *On the Threshold of Freedom*, 3–50.

23. On the masters' paternalism toward, and trust in, their slaves see Genovese, *Roll, Jordan, Roll*, 1–7, 97–98, and Jimerson, *Private Civil War*, 51–58.

24. The delayed secession of the Upper South is explained in Crofts, *Reluctant Confederates*.

25. Confederate mobilization and public enthusiasm are described in Ringold, *Role of the State Legislatures*, 13–20; Yearns, *Confederate Governors*; Winters, *Civil War in Louisiana*, 21–34; Barrett, *Civil War in North Carolina*, 17–29; and Dougan, *Confederate Arkansas*, 69–72.

26. Studies asserting or implying that white classes in the seceding states were, because of a shared perspective, more or less united in the secession crisis include Genovese, *Political Economy of Slavery*; Channing, *Crisis of Fear*; Greenberg, *Masters and Statesmen*; J. William Harris, *Plain Folk and Gentry*; and Ford, *Origins of Southern Radicalism*. Evidence of the radicalization of conservatives following Lincoln's call for troops is in Crofts, *Reluctant Confederates*, 308–52, and Dougan, *Confederate Arkansas*, 59–67.

27. Crofts, *Reluctant Confederates*, 345–47, 350–51; Marten, *Texas Divided*, 53–64; Klingberg, *Southern Claims Commission*, 10, 14; Tatum, *Disloyalty in the Confederacy*, 24–25, 36–37; Patton, *Unionism and Reconstruction in Tennessee*, 60–65; Bettersworth, *Confederate Mississippi*, 252–54.

28. Ringold, *Role of the State Legislatures*, 13, 57–59, 67–68; Litwack, *Been in the Storm So Long*, 27–30; Mohr, *On the Threshold of Freedom*, 50–55; Wiley, *Plain People of the Confederacy*, 92–93; Eaton, *History of the Southern Confederacy*, 244–45; Robinson, "In the Shadow of Old John Brown"; Ripley, *Slaves and Freedmen in Civil War Louisiana*, 8–9.

29. Dumond, *Southern Editorials on Secession*, 505–6; see also 509–11, 512.

30. Roark, *Masters Without Slaves*, 15, 26–27, 64–65, 75–76; Jimerson, *Private Civil War*, 22–25, 34, 126–29; Royster, *Destructive War*, 180–81; Dumond, *Southern Editorials on Secession*, 508.

CHAPTER ONE

1. *OR* 51(2):66–67, 58–59.

2. Ibid., 278–79, 322–23.

3. Ibid., 279; Susan Gouldin to John Letcher, February 8, 1862, Virginia Executive Papers, VSL; *OR* 2:915–16, 51(2):330, 5:994.

4. Bragg, *Louisiana in the Confederacy*, 101–2; Winters, *Civil War in Louisiana*, 71, 77, 79–80, 82.

5. Messner, "Black Violence and White Response," 20; Perquimans County Court Minutes, November 1861 (microfilm), NCDAH; Thomas McCandlish to John Letcher, April 27, 1862, and James Evans to William Smith, December 14, 1864, Virginia Executive Papers, VSL; Mohr, *On the Threshold of Freedom*, 99–100; Wish, "Slave Disloyalty under the Confederacy," 442; *OR* 11(3):561–62; William Watson Davis, *Civil War and Reconstruction in Florida*, 164–65.

6. Winters, *Civil War in Louisiana*, 57–59, 71–74; William Johnston et al. to John Pettus, April 28, 1862, R. Brown to Pettus, May 8, 1862, R. Watson and Lawrence Johnson to Pettus, May 20, 1862, and J. Clapp to Pettus, June 2, 1862, all in Pettus Correspondence, MDAH; John Ransom case, LL1996, ROJAG.

7. *OR* 2:907.

8. "Diary of John Berkley Grimball," 158; Power Diary, April 26, 1862 (typescript), SHC; Sperry Diary, March 7, 1862 (typescript), VSL.

9. Porter Journal, February 16–17, 1862 (MS), SHC. See also Overton Diary, February 8–17, 1862 (MS), MDAH.

10. Hoobler, "Civil War Diary," 313–17; Durham, *Nashville*, 6–13, 23–24, 29, 31–32, 37.

11. Lang, "Gloom Envelops New Orleans," 283–84; Capers, *Occupied City*, 44–45; Winters, *Civil War in Louisiana*, 96–97.

12. Lang, "Gloom Envelops New Orleans," 284–87; Porter Journal, March 20, 1862, SHC; Leak Books, June 5, 30, 1862 (MS), SHC; *OR Navy* 6:607–8, 7:110–12, 379–82; Winters, *Civil War in Louisiana*, 103; Bragg, *Louisiana in the Confederacy*, 126; Durham, *Nashville*, 30, 33–34; Maury Diary, April 18, 1862 (microfilm), LC; William Watson Davis, *Civil War and Reconstruction in Florida*, 157, 167–68; Graf, Haskins, and Bergeron, *Papers of Andrew Johnson*, 5:168; Hoobler, "Civil War Diary," 313, 315, 317.

13. Massey, *Refugee Life*, 12–14; *Diary of a Southern Refugee*, 13–20; Durham, *Nashville*, 17–18, 29; *OR* 6:22–23; Porter Journal, February 20, 1862, SHC.

14. Sallie Dillard to Priscilla Bailey, March 26, 1863, Bailey Papers, SHC; *OR Navy* 5:37; Graf, Haskins, and Bergeron, *Papers of Andrew Johnson*, 5:573; H. Titcomb to

George Gordon, March 2, 1862, Gordon and Avery Papers, TSLA; Durham, *Nashville*, 9–11, 17–18, 27–29, 38; Massey, *Refugee Life*, 15–16, 28; Porter Journal, February 20, 1862, SHC.

15. Massey, *Refugee Life*, 28–29; James Melvin to Audley Britton, November 20, 1862, Britton and Family Papers, LSU; Crabtree and Patton, *"Journal of a Secesh Lady,"* 115.

16. Journal of unknown man, August 17, 1862, Pettigrew Family Papers, SHC; Colin Clarke to Maxwell Clarke, September 14, 1862, Clarke Papers, SHC; Jay Clay to Clement Clay, March 30, 1862, Clay Papers, Duke; Massey, *Refugee Life*, 23–27.

17. H. Titcomb to George Gordon, March 2, 1862, Gordon and Avery Papers, TSLA; Durham, *Nashville*, 29–30; East Baton Rouge Parish Police Jury Minutes, May 23, 26, 1862 (MS), LSU.

18. William Loftin to Ann Bryan, March 18, 1862, Loftin Papers, Duke; Jay Clay to Clement Clay, March 30, 1862, Clay Papers, Duke; *OR* 6:94–95; Durham, *Nashville*, 11–12, 18–20; Massey, *Refugee Life*, 15–16, 27; Favill, *Diary of a Young Officer*, 72.

19. For reports of towns and communities mostly or entirely depopulated see J. Drake to father, June 25, 1861, Federal Soldiers' Letters, SHC; *OR Navy* 12:337; R. Creecy to Bettie Creecy, February 13, 19, 1862, Creecy Family Papers, SHC; S. Marrett to wife, March 1, 1862, Marrett Papers, Duke; and William Watson Davis, *Civil War and Reconstruction in Florida*, 163. On the flight of some refugees to nearby areas, and their eventual return home, see *OR Navy* 12:608; Durham, *Nashville*, 17, 20, 26; and Massey, *Refugee Life*, 16, 264, 266. One source (Rable, *Civil Wars*, 183) gives the number of Southern refugees during the war as "at least a quarter-million," but this presumably includes many from the border states and many who left their homes, or were expelled, after Federal occupation began.

20. *OR Navy* 12:596; Durham, *Nashville*, 20.

21. *OR Navy* 12:273; *OR* 6:6, 35(2):352.

22. J. Clay to Clement Clay, March 30, 1862, Clay Papers, Duke; French Diary, March 2, 1862 (MS), TSLA; M. Lovell to G. Randolph, June 19, 1862, Records of the Louisiana State Government, LSA.

23. A. Heise to James Bowman, July 5, 1862, Bowman Family Papers, LSU; Moore Diary, April 19, 1862 (MS), ADAH.

24. French Diary, March 2, 1862, TSLA; *OR Navy* 12:600–601; R. Creecy to Bettie Creecy, February 8, 1862, Creecy Family Papers, SHC; M. Lovell to G. Randolph, June 19, 1862, Records of the Louisiana State Government, LSA.

25. Maury Diary, April 25, 1862, LC; Pasquotank County Court Minutes, February 9, 1862 (microfilm), NCDAH; St. Charles Parish Police Jury Minutes, May 19, 1862 (typescript), LSU.

26. Southall Diary (MS), February 19, 1862, Southall and Bowen Papers, SHC; Martin, "Defeat in Victory," 13–17; Johns, *Florida during the Civil War*, 65–66.

27. *OR* 7:427–29; Durham, *Nashville*, 37–38; Hoobler, "Civil War Diary," 316–19; Lang, "Gloom Envelops New Orleans," 286–87; *New Orleans Daily Picayune*, April 30, May 1, 1862.

28. Hoobler, "Civil War Diary," 319; Maury Diary, April 20, 1862, LC.

29. Bond Papers and Diary, May 12, 1862 (MS), LSU; Charles Nathan to Loulou, May 1, 1862, Wharton Family Papers, LSU; Erwin Diary, June 17, 1862 (MS), LSU; Cox Diary, February 25, 1862 (microfilm), TSLA.

30. Taylor, *Cavalier and Yankee*, 15; Freidel, *Union Pamphlets*, 1:160; Foner, *Free Soil*, 40, 46–51, 64–73; David Brion Davis, *Slave Power Conspiracy*; Hess, *Liberty, Virtue, and Progress*, 18–19; Dunham, *Attitude of the Northern Clergy*, 81–83, 89–91; Perkins, *Northern Editorials on Secession*, 1:518, 532–33, 2:922–23.

31. Hess, *Liberty, Virtue, and Progress*, 4–5, 20–26, 29, 31; Paludan, *"People's Contest,"* 10–14; Royster, *Destructive War*, 144–56; Foner, *Free Soil*, 72, 316; Baker, *Affairs of Party*, 334–36; Perkins, *Northern Editorials on Secession*, 2:819.

32. Hess, *Liberty, Virtue, and Progress*, 28, 81–82; Dunham, *Attitude of the Northern Clergy*, 95–97; Foner, *Free Soil*, 41–51, 54–58; Paludan, *"People's Contest,"* 95–96; Foner, *Reconstruction*, 4.

33. Nevins, *War for the Union*, 1:190; Weigley, *American Way of War*, 132–33; Mitchell, *Civil War Soldiers*, 32–34.

34. Dunham, *Attitude of the Northern Clergy*, 191–92; Perkins, *Northern Editorials on Secession*, 1:535, 2:818–19, 975–76; S. Marrett to wife, May 17, 1862, Marrett Papers, Duke; William C. Harris, "Lincoln and Wartime Reconstruction," 149; Current, *Lincoln's Loyalists*, 4–5.

35. Weigley, *American Way of War*, 133–34; *OR* 7:669–70, 8:563, 10(2):34, and ser. 2, 2:139.

36. Fithian Diary, March 1, 1862 (MS), UTK.

37. Sperry Diary, March 12, April 3, 1862, VSL; Cooper Diary, April 17, 1862 (microfilm), ADAH.

38. Formal occupation ceremonies are documented in Hoobler, "Civil War Diary," 319 (Nashville); Porter Journal, April 26, 1862, SHC (Columbia, Tenn.); William Watson Davis, *Civil War and Reconstruction in Florida*, 167–69 (Pensacola); Lang, "Gloom Envelops New Orleans," 295; and Parks, "Memphis under Military Rule," 31–32.

39. *OR* 6:4–5, 5:431, 9:363–64.

40. For warnings against civilian resistance see General Order 4, August 24, 1861, E-1651, RUSACC, and *OR* 7:675–76. On the Federals' determination to protect Unionists see Chapter 4. Seizures of Rebel property, private and public, are noted in *Diary of a Southern Refugee*, 20; William Watson Davis, *Civil War and Reconstruction in Florida*, 156, 168; Durham, *Nashville*, 49, 56; Winters, *Civil War in Louisiana*, 101–2; and Parks, "Memphis under Military Rule," 38.

41. Graf, Haskins, and Bergeron, *Papers of Andrew Johnson*, 5:325–26; *OR* 7:675–76, 9:200; Durham, *Nashville*, 50; *OR* 5:428–29, 7:669–70, 8:564, 16(2):155–56. The military governorships and wartime reconstruction are discussed in Chapter 4. On the economy and local institutions under Federal occupation see Chapter 3.

42. Linderman, *Embattled Courage*, 180–84, 204–5; *OR* 2:663, 743–44; Bills Diary, June 10, 1862 (typescript), SHC; Maury Diary, May 22, 1862, LC.

43. *OR Navy* 12:595–96; Favill, *Diary of a Young Officer*, 80; Alvin Voris to wife, May 1, 1862, Voris Papers, VHS.

44. Maury Diary, May 13, 1862, LC; R. Creecy to Bettie Creecy, April 12, 1862, and Edward Creecy to Bettie Creecy, April 12, 1862, Creecy Family Papers, SHC; Lizzie Rogers to G. Gordon, May 18, 1862, Gordon and Avery Papers, TSLA.

45. [?] to mother, April 21, 1862, Bedinger-Dandridge Family Papers, Duke; Roxa Cole to mother, July 15, 1862, Cole Family Letters, MDAH.

46. J. Clay to C. Clay, May 15, 1862, Clay Papers, Duke; Calvin Hendrick to J. Ragwell, May 19, 1862, Hendrick Letter, LSU.

47. *OR* 9:199; Beatty, *Memoirs of a Volunteer*, 93; *OR Navy* 12:337; Moore Diary, April 19, 26, 1862, ADAH; Ready Diary, March 22, 1862 (typescript), SHC; Rawick, *American Slave*, 5(3):275, 19:111; Chadick, "Civil War Days in Huntsville," 201; Maury Diary, May 5, 1862, LC.

48. *OR* 5:431–32; *Senate Reports*, 37th Cong., 3d sess., no. 108, pp. 391, 394–95; Ames, "Federal Policy toward the Eastern Shore," 452–53. See also Berlin et al., *Destruction of Slavery*, 273, and Rawick, *American Slave*, 18:58.

49. Gerteis, *From Contraband to Freedman*, 66–68; Berlin et al., *Destruction of Slavery*, 12–29; Nevins, *War for the Union*, 1:331–35, 2:116–17.

50. Ready Diary, March 23–24, 1862, SHC. See also Rawick, *American Slave*, 8(1):110.

51. Moore Diary, April 19, 1862, ADAH; J. Willcox to Susannah Willcox, June 10, 1862, Willcox Papers, Duke.

52. For two Union officers' comments on the submissiveness of the citizens see *OR* 5:436–37, 9:365. Reports of white flags are in Norton, *Army Letters*, 79; Maury Diary, April 19, 1862, LC; and *OR* 7:423–24. The surrender of towns by municipal officials is documented in *OR* 7:422–23, 51(1):626–27; Maury Diary, April 18, 19, 1862, LC; William Watson Davis, *Civil War and Reconstruction in Florida*, 157–60, 167–68; Martin, "Defeat in Victory," 18; and East, "St. Augustine during the Civil War," 79–82. For evidence that the first civilians seen were mostly women, children, and older men see F. Colburn Adams, *Story of a Trooper*, 383, and Favill, *Diary of a Young Officer*, 72. Guerrilla warfare is discussed in Chapter 2.

53. Mitchell, *Civil War Soldiers*, 90–117; Cook, *Siege of Richmond*, 151–52, 164–67; Blegen, *Civil War Letters of Colonel . . . Heg*, 82, 81; Beatty, *Memoirs of a Volunteer*, 96; Alvin Voris to wife, March 8, 1862, Voris Papers, VHS. See also S. Marrett to wife, March 1, 1862, Marrett Papers, Duke, and *OR* 16(1):634. Chapter 6 has more on the invaders' reactions to Southern society and culture.

54. *OR* 13:66, 9:365; *OR Navy* 23:244–45.

55. *OR* 5:733, 7:155, 51(1):98.

56. Ibid., 7:425; Adams, *Story of a Trooper*, 383; Alvin Voris to wife, May 1, 1862, Voris Papers, VHS. See also Smart, *Radical View*, 1:111.

57. *OR* 5:549; Graf, Haskins, and Bergeron, *Papers of Andrew Johnson*, 5:325–26, 311.

CHAPTER TWO

1. Ready Diary, March 22, 1862, SHC.

2. Rable, *Civil Wars*, 42–49; Fellman, *Inside War*, 193–95; Ready Diary, March 22, April 15, 1862, SHC.

3. Graf, Haskins, and Bergeron, *Papers of Andrew Johnson*, 5:322–23, 346–47; M. Southall to William Harding, July 30, 1862, Harding-Jackson Papers, SHC; Sutherland, "Introduction to War," 130; Fithian Diary, March 28, 1862, UTK; Fielding Diary, May 5, 1862 (MS), ADAH.

4. Fielding Diary, May 5, 13, 1862, ADAH. See also J. Boardman to brother, April 8, 1862, Boardman Letter, LSU.

5. Fitch, *Annals of the Army*, 130; *OR* 16(2):403; journal of unknown man, September 8, 1862, Pettigrew Family Papers, SHC.

6. Worthington Diary, December 6, 1862 (microfilm), SHC; Stribling Diary, May 7, 1862 (MS), VSL; Loula to Poss, May 22, 1865, Graves Family Papers, SHC.

7. Maury Diary, June 22, 1862, LC. On secession as an act of purification see Faust, *Creation of Confederate Nationalism*, 41–44.

8. Cartmell Diary, January 25, 1863 (MS), TSLA; Colin Clarke to Maxwell Clarke, May 10, August 24, 1862, Clarke Papers, SHC. On the centrality of liberty to Confederate ideology see Jimerson, *Private Civil War*, 16–18. On the masculine cult of personal honor see Wyatt-Brown, *Southern Honor*.

9. Journal of unknown man, August 17, 1862, Pettigrew Family Papers, SHC; Cartmell Diary, March 12, 1863, TSLA.

10. T. Clarke to J. Leibman, August 20, 24, 1862, E-5175, RUSACC; *Williamsburg Cavalier*, June 25, 1862; Sperry Diary, March 16, 1862, VSL; Beatty, *Memoirs of a Volunteer*, 91; Blake, *Army of the Potomac*, 32–33, 87–88; Capers, *Occupied City*, 195–96; *OR Navy* 5:106–7; Simkins and Patton, *Women of the Confederacy*, 46.

11. Mitchell, *Vacant Chair*, 97–100; French Diary, June 15, 1862, TSLA; Robert Finley to Mollie Cabeen, September 6, 1862, Finley Papers, SHC.

12. Chadick, "Civil War Days in Huntsville," 209; Durham, *Nashville*, 89.

13. Maury Diary, May 22, 1862, LC; Cox Diary, March 15, 1863, TSLA.

14. Fielding Diary, August 12, 1862, ADAH.

15. Alvin Voris to wife, May 4, 1862, Voris Papers, VHS; *OR Navy* 12:596; Wiley, *Confederate Women*, 152. See also Wiley, "Southern Reaction to Federal Invasion," 492–95.

16. Sallie Dillard to Priscilla Bailey, March 26, 1863, Bailey Papers, SHC; Graf, Haskins, and Bergeron, *Papers of Andrew Johnson*, 5:480; *OR* 11(1):1035; Ward Diary, February 9, 1862 (MS), LC.

17. Ready Diary, March 23, 31, 1862, SHC; Maury Diary, May 4, 1862, LC; Capers, *Occupied City*, 177–78; Lay Diary, May 4–15, 1862 (MS), SHC; Durham, *Nashville*, 61–62.

18. Wyatt-Brown, *Southern Honor*, 55–57; Hyman, *Era of the Oath*, 35–47, and "Deceit in Dixie," 68–69; Dorris, *Pardon and Amnesty*, 1–94; Graf, Haskins, and Berg-

eron, *Papers of Andrew Johnson*, 5:346; Carney Diary, June 20, 1862, SHC; Skipper and Gove, " 'Stray Thoughts,' " 41:116; Maslowski, *Treason Must Be Made Odious*, 53–55; Durham, *Nashville*, 63, 73–74, 154–56; Spain, "R. B. C. Howell," 335–37.

19. Wyatt-Brown, *Southern Honor*, 14–15; Ayers, *Vengeance and Justice*, 12–20; Graf, Haskins, and Bergeron, *Papers of Andrew Johnson*, 5:475.

20. Matthews Journal, July 31–August 5, 1862 (MS), TSLA; *OR* 16(1):854, 52(1):106.

21. Journal of unknown man, August 17, 1862, Pettigrew Family Papers, SHC; Chadick, "Civil War Days in Huntsville," 202; *OR* 29(2):551.

22. Anonymous Diary, July 14, 1863 (typescript), MDAH.

23. James Tait to Colonel Doster, December 4, 1862, January 14, 1863, and H. Wells to J. Taylor, January 29, 1865, E-1457, RUSACC; J. Greene to W. Putnam, April 3, 1865, E-1472, ibid.; *Beaufort Old North State*, February 18, 1865; George Cadman to wife, May 24, 1863, Cadman Papers, SHC; Ward Diary, February 28, 1862, LC; *OR* 42(1):684; F. Harper to mother, February 15, 1865, Harper Papers, NCDAH; George Brush to W. French, September 26, 1864, E-1729, RUSACC; Bond Diary, February 17, 1865, LSU; [?] to James Bell, June 14, 1862, Holland Collection, NCDAH.

24. Accounts of guerrilla attacks are innumerable; illustrative examples may be found in *OR* 10(2):161–62; *Nashville Daily Press*, May 25, 1863; B. Ramsay case, OO1227, ROJAG; W. Winship to Colonel Taylor, January 28, 1864, E-1457, RUSACC; *Fort Smith New Era*, March 26, May 14, 28, 1864; and Herbert Cooley to father, May 8, 1863, Cooley Letters, SHC. The best analysis of the strategic role of guerrilla warfare in the Civil War is Archer Jones, *Civil War Command and Strategy*, especially 86–88, 144–45, 151–52. It should be pointed out here that pro-Confederate guerrilla warfare in the occupied South was confined to no-man's-land, as defined in Chapter 3.

25. The most perceptive analysis of the motives of pro-Confederate guerrillas is in Fellman, *Inside War*, 132–42, 189, 205–6. On masculine violence see Franklin, *Militant South*; Bruce, *Violence and Culture*; and Wyatt-Brown, *Southern Honor*, 34–44, 350–461.

26. Graf, Haskins, and Bergeron, *Papers of Andrew Johnson*, 5:423–24; Thomas Carrick file, Civil War Questionnaires, Confederate, TSLA; John Rhodin case, LL1996, Joseph Hardwick case, LL2835, and John Sailor case, MM557, ROJAG; *OR* 31(1):624; Huff, "Guerrillas, Jayhawkers, and Bushwhackers," 132, 136.

27. Fitch, *Annals of the Army*, 130; *OR* 16(2):417, 232.

28. On the distinctions between Confederate cavalry raiders and guerrillas see Jones, *Civil War Command and Strategy*, 87–88, 151–52, 221, and Gildrie, "Guerrilla Warfare," 161–63, 173. On the distinctions between partisan rangers and guerrillas see Fellman, *Inside War*, 82, 97–100, 107, 112; Linderman, *Embattled Courage*, 197–98; and Huff, "Guerrillas, Jayhawkers, and Bushwhackers," 130–31.

29. T. Sweet to James Hall, March 17, 1864, E-1611, RUSACC; *OR* 15:20–21; Thomas Carrick file, Civil War Questionnaires, Confederate, TSLA; Sutherland, "Guerrillas," 262–65; King Diary, August 15, 1864 (MS), SHC; *Fort Smith New Era*, May 13, 1865; Graf, Haskins, and Bergeron, *Papers of Andrew Johnson*, 5:424; Cordelia Scales to Loulie, January 27, 1863, Scales Letters, MDAH; *OR* 24(2):434; Porter Journal, July 18,

1863, SHC; H. Wells to J. Taylor, May 5, 1864, January 29, February 11, 1865, E-1457, RUSACC; Joseph Conrad and Joseph Matthews cases, LL902, John Rhodin case, LL1996, Reason Perdue case, LL2694, James Nolen case, LL2731, Joseph Hardwick case, LL2835, Peter Gregory case, LL2537, Thomas Elliott case, LL3195, John Sailor case, MM557, E. Dean case, MM1743, and Cornelius Peacher case, OO1188, ROJAG.

30. Mitchell, *Civil War Soldiers*, 132–34; *OR* 34(4):231, 24(2):423. See also F. Twitchell to sister, April 3, 1864, Twitchell Letter, LSU.

31. Hess, *Liberty, Virtue, and Progress*, 82; Weigley, *American Way of War*, 146–47; Freidel, *Union Pamphlets*, 1:303.

32. *OR* 10(1):877; *Senate Reports*, 37th Cong., 3d sess., no. 108, pp. 347–48, 434. The failure of Unionism in the occupied regions is discussed in Chapter 4.

33. *Senate Reports*, 37th Cong., 3d sess., no. 108, p. 434; *OR* 24(3):157. See also Sutherland, "Abraham Lincoln, John Pope, and the Origins of Total War."

34. Walters, "General William T. Sherman and Total War," 456–61; Barrett, *Sherman's March through the Carolinas*, 14–15; Royster, *Destructive War*, 89–90, 95, 106–9, 116; *OR* 10(2):34, 30(3):402.

35. Royster, *Destructive War*, 117, 352–59; Marszalek, *Sherman*, 223, 251; Linderman, *Embattled Courage*, 201–11; Weigley, *American Way of War*, 133–34; *OR* 32(2):280, 32(1):185, 30(3):698.

36. *OR* 32(2):278–79, 30(3):698, 44:799; Marszalek, *Sherman*, 189, 194–96, 250–51, 293–94, 308–9, 331–33; Royster, *Destructive War*, 108–10, 117–19, 340–42; Weigley, *American Way of War*, 145–52; Walters, "General William T. Sherman and Total War," 447–48, 458–67, 473; Linderman, *Embattled Courage*, 211–13.

37. Royster, *Destructive War*, 39, 360–64; Henry Hitchcock to Mary Hitchcock, April 7, 1865, Hitchcock Papers, LC.

38. Royster, *Destructive War*, 86–89; Harry Cushing to mother, March 30, 1862, Cushing Letters, UTK. See also *OR* 31(3):262, and Alfred Atkins to [?], March 22, 1865, Atkins Collection, GDAH.

39. *OR* 20(1):51, 24(2):423; Mitchell, *Civil War Soldiers*, 132–34.

40. The wartime campaign to reform Southern society is discussed in Chapters 5 and 6.

41. Royster, *Destructive War*, 85; *OR* 12(2):50, 16(2):640–41; Sutherland, "Abraham Lincoln, John Pope, and the Origins of Total War," 574–82. Such unrecompensed property seizures by the military were authorized by President Lincoln a few days after Pope's order: see Sutherland, "Abraham Lincoln, John Pope, and the Origins of Total War," 581, and Byrne, " 'A Terrible Machine,' " 8.

42. *OR* 39(2):503, 24(2):436. Though its substantive impact was very limited, the Confiscation Act passed by the U.S. Congress in July 1862 (authorizing the Federal government to seize and condemn the property of secessionists) was an important symbol of the new Northern attitude toward Southern property. See Nevins, *War for the Union*, 2:145–46, 203–4, and McPherson, *Battle Cry of Freedom*, 499–500.

43. *OR* 45(2):621–22; Henry Hitchcock to Mary Hitchcock, November 4, 1864, Hitchcock Papers, LC. See also J. Woods to [?], April 14, 1865, Woods Papers, Duke.

44. Mitchell, *Civil War Soldiers*, 137–47; Linderman, *Embattled Courage*, 183–84, 187–96, 213–15; Royster, *Destructive War*, 85–86; Elias Brady to wife, November 24, 1862, Brady Papers, SHC.

45. Roxa Cole to Cousin Blanche, November 2, 1862, Cole Family Letters, MDAH; R. Hoadley to Cousin Em, May 29, 1863, Hoadley Papers, Duke. Other examples are numerous, but see especially J. Dunn to H. Blackmon, January 5, 1864, Blackmon Papers, Duke; P. Willis to Sam Carey, February 3, 1862 [actually 1863], and enclosure, Walter Papers, SHC; and Wills, *Army Life of an Illinois Soldier*, 136. One of the most notorious instances of Northern destructiveness was the sacking and burning of Darien, Georgia, in 1863: see Coulter, "Robert Gould Shaw and the Burning of Darien," and King, *Darien*, 64–71.

46. Walters, "General William T. Sherman and Total War," 474–77; *OR* 44:13–14.

47. Jackson, *The Colonel's Diary*, 191. The most thorough account is in Glatthaar, *March to the Sea and Beyond*, 119–51, but see also Harwell and Racine, *Fiery Trail*, especially 92–93, 134, 153.

48. Randall, *Constitutional Problems under Lincoln*, 215–27, 234–36; Carpenter, "Military Government of Southern Territory," 1:468–70.

49. Gabriel, "American Experience with Military Government," 630–38; *OR*, ser. 3, 3:148–64; Freidel, "General Orders 100 and Military Government"; Futrell, "Federal Military Government in the South," 181–82.

50. *Washington New Era*, August 14, 1862; Robert Glasscock case, LL2804, ROJAG; Currie, *Enclave*, 6.

51. Waddel Diary, December 13, 1862 (MS), LC; King Diary, July 10, 1864, SHC. See also Ransdell Diary, January 12, 1863 (MS), SHC.

52. Durham, *Nashville*, 61–62, 75; Hardison, "In the Toils of War," 79–80; Capers, *Occupied City*, 176–78; Parks, "Memphis under Military Rule," 34; Lawrence, *A Present for Mr. Lincoln*, 215–16; *OR* 44:813.

53. George Cadman to Esther Cadman, June 3, 1863, Cadman Papers, SHC; Agnew Diary, September 10, 1863 (typescript), SHC; Cleveland Diary, April 11, 1865 (typescript), SHC.

54. Jane Warren to Electa Ames, August 27, 1863, Ames Papers, Duke; Provost Order 12, October 29, 1864, E-1417, RUSACC; Fielding Diary, August 8, 1862, ADAH; Special Order 5, March 6, 1864, and Special Order 13, May 12, 1864, E-1701, RUSACC; King Diary, July 18, 29, 31, August 17, 1864, SHC.

55. H. Wells to S. Heintzelman, April 5, 1863, E-1457, RUSACC; John Hatch to provost marshal, September 26, 1864, E-1729, ibid.; *OR* 31(3):199.

56. Favill, *Diary of a Young Officer*, 204; Russ, "Administrative Activities of the Union Army," 74; descriptive list of citizens, n.d., vol. 53, E-1614, RUSACC. See also list of Walker County, Georgia, Rebel citizens, n.d., no. 22213, Union Provost Marshals' File of Papers Relating to Two or More Civilians, M-416, War Department Collection of Confederate Records, RG 109, NA. This last set of documents and its companion set (Union Provost Marshals' File of Papers Relating to Individual Civilians, M-345) contain many thousands of dossiers on citizens, compiled by provost marshals in the occupied South.

57. John Clark to William Smith, September 25, 1864, Virginia Executive Papers, VSL; *OR* 41(2):196–97; Hendricks, "Union Army Occupation of the Southern Seaboard," 185; James Smith and Jesse Miller cases, LL391, and James Poteet case, LL2804, ROJAG; William Wood to Allan Pinkerton, August 5, 1864, January 5, 1865, and William Wood to Captain White, March 27, 1865, E-5545, RUSACC; Fitch, *Annals of the Army*, 350–52; Maslowski, *Treason Must Be Made Odious*, 62–64.

58. Graf, Haskins, and Bergeron, *Papers of Andrew Johnson*, 5:614; wife to W. Harding, August 5, 1862, Harding-Jackson Papers, SHC; George Cadman to Esther Cadman, June 3, 1863, Cadman Papers, SHC; Edmonson Diary, November 25, 1863 (typescript), AHC; *Nashville Daily Times and True Union*, November 28, 1864; Circular 5, September 23, 1864, E-1411, RUSACC; Hyman, *Era of the Oath*, 41–44.

59. Massey, *Refugee Life*, 205, 209–10; Maslowski, *Treason Must Be Made Odious*, 60–62; Parks, "Memphis under Military Rule," 35–38; John Ela to James Bowen, May 11, 1863, E-1482, RUSACC; Lewis Weld to provost marshal, April 26, 1864, E-1599, RUSACC; *Little Rock National Democrat*, February 11, 1865; *OR* 23(2):107–8, 121. The two best-known incidents of mass deportation during the war—Sherman's expulsion of the residents of Atlanta and of the workers in the Confederate textile factories of Roswell, Georgia, both in 1864—originated in motives different from those discussed here. The oath was not an issue in these two cases; Sherman simply desired, for military reasons, to move all civilians out of Atlanta and to send the Roswell workers where they could no longer be of use to the Confederacy. (The Roswell workers were, in fact, sent north.) See Massey, *Refugee Life*, 211–13, and Bynum, "Sherman's Expulsion of the Roswell Women," 169–80.

60. Graf, Haskins, and Bergeron, *Papers of Andrew Johnson*, 5:605; Royster, *Destructive War*, 20, 22, 86–87. See also Stewart, *Camp, March and Battle-field*, 404; Henry Hitchcock to Mary Hitchcock, April 7, 1865, Hitchcock Papers, LC; and Mitchell, *Vacant Chair*, 100–104.

61. S. Marrett to wife, n.d. (probably May 1862), June 15, 1862, Marrett Papers, Duke; Beatty, *Memoirs of a Volunteer*, 219; *OR* 24(3):209; Fellman, *Inside War*, 199–205.

62. Henry Hitchcock Diary, November 17, 1864, Hitchcock Papers, LC; J. Strong to E. White, November 21, 1864, E-1700, RUSACC. See also Volwiler, "Documents," 512.

63. J. Strong to Frank White, August 24, 1864, E-1700, RUSACC; French Diary, September 5, 1862, TSLA; Lemke, *Mecklin Letters*, 35.

64. Maria Tabb case, LL391, ROJAG. For an example of a woman who received a lesser punishment for an offense that might have earned a man the death penalty see *Yorktown Cavalier*, May 12, 1863.

65. General Order 2, October 16, 1863, E-1461, RUSACC; endorsement by H. Wells, November 25, 1863, E-1457, ibid.; *Nashville Daily Times and True Union*, August 20, 1864; *OR* 25(2):511, 31(1):713; William T. Palfrey Plantation Diary (MS), September 23, 1863, Palfrey Account Books, LSU.

66. James Wright case, LL2765, and E. Dean case, MM1743, ROJAG; A. Smith to B. Polk, October 15, 1864, E-3023, RUSACC; Peter Gregory case, LL2537, ROJAG; *OR* 29(1):69; J. Strong to Frank White, March 24, August 25, 1864, E-1700, RUSACC.

67. *OR*, ser. 3, 3:157, and ser. 1, 24(3):538. See also William Yant case, LL3288, ROJAG, and *OR* 43(2):470.

68. *Fort Smith New Era*, November 21, 1863; *OR* 52(1):114.

69. *OR* 10(1):877, 16(2):484.

70. Ibid., 15:312.

71. Fisher, "'Prepare Them for My Coming,'" 78–81; Sutherland, "Guerrillas," 278–80; *OR* 17(2):69, 30(3):33–34, 13:106.

72. *OR* 12(2):51; Sutherland, "Introduction to War," 124–25, and "Abraham Lincoln, John Pope, and the Origins of Total War," 577–86; *Nashville Daily Times and True Union*, July 26–27, August 8, 1864; *OR* 31(1):623–24, 32(2):37–38. See also H. Van Cleve to B. Polk, June 13, 1864, E-3071, RUSACC; "List of the names of disloyal citizens . . . assessed," n.d., no. 22180, and order of January 20, 1865, no. 13981, Union Provost Marshals' File, M-416, NA.

73. *OR* 17(1):720, 43(1):30, (2):679.

74. Ibid., 17(2):285, 525.

75. Durham, *Rebellion Revisited*, 208; *OR* 15:312, 43(2):909. See also *Shelbyville Tri-Weekly News*, June 21, 1862, and journal of events, April 15, 1864, vol. 52, E-1614, RUSACC.

76. *OR* 43(1):32, 29(1):90.

77. Ibid., 17(1):144–45, 22(1):230; Demuth, "Burning of Hopefield," 125–27; *OR* 41(1):295, 45(1):356.

78. *OR* 43(2):348.

79. Lucy Johnson Ambler Diary, July 27–28, 1863 (typescript), Ambler-Brown Family Papers, Duke; Cartmell Diary, April 17, 1863, TSLA.

80. Moore Diary, September 15, 1862, ADAH; *OR* 48(1):741. See also William Smith to Christopher Tompkins, August 12, 1862, William Patterson Smith Papers, Duke.

81. James Willcox to Susa, July 25, 1864, Willcox Papers, Duke; Ambler Diary, August 2, 1863, Ambler-Brown Family Papers, Duke; Colin Clarke to Maxwell Clarke, July 22, 1862, Clarke Papers, SHC. See also Cornelia Grinnan to the Duke of Argyll, September 12, 1863, Grinnan Letter, VSL.

82. Unknown Confederate Diary, May 29, June 7, 1864 (photostat), VSL; Roxa Cole to Cousin Blanche, December 28, 1862, Cole Family Letters, MDAH; French Diary, September 3, 1862, TSLA. See also Amanda Hall to B. Hall, June 11, 1863, Clark Collection, SHC.

83. Fleet and Fuller, *Green Mount*, 330; Cox Diary, June 29, 1862, TSLA.

84. Fleet and Fuller, *Green Mount*, 330; French Diary, July 17, 1862, TSLA; Wiley, *Confederate Women*, 152; Cordelia Scales to Loulie, January 27, 1863, Scales Letters, MDAH.

85. William Smith to Christopher Tompkins, October 15, 1863, William Patterson Smith Papers, Duke; Waddel Diary, December 10, 13, 17, 1862, LC; Parks, "Memphis under Military Rule," 36–37; *Nashville Daily Press*, May 12, 1863; Capers, *Occupied City*, 200–201.

86. Lemke, *Mecklin Letters*, 17–18; R. Creecy to Bettie Creecy, August 1, 1864, Creecy Family Papers, SHC; French Diary, August 10, 1862, TSLA.

87. Charles Mann to [?], April 6, 1863, William Patterson Smith Papers, Duke; Porter Journal, March 16, 1865, SHC; Lemke, *Mecklin Letters*, 9. See also Helen Sawyer to Sallie, March 28, 1864, Daugherty Papers, Duke.

88. Stevens, *Three Years in the Sixth Corps*, 342–43; Chappelear Diary, February 10, 1863 (MS), VHS. See also Cy Titus to Nannie Slater, n.d. (probably March 1865), Bentley Papers, TSLA.

89. "Diary of Miss Harriette Cary," 105; George Cadman to Esther Cadman, November 5, 1863, Cadman Papers, SHC; Smith, "Yankees in New Albany," 45.

90. R. Creecy to Bettie Creecy, August 1, 1864, Creecy Family Papers, SHC; James Wright case, LL2765, ROJAG. See also Robert Glasscock case, LL2804, ROJAG, and the discussion of lying as a survival strategy in Fellman, *Inside War*, 48–49, 195–98.

91. *OR* 29(1):138, 24(2):434, 18:552.

92. Waddel Diary, November 8, 1862, LC; Roxa Cole to mother, July 27, 1862, Cole Family Letters, MDAH. See also A. Beans to Thomas Watts, November 30, 1864, Watts Papers, ADAH.

93. For examples of citizens who repudiated Federal authority in matters of honor see journal of events, April 25, 1864, vol. 52, E-1614, RUSACC; Peter Gregory case, LL2537, ROJAG; and *OR* 11(1):1035.

94. H. Wells to J. Devereux, December 7, 1863, E-1457, RUSACC; Matthews Journal, August 6, 1862, TSLA; Harrison Tunstall to brother, April 17, 1864, Harrison Tunstall case, LL2240, ROJAG. See also Cox Diary, February 16, 1864, TSLA; Tilney, *My Life in the Army*, 62; and S. Garrett to Quitman, November 30, 1863, Garrett Papers, MDAH.

95. John Burruss to Edward Burruss, May 23, 1864, Burruss Family Papers, LSU; George Cadman to Esther Cadman, June 3, 1863, Cadman Papers, SHC. See also Amanda Worthington Diary, May 26, 1863 (typescript), Worthington Family Papers, MDAH.

96. On the role of institutional propaganda in the Confederacy see Faust, *Creation of Confederate Nationalism*; Andrews, "The Confederate Press and Public Morale"; Daniel, "Protestantism and Patriotism in the Confederacy"; Silver, "Propaganda in the Confederacy" and *Confederate Morale and Church Propaganda*; and Wight, "Churches and the Confederate Cause."

97. Harrison Tunstall to brother, April 17, 1864, Harrison Tunstall case, LL2240, ROJAG; Sanford, "Virginian's Diary," 368; William Smith to Christopher Tompkins, August 12, 1862, William Patterson Smith Papers, Duke. See also James Earl Bradley Diary, October 28, 1863 (microfilm), LSU, and Roxa Cole to mother, August 15, 1864, Cole Family Letters, MDAH.

98. Sallie to John Minor, May 15, 1864, Sailor's Rest Plantation Papers, TSLA. See also Louis to sister, April 9, 1863, Talbot and Related Families Papers, TSLA, and *OR* 39(2):482, 16(1):816. The powerful influence of battlefield events on civilian morale is discussed in Gallagher, "Generals."

99. *OR* 31(1):623–24; John Sailor case, MM557, ROJAG. Other examples of guerrilla brutality are in Dick Davis case, LL2904, ROJAG, and *Nashville Daily Times and True*

Union, July 26–27, August 5, 1864. See also the discussion of the mutilation of corpses in Fellman, *Inside War*, 189.

CHAPTER THREE

1. A. Beans to Thomas Watts, November 30, 1864, Watts Papers, ADAH; Alvin Voris to wife, January 12, 1863, Voris Papers, VHS; Capers, *Occupied City*, 150; Durham, *Nashville*, 204, 206–7, 273–75; Currie, *Enclave*, 10; *New Orleans Daily Picayune*, June 10, 1862; Doyle, "Greenbacks," 348–53; *Nashville Dispatch*, May 18, September 27, November 1, December 7, 1862, May 31, 1863; Graf, Haskins, and Bergeron, *Papers of Andrew Johnson*, 6:450.

2. Capers, *Occupied City*, 150–53, 197; Maslowski, *Treason Must Be Made Odious*, 136; Leslie, "Arabella Lanktree Wilson's Civil War Letter," 269; Spencer Diary, May 27, 1864 (MS), LC; H. Burleigh to P. Davis, January 22, 1862, E-5175, RUSACC; J. Sturtevant to [?], May 18, 1864, E-1480, RUSACC; Cleveland Diary, April 5–6, 1865, SHC; George Cadman to Esther Cadman, May 18, 1863, Cadman Papers, SHC; *New Orleans Daily Picayune*, May 9, 1862; John Watkins to John Probert, December 14, 1864, Watkins Papers, UTK.

3. Evidence of the influx of Northern civilians is in *Alexandria Gazette*, September 5, 1862, April 2, 1863; Doyle, "Greenbacks," 350–52; George Cadman to Esther Cadman, August 4, 1863, Cadman Papers, SHC; Maury Diary, June 22, 1862, LC; *Nashville Dispatch*, April 14, 1862, May 31, 1863; and Leslie, "Arabella Lanktree Wilson's Civil War Letter," 269.

4. Parks, "Confederate Trade Center"; Ludwell H. Johnson III, "Blockade or Trade Monopoly?"; Maslowski, *Treason Must Be Made Odious*, 135; *OR* 20(2):104–5, 39(2):314–15. General studies of wartime trade policy include Coulter, "Commercial Intercourse with the Confederacy"; Ludwell H. Johnson III, "Contraband Trade"; O'Connor, "Lincoln and the Cotton Trade"; and Roberts, "The Federal Government and Confederate Cotton."

5. Doyle, "Greenbacks," 354–58; Carpenter, "Military Government of Southern Territory," 492–93; *OR* 23(2):189, 27(3):851, 47(3):70; *Calendar of Virginia State Papers*, 11:230; Leslie, "Arabella Lanktree Wilson's Civil War Letter," 269; Martha Hooff to Mary Ward, December 4, 1864, Ward Family of Richmond County, Va., Papers, LC.

6. Parks, "Memphis under Military Rule," 53–54; Capers, *Occupied City*, 151; Nancy Smith to James Smith, May 26, 1864, Smith Letters, TSLA; Patten Diary, February 13, 1863 (microfilm), TSLA; *Nashville Daily Press*, June 5, 1863; *OR* 18:382–83, 406–7.

7. Parks, "Memphis under Military Rule," 31, 54; Durham, *Nashville*, 3, 49, 56, 87, 180–81; Durham, *Reluctant Partners*, 152–54, 277; Cleveland Diary, March 13, 1865, SHC; William Hackley to wife, December 7, 1863, Hackley Letters, UTK; Norton Diary, July 13, August 18, 1864 (microfilm), GDAH; Capers, *Occupied City*, 151–52; Currie, *Enclave*, 12; *Nashville Dispatch*, May 31, November 19, 1863.

8. *OR* 18:382–83.

9. Ibid., 384, 47(2):88. See also Provost Marshal to Thomas Robinson, November 24, 1864, E-1611, RUSACC.

10. *OR* 18:384.

11. Ibid., 24(3):501–2; "Issue of Rations to Families resident," July 1864–May 1865, E-1409, RUSACC; journal of provost marshal's office, October 1863–November 1865, E-1600, RUSACC; *OR* 27(3):851; Durham, *Reluctant Partners*, 67–68; *Nashville Dispatch*, November 1, 3, 1863; Winters, *Civil War in Louisiana*, 126–27; *OR* 26(1):765.

12. On the establishment of markets see Frank White to Lieutenant Thomas, December 21, 1864, E-1700, RUSACC; *OR* 30(3):34–35; *Pulaski Chanticleer*, January 7, 1864; and *Yorktown Cavalier*, September 21, 1863. On the regulation of prices and rents see *Vicksburg Daily Herald*, August 20, October 14, 1864; Currie, *Enclave*, 10–12; *Savannah Daily Herald*, January 12, 18, 1865; R. Loveridge to R. Thompson, April 3, 1865, E-1598, RUSACC; and Capers, *Occupied City*, 152.

13. For examples of the governmental problems facing the Federals on their arrival see *Calendar of Virginia State Papers*, 11:370–71, and Graf, Haskins, and Bergeron, *Papers of Andrew Johnson*, 5:511–12, 573, 592. For evidence of the citizens' desire for the Federals to assume municipal functions see H. Weymouth to Edward Smith, January 7, 1865, U.S. Army Provost Marshal, Portsmouth, Va., Letterpress Book, 1864–65, Duke.

14. Currie, *Enclave*, 25; *Fort Smith New Era*, April 29, 1865; James Gilfillan to B. Polk, November 23, 1864, E-3048, RUSACC; Durham, *Rebellion Revisited*, 58, 250; Ash, *Middle Tennessee Society Transformed*, 100n; Carpenter, "Military Government of Southern Territory," 493; Benjamin F. Butler, *Private and Official Correspondence*, 4:589–90; Futrell, "Federal Military Government in the South," 190–91; R. Loveridge to Frank Geise, April 3, 1865, E-1598, RUSACC; A. Bowman to James Sandom, February 10, 1865, E-1700, RUSACC; *Senate Reports*, 38th Cong., 1st sess., no. 54, p. 3.

15. On the role of the provost marshal see Wilton P. Moore, "Union Army Provost Marshals"; Hendricks, "Union Army Occupation of the Southern Seaboard," 179–85; Hyman, "Deceit in Dixie," 65–68; and *OR* 32(3):537–41. For examples of the provost marshal's daily routine see journal of provost marshal's office, 1863–65, E-1600, RUSACC; journal of events of provost marshal, 1862, E-1711, RUSACC; and Fitch, *Annals of the Army*, 282–83.

16. *OR* 32(1):179–80. See also ibid., 5:428–29. On the seven cities named see Maslowski, *Treason Must Be Made Odious*, 121–23; Winters, *Civil War in Louisiana*, 125–26; Parks, "Memphis under Military Rule," 32, 39; Wilson, "Experiment in Reunion," 92–137; Norfolk Hustings Court Order Book, 1862–65 (microfilm), VSL; Portsmouth City Council Minutes, 1862–65, (microfilm), VSL; *Murfreesboro Union Volunteer*, May 20, 1862; and Dyer, "Northern Relief for Savannah," 461–62.

17. Maslowski, *Treason Must Be Made Odious*, 125–26; *Alexandria Gazette*, June 28, 1864; *Savannah Daily Herald*, January 17, 1865; Benjamin F. Butler, *Private and Official Correspondence*, 4:577–78, 589; H. Weymouth to Edward Smith, January 7, 1865, U.S. Army Provost Marshal Book, Duke; and statement of expenditures, February 26, 1865, E-1416, Alexander Bailie to H. Robinson, January 7, 1865, E-1408, and C. Newton to Harai Robinson, October 20, 1864, E-1469, all in RUSACC.

18. Parks, "Memphis under Military Rule," 54; Futrell, "Federal Military Government in the South," 191; Currie, *Enclave*, 14–15; Maslowski, *Treason Must Be Made Odious*, 126–27; *Alexandria Gazette*, June 25, 1864; *Washington New Era*, August 14, 1862; *Vicksburg Daily Herald*, December 20, 1864; Aaron Seeley to J. Leibman, September 11, 1862, E-5175, RUSACC; statement of expenditures, February 3, 1865, and receipt, February 27, 1865, E-1416, RUSACC; McCrary, *Abraham Lincoln and Reconstruction*, 82; Nash, *Stormy Petrel*, 186–87.

19. Futrell, "Federal Military Government in the South," 191; *Alexandria Gazette*, January 9, 1864; *Nashville Dispatch*, November 24, 1863; Davidson County Court Minutes, book 1, 224 (microfilm), TSLA; Circular 17, October 25, 1864, and H. Hendrick to J. Atwater, May 4, 1864, E-1599, RUSACC; Carrigan, "Yankees versus Yellow Jack."

20. James Boyd Jones Jr., "A Tale of Two Cities"; Durham, *Reluctant Partners*, 46–49, 112–14; T. Harris to O. Mann, April 12, 1865, E-5175, RUSACC.

21. Capers, *Occupied City*, 73; *Nashville Daily Times and True Union*, November 21, 1864, February 2, 1865; *Senate Reports*, 38th Cong., 1st sess., no. 54, pp. 1–3; *Alexandria Gazette*, December 10, 1862.

22. C. Porter to R. Brown, October 1, 1863, E-1482, RUSACC; Parks, "Memphis under Military Rule," 39, 43–44; Durham, *Nashville*, 239; Currie, *Enclave*, 25–26; Benjamin F. Butler, *Private and Official Correspondence*, 4:589; Joseph Bly case, KK872, ROJAG.

23. Futrell, "Federal Military Government in the South," 186–87; Helis, "Of Generals and Jurists," 143, 146–51, 159–62; Durham, *Nashville*, 236; Currie, *Enclave*, 25; Circular 3, August 24, 1864, E-1411, RUSACC; Hendricks, "Union Army Occupation of the Southern Seaboard," 183–87, 201–2; Doyle, "New Orleans Courts," 185–89; Benjamin F. Butler, *Private and Official Correspondence*, 4:589; H. Wells to J. Taylor, July 28, 1864, E-1457, RUSACC.

24. Civilian courts authorized to try serious crimes reopened in New Orleans, Nashville, and a few other Tennessee towns before the war ended. In New Orleans, President Lincoln established a special "Provisional Court" with broad authority over criminal and other cases. See Helis, "Of Generals and Jurists," 145–49, 151–59, 161; Ash, *Middle Tennessee Society Transformed*, 99; and Doyle, "New Orleans Courts," 190–92. On military commissions see Randall, *Constitutional Problems under Lincoln*, 230; Neely, *Fate of Liberty*, 40–44, 168–69; St. Clair, "Military Justice in North Carolina," 341–42; Carpenter, "Military Government of Southern Territory," 483–85; Futrell, "Federal Military Government in the South," 186–87; and *OR*, ser. 3, 3:77–78.

25. Helis, "Of Generals and Jurists," 149–51; Hendricks, "Union Army Occupation of the Southern Seaboard," 199–203; case of Richard Wiggins v. John Edmonson, September 1, 1864, E-1416, RUSACC; Edward Bigelow to Mr. Guillot, February 17, 1865, E-1486, RUSACC.

26. *New Bern North Carolina Times*, January 23, 1864; Winters, *Civil War in Louisiana*, 126; Davidson County Court Minutes, book 1, 56, TSLA; Gaston, "World Overturned," 5, 8. See also John Brooks to E. Paine, February 24, 1864, and E. Paine to B. Polk, March 2, 1864, Johnson Papers, LC; *Calendar of Virginia State Papers*, 11:228–30,

236–37; and *OR* 46(2):503. (These last two citations deal with the Virginia State Lunatic Asylum, at Williamsburg, which was put under the authority of a Federal army surgeon and maintained with money drawn from the post fund.)

27. *New Bern North Carolina Times*, March 16, April 2–3, 1864; Currie, *Enclave*, 23; J. Johnson to E. Woodruff, June 9, 1865, E-1612, RUSACC; Benjamin F. Butler, *Private and Official Correspondence*, 4:589; Doyle, "Nurseries of Treason," 161–69; Capers, *Occupied City*, 185–88. Nashville's school system was an exception to the rule; all the city's public schools closed on the arrival of the Yankees and were not revived until after the war. See Durham, *Nashville*, 195–96, and *Reluctant Partners*, 51, 77–78, 142–43.

28. *Nashville Dispatch*, November 26, 1862; Durham, *Reluctant Partners*, 51–52, 141–42; Currie, *Enclave*, 23–24; Doyle, "Nurseries of Treason," 169–74. These generalizations apply only to elementary education. Academies and colleges in the garrisoned towns, many of whose students were nonresidents, were generally disrupted for the whole period of occupation. See, for example, William Hackley to wife, December 7, 1863, Hackley Letters, UTK; Capers, *Occupied City*, 190; and Ash, *Middle Tennessee Society Transformed*, 96.

29. David Pise Journal, December 8–9, 1863, May 10, June 11, 1865 (MS), SHC. See also Capers, *Occupied City*, 182–83.

30. Capers, *Occupied City*, 181–82, 184–85.

31. Spain, "R. B. C. Howell," 337–38; Brydon, "Diocese of Virginia," 392; Daniel, "Effects of the Civil War on Southern Protestantism," 47–49; Norton Diary, October 20, 1864, Enon Baptist Church, Rome, Floyd County, Minutes, 1864 (microfilm), and St. Peter's Episcopal Church, Rome, Floyd County, Vestry Minutes, 1864–65 (microfilm), all in GDAH; Durham, *Nashville*, 278–79, and *Reluctant Partners*, 49–51, 139–40, 279–80; Christ (Episcopal) Church, Norfolk, Vestry Minutes, 1863–65 (microfilm), VSL. For other examples of urban churches that continued to operate under Federal occupation see S. Clay to Clement Clay, March 24, 1865, Clay Papers, Duke, and Trinity Episcopal Church (Natchez) Records, 1863–65 (microfilm), MDAH.

32. For a good illustration of the normality of daily life in one town (Vicksburg) see Roach Diary, 1864–65 (MS), VHS.

33. Norton Diary, June 8, July 13, August 18, October 4, November 13, 1864, GDAH; R. Minor to wife, February 24, 1863, Minor Correspondence, VSL; petition no. 394, November 1864, Memorials and Petitions, E-175, Legislative Records (Confederate), War Department Collection of Confederate Records, RG 109, NA; Stevens, *Three Years in the Sixth Corps*, 340; Coffin, *Four Years of Fighting*, 326; George Cadman to Esther Cadman, April 18, 1864, Cadman Papers, SHC; *OR* 32(3):94–95.

34. Ward Diary, January 25, 1862, LC; Capers, *Occupied City*, 72; Somers, "War and Play"; Currie, *Enclave*, 21–22; Cleveland Diary, February 16, 1865, SHC; *Clarksville Gazette*, February 27, 1864. See also *Little Rock National Democrat*, February 13, 1864.

35. Barrett, *Civil War in North Carolina*, 124, 137–38; Hassell Diary and Papers, November 3–4, 13, 1862, February 13, 1863 (MS), SHC; John Laurence to Thomas Watts, July 29, 1864, Watts Papers, ADAH; Espy Diary, October 24–25, 27, 1864, March 31, 1865 (MS), ADAH. Other examples are numerous, but see especially R. Dixon to Harry Dixon, March 6, 1863, Dixon Papers, SHC.

36. [?] to mother, January 4, 1863, Burrus Papers, MDAH. See also Crabtree and Patton, *Journal of a Secesh Lady*, 442, 445.

37. Fleet and Fuller, *Green Mount*, 235; Hassell Diary, November 28, December 10, 13, 1862, April 7, July 24, 27, 1863, Agnew Diary, May 7, 1863, Eliza Sivley to Jane Sivley, February 2, 14, 1864, February 20, 1865, Jane Sivley Papers, and Dwight Reinhardt to Mary Dalton, March 12, 1864, Kennedy Papers, all in SHC; petition of De Soto County citizens, February 27, 1863, Pettus Correspondence, MDAH.

38. Mary Forman to Sarah Newell, February 22, 1864, Newell Papers, LSU; Espy Diary, August 10, 1864, ADAH. On the attitude of the Confederate high command concerning the frontier districts see *OR* 11(3):669-70.

39. Berlin et al., *Destruction of Slavery*, 701, 751, 765-66; J. Sheffield to Thomas Watts, April 22, 1864, Watts Papers, ADAH. See also petition of Tishomingo County citizens, n.d., Clark Correspondence, MDAH. On the Confederate government's policy see *OR* 11(3):670, 22(2):990, and De Saussure Plantation Record, April 14, 1862 (MS), SHC.

40. Roxa Cole to mother, August 15, 1864, Cole Family Letters, MDAH; petition no. 395, n.d., E-175, Legislative Records (Confederate), NA. See also *OR* 32(3):804, 36(1): 778. Two general studies of food production in the Confederacy that touch on the distinctive conditions in what is here designated the frontier are Gates, *Agriculture and the Civil War*, 73-108, and Massey, *Ersatz in the Confederacy*, 27-29, 55-56.

41. W. Nugent to John Pettus, September 29, 1863, Pettus Correspondence, MDAH. See also petition of Coahoma County planter, n.d., Confederate States of America Congress Papers, 1862-65, Duke, and Maria Swanson to Alexander Swanson, January 13, 1864, and n.d., Swanson-Yates Family Papers, MDAH. On the Confederate government's trade policy see Ludwell H. Johnson, "Trading with the Union."

42. Mary Tribble to William Smith, August 24, 1864, Virginia Executive Papers, VSL. Other complaints and petitions concerning taxes, impressment, and conscription on the frontier are in Bertie County Court Minutes, December 12, 1863 (microfilm), NCDAH; petition no. 368, November 1864, E-175, Legislative Records (Confederate), NA; and St. Landry Parish Police Jury Minutes, October 3, 1864 (MS), LSU.

43. Tippah County Minutes of Police Board, 1863-65 (microfilm), MDAH; Roxa Cole to mother, August 15, 1864, Cole Family Letters, MDAH. Other examples of the persistence of local government in frontier districts are in Morgan County Commissioners' Court Minutes, 1862-65 (MS), ADAH; Cherokee County Inferior Court Minutes, 1864 (microfilm), GDAH; Fredericksburg City Council Minutes, June 1864-April 1865 (microfilm), VSL; and Chowan County Court Minutes, 1862-65 (microfilm), NCDAH. Many of the Rebel state legislatures enacted special laws to deal with the disruption of local government in the invaded regions; some, for instance, authorized county magistrates to meet elsewhere if the county seat was in enemy hands: see Ringold, *Role of the State Legislatures*, 60-61. For examples of the activities of Confederate and state military and civil officials that helped preserve order on the frontier—including arresting army deserters and other outlaws, holding elections, and operating post offices—see John Burruss to Edward Burruss, June 1, 1864, Burruss Family Papers,

LSU; T. Sparks to Henry Allen, July 5, 1864, Records of the Louisiana State Government, LSA; and *OR* 25(1):13.

44. Agnew Diary, May 7, 1863, SHC; A. Bradford to Charles Clark, August 27, 1864, and petition of Coahoma County citizens, August 29, 1864, Clark Correspondence, MDAH; Hassell Diary, January 29, July 21, 1863, SHC; Lafayette Parish Police Jury Minutes, October 6, 1864 (typescript), LSU; *OR Navy* 5:487–88; Fleet and Fuller, *Green Mount*, 235–48, 260.

45. Ramsdell, *Behind the Lines*, 25–26; Massey, *Ersatz in the Confederacy*, 33–53; Fleming, *Civil War and Reconstruction in Alabama*, 196–202; McMillan, *Disintegration of a Confederate State*, 43–44, 92–93, 132–33; Yearns, *Confederate Governors*, 26–28, 36, 67–68, 77, 157–58, 229–30; Thomas Ashby to John Letcher, October 14, 1862, Virginia Executive Papers, VSL; T. Sparks to Henry Allen, July 5, 1864, Records of the Louisiana State Government, LSA; petition no. 368, November 1864, E-175, Legislative Records (Confederate), NA.

46. Tippah County Minutes of Police Board, March 1864–May 1865, MDAH; proclamation, April 25, 1864, Watts Papers, ADAH; G. Moore to Zebulon Vance, February 28, 1865, Vance Papers, NCDAH. See also Avoyelles Parish Police Jury Minutes, October 19, 1863, July 11, September 5, 1864, January 28, 1865 (typescript), LSU.

47. Hephzibah Church Record Book, October 1864, and 1862–65 (typescript), LSU; Luray (Main Street) Baptist Church, Page County, Minute Book, April 5, 1862, and 1862–65 (microfilm), VSL. See also Mount Joy Primitive Baptist Church, Blount County, Minutes, 1862–65 (MS), ADAH; Battle Run Baptist Church (Rappahannock County), Minute Book, 1862–65 (MS), VSL; Meherrin Baptist Church, Murfreesboro (Hertford County), Minutes, 1862–65 (microfilm), NCDAH; and Union Church Presbyterian Church Records, 1862–65 (microfilm), MDAH.

48. Mount Tabor Baptist Church, Murfreesboro, Hertford County, Minutes, October 1862, September 1863 (microfilm), NCDAH; Espy Diary, November 13, 1864, ADAH.

49. Espy Diary, November 20, December 31, 1864, ADAH; Lemke, *Mecklin Letters*, 9, 14. See also Fleet and Fuller, *Green Mount*, 331, and Mary Tribble to William Smith, August 24, 1864, Virginia Executive Papers, VSL.

50. Thomas Batchelor to Albert Batchelor, September 7, 1864, Batchelor Papers, LSU. For good illustrations of the persistence of rural community life on the Confederate frontier see Erwin Diary, 1863–65, LSU; Hassell Diary, 1862–65, SHC; and Henry Marston Jr. Diary, 1864, Marston and Family Papers, LSU.

51. Thomas Batchelor to Albert Batchelor, September 21, December 26, 1864, Batchelor Papers, LSU. For a study of one Southern county that exemplifies many of the generalizations made here about the Confederate frontier see Crofts, *Old Southampton*, chap. 7.

52. On the difficulty of establishing Federal authority in no-man's-land see C. Newton to C. Miller, November 29, 1864, E-1469, RUSACC, and Graf, Haskins, and Bergeron, *Papers of Andrew Johnson*, 7:173, 201. For evidence of the inability of Confederate authority to penetrate no-man's-land see J. Taliaferro to John Letcher, September 26,

1862, and order of Madison County Court, February 25, 1864, Virginia Executive Papers, VSL; Johns, *Florida during the Civil War*, 80; and McMillan, *Disintegration of a Confederate State*, 91, 101.

53. Lemke, *Mecklin Letters*, 26–27. For a study of disruption in a region that was no-man's-land for most of the war see Edward H. Phillips, "Lower Shenandoah Valley during the Civil War," chaps. 6–11.

54. Cox Diary, March 15, 24, 29, 1863, and 1863–64, TSLA; Graf, Haskins, and Bergeron, *Papers of Andrew Johnson*, 6:10–11. See also Nourse Diary, 1862 (MS), VHS; Sanford, "Virginian's Diary," 362; Hughes, "Wartime Gristmill Destruction," 175–78; and Moneyhon, *Impact of the Civil War*, 128–30, 134–35.

55. Roland, "Difficulties of Civil War Sugar Planting," 44–47; Moneyhon, "Impact of the Civil War in Arkansas," 110; *OR* 32(2):269; Lemke, *Mecklin Letters*, 37.

56. Simon McCartney to J. Conn, May 24, 1864, Federal Soldiers' Letters, SHC. See also George Cadman to Esther Cadman, November 23, 1862, Cadman Papers, SHC, and report of William Palfrey, February 1864, Palfrey Papers, LSU. A related problem was the deterioration and destruction of levees, which plagued planters along the Mississippi River. See Roland, "Difficulties of Civil War Sugar Planting," 54–55, and Concordia Parish Police Jury Minutes, October 16, 1865 (typescript), LSU.

57. Roland, "Difficulties of Civil War Sugar Planting," 41–44; Moneyhon, "Impact of the Civil War in Arkansas," 109; *Clarksville Gazette*, February 20, 1864; Peter Yawyer to brother, January 10, 1863, Yawyer Letter, LSU.

58. Bills Diary, March 14, 1863, SHC. See also [?] to Frank Nicholls, January 8, 1865, Emily Sparks case, MM2049, ROJAG.

59. See, for example, Henry Jones to J. Donnell, April 5, September 2, October 24, 1863, Bryan Family Papers, Duke.

60. Colin Clarke to Maxwell Clarke, September 24, December 7, 29, 1863, Clarke Papers, SHC.

61. For examples of citizens bringing in produce to the garrisoned towns from the countryside see "Documents: Civil War Diary of Jabez T. Cox," 49–50, and Handy Diary, February 3, 1865 (MS), Duke. Restrictions on the purchase and transportation of supplies by citizens living outside the garrisoned towns are documented in H. Wells to J. Taylor, May 30, 1864, E-1457, RUSACC; *OR* 39(2):30–31; and William Hackley to wife, November 29, 1863, Hackley Letters, UTK. Illegal trade with the North is evidenced in Graf, Haskins, and Bergeron, *Papers of Andrew Johnson*, 7:318, and H. Wells to T. Gaines, April 6, 1864, E-1457, RUSACC.

62. For examples of problems involving currency faced by the residents of no-man's-land see Colin Clarke to Maxwell Clarke, December 7, 1863, Clarke Papers, SHC, and John Evans to William Smith, May 7, 1864, Virginia Executive Papers, VSL.

63. King Diary, July 16, August 3, 1864, SHC; *OR* 51(1):1137–38, 43(2):830–31; Giles Ward to father, May 10, 1863, Ward Papers, Duke.

64. King Diary, July 16, 23, 25, August 3, 18, 21, 1864, SHC; Lemke, *Mecklin Letters*, 19, 37.

65. On the loss of wagons and the destruction of bridges and boats see George

Cadman to Esther Cadman, November 23, 1862, Cadman Papers, SHC; "Documents: The Shelly Papers," 190; report of William Palfrey, February 1864, Palfrey Papers, LSU; and Edward H. Phillips, "Lower Shenandoah Valley during the Civil War," chap. 10. Road maintenance was customarily carried out under the authority of county government, on the fate of which see below.

66. Rebecca Ballou to parents, July 1, 1863, Ballou Family of Virginia Papers, LC. See also Colin Clarke to Maxwell Clarke, July 16, 1863, Clarke Papers, SHC.

67. Norton Diary, June 27, 1864, GDAH; King Diary, July–September 1864, especially July 21, 27–28, August 1, 27, September 1, SHC. See also *Nashville Dispatch*, September 11, October 31, 1862.

68. Cox Diary, June 16, 1863, TSLA; King Diary, July 10, 22, August 1, 4, 27, 1864, SHC.

69. For evidence of the disruption of schools in no-man's-land see Sanford, "Virginian's Diary," 360; Hopewell Meeting of Friends (Frederick County) Monthly Meeting Record Book, March 7, 1866 (MS), VSL; and Edward H. Phillips, "Lower Shenandoah Valley during the Civil War," chap. 7. On church disruption see Edmonson Diary, September 19, 1863, AHC; Brydon, "Diocese of Virginia," 400; Edward H. Phillips, "Lower Shenandoah Valley during the Civil War," chap. 8; and the church records cited in the following note. For an example of a rural fraternal organization that was disrupted see Woodbury [Masonic] Lodge no. 235 Minutes, 1862–65 (microfilm), TSLA.

70. Christian Chapel Church of Christ, Henderson County, Minute Book, n.d. (probably August 1866) (microfilm), TSLA; Ebenezer Baptist Church, Loudoun County, Minute Book, July 1865 (microfilm), VSL. For other examples of churches that were wholly or mostly disrupted during the time they were in no-man's-land see Hopewell Meeting Monthly Record Book, October 5, 1864, VSL; West Station Primitive Baptist Church, Sumner County, Session Minutes, 1862–65 (microfilm), TSLA; Ebenezer Primitive Baptist Church, Dunwoody, De Kalb County, Minutes, 1864 (microfilm), GDAH; Rodney Presbyterian Church Records, 1862–65 (microfilm), MDAH; and Thumb Run Primitive Baptist Church, Fauquier County, Minute Book, 1862–65 (microfilm), VSL.

71. Edward H. Phillips, "Lower Shenandoah Valley during the Civil War," chap. 6; *OR* 32(2):261; West Feliciana Parish Police Jury Minutes, 1862–65 (MS), LSU; Loudoun County Court Minute Book, 1862–65 (microfilm), VSL. For other examples of the disruption of local government in counties and parishes within no-man's-land see Bartow County Ordinary Court Minutes, 1864 (microfilm), GDAH; Madison County Court Minutes, 1862–65 (microfilm), TSLA; St. John the Baptist Parish Police Jury Minutes, 1862–65 (MS), LSU; and Stafford County Court Minute Book, 1862–65 (microfilm), VSL.

72. W. Little to William Smith, February 27, 1864, Virginia Executive Papers, VSL.

73. Ibid.; Sanford, "Virginian's Diary," 364.

74. John Evans to William Smith, May 7, 1864, Virginia Executive Papers, VSL; *OR* 32(1):156. See also Norton, *Army Letters*, 160, and *Nashville Dispatch*, January 12, 1864.

75. Bickham, *Rosecrans' Campaign with the Fourteenth Army Corps*, 50; Sanford,

"Virginian's Diary," 366. See also Jay Caldwell Butler, *Letters Home*, 33–34, and Beck Diary, December 23, 1862, January 9, 1863 (microfilm), Clark Collection, LC.

CHAPTER FOUR

1. Durham, *Nashville*, 47; Graf, Haskins, and Bergeron, *Papers of Andrew Johnson*, 5:462; Blegen, *Civil War Letters of Colonel . . . Heg*, 241.

2. See, besides the citations in the Prologue and Chapter 1, *Nashville Daily Times and True Union*, September 8, 1864, January 11, 1865, and Moore Diary, May 23, 1865, ADAH.

3. Graf, Haskins, and Bergeron, *Papers of Andrew Johnson*, 5:462.

4. William Watson Davis, *Civil War and Reconstruction in Florida*, 244–45; Henry Barker to wife, July 1, 1862, Barker Papers, TSLA.

5. Klingberg, *Southern Claims Commission*, 5–8, and "Operation Reconstruction," 467, 472; *Nashville Dispatch*, November 28, 1862; Graf, Haskins, and Bergeron, *Papers of Andrew Johnson*, 5:344–45.

6. Tatum, *Disloyalty in the Confederacy*, 4–5; Honey, "War within the Confederacy," 75–79, 84–90; Klingberg, *Southern Claims Commission*, 2; *OR* 23(2):54–55.

7. Martin, "Defeat in Victory," 21–22; William Watson Davis, *Civil War and Reconstruction in Florida*, 250–51; *OR* 6:251–52. See also *Calendar of Virginia State Papers*, 11:370–71, and Delaney, "Charles Henry Foster," 355.

8. Graf, Haskins, and Bergeron, *Papers of Andrew Johnson*, 6:135, 5:246.

9. *OR* 25(2):114, 29(1):71; William Russell case, NN3272, ROJAG; Graf, Haskins, and Bergeron, *Papers of Andrew Johnson*, 5:407–8.

10. Parks, "Memphis under Military Rule," 42–43; Fitch, *Annals of the Army*, 449; "Major Connolly's Letters to His Wife," 271.

11. *Senate Reports*, 37th Cong., 3d sess., no. 108, p. 433; *OR* 9:200; Durrill, *War of Another Kind*, 98, 103.

12. William Watson Davis, *Civil War and Reconstruction in Florida*, 159, 250–53; Martin, "Defeat in Victory," 14–28.

13. *OR* 7:671, and ser. 2, 2:61–62.

14. See, for example, ibid., ser. 1, 51(1):96.

15. Blegen, *Civil War Letters of Colonel . . . Heg*, 241–42. See also George Cadman to Esther Cadman, November 5, 1863, Cadman Papers, SHC, and *OR* 19(2):26.

16. Simeon Evans to mother, June 3, 1862, Evans Letters, LSU; *OR* 22(1):241.

17. *Nashville Dispatch*, November 14, 1863; *OR* 47(2):50. See also petition, March 1865, no. 15461, and "List of the names of disloyal citizens . . .," n.d., no. 22180, Union Provost Marshals' File, M-416, NA.

18. *Fort Smith New Era*, November 14, 1863, May 28, 1864; S. Harrison to wife, August 1, 1862, Harrison Papers, Duke; *OR* 16(2):252, 38(4):50; Marten, "Wearying Existence"; *OR* 6:125, 22(2):825, 31(3):58. For more on the refugee camps see Chapter 6.

19. Doyle, "Nurseries of Treason," 164; Capers, *Occupied City*, 178, 186–87; Gaston,

"World Overturned," 8; Durham, *Nashville*, 80n, 156–57; Avery, "Second Presbyterian Church of Nashville."

20. Hesseltine, *Lincoln's Plan of Reconstruction*; Belz, *Reconstructing the Union*, 291–304; Abbott, *Republican Party and the South*, 20, 29, 40–41.

21. Hesseltine, *Lincoln's Plan of Reconstruction*, especially 136, 139; Belz, *Reconstructing the Union*, 43–44, 285; Abbott, *Republican Party and the South*, 29–30; Foner, *Reconstruction*, 35–37.

22. Belz, *Reconstructing the Union*, 43–44, 285–86; Abbott, *Republican Party and the South*, 29–30, 39–40; William C. Harris, "Lincoln and Wartime Reconstruction," 168; Maslowski, "From Reconciliation to Reconstruction," 349; Hendricks, "Union Army Occupation of the Southern Seaboard," 215; *OR* 18:649.

23. See, for example, Graf, Haskins, and Bergeron, *Papers of Andrew Johnson*, 7:201, 261, 470–71.

24. Abbott, *Republican Party and the South*, 31; Alexander, *Political Reconstruction in Tennessee*, 16, 30–31, 39; Maslowski, "From Reconciliation to Reconstruction," 343–46; Dawson, *Army Generals and Reconstruction*, 15–16.

25. Ambler, *Francis H. Pierpont*, 213–30; Norman D. Brown, *Edward Stanly*, 201–53; Harris, "Lincoln and Wartime Reconstruction," 149–68; Abbott, *Republican Party and the South*, 30–31; Cowan, "Reorganization of Federal Arkansas"; Moneyhon, *Impact of the Civil War*, 156–69.

26. Alexander, *Political Reconstruction in Tennessee*, 15–48; Patton, *Unionism and Reconstruction in Tennessee*, 30–50; Maslowski, "From Reconciliation to Reconstruction," 281–99, 343–61.

27. Joe Gray Taylor, *Louisiana Reconstructed*, 13–52; McCrary, *Abraham Lincoln and Reconstruction*, 347–51; Tunnell, *Crucible of Reconstruction*, 19, 26–65; Dawson, *Army Generals and Reconstruction*, 11–23.

28. Graf, Haskins, and Bergeron, *Papers of Andrew Johnson*, 7:470–71, 6:459.

29. *OR* 48(1):1120, 12(1):51. See also Cartmell Diary, December 31, 1863, TSLA; Graf, Haskins, and Bergeron, *Papers of Andrew Johnson*, 6:310; and Klingberg, "Operation Reconstruction," 475–79.

30. Graf, Haskins, and Bergeron, *Papers of Andrew Johnson*, 6:135; *Clarksville Gazette*, February 20, 1864.

31. Capers, *Occupied City*, 123–25; Graf, Haskins, and Bergeron, *Papers of Andrew Johnson*, 7:296.

32. Ambler, *Francis H. Pierpont*, 231–47; Wilson, "Experiment in Reunion," 184–235; *Calendar of Virginia State Papers*, 11:419, 422–23.

33. Alexander, *Political Reconstruction in Tennessee*, 39–42; Nourse Diary, July 31, 1862, VHS; Maslowski, "From Reconciliation to Reconstruction," 345.

34. Benjamin F. Butler, *Private and Official Correspondence*, 1:449; Crabtree and Patton, *Journal of a Secesh Lady*, 242–43. See also Ward Diary, February 7, 1862, LC.

35. Crabtree and Patton, *Journal of a Secesh Lady*, 303; *OR* 10(1):81; Bernard Diary, April 20, 1863 (MS), SHC.

36. Benjamin F. Butler, *Private and Official Correspondence*, 1:485; *Memphis Bulletin*, July 6, 1862; Graf, Haskins, and Bergeron, *Papers of Andrew Johnson*, 5:346–47.

37. Graf, Haskins, and Bergeron, *Papers of Andrew Johnson*, 5:547–48; *Memphis Union Appeal*, July 23, 1862.

38. *Memphis Bulletin*, July 10, 1862; Ward Diary, November 19, December 1, 8, 1861, LC; Spain, "R. B. C. Howell," 334.

39. Proclamation, April 24, 1862, Virginia Executive Papers, VSL; Orders 681 and 682, June 20, 1862, Records of the Louisiana State Government, LSA; Lathrop, "Lafourche District in 1862," 231–32, 239–43.

40. William Watson Davis, *Civil War and Reconstruction in Florida*, 257–58; Hopewell Meeting Monthly Record Book, March 7, 1866, VSL; Sterling Scroggs case, MM2887, ROJAG.

41. Agnew Diary, April 7, 1863, SHC; Cool Springs Baptist Church, Eure, Gates County, Minutes, July 1864 (microfilm), NCDAH.

42. *OR* 10(2):407–8. See also William Bonner to George Wortham, June 16, 1864, Pittman Collection, NCDAH.

43. Graf, Haskins, and Bergeron, *Papers of Andrew Johnson*, 5:460–61; *OR Navy* 5:279; Amanda to Mary, September 12, 1862, Clarksville Correspondence Concerning Civil War Guerrillas, TSLA; Sperry Diary, January 14, 1864, VSL.

44. Joseph Matthews case, LL902, and James Cannemore case, OO662, ROJAG. See also *Fort Smith New Era*, November 14, 1863, April 9, 1864; Graf, Haskins, and Bergeron, *Papers of Andrew Johnson*, 5:545–46; *OR* 17(2):365; and Sutherland, "Guerrillas," 267–69, 273.

45. Winn McGrew case, OO873, ROJAG. Other examples are in Cornelius Peacher case, OO1188, and Thomas Elliott case, LL3195, ibid., and Porter Journal, July 18, 1863, SHC.

46. *Fort Smith New Era*, November 14, 1863, May 28, 1864; Harrison to mother, September 15, 1863, Harrison Papers, Duke; *Nashville Daily Times and True Union*, August 10, 1864; *OR* 34(4):561.

47. Powhatan Hardiman case, OO847, ROJAG. See also S. Harrison to wife, August 1, 1862, Harrison Papers, Duke.

48. Killings of Unionist men by guerrillas are noted in John Sailor case, MM557, ROJAG; James Tait to E. Parker, February 12, 1863, E-1457, RUSACC; *OR* 16(1):636; and *Nashville Daily Times and True Union*, June 14, 1864.

49. Graf, Haskins, and Bergeron, *Papers of Andrew Johnson*, 7:431–32; *OR* 39(2):56; *Fort Smith New Era*, April 9, 1864.

50. Graf, Haskins, and Bergeron, *Papers of Andrew Johnson*, 5:460–61.

51. *Diary of a Southern Refugee*, 20; Leslie, "Arabella Lanktree Wilson's Civil War Letter," 261–63. See also *OR* 7:659–60.

52. Gordon, *War Diary*, 301; *OR* 37(1):599, 26(1):532, 29(1):478–79; statement of Samuel Berek, January 22, 1864, E-949, RUSACC; Henry Saules case, MM1969, ROJAG; Auman and Scarboro, "Heroes of America."

53. Bradford Hambrick case, LL2953, ROJAG. See also Harrison to mother, September 15, 1863, Harrison Papers, Duke, and Charles Stevenson to Tom Heckstall, n.d., Heckstall Papers, NCDAH.

54. *OR Navy* 7:153; *OR* 16(1):785–88.

55. Current, *Lincoln's Loyalists* (enlistment figures, pp. 213–18); Fitch, *Annals of the Army*, 213–15.

56. Bettersworth, *Confederate Mississippi*, 216–17; Huff, "Guerrillas, Jayhawkers, and Bushwhackers," 129–30, 137–38; Albert Burton Moore, *Conscription and Conflict in the Confederacy*, 151–53; Espy Diary, July 22, 27, 29, August 19, December 2, 1864, ADAH. These bands, it should be noted, often included men who were not Unionists strictly speaking but were instead what might be called anti-Confederates, including deserters from the Rebel army and men evading Confederate conscription.

57. H. Wells to Samuel Heintzelman, July 20, 1863, E-1457, RUSACC.

58. *OR Navy* 22:648; Durrill, *War of Another Kind*, 98–99; *OR* 38(5):299. See also Maury County refugees to Andrew Johnson, July 8, 1863, Johnson Papers, LC, and *OR* 22(2):543.

59. *Fayetteville Union Herald*, June 18, 1862; Maslowski, *Treason Must Be Made Odious*, 41–43; *OR* 22(2):533; H. Wells to J. Taylor, October 14, 1863, E-1457, RUSACC.

60. Graf, Haskins, and Bergeron, *Papers of Andrew Johnson*, 7:86–87; *Fort Smith New Era*, April 23, May 14, 1864. See also H. Wells to J. Taylor, November 17, 1863, E-1457, RUSACC, and *OR* 49(1):34.

CHAPTER FIVE

1. Moore Diary, April 26, 30, 1862, ADAH.

2. *Senate Reports*, 37th Cong., 3d sess., no. 108, p. 352; Hess, *Liberty, Virtue, and Progress*, 97; journal of unknown man, September 10, 1862 (misdated August 10), Pettigrew Family Papers, SHC.

3. Berlin et al., *Destruction of Slavery*, 23, 27, 32–34, 59–68, 103–10, 187–98, 249–60; Cimprich, *Slavery's End in Tennessee*, 33–38; Ripley, *Slaves and Freedmen in Civil War Louisiana*, 25–39; Mitchell, *Civil War Soldiers*, 126–29; Hess, *Liberty, Virtue, and Progress*, 96–100; Jimerson, *Private Civil War*, 80–81; "Major Connolly's Letters," 248.

4. On the Federal government's policy toward slavery from the second Confiscation Act to the Emancipation Proclamation see Gerteis, *From Contraband to Freedman*; Berlin et al., *Destruction of Slavery*, 1–51, 65, 67n, 109–10, 195–96, 198n, 258; and McPherson, *Battle Cry of Freedom*, 354–58, 494–510, 557–58, 563–66. The forty-eight counties of western Virginia, soon to be granted statehood, were also exempted from the proclamation.

5. Berlin et al., *Destruction of Slavery*, 67–69, 109–10, 112–13, 198–99, 250–51, 261–69; Fitch, *Annals of the Army*, 270; Cimprich, *Slavery's End in Tennessee*, 38–45; testimony of George Stearns, November 1863, American Freedmen's Inquiry Commission, Preliminary and Final Reports, M-619, RG 94, NA.

6. Gerteis, *From Contraband to Freedman*, 58–62, 83–85, 135–45; Cimprich, *Slavery's End in Tennessee*, 60–72; Currie, *Enclave*, 56–62, 75; Moneyhon, *Impact of the Civil War*, 142–51; Ronald L. F. Davis, *Good and Faithful Labor*, 62–73; Ripley, *Slaves*

and Freedmen in Civil War Louisiana, 40–68, 90–91, 126–45; Powell, *New Masters*, 1–7; Foner, *Reconstruction*, 50–60.

7. Gerteis, *From Contraband to Freedman*, 59–60, 153–54, 169, 181, 183–85; Foner, *Reconstruction*, 55, 58; Ripley, *Slaves and Freedmen in Civil War Louisiana*, 58, 90–91; Mitchell, *Civil War Soldiers*, 121–23, 128–31; *OR* 30(3):277.

8. Litwack, *Been in the Storm So Long*, 52–59; Engs, *Freedom's First Generation*, 68–70; Mohr, *On the Threshold of Freedom*, 70–75; Pugh Plantation Diary, July 7–8, 1862 (typescript), LSU; Colin Clarke to Maxwell Clarke, July 22, 1862, Clarke Papers, SHC. See also Rawick, *American Slave*, 8(1):168–69, 19:112–16; Eliza Brockenbrough to Alice Aylett, November 4, 1862, Brockenbrough Letters, VHS; and George Wallace to James Saunders, June 25, 1862, Wallace Papers, Duke.

9. Wiley, *Southern Negroes*, 72–83; Ripley, *Slaves and Freedmen in Civil War Louisiana*, 22–23; E. McCollam to Andrew McCollam, March 26, 1863, McCollam Papers, SHC; wife to William Harding, May 15, 1862, Harding-Jackson Papers, SHC; *OR* 10(1):82; Dulany Diary, June 11, 1862 (MS), VHS; Berlin et al., *Destruction of Slavery*, 219–20; Bills Diary, July 30, November 5, 1862, SHC.

10. John Ela to James Bowen, June 11, 1863, E-1482, RUSACC; Samuel Dwyer case, MM2135, ROJAG.

11. John Ransdell to Thomas Moore, May 24, 1863, Moore Papers, LSU; Fonsylvania Plantation Journal, May 6–June 13, 1863 (MS), MDAH. See also Palfrey Plantation Diary, April 25, 1863, Palfrey Account Books, LSU, and Rawick, *American Slave*, 14(1):24–25.

12. Messner, "Black Violence and White Response," 21–23; James Evans to William Smith, December 14, 1864, Virginia Executive Papers, VSL; James Ela to [?], February 23, 1863, E-1482, RUSACC.

13. *Alexandria Gazette*, September 12, 18, 1862.

14. Cimprich, *Slavery's End in Tennessee*, 46–47; *Alexandria Gazette*, January 10, 1865; Bernard Diary, January 1, 1863, SHC; Handy Diary, March 20, 1865, Duke.

15. Blegen, *Civil War Letters of Colonel . . . Heg*, 79; Fleet and Fuller, *Green Mount*, 133.

16. Waddel Diary, November 23, 1862, LC; Graf, Haskins, and Bergeron, *Papers of Andrew Johnson*, 6:318–19.

17. Roark, *Masters Without Slaves*, 71–72; Bernard Diary, August 8, 1863, SHC.

18. Roark, *Masters Without Slaves*, 71–72; Jimerson, *Private Civil War*, 73–74, 76; Bond Diary, September 2, 1863, LSU. See also Lemke, *Mecklin Letters*, 23.

19. Skipper and Gove, "'Stray Thoughts,'" 1:136; Moore Diary, January 1, 1863 (microfilm), SHC. See also Harry to Willis Claiborne, October 16, 1862, Claiborne Papers, LC.

20. Graf, Haskins, and Bergeron, *Papers of Andrew Johnson*, 5:371–72, 6:526; Rebecca Ballou to parents, July 1, 1863, Ballou Family Papers, LC; Anonymous Diary, July 25, 1863, MDAH; Maud Morrow Brown, "War Comes to College Hill," 26–27; Hugh Torrance to Mrs. T. Reid, February 16, 1863, Davidson Papers, Duke; Davis Diary, June 15, July 1, 1862 (MS), VHS.

21. William Lewis to George Washington, February 24, March 6, 1863, Washington Family Papers, TSLA; Agnew Diary, December 7, 1863, SHC; Anonymous Diary, September 20, 1863, MDAH; Crabtree and Patton, *Journal of a Secesh Lady*, 446; William Smith to Christopher Tompkins, December 5, 1862, William Patterson Smith Papers, Duke; Priscilla Bond to mother, September 2, 1863, Bond Papers, LSU.

22. Anonymous Diary, July 16, 28, 1863, MDAH; Berlin et al., *Destruction of Slavery*, 220; Alvin Voris to wife, January 12, 1863, Voris Papers, VHS; Rable, *Civil Wars*, 118; Carney Diary, July 21, 1862, SHC.

23. Litwack, *Been in the Storm So Long*, 147–49; Roark, *Masters Without Slaves*, 75–76; Moore Diary, April 26, 1862, ADAH; Palfrey Plantation Diary, March 16, 1864, Palfrey Account Books, LSU; Bernard Diary, December 25, 1862, SHC; Berlin et al., *Destruction of Slavery*, 232; Rable, *Civil Wars*, 158; Lititia Andrews to John Pettus, March 28, 1863, Pettus Correspondence, MDAH.

24. Jimerson, *Private Civil War*, 111–12, 115–16; Espy Diary, June 7, 1864, ADAH; Cyrus Branch to William Smith, May 15, 1864, Virginia Executive Papers, VSL.

25. Cartmell Diary, October 1, November 13, 1862, TSLA; Colin Clarke to Maxwell Clarke, September 16, 1862, Clarke Papers, SHC.

26. Coffin, *Four Years of Fighting*, 431; John Ela to James Bowen, June 11, 1863, E-1482, RUSACC. See also *OR* 48(1):1290.

27. Testimony of George Stearns, November 1863, American Freedmen's Inquiry Commission Reports, NA; Hardy Hardison to Josiah Collins, March 27, 1863, and G. Spruill to Josiah Collins, May 16, 1863, Collins Papers, NCDAH. See also *Nashville Daily Times and True Union*, May 20, 1864; N. Gill to [?], February 19, 1865, E-1488, RUSACC; and *OR* 34(4):232.

28. Jane Warren to Electa Ames, August 27, 1863, Ames Papers, Duke.

29. See *Nashville Dispatch*, April–December 1862.

30. Ibid., November 26, 1862, January 18, 1863.

31. Maury Diary, May 16, 1862, LC; T. Clarke to J. Liebman, August 21, 1862, E-5175, RUSACC.

32. *Nashville Dispatch*, November 26, December 11, 1862, February 11, 27, 1863; Bernard Diary, January 2, 1863, SHC.

33. Cartmell Diary, August 20, 1862, TSLA; petition no. 231, December 8, 1862, E-175, Legislative Records (Confederate), NA. See also Coffin, *Four Years of Fighting*, 482.

34. In addition to the sources cited in Chapter 3, note 39, see Rawick, *American Slave*, 7:162–63, 8(1):110, 14(1):136; A. Bradford to Charles Clark, August 27, 1864, Clark Correspondence, MDAH; Roxa Cole to Cousin Blanche, November 2, 1862, Cole Family Letters, MDAH; Thomas Batchelor to Albert Batchelor, September 21, 1864, Batchelor Papers, LSU; and L. Gambill to John Letcher, n.d. (probably December 1862), Virginia Executive Papers, VSL.

35. See, for example, H. Cassedy to Charles Clark, September 12, 1864, Clark Correspondence, MDAH.

36. Fleet and Fuller, *Green Mount*, 260; J. Wilson to John Chesson, n.d., Chesson

Papers, NCDAH; Lafayette Parish Police Jury Minutes, October 6, 1864, LSU; Berlin et al., *Destruction of Slavery*, 300; *OR* 14:293, 541, 46(2):1139; Agnew Diary, May 12, 1863, SHC.

37. Berlin et al., *Destruction of Slavery*, 94–95.

38. Litwack, *Been in the Storm So Long*, 172–77; John Ransdell to Thomas Moore, May 24, 26, 1863, Moore Papers, LSU.

39. Berlin et al., *Destruction of Slavery*, 795–98; statement of Washington Someroy, November 26, 1864, E-1599, RUSACC; *OR* 42(2):653; Maud Morrow Brown, "War Comes to College Hill," 28–30.

40. Berlin et al., *Destruction of Slavery*, 701, 775; order of Madison County court, February 25, 1864, Hiram Yugee et al. to William Smith, November 2, 1864, and resolution of Rockingham County court, September 28, 1863, all in Virginia Executive Papers, VSL; John Burruss to Edward Burruss, May 23, 1864, Burruss Family Papers, LSU.

41. Hassell Diary, 1862–65, especially November 13, 26, 1862, August 4, 1863, March 15, 1864, February 3, 28, May 8, 1865, SHC.

42. Cimprich, *Slavery's End in Tennessee*, 27–29; George Wallace to James Saunders, July 1, 1862, Wallace Papers, Duke; Rawick, *American Slave*, 14(1):214; journal of events of provost marshal, June 17, 1862, E-1711, RUSACC; William Lewis to George Washington, March 6, May 1, 1863, Washington Family Papers, TSLA. On the ease with which slaves in no-man's-land could run off to Federal posts see Henderson Diary, 1862–63 (microfilm), TSLA.

43. Graf, Haskins, and Bergeron, *Papers of Andrew Johnson*, 6:426; Henry Jones to J. Donnell, September 14, 1862, Bryan Family Papers, Duke; Berlin et al., *Destruction of Slavery*, 301; Colin Clarke to Maxwell Clarke, August 10, 1862, Clarke Papers, SHC; testimony concerning Silas Norris case, January 15, 1863, Johnson Papers, LC.

44. Cimprich, *Slavery's End in Tennessee*, 30; T. Clarke to T. Christensen, July 17, 1862, E-5175, RUSACC; E. Dean case, MM1743, ROJAG; Porter Journal, August 17, 1863, SHC.

45. P. Cox to J. Rudyard, May 26, 1863, E-1474, RUSACC.

46. Crabtree and Patton, *Journal of a Secesh Lady*, 463; Bills Diary, August 29, September 3, October 17, 1863, SHC. See also Colin Clarke to Maxwell Clarke, September 14, 1862, Clarke Papers, SHC.

47. Stephen Duncan Jr. to father, January 11, 1864 (misdated 1863), Duncan Correspondence, LSU; Pugh Plantation Diary, February 19, April 14, 1865, LSU.

48. Gerteis, *From Contraband to Freedman*, 91–98, 114–15; W. Allen to C. Newton, February 4, 1864, and Thomas Tileston to Major Remington, May 20, 1864, E-1471, RUSACC. See also Henry Wood to Simon Jerrard, April 30, 1863, Jerrard Papers, LSU, and Pugh Plantation Diary, April 25, 1865, LSU.

49. Ripley, *Slaves and Freedmen in Civil War Louisiana*, 57, 61–62, 66–67, 99–101; Porter Journal, May 16, 1864, March 8, 1865, SHC; Edward Bigelow to F. Starring, May 19, 1865, E-1486, RUSACC.

50. Gerteis, *From Contraband to Freedman*, 85, 145, 158–60; Powell, *New Masters*,

45–46; Currie, *Enclave*, 62–66; Porter Journal, May 26, 30, 1864, SHC; *OR* 41(3):402; David Sink case, LL2862, ROJAG.

51. William Murray case, MM2682, ROJAG.

CHAPTER SIX

1. *OR* 18:745–47; Durrill, *War of Another Kind*, 180.

2. Mitchell, *Civil War Soldiers*, 91, 95; Current, *Northernizing the South*, 50–57; Royster, *Destructive War*, 81–82; Jimerson, *Private Civil War*, 134–35; Corporal, *Letters from the Forty-fourth Regiment*, 90.

3. Ira V. Brown, *Lyman Abbott*, 37; Simeon Evans to mother, June 3, 1862, Evans Letters, LSU; Coffin, *Four Years of Fighting*, 95.

4. Powell, *New Masters*, 13, 24–32; Overy, "Wisconsin Carpetbagger," 19–22; William Watson Davis, *Civil War and Reconstruction in Florida*, 255–57.

5. American Union Commission, *Speeches*, 22; Dunham, *Attitude of the Northern Clergy*, 204–12.

6. Capers, *Occupied City*, 178–79, 183–84; Parks, "Memphis under Military Rule," 34; Harris, "Lincoln and Wartime Reconstruction," 157; Cleveland Diary, February 19, 1865, SHC; Matthias Willing case, LL3250, ROJAG; Fleming, *Documentary History of Reconstruction*, 2:221–23; Brydon, "Diocese of Virginia," 389–90, 394–95; Somers, "War and Play," 14–15.

7. Mitchell, *Civil War Soldiers*, 113–15; Chancellor, *Englishman in the American Civil War*, 141; Knox, *Camp-Fire and Cotton-Field*, 222; Agassiz, *Meade's Headquarters*, 133.

8. Henry Hitchcock to wife, April 7, 1865, Hitchcock Papers, LC; Graf, Haskins, and Bergeron, *Papers of Andrew Johnson*, 5:457–58. See also *OR* 11(1):1055, 23(2):56.

9. Hardison, "In the Toils of War," 82–90; *OR* 34(2):797, 23(1):270, 12(1):453.

10. Mitchell, *Civil War Soldiers*, 109–11; Cook, *Siege of Richmond*, 164–67; Favill, *Diary of a Young Officer*, 204–5; Spencer Diary, August 2, 1864, LC; Alvin Voris to wife, September 20, 1862, Voris Papers, VHS.

11. Richardson, " 'We Are Truly Doing Missionary Work,' " 183; American Union Commission, *Speeches*, 18.

12. Bearss, "Civil War Letters of Major William G. Thompson," 449; *OR* 33:668–69; S. Marrett to wife, May 17, 1862, Marrett Papers, Duke; *New Bern North Carolina Times*, March 16, April 2–3, 1864; Swint, *Dear Ones at Home*, 104, 143, 147; Graf, Haskins, and Bergeron, *Papers of Andrew Johnson*, 7:331; American Union Commission, *Speeches*, 18.

13. Coffin, *Four Years of Fighting*, 432–33; Harwell and Racine, *Fiery Trail*, 102; Swint, *Dear Ones at Home*, 143; Schwartz, *Woman Doctor's Civil War*, 108–11; *OR* 6:506.

14. *Fort Smith New Era*, October 8, 1863. See also *New Bern North Carolina Times*, January 9, 1864.

15. Norton, *Army Letters*, 160. See also Graf, Haskins, and Bergeron, *Papers of Andrew Johnson*, 6:611. For an example of an aristocrat whose supplies held out at least through the first year of occupation see Colin Clarke to Maxwell Clarke, May 21, 1863, Clarke Papers, SHC.

16. See, for example, James Gilfillan to B. Polk, November 23, 1864, E-3048, RUSACC, and *OR* 18:384.

17. *OR Navy* 23:245; Robert Baylor to John Letcher, October 12, 1861, Virginia Executive Papers, VSL; C. Beckerdite to John Pettus, November 23, 1862, Pettus Correspondence, MDAH. The literature on plain folk disaffection in the Confederacy is extensive; see especially Escott, *After Secession*, 94–98, 113–21; Wiley, *Plain People of the Confederacy*, 36–38, 64–69; and Wesley, *Collapse of the Confederacy*, 82.

18. Fielding Diary, July 13, 1862, ADAH; King Diary, August 21, 24, 29, 1864, SHC; Norton Diary, November 12, 1864, GDAH.

19. American Union Commission, *Speeches*, 9, 13–15; J. Sheffield to Thomas Watts, April 22, 1864, Watts Papers, ADAH; *OR* 33:641; King Diary, July 15–16, August 29, 1864, SHC; journal of events of provost marshal, May 30, June 3, 20, September 19, 1862, E-1711, RUSACC; statement of L. Clay, December 28, 1864, E-4294, RUSACC. See also statements of refugees, 1863–64, E-949, RUSACC, and "List of Refugees reporting . . . at Savannah," March 1865, no. 15515, Union Provost Marshals' File, M-416, NA.

20. *OR* 41(2):465; *Nashville Daily Times and True Union*, March 14, 23, May 4, 1864; *New Bern North Carolina Times*, April 4, 1865; "Assessment of Property," April 1863, no. 4487, Union Provost Marshals' File, M-416, NA; William C. Harris, "East Tennessee's Civil War Refugees," 13–15; *Memphis Bulletin*, April 13, 1865; James Hall to W. Burger, October 25, 1864, and Stewart Woodford to M. Littlefield, February 7, 1865, E-4270, RUSACC; American Union Commission, *American Union Commission*; Bremner, *Public Good*, 91–94; *Fort Smith New Era*, March 18, 1865.

21. *OR* 4:619; statement of William Eddins, December 4, 1863, E-949, RUSACC. See also statement of Oliver Webster, January 3, 1864, E-949, RUSACC, and *OR* 6:666.

22. Report of D. Johnson, April 30, 1863, E-1482, RUSACC; Wiley Barren case, MM2887, ROJAG.

23. Pointe Coupee Parish Police Jury Minutes, October 2, 1865 (typescript), LSU; Charles Coolidge to [?], June 13, 1865, E-1598, RUSACC; W. Montgomery to Charles Clark, January 26, 1864, Clark Correspondence, MDAH; Shofner, "Andrew Johnson and the Fernandina Unionists," 211–14; Staudenraus, "War Correspondent's View of St. Augustine," 65.

24. Guerrilla attacks against Northern lessees are noted in *OR* 41(3):208–9; Currie, *Enclave*, 64–65; Overy, "Wisconsin Carpetbagger," 28–29; and Powell and Wayne, "Self-Interest and the Decline of Confederate Nationalism," 42. The resistance of poor whites and others to Northern reform efforts is documented in Richardson, " 'We Are Truly Doing Missionary Work,' " 185–86; Schwartz, *Woman Doctor's Civil War*, 111; and Swint, *Dear Ones at Home*, 143.

25. Archibald Atkinson to John Letcher, August 21, 1862, Virginia Executive Papers, VSL; Knox, *Camp-Fire and Cotton-Field*, 221–22.

26. Potts, *Address to the People*, 3–4; *Nashville Daily Times and True Union*, February 26, 22, 1864.

27. *OR* 25(2):526, 541, 571.

28. *Memphis Union Appeal*, July 18, 1862; Delaney, "Charles Henry Foster," 348–66; Honey, "War within the Confederacy," 88; Norman D. Brown, *Edward Stanly*, 244–46. See also *Nashville Daily Times and True Union*, August 25, 1864.

29. Graf, Haskins, and Bergeron, *Papers of Andrew Johnson*, 6:611; [?] to [?], April 8, 1864, Anonymous Letter, TSLA.

30. Colin Clarke to Powhatan Page, n.d., Clarke Papers, SHC; *OR* 21:776. See also E. Dean case, MM1743, ROJAG.

31. John Evans to William Smith, May 7, 1864, Virginia Executive Papers, VSL; James Limmons to J. Donnell, March 28, May 2, 1864, Bryan Family Papers, Duke. See also William Everitt to George Wortham, May 31, 1864, Pittman Collection, NCDAH, and Durrill, *War of Another Kind*, 106, 112–13.

32. Sallie Dillard to Priscilla Bailey, March 26, 1863, Bailey Papers, SHC; M. Lovell to G. Randolph, June 19, 1862, Records of the Louisiana State Government, LSA; P. Stratton to George Gordon, June 28, 1862, Gordon and Avery Papers, TSLA.

33. Kenelm Lewis to wife, July 27, 1863, Lewis Papers, NCDAH.

34. Daniel Jones to John Letcher, November 6, 1862, Virginia Executive Papers, VSL; petition of planters, January 1, 1864, E-1482, RUSACC.

35. Special Order 8, January 17, 1863, E-1461, RUSACC; *Nashville Dispatch*, January 27, 1863; Cartmell Diary, April 29, 1863, TSLA.

36. Crabtree and Patton, *Journal of a Secesh Lady*, 242–43.

37. Coffin, *Four Years of Fighting*, 429–30. For an example of the banishing of aristocrats see Graf, Haskins, and Bergeron, *Papers of Andrew Johnson*, 5:519. On aristocratic refugees see Chapter 1; on the fate of political institutions see Chapter 3.

38. *OR* 48(1):706–7; William Loftin to mother, October 2, 1862, Loftin Papers, Duke; Bills Diary, July 31, August 29, 1862, SHC; James Willcox to Susa, June 26, 1865, May 30, 1864, Willcox Papers, Duke.

39. Harry to Willis Claiborne, October 16, 1862, Claiborne Papers, LC; Bickham, *Rosecrans' Campaign*, 56; Coffin, *Four Years of Fighting*, 406; *OR* 9:200.

40. Oscar to Gustave Lauve, June 26, 1863, Lauve Letter, LSU; Agnes Whiteside to E. Peacock, November 30, 1863, Whiteside Family Papers, TSLA; Colin Clarke to Maxwell Clarke, August 31, 1862, December 7, 1863, Clarke Papers, SHC.

41. Sanford, "Virginian's Diary," 368; Jane Washington to son, December 18, 1864, Washington Letter, TSLA; Berlin et al., *Destruction of Slavery*, 96–97. See also Royster, *Destructive War*, 27.

42. Testimony of George Stearns, November 1863, American Freedmen's Inquiry Commission Reports, NA; Elizabeth Harding to William Harding, June 16, 1862, Harding-Jackson Papers, SHC.

43. Rable (*Civil Wars*, 184) makes this point in a somewhat different context.

44. Petition of planters, January 1, 1864, E-1482, RUSACC; R. Hudson to Charles Clark, May 24, June 13, 25, 1864, Clark Correspondence, MDAH.

45. Durrill, *War of Another Kind*, 91.

46. Similar outbreaks occurred in the Confederate interior, but they were undoubtedly less common there because suffering and disruption, though considerable, were less extensive than in the occupied regions. On the Confederate interior see Thomas, *Confederate Nation*, 233–35; Escott, *Many Excellent People*, 67–84; and Rable, *Civil Wars*, 108–11.

47. *OR* 44:280, 793; Lawrence, *A Present for Mr. Lincoln*, 209–10; Special Order 8, January 17, 1863, E-1461, RUSACC.

48. Ellen Cooley to Julia Brookes, March 11, 1865, Brookes Papers, Duke; Minerva McClatchey Diary (MS), January 1, 1865, McClatchey Family Papers, GDAH; Norton Diary, November 13, 1864, GDAH.

49. Durrill, *War of Another Kind*, 180; M. Baker to Joseph Finegan, January 14, 1864, E-1710, RUSACC. See also *OR* 35(2):544.

50. Espy Diary, July 29, 1864, ADAH; Durrill, *War of Another Kind*, 180–81.

51. Plantation journal, May 11, 1863, Bayside Plantation Records, SHC; Kenelm Lewis to wife, July 27, 1863, Lewis Papers, NCDAH; King Diary, July 10, 1864, SHC; Roswell Manufacturing Company, Minutes of Stockholders' Meetings, July 19, 1865 (microfilm), GDAH.

52. J. Spruill to Josiah Collins, April 22, 1863, and Girard Phelps to Josiah Collins, March 14, 1863, Collins Papers, NCDAH; Durrill, *War of Another Kind*, 105–14, 131–36, 172–73, 179–84, 211–12, 216; Escott, *Many Excellent People*, 62–63. See also Sallie Dillard to Priscilla Bailey, March 26, 1863, Bailey Papers, SHC.

53. Gower, "Beersheba Diary," 91.

54. French Diary, June 10, 22, July 7, 20, 23, 25–27, October 12, 1863, TSLA.

CHAPTER SEVEN

1. Sallie to John Minor, May 15, 1864, Sailor's Rest Plantation Papers, TSLA.

2. For examples of men's concerns, efforts, and failures with regard to their families see Berlin et al., *Destruction of Slavery*, 219–20; Hassell Diary, November 3, 1862, SHC; King Diary, August 4, 23, 1864, SHC; and Fielding Diary, January 15, 1865, ADAH.

3. Beck Diary, January 9, 1863, Clark Collection, LC; *OR* 31(1):592; King Diary, August 3, 1864, SHC; petition no. 368, November 1864, E-175, Legislative Records (Confederate), NA; W. Holder to Charles Clark, September 15, 1864, Clark Correspondence, MDAH.

4. Hassell Diary, November 3–13, 1862, SHC; Roxa Cole to mother, September 14, August 4, 1862, Cole Family Letters, MDAH; Graf, Haskins, and Bergeron, *Papers of Andrew Johnson*, 6:367.

5. Emily Hewlett to John Shorter, August 13, 1862, Shorter Papers, ADAH; Crabtree and Patton, *Journal of a Secesh Lady*, 464; Stella Bringier to Louis Bringier, July 28, 1862, Bringier and Family Papers, LSU.

6. Anonymous Diary, July 14, 1863, MDAH; Roxa Cole to Cousin Blanche, Novem-

ber 2, 1862, Cole Family Letters, MDAH. On the "woman order" see Massey, *Bonnet Brigades*, 228–30, and Simkins and Patton, *Women of the Confederacy*, 56–58.

7. Lemke, *Mecklin Letters*, 18; Edmonson Diary, September 19, 1863, AHC; French Diary, June 29, 1862, April 17, 1864, TSLA; Kate Burruss to Edward Burruss, February 18, 1864, Burruss Family Papers, LSU.

8. Petition no. 395, n.d. (1864), E-175, Legislative Records (Confederate), NA; Maria Kehoe to Robert Brown, December 7, 1862, E-1482, RUSACC; Nott, *Sketches of the War*, 98.

9. Hassell Diary, November 26, 1862, July 9, August 11, 1863, January 25, April 14, May 11, 1864, SHC; King Diary, August 3, 1864, SHC; H. Burleigh to John Wool, October 20, 1861, E-5175, RUSACC.

10. Rable, *Civil Wars*, 115–19; Mohr, *On the Threshold of Freedom*, 221–22, 224–32; Joyce Davis to Jane Washington, February 19, 1865, Mary Washington to Jane Washington, March 3, 11, 17, 1865, and Joseph Washington to Jane Washington, March 11, 27, 1865, Washington Family Papers, TSLA.

11. *Fort Smith New Era*, July 15, 1865; *Nashville Dispatch*, July 23, 1863; T. Clarke to J. Leibman, August 21, 30, 1862, E-5175, RUSACC.

12. On the rarity of rape and the Federals' disapproval of the molestation of women see Mitchell, *Vacant Chair*, 104–6, 109; Coffin, *Four Years of Fighting*, 399; Fellman, *Inside War*, 189, 201–6; and Glatthaar, *March to the Sea and Beyond*, 73–74. On body searches see Sperry Diary, February 11, 1863, VSL; *Beaufort Old North State*, February 18, 1865; and Cleveland Diary, February 9, 1865, SHC. Instances of rape or attempted rape are documented in James Sibley case, LL2449, ROJAG; Fleet and Fuller, *Green Mount*, 328–30; and *OR* 12(1):51, 78. On executions for rape see Alotta, *Civil War Justice*, 30–32, 97–99, 158–59.

13. Rable, *Civil Wars*, 161; Charlotte Wright to Mary Ward, July 9, 1864, Ward Family Papers, LC; Nancy Smith to James Smith, May 18, 1864, Smith Letters, TSLA.

14. On symbolic rape see Fellman, *Inside War*, 207–8. For examples see Maud Morrow Brown, "War Comes to College Hill," 26; Chadick, "Civil War Days in Huntsville," 218; and Fielding Diary, May 27, 1862, ADAH.

15. Espy Diary, June 3, 1864, ADAH; Roxa Cole to Cousin Blanche, November 2, 1862, Cole Family Letters, MDAH; Crabtree and Patton, *Journal of a Secesh Lady*, 464.

16. Lemke, *Mecklin Letters*, 25–26.

17. *Memphis Bulletin*, April 13, 1865; *OR Navy* 5:362–64; Graf, Haskins, and Bergeron, *Papers of Andrew Johnson*, 7:5–6, 310.

18. See, for example, *OR* 35(2):616; William Russell case, NN3272, ROJAG; and Corporal, *Letters from the Forty-fourth Regiment*, 51.

19. Mary Washington to Jane Washington, March 18, 31, 1865, Washington Family Papers, TSLA; Cartmell Diary, October 28, 1864, TSLA; King Diary, July 18, August 3, 1864, SHC.

20. Carney Diary, May 12, 1862, SHC; Mary Washington to Jane Washington, March 31, 1865, Washington Family Papers, TSLA; James Garner case, OO1235, ROJAG. See also Michael Dambacker case, LL3288, ROJAG, and Bond Diary, June 29, 1862, LSU.

21. King Diary, July 18, August 1, 10, 1864, SHC; Wilmer Shields to William Mercer, December 11, 1863, Mercer Papers, LSU; Cartmell Diary, November 16, 1863, TSLA. On depopulation, the vacuum of authority, immobility, and institutional disruption in no-man's-land see Chapter 3.

22. *Nashville Dispatch*, December 11, 1862, July 26, 28, November 29, December 17, 1863; William Whitney to Frank Whitney, January 21, 1864, Whitney Papers, LSU; Benjamin Halbrook case, LL1996, ROJAG. See also John Clark case, LL2953, ROJAG, and French Diary, June 10, 1863, TSLA.

23. On deserters who turned to banditry see William Hackley to wife, March 12, 1865, Hackley Letters, UTK; King Diary, August 1, 1864, SHC; and W. Winship to C. Moore, November 7, 1864, E-1457, RUSACC. For evidence of bandits who were long-time members of the community, often well known to their victims, see William Perdue case, NN3272, Henry Stolzy case, NN3687, and Oscar Fraley case, OO873, ROJAG. Teenage bandits as young as fifteen are noted in *Nashville Dispatch*, March 12, 1863, and in Andrew Hibarger case, LL1996, and Hervey Whitfield case, MM2054, ROJAG. For evidence of guerrillas who became bandits see William Walker case, OO1235, Calvin Boyle case, MM2566, and James Nolen case, LL2731, ROJAG. Some blacks, too, turned to banditry: see, for example, affidavits, April 1863, Jerrard Papers, LSU, and Fred Baker case, LL2530, ROJAG.

24. Benjamin Halbrook case, LL1996, and Hervey Whitfield case, MM2054, ROJAG; King Diary, August 25, 1864, SHC; Michael Dambacker case, LL3288, ROJAG. Robberies of poor blacks are documented in Henderson Diary, April 11, 1864, TSLA, and [?] to R. Goodwin, March 26, 1865, E-1411, RUSACC.

25. Porter Journal, February 6, 1864, SHC; *Nashville Daily Times and True Union*, October 6, 1864; James Roden case, LL3182, ROJAG.

26. James Hill case, OO802, ROJAG; Graf, Haskins, and Bergeron, *Papers of Andrew Johnson*, 7:411. See also J. Cunningham to T. Harris, May 19, 1865, U.S. Army Provost Marshal Book, Duke.

27. King Diary, August 27, 1864, SHC; Porter Journal, January 1, 1864, January 20, 1865, SHC. See also Wilmer Shields to William Mercer, January 25, 1864, Mercer Papers, LSU.

28. William Housden case, LL3288, ROJAG; Norton Diary, November 15–16, 1864, GDAH.

29. Cartmell Diary, March 1, 1865, French Diary, October 12, 1863, and Jane Washington to George Washington, July 25, 27, 31, 1864, Washington Family Papers, all in TSLA.

30. French Diary, December 6, 1863, TSLA; King Diary, August 1, 10, September 3, 1864, SHC.

31. [?] to William Moore, February 25, 1865, E-1411, RUSACC; *Nashville Dispatch*, March 4, 1863; Jane Washington to George Washington, July 27, 1864, Washington Family Papers, TSLA; Williamson County citizens to Andrew Johnson, December 25, 1863, Johnson Papers, LC; Cartmell Diary, March 4, 1864, TSLA.

32. Calvin Boyle case, MM2566, ROJAG; *Nashville Daily Times and True Union*, February 8, 1865.

33. Graf, Haskins, and Bergeron, *Papers of Andrew Johnson*, 6:174, 340. See also ibid., 71; Coffee County Court Minutes, December 7, 1863 (microfilm), TSLA; and Andrew Hibarger case, LL1996, ROJAG.

34. *OR* 32(3):274, 49(1):510–11, 26(1):763, 49(2):106; petition of Bayou Petit Anse planters, n.d., Jerrard Papers, LSU.

35. *OR* 49(2):291–93.

36. Union Adjutant Diary, April 7, 1864 (MS), AHC; *Fort Smith New Era*, March 11, 25, 1865; *OR* 48(1):1179, 1293–94; Huff, "Guerrillas, Jayhawkers, and Bushwhackers," 146–47; Hughes, "Wartime Gristmill Destruction," 179–86.

37. Mary Govan to [?], April 18, 1863, Graves Family Papers, SHC.

38. Pugh Plantation Diary, November 26, December 20, 1862, LSU; King Diary, July 24, 1864, SHC.

39. King Diary, July 4, 1864, SHC; *Alexandria Gazette*, April 2, 1863. See also Roach Diary, February 12, 1865, VHS, and *Nashville Dispatch*, May 21, 1863.

40. Mary Johnson to Sarah Cain, August 22, 1863, Bailey Papers, SHC; Colin Clarke to Powhatan Page, n.d., Clarke Papers, SHC; McClatchey Diary, July 3, 22, 1864, McClatchey Family Papers, GDAH.

41. John Downey to L. Burwell, February 24, 1863, Downey Papers, Duke; Graf, Haskins, and Bergeron, *Papers of Andrew Johnson*, 6:525–26; Eliza Sivley to Jane Sivley, March 10, 1864, Sivley Papers, SHC.

42. Cox Diary, December 31, 1863, TSLA; Erwin Diary, May 17, 1863, LSU; record of sermons, April 8, 1865, Hassell Papers, SHC.

CHAPTER EIGHT

1. Porter Journal, October 22, 1864, SHC.

2. Bills Diary, December 26, 1862, SHC; Erwin Diary, May 14, December 1, 1864, LSU.

3. Porter Journal, January 1, 1864, SHC; Cartmell Diary, March 3, 1863, TSLA. See also Colin Clarke to Powhatan Page, n.d., Clarke Papers, SHC.

4. "Documents: The Shelly Papers," 187; Academy Baptist Church Minute Books, November 1864 (typescript), MDAH.

5. Moore Diary, August 17, 1862, ADAH; Espy Diary, August 1, 1864, ADAH. See also Erwin Diary, January 1, 1864, LSU.

6. Joseph Hynson to James Wise, May 1, 1865, Wise Papers, LSU; Colin Clarke to Maxwell Clarke, August 24, 1862, Clarke Papers, SHC.

7. Porter Journal, February 19, 1865, SHC; Rose Bradford to Robert Bradford, November 26, 1864, Emily Sparks case, MM2049, ROJAG; Cartmell Diary, October 28, 1864, TSLA. See also Bond Diary, October 28, 1864, LSU; Edward Morley to Sardis and Anna Morley, November 1, 1864, Morley Papers, LC; and *OR* 32(2):268.

8. *OR* 32(3):634–35; George Wortham to Zebulon Vance, May 10, 1864, Pittman Collection, NCDAH.

9. Powell and Wayne, "Self-Interest and the Decline of Confederate Nationalism," 29–45; *OR* 31(3):690–91.

10. Henry Wood to Simon Jerrard, April 28, 1863, and manuscript notes by Jerrard, n.d., Jerrard Papers, LSU.

11. Wiley, "Southern Reaction to Federal Invasion," 508–10; George Cadman to Esther Cadman, April 2, 1864, Cadman Papers, SHC; Anonymous Diary, September 20, 1863, MDAH.

12. Porter Journal, March 21, 1864, SHC; *Yorktown Cavalier*, September 21, 1863; Roach Diary, February 24, 1865, VHS; George Cadman to Esther Cadman, October 3, 1863, March 19, 1864, Cadman Papers, SHC; *Nashville Dispatch*, June 10, 1863.

13. Handy Diary, February 19, March 4, 1865, Duke; Cleveland Diary, November 4, 1864, January 12, April 9, 1865, SHC; Roach Diary, February 19, 1865, VHS; St. Paul's Episcopal Church, Beaufort, Carteret County, Minutes, January 1, 1863, March 21, 1865 (microfilm), NCDAH; "Remarks of the Master," January 10, 1863, Louisiana Masonic Lodge Collection, St. James Lodge no. 47 (Baton Rouge), LSU.

14. Chadick, "Civil War Days in Huntsville," 305; Harry Cushing to mother, March 9, 1862, Cushing Letters, UTK; Leslie, "Arabella Lanktree Wilson's Civil War Letter," 265; Roach Diary, October 24, 1864–January 24, 1865, VHS; Waddel Diary, November 4, 1862, LC.

15. Union Adjutant Diary, February 18, 1864, AHC; Blegen, *Civil War Letters of Colonel . . . Heg*, 211. On the soldiers' perception of poor white women see Robert Hoadley to Cousin Em, March 15, 1864, Hoadley Papers, Duke, and Nott, *Sketches of the War*, 100–101. For examples of courtship and marriage see [?] to [?], December 28, 1863, Hunter-Taylor Family Papers, LSU; Corporal, *Letters from the Forty-fourth Regiment*, 90; Massey, *Bonnet Brigades*, 230–33; and Rable, *Civil Wars*, 164–67.

16. Anonymous Diary, September 20, 1863, MDAH.

17. See, for example, George Cadman to Esther Cadman, March 23, June 20, August 20, 1864, Cadman Papers, SHC, and E. Cheney to Sarah Newell, February 3, 1864, Newell Papers, LSU.

18. Beringer et al., *Why the South Lost*, 82–102, 270–76; Wight, "Churches and the Confederate Cause," 361–63, 366–67; Daniel, "Southern Protestantism," 278–79; Anonymous Diary, July 9, 1863, MDAH; S. Clay to C. Clay, July 24, 1863, Clay Papers, Duke; Hassell Diary, July 16, 1863, SHC.

19. Beringer et al., *Why the South Lost*, 276–93, 351; Rable, *Civil Wars*, 213–14, 216–17; Roxa Cole to mother, August 15, 1864, Cole Family Letters, MDAH; Espy Diary, January 22, 1865, ADAH.

20. Fielding Diary, December 28, 1864, ADAH; Coffin, *Four Years of Fighting*, 430. See also D. Schreckhise to brother, October 17, 1864, Schreckhise Papers, Duke, and *OR* 45(2):471, 732.

21. George Cadman to Esther Cadman, August 4, 1863, Cadman Papers, SHC; Gatell, "Yankee Views the Agony of Savannah," 430.

22. *OR* 32(2):86; Robert Glasscock case, LL2804, ROJAG.

23. Genovese, *Roll, Jordan, Roll*, 97–112; Litwack, *Been in the Storm So Long*, 151–

62; Charlotte Wright to Mary Ward, July 9, 1864, Ward Family Papers, LC; Crabtree and Patton, *Journal of a Secesh Lady*, 463; Colin Clarke to Maxwell Clarke, August 10, 1862, August 23, 1863, Clarke Papers, SHC.

24. Charlotte Wright to Mary Ward, July 9, 1864, Ward Family Papers, LC; Graf, Haskins, and Bergeron, *Papers of Andrew Johnson*, 6:446 (see also p. 342).

25. Chappelear Diary, April 19, 1862, VHS; Ambler Diary, July 28, 1863, Ambler-Brown Family Papers, Duke; Mary Dickinson to Sis, June 8, 1863, Gay and Family Papers, LSU. See also [?] to [?], April 21, 1864, Anna Maria (Smith) Smith Papers, Duke; Pugh Plantation Diary, February 26, 1865, LSU; A. Smith to B. Polk, April 19, 1864, E-3023, RUSACC; and Ash, *Middle Tennessee Society Transformed*, 128–31.

26. *OR* 49(1):590–91; W. Rivers to Sarah Trotter, March 25, 1864, Pope-Carter Family Papers, Duke.

27. Eliza Sivley to Jane Sivley, February 14, 1864, February 20, 1865, Sivley Papers, SHC.

28. Agnew Diary, May 8, 1865, SHC; Espy Diary, May 20, 1865, ADAH.

29. Espy Diary, June 21, 1865, ADAH. On the dissolution of Confederate and state authority and the gradual extension of Federal control see *OR* 46(3):694–95, 1166, 1295; Yearns, *Confederate Governors*, 37, 56, 106–7, 129, 159–60, 183–84, 214–15, 230–31; Winters, *Civil War in Louisiana*, 418–29; Carter, *When the War Was Over*, 11–12; and Sefton, *United States Army and Reconstruction*, 8–24.

30. Bond Diary, May 21, 1865, LSU; D. Boyd to Louis Bringier, May 17, 1865, and Louis Bringier to Stella Bringier, May 11, 1865, Bringier and Family Papers, LSU; Espy Diary, May 14, 1865, ADAH; *OR* 46(3):1295; Winters, *Civil War in Louisiana*, 422–25.

31. *OR* 46(3):1166; resolution of Itawamba County citizens, n.d. (June 1865), Sharkey Correspondence, MDAH; Agnew Diary, May 12, 1865, SHC. On no-man's-land see H. Wells to J. Taylor, June 19, 1865, E-1457, RUSACC, and *OR* 47(3):595–96, 48(2):684.

32. Carter, *When the War Was Over*, 15; *OR* 47(3):396; Greenough, "Aftermath at Appomattox," 6–9; *OR* 49(2):863; H. Wells to Captain Pierson, May 5, 1865, E-1457, RUSACC; Hassell Diary, May 24–June 3, 1865, SHC.

33. Beringer et al., *Why the South Lost*, 338–46; Henry Hitchcock to Mary Hitchcock, April 15, 1865, Hitchcock Papers, LC; *OR Navy* 5:550–51. See also James Scudder to Andrew Johnson, July 7, 1865, Johnson Papers, LC; resolution of Warren County citizens, May 15, 1865, and P. Williams to Francis Pierpont, May 30, 1865, Pierpont Executive Papers, VSL; and *OR* 46(3):714, 1006.

34. F. Surget to Stephen Duncan, June 12, 14, 1865, Duncan Correspondence, LSU. For more evidence of oath taking see James Fuqua to James Kilbourne, June 8, 1865, Kilbourne Correspondence, LSU, and R. Loveridge to B. Thompson, May 12, 1865, E-1598, RUSACC. On the surrender of guerrillas see Thomas Carrick file, Civil War Questionnaires, Confederate, TSLA; James Gilfillan to B. Polk, May 10, 1865, E-3048, RUSACC; *OR* 49(2):549, 710; and Bearss and Gibson, *Fort Smith*, 302–3.

35. Hassell Diary, May 16, 22, 1865, SHC; O. Davis to William Sharkey, June 28, 1865, Sharkey Correspondence, MDAH. See also Moore Diary, April 24, 1865, ADAH. On the persistence of proslavery beliefs see Roark, *Masters Without Slaves*, 94–108.

36. Erwin Diary, May 28, 1865, LSU; Worthington Diary, July 31, 1865, Worthington Family Papers, MDAH; Porter Journal, April 29, 1865, SHC.

37. Espy Diary, May 10, 1865, ADAH; Erwin Diary, April 19, May 31, 1865, LSU; Porter Journal, April 17-18, 1865, SHC; Moore Diary, April 24, 1865, ADAH; O. Davis to William Sharkey, June 28, 1865, Sharkey Correspondence, MDAH.

38. Smith Diary, April 12, 3, 1865 (MS), VHS.

EPILOGUE

1. Hill Carter to Peyton Johnson, June 24, 1865, Pierpont Papers, VSL.

2. Trowbridge, *The South*, 100-101, 121-22, 133-34, 141.

3. Ash, *Middle Tennessee Society Transformed*, 175-83; Porter Journal, June 8, 1865, SHC; Fielding Diary, August 8, 1865, ADAH. See also Bond Diary, June 27, 1865, LSU, and Hassell Diary, June-September 1865, SHC.

4. Perman, *Reunion Without Compromise*, 57-67; Carter, *When the War Was Over*, 24-95; H. Enry to Robert Reed, August 1865, E-3071, RUSACC; W. Kennedy to M. Schmidt, August 9, 1865, E-1411, RUSACC; *OR* 47(3):625, 49(2):1028-29; Fleming, *Civil War and Reconstruction in Alabama*, 353; Neander Rice to Lewis Parsons, August 5, 1865, Parsons Papers, ADAH.

5. D. Bulman to F. Pierpont, July 23, 1865, Pierpont Papers, VSL; John Holman to W. Goodrich, September 12, 1865, no. 17830, Union Provost Marshals' File, M-416, NA. See also A. Whitehurst et al. to William Sharkey, July 15, 1865, Sharkey Correspondence, MDAH, and B. Peart to Andrew Johnson, July 15, 1865, Johnson Papers, LC. On Johnson's reconstruction policy see Foner, *Reconstruction*, 176-84, and Carter, *When the War Was Over*, 24-31.

6. Dennett, *The South as It Is*, 5-6; Joseph Bradley to Lewis Parsons, September 5, 1865, Parsons Papers, ADAH. See also John Terrell to W. Fairbanks, July 12, 1865, E-1416, RUSACC.

7. *OR* 48(2):844; Joseph Defoore and Sterling Scroggs cases, MM2887, ROJAG. See also Espy Diary, July 10-11, 1865, ADAH.

8. East Baton Rouge Parish Police Jury Minutes, August 1, 1865, LSU; Moore Diary, June 3, 1865, ADAH. See also Trowbridge, *The South*, 228-29, and Berlin et al., *The Black Military Experience*, 699-700.

9. Alex Bailey to Thomas Conway, June 26, July 20, 1865, E-1718, RUSACC; West Baton Rouge Parish Police Jury Minutes, August 17, 1865 (MS), LSU. For further examples of the mistreatment of black workers see George Southworth case, MM2655, ROJAG, and record of civilian disputes, September 1865, E-1410, RUSACC.

10. Endorsements by R. Johnson in William Bonner case, MM2887, ROJAG; D. Bulman to Francis Pierpont, July 23, 1865, Pierpont Papers, VSL. More evidence of the Federal authorities' determination to protect blacks is in Agnew Diary, July 20, 1865, SHC; William Nalle Diary, August 25, 1865 (MS), VHS; *OR* 49(2):1043; and Alex Bailie to S. Granger, September 8, 1865, E-1718, RUSACC.

11. East Baton Rouge Parish Police Jury Minutes, August 1, 1865, LSU; Trowbridge, *The South*, 134–35; Charles Coolidge to [?], June 13, 1865, E-1598, RUSACC; Ash, "Poor Whites in the Occupied South," 59–62.

12. *Fort Smith New Era*, June 10, 1865.

13. Trowbridge, *The South*, 115–16.

Bibliography

MANUSCRIPT COLLECTIONS

Alabama Department of Archives and History, Montgomery
  William Cooper Diary
  Sarah R. Espy Diary
  Mary Fielding Diary
  Joshua Burns Moore Diary
  Morgan County Commissioners' Court Minutes
  Mount Joy Primitive Baptist Church, Blount County, Minutes
  Provisional Governor Lewis Parsons Papers
  Governor John G. Shorter Papers
  Governor Thomas H. Watts Papers
Arkansas History Commission, Little Rock
  Mrs. Albert G. Edmonson Diary
  Union Adjutant Diary
William R. Perkins Library, Duke University, Durham, N.C.
  Ambler-Brown Family Papers
  Electa Ames Papers
  Bedinger-Dandridge Family Papers
  Homer Blackmon Papers
  Iveson L. Brookes Papers
  Bryan Family Papers
  Clement Claiborne Clay Papers
  Confederate States of America Congress Papers, Confederate States of America
    Archives
  Helen J. (Thompson) Sawyer Daugherty Papers
  George F. Davidson Papers
  Samuel Smith Downey Papers
  Frank A. Handy Diary
  Jesse Harrison Papers
  Robert Bruce Hoadley Papers
  William F. Loftin Papers
  S. S. Marrett Papers
  Pope-Carter Family Papers
  James M. Schreckhise Papers
  Anna Maria (Smith) Smith Papers
  William Patterson Smith Papers

U.S. Army Provost Marshal, Portsmouth, Va., Letterpress Book
George T. Wallace Papers
Giles Frederick Ward Jr. Papers
James M. Willcox Papers
J. F. Woods Papers
Georgia Department of Archives and History, Atlanta
Alfred A. Atkins Collection
Bartow County Ordinary Court Minutes
Cherokee County Inferior Court Minutes
Ebenezer Primitive Baptist Church, Dunwoody, De Kalb County, Minutes
Enon Baptist Church, Rome, Floyd County, Minutes
McClatchey Family Papers
Reuben S. Norton Diary
Roswell Manufacturing Company Minutes of Stockholders' Meetings
St. Peter's Episcopal Church, Rome, Floyd County, Vestry Minutes
Library of Congress, Washington
Ballou Family of Virginia Papers
John Francis Hamtramck Claiborne Papers
(Mrs.) Douglas W. Clark Collection
Henry Hitchcock Papers
Andrew Johnson Papers
Betty Herndon Maury Diary
Edward Williams Morley Papers
Lyman Potter Spencer Diary
John Newton Waddel Diary
James Thomas Ward Diary
Ward Family of Richmond County, Va., Papers
Louisiana State Archives, Baton Rouge
Records of the Louisiana State Government, 1850–88 ("Rebel Archives")
Hill Memorial Library, Louisiana State University, Baton Rouge
Avoyelles Parish Police Jury Minutes
Albert A. Batchelor Papers
J. G. Boardman Letter
Priscilla "Mittie" Munnikhuysen Bond Papers and Diary
James P. Bowman Family Papers
James Earl Bradley Diary
Louis A. Bringier and Family Papers
Audley Clark Britton and Family Papers
John C. Burruss Family Papers
Concordia Parish Police Jury Minutes
Stephen Duncan Correspondence
East Baton Rouge Parish Police Jury Minutes
Isaac Erwin Diary

Simeon A. Evans Letters
Andrew Hynes Gay and Family Papers
Calvin S. Hendrick Letter
Hephzibah Church Record Book
Hunter-Taylor Family Papers
Simon G. Jerrard Papers
James Gilliam Kilbourne Correspondence
Lafayette Parish Police Jury Minutes
Gustave Lauve Letter
Louisiana Masonic Lodge Collection
Henry W. Marston and Family Papers
William N. Mercer Papers
Thomas O. Moore Papers
Robert A. Newell Papers
William T. Palfrey Papers
William T. and George D. Palfrey Account Books
Pointe Coupee Parish Police Jury Minutes
Alexander Franklin Pugh Plantation Diary
St. Charles Parish Police Jury Minutes
St. John the Baptist Parish Police Jury Minutes
St. Landry Parish Police Jury Minutes
Franklin S. Twitchell Letter
West Baton Rouge Parish Police Jury Minutes
West Feliciana Parish Police Jury Minutes
Edward Clifton Wharton Family Papers
William H. Whitney Letters
James Calvert Wise Papers
Peter M. Yawyer Letter
Mississippi Department of Archives and History, Jackson
Academy Baptist Church Minute Books
Anonymous Diary
John C. Burrus Papers
Charles Clark Correspondence, Mississippi Governors' Papers
Cole Family Letters
Fonsylvania Plantation Journal
Louisiana D. Garrett Papers
Walter Alexander Overton Diary
John J. Pettus Correspondence, Mississippi Governors' Papers
Rodney Presbyterian Church Records
Cordelia Lewis Scales Letters
William L. Sharkey Correspondence, Mississippi Governors' Papers
Swanson-Yates Family Papers
Tippah County Minutes of Police Board

Trinity Episcopal Church (Natchez) Records
Union Church Presbyterian Church Records
Worthington Family Papers
National Archives, Washington
American Freedmen's Inquiry Commission Preliminary and Final Reports (M-619, RG 94)
Legislative Records (Confederate), Memorials and Petitions (E-175, RG 109)
Records of the Office of Judge Advocate General, Court Martial Files (E-15, RG 153)
Records of U.S. Army Continental Commands, 1821–1920 (RG 393)
Union Provost Marshals' File of Papers Relating to Individual Civilians (M-345, RG 109)
Union Provost Marshals' File of Papers Relating to Two or More Civilians (M-416, RG 109)
North Carolina Division of Archives and History, Raleigh
Bertie County Court Minutes
John B. Chesson Papers
Chowan County Court Minutes
Josiah Collins Papers
Cool Springs Baptist Church, Eure, Gates County, Minutes
F. M. Harper Papers
Heckstall Papers
George Holland Collection
Kenelm H. Lewis Papers
Meherrin Baptist Church, Murfreesboro (Hertford County), Minutes
Mount Tabor Baptist Church, Murfreesboro, Hertford County, Minutes
Pasquotank County Court Minutes
Perquimans County Court Minutes
Thomas Merritt Pittman Collection
St. Paul's Episcopal Church, Beaufort, Carteret County, Minutes
Zebulon Baird Vance Papers
Southern Historical Collection, University of North Carolina, Chapel Hill
Samuel Andrew Agnew Diary
John Lancaster Bailey Papers
Bayside Plantation Records
Overton and Jessie Bernard Diary
John Houston Bills Diary
Elias Brady Papers
George Hovey Cadman Papers
Kate S. Carney Diary
Lulah A. Clark Collection
Maxwell Troax Clarke Papers
Edmund J. Cleveland Diary

Herbert Arthur Cooley Letters
Creecy Family Papers
Louis M. De Saussure Plantation Record
Harry St. John Dixon Papers
Federal Soldiers' Letters (Miscellaneous)
Robert Stuart Finley Papers
Graves Family Papers
Harding-Jackson Papers
Cushing Biggs Hassell Diary and Papers
Mary Hunter Kennedy Papers
William King Diary
Henry Champlin Lay Diary
Francis Terry Leak Books
Andrew McCollam Papers
Harriet Ellen Moore Diary
Pettigrew Family Papers
David Pise Journal
Nimrod Porter Journal
Ellen Louise Power Diary
D. M. Ransdell Diary
C. Alice Ready Diary
Jane Sivley Papers
Southall and Bowen Papers
Harvey W. Walter Papers
Amanda (Daugherty) Worthington Diary
Tennessee State Library and Archives, Nashville
Anonymous Letter, Civil War Collection
Henry J. Barker Papers
Blanch Spurlock Bentley Papers
Robert H. Cartmell Diary
Christian Chapel Church of Christ, Henderson County, Minute Book
Civil War Questionnaires, Confederate
Clarksville Correspondence concerning Civil War Guerrillas
Coffee County Court Minutes
Jesse Cox Diary
Davidson County Court Minutes
L. Virginia French Diary
George W. Gordon and William T. Avery Papers
Samuel Henderson Diary
Madison County Court Minutes
James W. Matthews Journal
Zeboim Carter Patten Diary

Sailor's Rest Plantation Papers
Nancy B. Smith Letters
Talbot and Related Families Papers
Washington Family Papers
Jane S. Washington Letter
West Station Primitive Baptist Church, Sumner County, Session Minutes
Whiteside Family Papers
Woodbury [Masonic] Lodge no. 235 Minutes
Special Collections, University of Tennessee, Knoxville
Harry C. Cushing Letters
William Henry Harrison Fithian Diary
William Beverly Randolph Hackley Letters
John Watkins Papers
Virginia Historical Society, Richmond
Eliza Bland (Smith) Brockenbrough Letters
Amanda Virginia (Edmonds) Chappelear Diary
Caroline Kean (Hill) Davis Diary
Mary Eliza (Powell) Dulany Diary
William Nalle Diary
Margaret Tilloston (Kemble) Nourse Diary
Mahala Perkins Harding (Eggleston) Roach Diary
Eliza Chew (French) Smith Diary
Alvin Coe Voris Papers
Virginia State Library, Richmond
Battle Run Baptist Church (Rappahannock County) Minute Book
Christ (Episcopal) Church, Norfolk, Vestry Minutes
Ebenezer Baptist Church, Loudoun County, Minute Book
Fredericksburg City Council Minutes
Grinnan Letter
Hopewell Meeting of Friends (Frederick County) Monthly Meeting Record Book
Loudoun County Court Minute Book
Luray (Main Street) Baptist Church, Page County, Minute Book
R. D. Minor Correspondence
Norfolk Hustings Court Order Book
Francis H. Pierpont Executive Papers
Portsmouth City Council Minutes
Kate S. Sperry Diary
Stafford County Court Minute Book
Mary Cary Ambling Stribling Diary
Thumb Run Primitive Baptist Church, Fauquier County, Minute Book
Unknown Confederate Diary
Virginia Executive Papers

NEWSPAPERS

Alexandria Gazette
Beaufort (North Carolina) Old North State
Clarksville (Tennessee) Gazette
Fayetteville (Tennessee) Union Herald
Fort Smith (Arkansas) New Era
Little Rock National Democrat
Memphis Bulletin
Memphis Union Appeal
Murfreesboro (Tennessee) Union Volunteer
Nashville Daily Press
Nashville Daily Times and True Union
Nashville Dispatch
New Bern North Carolina Times
New Orleans Daily Picayune
Pulaski (Tennessee) Chanticleer
Savannah Daily Herald
Shelbyville (Tennessee) Tri-Weekly News
Vicksburg Daily Herald
Washington (North Carolina) New Era
Williamsburg (Virginia) Cavalier
Yorktown (Virginia) Cavalier

PUBLISHED PRIMARY SOURCES

Adams, F. Colburn. *The Story of a Trooper . . .* New York, 1865.
Agassiz, George R., ed. *Meade's Headquarters, 1863–1865: Letters of Colonel Theodore Lyman from the Wilderness to Appomattox.* Boston, 1922.
American Union Commission. *Speeches . . . in the Hall of Representatives, Washington, Feb. 12, 1865.* New York, 1865.
Bearss, Edwin C., ed. "The Civil War Letters of Major William G. Thompson." *Annals of Iowa* 38 (1966): 431–55.
Beatty, John. *Memoirs of a Volunteer, 1861–1863.* New York, 1946.
Berlin, Ira, Joseph P. Reidy, and Leslie S. Rowland, eds. *The Black Military Experience.* Cambridge, 1982.
Berlin, Ira, Barbara J. Fields, Thavolia Glymph, Joseph P. Reidy, and Leslie S. Rowland, eds. *The Destruction of Slavery.* Cambridge, 1985.
Bickham, William D. *Rosecrans' Campaign with the Fourteenth Army Corps . . .* Cincinnati, 1863.
Blake, Henry N. *Three Years in the Army of the Potomac.* Boston, 1865.
Blegen, Theodore C., ed. *The Civil War Letters of Colonel Hans Christian Heg.* Northfield, 1936.

Brown, Maud Morrow, ed. "The War Comes to College Hill." *Journal of Mississippi History* 16 (1954): 22–30.

Butler, Benjamin F. *Private and Official Correspondence* . . . 5 vols. Norwood, 1917.

Butler, Jay Caldwell. *Letters Home [by] Jay Caldwell Butler, Captain, 101st Ohio Volunteer Infantry*. Binghamton, 1930.

Calendar of Virginia State Papers and Other Manuscripts . . . 11 vols. Richmond, 1875–93.

Chadick, Mrs. W. D. "Civil War Days in Huntsville." *Alabama Historical Quarterly* 9 (1947): 199–333.

Chancellor, Sir Christopher, ed. *An Englishman in the American Civil War: The Diaries of Henry Yates Thompson, 1863*. New York, 1971.

Coffin, Charles Carleton. *Four Years of Fighting: A Volume of Personal Observation with the Army and Navy* . . . Boston, 1866.

Cook, Joel. *The Siege of Richmond: A Narrative* . . . Philadelphia, 1862.

Corporal [Zenas T. Haines]. *Letters from the Forty-fourth Regiment M. V. M.* Boston, 1863.

Crabtree, Beth G., and James W. Patton, eds. *"Journal of a Secesh Lady": The Diary of Catherine Ann Devereaux Edmondston, 1860–1866*. Raleigh, 1979.

Dennett, John Richard. *The South as It Is, 1865–1866*. New York, 1965.

"Diary of John Berkley Grimball, 1858–1865." *South Carolina Historical Magazine* 56 (1955): 157–77.

"Diary of Miss Harriette Cary, Kept by Her from May 6, 1862, to July 24, 1862." *Tyler's Quarterly Historical and Genealogical Magazine* 9 (1927): 104–15.

Diary of a Southern Refugee, during the War. 2d ed. New York, 1868.

"Documents: Civil War Diary of Jabez T. Cox." *Indiana Magazine of History* 28 (1932): 40–54.

"Documents: The Shelly Papers." *Indiana Magazine of History* 44 (1948): 181–98.

Dumond, Dwight Lowell, ed. *Southern Editorials on Secession*. New York, 1931.

Favill, Josiah Marshall. *The Diary of a Young Officer Serving with the Armies of the United States during the War of the Rebellion*. Chicago, 1909.

Fitch, John. *Annals of the Army of the Cumberland* . . . Philadelphia, 1864.

Fleet, Betsy, and John D. P. Fuller, eds. *Green Mount: A Virginia Plantation Family during the Civil War* . . . Lexington, 1962.

Fleming, Walter L., ed. *Documentary History of Reconstruction* . . . 2 vols. Cleveland, 1906.

Freidel, Frank, ed. *Union Pamphlets of the Civil War, 1861–1865*. 2 vols. Cambridge, 1967.

Gatell, Frank Otto, ed. "A Yankee Views the Agony of Savannah." *Georgia Historical Quarterly* 43 (1959): 428–31.

Gordon, George H. *A War Diary of Events in the War of the Great Rebellion, 1863–1865*. Boston, 1882.

Gower, Herschel, ed. "The Beersheba Diary of L. Virginia French." East Tennessee Historical Society's *Publications* 52–53 (1981–82): 89–107.

Graf, LeRoy P., Ralph W. Haskins, and Paul H. Bergeron, eds. *The Papers of Andrew Johnson.* 10 vols. to date. Knoxville, 1967–.

Harwell, Richard, and Philip N. Racine, eds. *The Fiery Trail: A Union Officer's Account of Sherman's Last Campaigns.* Knoxville, 1986.

Hoobler, James A., ed. "The Civil War Diary of Louisa Brown Pearl." *Tennessee Historical Quarterly* 38 (1979): 308–21.

Jackson, Oscar L. *The Colonel's Diary: Journals Kept before and during the Civil War . . .* Sharon, 1922.

Knox, Thomas W. *Camp-Fire and Cotton-Field: Southern Adventure in Time of War . . .* 1865. Reprint, New York, 1969.

Lemke, W. J., ed. *The Mecklin Letters Written in 1863–64 at Mt. Comfort by Robert W. Mecklin . . .* Fayetteville, 1955.

Leslie, James W., ed. "Arabella Lanktree Wilson's Civil War Letter." *Arkansas Historical Quarterly* 47 (1988): 257–72.

"Major Connolly's Letters to His Wife, 1862–1865." *Transactions of the Illinois State Historical Society* (1928), 217–383.

Norton, Oliver Willcox. *Army Letters, 1861–1865 . . .* Chicago, 1903.

Nott, Charles C. *Sketches of the War: A Series of Letters to the North Moore Street School of New York.* New York, 1865.

Official Records of the Union and Confederate Navies in the War of the Rebellion. 30 vols. Washington, 1894–1922.

Perkins, Howard Cecil, ed. *Northern Editorials on Secession.* 2 vols. New York, 1942.

Potts, J. G. *Address to the People of the Counties of Accomac and Northampton in General, and Particularly to the Mechanics, Tenants, and Laborers.* Baltimore, 1862.

Rawick, George P., ed. *The American Slave: A Composite Autobiography.* 41 vols. Westport, 1972–79.

Richardson, Joe M., ed. " 'We Are Truly Doing Missionary Work': Letters from American Missionary Association Teachers in Florida, 1864–1874." *Florida Historical Quarterly* 54 (1975): 178–95.

Sanford, Orlin M., ed. "A Virginian's Diary in Civil War Days." *Americana* 18 (1924): 353–68.

Schwartz, Gerald, ed. *A Woman Doctor's Civil War: Esther Hill Hawks' Diary.* Columbia, 1984.

Senate Reports, 37th Cong., 3d sess., no. 108; 38th Cong., 1st sess., no. 54.

Skipper, Elvie Eagleton, and Ruth Gove, eds. " 'Stray Thoughts': The Civil War Diary of Ethie M. Foute Eagleton." *East Tennessee Historical Society's Publications* 40 (1968): 128–37; 41 (1969): 116–28.

Smart, James G., ed. *A Radical View: The "Agate" Dispatches of Whitelaw Reid, 1861–1865.* 2 vols. Memphis, 1976.

Smith, Mrs. W. F., ed. "The Yankees in New Albany: Letter of Elizabeth Jane Beach, July 29, 1864." *Journal of Mississippi History* 2 (1940): 42–48.

Staudenraus, P. J., ed. "A War Correspondent's View of St. Augustine and Fernandina, 1863." *Florida Historical Quarterly* 41 (1962): 60–65.

Stevens, George T. *Three Years in the Sixth Corps* . . . Albany, 1866.

Stewart, A. M. *Camp, March, and Battle-field; Or, Three Years and a Half with the Army of the Potomac.* Philadelphia, 1865.

Swint, Henry L., ed. *Dear Ones at Home: Letters from Contraband Camps.* Nashville, 1966.

Tilney, Robert. *My Life in the Army: Three Years and a Half with the Fifth Army Corps* . . . Philadelphia, 1912.

Trowbridge, J. T. *The South: A Tour of Its Battlefields and Ruined Cities* . . . Hartford, 1866.

U.S. War Department. *The War of the Rebellion: A Compilation of the Official Records of the Union and Confederate Armies.* 70 vols. in 128 pts. Washington, 1880–1901.

Volwiler, A. T., ed. "Documents: Letters from a Civil War Officer." *Mississippi Valley Historical Review* 14 (1928): 508–29.

Wills, Charles W. *Army Life of an Illinois Soldier* . . . Washington, 1906.

SECONDARY SOURCES

Abbott, Richard H. *The Republican Party and the South, 1855–1877: The First Southern Strategy.* Chapel Hill, 1986.

Adams, Michael C. C. *Our Masters the Rebels: A Speculation on Union Military Failure in the East, 1861–1865.* Cambridge, 1978.

Alexander, Thomas B. *Political Reconstruction in Tennessee.* Nashville, 1950.

Alotta, Robert I. *Civil War Justice: Union Army Executions under Lincoln.* Shippensburg, 1989.

Ambler, Charles H. *Francis H. Pierpont: Union War Governor of Virginia and Father of West Virginia.* Chapel Hill, 1937.

American Union Commission. *The American Union Commission: Its Origin, Operations, and Purposes* . . . New York, 1865.

Ames, Susie May. "Federal Policy toward the Eastern Shore of Virginia in 1861." *Virginia Magazine of History and Biography* 69 (1961): 432–59.

Andrews, J. Cutler. "The Confederate Press and Public Morale." *Journal of Southern History* 32 (1966): 445–65.

Ash, Stephen V. *Middle Tennessee Society Transformed, 1860–1870: War and Peace in the Upper South.* Baton Rouge, 1988.

———. "Poor Whites in the Occupied South, 1861–1865." *Journal of Southern History* 57 (1991): 39–62.

Auman, William T., and David D. Scarboro. "The Heroes of America in Civil War North Carolina." *North Carolina Historical Review* 58 (1981): 327–63.

Avery, Mrs. Roy C. "The Second Presbyterian Church of Nashville during the Civil War." *Tennessee Historical Quarterly* 11 (1952): 356–75.

Ayers, Edward L. *Vengeance and Justice: Crime and Punishment in the Nineteenth-Century American South.* New York, 1984.

Bailey, Fred Arthur. *Class and Tennessee's Confederate Generation*. Chapel Hill, 1987.

Baker, Jean. *Affairs of Party: The Political Culture of Northern Democrats in the Mid-Nineteenth Century*. Ithaca, 1983.

Barrett, John G. *The Civil War in North Carolina*. Chapel Hill, 1963.

——. *Sherman's March through the Carolinas*. Chapel Hill, 1956.

Bearss, Ed, and Arrell M. Gibson. *Fort Smith: Little Gibraltar on the Arkansas*. Norman, 1969.

Belz, Herman. *Reconstructing the Union: Theory and Policy during the Civil War*. Ithaca, 1969.

Beringer, Richard E., Herman Hattaway, Archer Jones, and William N. Still Jr. *Why the South Lost the Civil War*. Athens, 1986.

Bettersworth, John Knox. *Confederate Mississippi: The People and Policies of a Cotton State in Wartime*. Baton Rouge, 1943.

Bolton, Charles. *Poor Whites of the Antebellum South: Tenants and Laborers in Central North Carolina and Northeast Mississippi*. Durham, 1994.

Bragg, Jefferson Davis. *Louisiana in the Confederacy*. Baton Rouge, 1941.

Bremner, Robert H. *The Public Good: Philanthropy and Welfare in the Civil War Era*. New York, 1980.

Brown, Ira V. *Lyman Abbott, Christian Evolutionist: A Study in Religious Liberalism*. Cambridge, 1953.

Brown, Norman D. *Edward Stanly: Whiggery's Tarheel "Conqueror"*. University, 1974.

Bruce, Dickson D., Jr. *Violence and Culture in the Antebellum South*. Austin, 1979.

Brydon, G. MacLaren. "The Diocese of Virginia in the Southern Confederacy." *Historical Magazine of the Protestant Episcopal Church* 17 (1948): 384–410.

Buck, Paul H. "The Poor Whites of the Ante-bellum South." *American Historical Review* 31 (1925): 41–54.

Burton, Orville Vernon. *In My Father's House Are Many Mansions: Family and Community in Edgefield, South Carolina*. Chapel Hill, 1985.

Bynum, Hartwell T. "Sherman's Expulsion of the Roswell Women, in 1864." *Georgia Historical Quarterly* 54 (1970): 169–82.

Byrne, Frank L. "'A Terrible Machine': General Neal Dow's Military Government on the Gulf Coast." *Civil War History* 12 (1966): 5–22.

Campbell, Randolph B., and Richard G. Lowe. *Wealth and Power in Antebellum Texas*. College Station, 1977.

Capers, Gerald M. *Occupied City: New Orleans under the Federals, 1862–1865*. Lexington, 1965.

Carpenter, A. H. "Military Government of Southern Territory, 1861–1865." In American Historical Association, *Annual Report . . . for the year 1900*, 1:467–98. 2 vols. Washington, 1901.

Carrigan, Jo Ann. "Yankees versus Yellow Jack in New Orleans, 1862–1866." *Civil War History* 9 (1963): 248–60.

Carter, Dan T. *When the War Was Over: The Failure of Self-Reconstruction in the South*. Baton Rouge, 1985.

Cash, W. J. *The Mind of the South*. New York, 1941.

Cecil-Fronsman, Bill. *Common Whites: Class and Culture in Antebellum North Carolina*. Lexington, 1992.

Censer, Jane Turner. *North Carolina Planters and Their Children, 1800–1860*. Baton Rouge, 1984.

Channing, Steven A. *Crisis of Fear: Secession in South Carolina*. New York, 1970.

Cimprich, John. *Slavery's End in Tennessee, 1861–1865*. University, 1985.

Clinton, Catherine. *The Plantation Mistress: Woman's World in the Old South*. New York, 1982.

Collins, Bruce. *White Society in the Antebellum South*. New York, 1985.

Coulter, E. Merton. "Commercial Intercourse with the Confederacy in the Mississippi Valley." *Mississippi Valley Historical Review* 5 (1919): 377–95.

——. "Robert Gould Shaw and the Burning of Darien, Georgia." *Civil War History* 5 (1959): 363–73.

Cowan, Ruth Caroline. "Reorganization of Federal Arkansas, 1862–1865." *Arkansas Historical Quarterly* 18 (1959): 32–57.

Crofts, Daniel W. *Old Southampton: Politics and Society in a Virginia County, 1834–1869*. Charlottesville, 1992.

——. *Reluctant Confederates: Upper South Unionists in the Secession Crisis*. Chapel Hill, 1989.

Current, Richard N. *Lincoln's Loyalists: Union Soldiers from the Confederacy*. Boston, 1992.

——. *Northernizing the South*. Athens, 1983.

Currie, James T. *Enclave: Vicksburg and Her Plantations, 1863–1870*. Jackson, 1980.

Daniel, W. Harrison. "The Effects of the Civil War on Southern Protestantism." *Maryland Historical Magazine* 69 (1974): 44–63.

——. "Protestantism and Patriotism in the Confederacy." *Mississippi Quarterly* 24 (1971): 117–34.

——. "Southern Protestantism—1861 and After." *Civil War History* 5 (1959): 276–82.

Davis, David Brion. *The Slave Power Conspiracy and the Paranoid Style*. Baton Rouge, 1969.

Davis, Ronald L. F. *Good and Faithful Labor: From Slavery to Sharecropping in the Natchez District, 1860–1890*. Westport, 1982.

Davis, William Watson. *The Civil War and Reconstruction in Florida*. New York, 1913.

Dawson, Joseph G., III. *Army Generals and Reconstruction: Louisiana, 1862–1877*. Baton Rouge, 1982.

Delaney, Norman C. "Charles Henry Foster and the Unionists of Eastern North Carolina." *North Carolina Historical Review* 37 (1960): 348–66.

Demuth, David O. "The Burning of Hopefield." *Arkansas Historical Quarterly* 36 (1977): 123–29.

Dorris, Jonathan T. *Pardon and Amnesty under Lincoln and Johnson: The Restoration of the Confederates to Their Rights and Privileges, 1861–1898*. Chapel Hill, 1953.

Dougan, Michael B. *Confederate Arkansas: The People and Policies of a Frontier State in Wartime.* University, 1976.

Doyle, Elizabeth Joan. "Greenbacks, Car Tickets, and the Pot of Gold: The Effects of Wartime Occupation on the Business Life of New Orleans." *Civil War History* 5 (1959): 347–62.

———. "New Orleans Courts under Military Occupation, 1861–1865." *Mid-America* 42 (1960): 185–92.

———. "Nurseries of Treason: Schools in Occupied New Orleans." *Journal of Southern History* 26 (1960): 161–79.

Dunham, Chester Forrester. *The Attitude of the Northern Clergy toward the South, 1860–1865.* Toledo, 1942.

Durham, Walter T. *Nashville, the Occupied City: The First Seventeen Months— February 16, 1862, to June 30, 1863.* Nashville, 1985.

———. *Rebellion Revisited: A History of Sumner County, Tennessee, from 1861 to 1870.* Gallatin, 1982.

———. *Reluctant Partners: Nashville and the Union, July 1, 1863, to June 30, 1865.* Nashville, 1987.

Durrill, Wayne K. *War of Another Kind: A Southern Community in the Great Rebellion.* New York, 1990.

Dyer, John Percy. "Northern Relief for Savannah during Sherman's Occupation." *Journal of Southern History* 19 (1953): 457–72.

East, Omega G. "St. Augustine during the Civil War." *Florida Historical Quarterly* 31 (1952): 75–91.

Eaton, Clement. *A History of the Southern Confederacy.* New York, 1954.

———. *The Waning of the Old South Civilization, 1860–1880's.* Athens, 1968.

Engs, Robert Francis. *Freedom's First Generation: Black Hampton, Virginia, 1861–1890.* Philadelphia, 1979.

Escott, Paul D. *After Secession: Jefferson Davis and the Failure of Confederate Nationalism.* Baton Rouge, 1978.

———. *Many Excellent People: Power and Privilege in North Carolina, 1850–1900.* Chapel Hill, 1985.

Faust, Drew Gilpin. *The Creation of Confederate Nationalism: Ideology and Identity in the Civil War South.* Baton Rouge, 1988.

Fellman, Michael. *Inside War: The Guerrilla Conflict in Missouri during the American Civil War.* New York, 1989.

Fisher, Noel C. " 'Prepare Them for My Coming': General William T. Sherman, Total War, and Pacification in West Tennessee." *Tennessee Historical Quarterly* 51 (1992): 75–86.

Fleming, Walter L. *Civil War and Reconstruction in Alabama.* 1905. Reprint, New York, 1949.

Flynt, J. Wayne. *Dixie's Forgotten People: The South's Poor Whites.* Bloomington, 1979.

Foner, Eric. *Free Soil, Free Labor, Free Men: The Ideology of the Republican Party before the Civil War.* New York, 1970.

——. *Reconstruction: America's Unfinished Revolution, 1863–1877*. New York, 1988.

Ford, Lacy K., Jr. *Origins of Southern Radicalism: The South Carolina Upcountry, 1800–1860*. New York, 1988.

Fox-Genovese, Elizabeth. *Within the Plantation Household: Black and White Women of the Old South*. Chapel Hill, 1988.

Franklin, John Hope. *The Militant South*. Cambridge, 1956.

——. *A Southern Odyssey: Travelers in the Antebellum North*. Baton Rouge, 1976.

Frederickson, George M. *The Black Image in the White Mind: The Debate on Afro-American Character and Destiny, 1817–1914*. New York, 1971.

Freidel, Frank. "General Orders 100 and Military Government." *Mississippi Valley Historical Review* 32 (1946): 541–56.

Friedman, Jean E. *The Enclosed Garden: Women and Community in the Evangelical South, 1830–1900*. Chapel Hill, 1985.

Futrell, Robert J. "Federal Military Government in the South, 1861–1865." *Military Affairs* 15 (1951): 181–91.

Gabriel, Ralph H. "American Experience with Military Government." *American Historical Review* 49 (1944): 630–43.

Gallagher, Gary W. " 'Upon Their Success Hang Momentous Issues': Generals." In *Why the Confederacy Lost*, edited by Gabor S. Boritt, 79–108. New York, 1992.

Gaston, Kay Baker. "A World Overturned: The Civil War Experience of Dr. William A. Cheatham and His Family." *Tennessee Historical Quarterly* 50 (1991): 3–16.

Gates, Paul. *Agriculture and the Civil War*. New York, 1965.

Genovese, Eugene D. *The Political Economy of Slavery*. New York, 1965.

——. *Roll, Jordan, Roll: The World the Slaves Made*. New York, 1976.

——. "Yeomen Farmers in a Slaveholders' Democracy." *Agricultural History* 49 (1975): 331–42.

Gerteis, Louis S. *From Contraband to Freedman: Federal Policy toward Southern Blacks, 1861–1865*. Westport, 1973.

Gildrie, Richard P. "Guerrilla Warfare in the Lower Cumberland River Valley, 1862–1865." *Tennessee Historical Quarterly* 49 (1990): 161–76.

Glatthaar, Joseph T. *The March to the Sea and Beyond: Sherman's Troops in the Savannah and Carolinas Campaign*. New York, 1985.

Green, Fletcher M. "Democracy in the Old South." *Journal of Southern History* 12 (1946): 3–23.

Greenberg, Kenneth S. *Masters and Statesmen: The Political Culture of American Slavery*. Baltimore, 1985.

Greenough, Mark K. "Aftermath at Appomattox: Federal Military Occupation of Appomattox County, May–November, 1865." *Civil War History* 31 (1985): 5–23.

Hahn, Steven. *The Roots of Southern Populism: Yeoman Farmers and the Transformation of the Georgia Upcountry, 1850–1890*. New York, 1983.

Hardison, Edwin T. "In the Toils of War: Andrew Johnson and the Federal Occupation of Tennessee." Ph.D. dissertation, University of Tennessee, Knoxville, 1981.

Harris, J. William. *Plain Folk and Gentry in a Slave Society: White Liberty and Black Slavery in Augusta's Hinterlands*. Middletown, 1985.

Harris, William C. "East Tennessee's Civil War Refugees and the Impact of the War on Civilians." *Journal of East Tennessee History* 64 (1992): 3–19.

———. "Lincoln and Wartime Reconstruction in North Carolina, 1861–1863." *North Carolina Historical Review* 63 (1986): 149–68.

Helis, Thomas W. "Of Generals and Jurists: The Judicial System of New Orleans under Union Occupation, May 1862–April 1865." *Louisiana History* 29 (1988): 143–62.

Hendricks, George Linton. "Union Army Occupation of the Southern Seaboard, 1861–1865." Ph.D. dissertation, Columbia University, 1954.

Hess, Earl J. *Liberty, Virtue, and Progress: Northerners and Their War for the Union*. New York, 1988.

Hesseltine, William B. *Lincoln's Plan of Reconstruction*. 1960. Reprint, Gloucester, 1963.

Honey, Michael K. "The War within the Confederacy: White Unionists of North Carolina." *Prologue* 18 (1986): 74–93.

Huff, Leo E. "Guerrillas, Jayhawkers, and Bushwhackers in Northern Arkansas during the Civil War." *Arkansas Historical Quarterly* 24 (1965): 127–48.

Hughes, Michael A. "Wartime Gristmill Destruction in Northwest Arkansas and Military-Farm Colonies." *Arkansas Historical Quarterly* 46 (1987): 167–86.

Hundley, D. R. *Social Relations in Our Southern States*. New York, 1860.

Hyman, Harold M. "Deceit in Dixie." *Civil War History* 3 (1957): 65–82.

———. *Era of the Oath: Northern Loyalty Tests during the Civil War and Reconstruction*. Philadelphia, 1954.

Jenkins, William Sumner. *Pro-Slavery Thought in the Old South*. Chapel Hill, 1935.

Jimerson, Randall C. *The Private Civil War: Popular Thought during the Sectional Conflict*. Baton Rouge, 1988.

Johns, John E. *Florida during the Civil War*. Gainesville, 1963.

Johnson, Ludwell H., III. "Blockade or Trade Monopoly? John A. Dix and the Union Occupation of Norfolk." *Virginia Magazine of History and Biography* 93 (1985): 54–78.

———. "Contraband Trade during the Last Year of the Civil War." *Mississippi Valley Historical Review* 49 (1963): 635–52.

———. "Trading with the Union: The Evolution of Confederate Policy." *Virginia Magazine of History and Biography* 78 (1970): 308–25.

Johnson, Michael P. *Toward a Patriarchal Republic: The Secession of Georgia*. Baton Rouge, 1977.

Jones, Archer. *Civil War Command and Strategy: The Process of Victory and Defeat*. New York, 1992.

Jones, James Boyd, Jr. "A Tale of Two Cities: The Hidden Battle against Venereal Disease in Civil War Nashville and Memphis." *Civil War History* 31 (1985): 270–76.

Kenzer, Robert C. *Kinship and Neighborhood in a Southern Community: Orange County, South Carolina, 1849–1881.* Knoxville, 1987.

King, Spencer B., Jr. *Darien: The Death and Rebirth of a Southern Town.* Macon, 1981.

Klingberg, Frank W. "Operation Reconstruction: A Report on Southern Unionist Planters." *North Carolina Historical Review* 25 (1948): 466–84.

———. *The Southern Claims Commission.* Berkeley, 1955.

Lang, James O. "Gloom Envelops New Orleans, April 24 to May 2, 1862." *Louisiana History* 1 (1960): 281–99.

Lathrop, Barnes F. "The Lafourche District in 1862: Militia and Partisan Rangers." *Louisiana History* 1 (1960): 230–44.

Lawrence, Alexander A. *A Present for Mr. Lincoln: The Story of Savannah from Secession to Sherman.* Macon, 1961.

Lebsock, Suzanne D. *The Free Women of Petersburg: Status and Culture in a Southern Town, 1784–1860.* New York, 1984.

Levine, Lawrence W. *Black Culture and Black Consciousness: Afro-American Folk Thought from Slavery to Freedom.* New York, 1978.

Linderman, Gerald F. *Embattled Courage: The Experience of Combat in the American Civil War.* New York, 1987.

Litwack, Leon F. *Been in the Storm So Long: The Aftermath of Slavery.* New York, 1979.

Luraghi, Raimondo. "The Civil War and the Modernization of American Society: Social Structure and Industrial Revolution in the Old South before and during the War." *Civil War History* 18 (1972): 230–50.

McCardell, John. *The Idea of a Southern Nation: Southern Nationalists and Southern Nationalism, 1830–1860.* New York, 1979.

McCrary, Peyton. *Abraham Lincoln and Reconstruction: The Louisiana Experiment.* Princeton, 1978.

McIlwaine, Shields. *The Southern Poor-White from Lubberland to Tobacco Road.* Norman, 1939.

McMillan, Malcolm C. *The Disintegration of a Confederate State: Three Governors and Alabama's Wartime Home Front, 1861–1865.* Macon, 1986.

McPherson, James M. *Battle Cry of Freedom: The Civil War Era.* New York, 1988.

Marszalek, John F. *Sherman: A Soldier's Passion for Order.* New York, 1993.

Marten, James. *Texas Divided: Loyalty and Dissent in the Lone Star State, 1856–1874.* Lexington, 1990.

———. "A Wearying Existence: Texas Refugees in New Orleans, 1862–1865." *Louisiana History* 28 (1987): 343–56.

Martin, Richard A. "Defeat in Victory: Yankee Experience in Early Civil War Jacksonville." *Florida Historical Quarterly* 53 (1974): 1–32.

Maslowski, Peter. "From Reconciliation to Reconstruction: Lincoln, Johnson, and Tennessee." *Tennessee Historical Quarterly* 42 (1983): 281–98, 343–61.

———. *Treason Must Be Made Odious: Military Occupation and Wartime Reconstruction in Nashville, Tennessee.* Millwood, 1978.

Massey, Mary E. *Bonnet Brigades: Women and the Civil War*. New York, 1966.

——. *Ersatz in the Confederacy*. Columbia, 1952.

——. *Refugee Life in the Confederacy*. Baton Rouge, 1964.

Messner, William F. "Black Violence and White Response: Louisiana, 1862." *Journal of Southern History* 41 (1975): 19–38.

Mitchell, Reid. *Civil War Soldiers*. New York, 1988.

——. *The Vacant Chair: The Northern Soldier Leaves Home*. New York, 1993.

Mohr, Clarence L. *On the Threshold of Freedom: Masters and Slaves in Civil War Georgia*. Athens, 1986.

Moneyhon, Carl H. "The Impact of the Civil War in Arkansas: The Mississippi River Plantation Counties." *Arkansas Historical Quarterly* 51 (1992): 105–18.

——. *The Impact of the Civil War and Reconstruction on Arkansas: Persistence in the Midst of Ruin*. Baton Rouge, 1994.

Moore, Albert Burton. *Conscription and Conflict in the Confederacy*. New York, 1924.

Moore, Wilton P. "Union Army Provost Marshals in the Eastern Theater." *Military Affairs* 26 (1962): 120–26.

Nash, Howard P., Jr. *Stormy Petrel: The Life and Times of General Benjamin F. Butler, 1818–1893*. Rutherford, 1969.

Neely, Mark E., Jr. *The Fate of Liberty: Abraham Lincoln and Civil Liberties*. New York, 1991.

Nevins, Allan. *The War for the Union*. 4 vols. New York, 1959–71.

Oakes, James. *Slavery and Freedom: An Interpretation of the Old South*. New York, 1990.

O'Connor, Thomas H. "Lincoln and the Cotton Trade." *Civil War History* 7 (1961): 20–35.

Overy, David H., Jr. "The Wisconsin Carpetbagger: A Group Portrait." *Wisconsin Magazine of History* 44 (1960): 15–49.

Owsley, Frank. *Plain Folk of the Old South*. Baton Rouge, 1949.

Paludan, Philip Shaw. *"A People's Contest": The Union and Civil War, 1861–1865*. New York, 1988.

Parks, Joseph H. "A Confederate Trade Center under Federal Occupation: Memphis, 1862–1865." *Journal of Southern History* 7 (1941): 289–314.

——. "Memphis under Military Rule, 1862 to 1865." East Tennessee Historical Society's *Publications* 14 (1942): 31–58.

Patton, James W. *Unionism and Reconstruction in Tennessee, 1860–1869*. Chapel Hill, 1934.

Perman, Michael. *Reunion Without Compromise: The South and Reconstruction, 1865–1868*. Cambridge, 1973.

Phillips, Edward H. "The Lower Shenandoah Valley during the Civil War: The Impact of War upon the Civilian Population and upon Civil Institutions." Ph.D. dissertation, University of North Carolina, Chapel Hill, 1958.

Phillips, Ulrich B. "The Central Theme of Southern History." *American Historical Review* 34 (1928): 30–43.

Potter, David M. *The South and the Sectional Conflict*. Baton Rouge, 1968.

Powell, Lawrence N. *New Masters: Northern Planters during the Civil War and Reconstruction*. New Haven, 1980.

Powell, Lawrence N., and Michael S. Wayne. "Self-Interest and the Decline of Confederate Nationalism." In *The Old South in the Crucible of War*, edited by Harry P. Owens and James J. Cooke, 29–45. Jackson, 1983.

Rable, George C. *Civil Wars: Women and the Crisis of Southern Nationalism*. Urbana, 1989.

Ramsdell, Charles W. *Behind the Lines in the Southern Confederacy*. Baton Rouge, 1944.

Randall, James G. *Constitutional Problems under Lincoln*. Urbana, 1926.

Ringold, May Spencer. *The Role of the State Legislatures in the Confederacy*. Athens, 1966.

Ripley, C. Peter. *Slaves and Freedmen in Civil War Louisiana*. Baton Rouge, 1976.

Roark, James L. *Masters Without Slaves: Southern Planters in the Civil War and Reconstruction*. New York, 1977.

Roberts, A. Sellew. "The Federal Government and Confederate Cotton." *American Historical Review* 32 (1927): 262–75.

Robinson, Armstead L. "In the Shadow of Old John Brown: Insurrection Anxiety and Confederate Mobilization, 1861–1863." *Journal of Negro History* 65 (1980): 279–97.

Roland, Charles P. "Difficulties of Civil War Sugar Planting in Louisiana." *Louisiana Historical Quarterly* 38 (1955): 40–62.

Royster, Charles. *The Destructive War: William Tecumseh Sherman, Stonewall Jackson, and the Americans*. New York, 1991.

Russ, William A., Jr. "Administrative Activities of the Union Army during and after the Civil War." *Mississippi Law Journal* 17 (1945): 71–89.

Scott, Anne Firor. *The Southern Lady: From Pedestal to Politics, 1830–1930*. Chicago, 1970.

Sefton, James E. *The United States Army and Reconstruction, 1865–1877*. Baton Rouge, 1967.

Shofner, Jerrell H. "Andrew Johnson and the Fernandina Unionists." *Prologue* 10 (1978): 211–23.

Shugg, Roger W. *Origin of Class Struggle in Louisiana: A Social History of White Farmers and Laborers during Slavery and After, 1840–1875*. 1939. Reprint, Baton Rouge, 1968.

Silver, James W. *Confederate Morale and Church Propaganda*. Tuscaloosa, 1957.

———. "Propaganda in the Confederacy." *Journal of Southern History* 11 (1945): 487–503.

Simkins, Francis Butler, and James Welch Patton. *The Women of the Confederacy*. Richmond, 1936.

Somers, Dale A. "War and Play: The Civil War in New Orleans." *Mississippi Quarterly* 26 (1972–73): 3–28.

Spain, Rufus B. "R. B. C. Howell: Nashville Baptist Leader in the Civil War Period." *Tennessee Historical Quarterly* 14 (1955): 323–40.

Stampp, Kenneth M. *The Peculiar Institution: Slavery in the Ante-Bellum South*. New York, 1956.

St. Clair, Kenneth E. "Military Justice in North Carolina, 1865: A Microcosm of Reconstruction." *Civil War History* 11 (1965): 341–50.

Sutherland, Daniel E. "Abraham Lincoln, John Pope, and the Origins of Total War." *Journal of Military History* 56 (1992): 567–86.

——. "Guerrillas: The Real War in Arkansas." *Arkansas Historical Quarterly* 52 (1993): 257–85.

——. "Introduction to War: The Civilians of Culpeper County, Virginia." *Civil War History* 37 (1991): 120–37.

Tatum, Georgia Lee. *Disloyalty in the Confederacy*. Chapel Hill, 1934.

Taylor, Joe Gray. *Louisiana Reconstructed, 1863–1877*. Baton Rouge, 1974.

Taylor, William R. *Cavalier and Yankee: The Old South and American National Character*. New York, 1961.

Thomas, Emory M. *The Confederate Nation, 1861–1865*. New York, 1979.

Thornton, J. Mills. *Politics and Power in a Slave Society: Alabama, 1800–1860*. Baton Rouge, 1978.

Tunnell, Ted. *Crucible of Reconstruction: War, Radicalism, and Race in Louisiana, 1862–1877*. Baton Rouge, 1984.

Walters, John Bennett. "General William T. Sherman and Total War." *Journal of Southern History* 14 (1948): 447–80.

Wayne, Michael. *The Reshaping of Plantation Society: The Natchez District, 1860–1880*. Baton Rouge, 1983.

Weigley, Russell F. *The American Way of War: A History of United States Military Strategy and Policy*. New York, 1973.

Wesley, Charles H. *The Collapse of the Confederacy*. Washington, 1937.

Wight, Willard Eugene. "The Churches and the Confederate Cause." *Civil War History* 6 (1960): 361–73.

Wiley, Bell Irvin. *Confederate Women*. Westport, 1975.

——. *Plain People of the Confederacy*. Baton Rouge, 1943.

——. *Southern Negroes, 1861–65*. New Haven, 1938.

——. "Southern Reaction to Federal Invasion." *Journal of Southern History* 16 (1950): 491–510.

Williamson, Joel. *The Crucible of Race: Black-White Relations in the American South since Emancipation*. New York, 1984.

Wilson, Spencer. "Experiment in Reunion: The Union Army in Civil War Norfolk and Portsmouth, Virginia." Ph.D. dissertation, University of Maryland, 1973.

Winters, John D. *The Civil War in Louisiana*. Baton Rouge, 1963.

Wish, Harvey. "Slave Disloyalty under the Confederacy." *Journal of Negro History* 23 (1938): 435–50.

Wooster, Ralph A. *The People in Power: Courthouse and Statehouse in the Lower South, 1850–1860*. Knoxville, 1969.

———. *Politicians, Planters, and Plain Folk: Courthouse and Statehouse in the Upper South, 1850–1860*. Knoxville, 1975.

Wyatt-Brown, Bertram. *Southern Honor: Ethics and Behavior in the Old South*. New York, 1982.

Yearns, W. Buck, ed. *The Confederate Governors*. Athens, 1985.

Index

laging by, 17–18, 93; and civilian
morale, 39–40, 48, 74–75, 159, 215,
220–22, 226–27; cavalry raids by, 48,
75, 124–25; slave-catching by, 162; surrender of, 225. *See also* Confederate
government
Confederate frontier: defined, 76–77, 92;
destruction, disruption, uncertainty,
and privation on, 92–95, 98, 177–78,
191–92; economy on, 93, 94; slavery
and blacks on, 94, 95, 98, 162–65,
224–25, 227; resentment of Confederate government on, 94–95, 171, 178,
179, 217–18; local government on, 95,
96–97, 261 (n. 43); preservation of
order on, 95, 98, 162, 261 (n. 43); relief
efforts on, 96–97; churches on, 97, 98;
communalism on, 97–98, 162; schools
on, 98; Unionists on, 111, 114, 116,
122–24, 129; class conflict on, 170–71,
177–78, 190–92; Confederate morale
on, 217–18, 222–23, 226–27; at war's
end, 225–27
Confederate government: citizens'
resentment toward, 94–95, 109–10,
171, 178, 179, 217–18; persisting
authority of, on Confederate frontier,
95, 162, 261 (n. 43); collapse of,
225–26. *See also* Confederate army;
Morale, Confederate
Confiscation Acts, 32, 120, 150–51, 252
(n. 42)
Contraband camps, 152, 155
Contrabands. *See* Blacks
Crittenden Resolution, 26

Darien, Ga., 253 (n. 45)
Decatur, Ala., 21, 91, 128
Destruction. *See* Property, destruction
and seizure of
Dix, John A., 27, 28, 32, 81, 116
Dow, Neal, 113

Economy: in garrisoned towns, 77–81,
83; on Confederate frontier, 93, 94,
217–18; in no-man's-land, 100–102, 263
(n. 56); in postwar months, 229–31
Edgefield, Tenn., 219
Education. *See* Schools
Emancipation. *See* Blacks; Slaveholders;
Slavery
Emancipation Proclamation, 54, 117, 120,
151–52, 268 (n. 4)
Etheridge, Emerson, 120

Falmouth, Va., 59, 174
Families, 195–203. *See also* Children;
Men, civilian; Women
Fayetteville, Tenn., 37, 207
Federal army. *See* Union army; Union
soldiers
Fernandina, Fla., 82, 163, 180
Florence, Ala., 231
Forrest, Nathan Bedford, 48, 57
Fort Smith, Ark., 83, 127, 130, 176
Foster, Charles Henry, 182–83
Fredericksburg, Va., 22, 69, 71; capture
of, 17, 24; under Union occupation,
29, 31–32, 40–41, 91, 161; at war's end,
227, 230
Freedmen. *See* Blacks
Freedmen's Bureau, 233
Free Labor Associations, 182–83
Frémont, John C., 32

Gallatin, Tenn., 1, 83, 109
Garrisoned towns: defined, 76–77;
destruction, privation, and overcrowding in, 77, 79–81, 91, 177, 190; slavery
and blacks in, 77, 79, 155–56, 160–62,
223–24; economy in, 77–81, 83; relief
efforts in, 81–83, 178–79; preservation
of order in, 82, 86–88, 90, 91–92;
local government in, 83–88, 160, 259
(n. 24), 260 (n. 26); health and safety

measures in, 84–86; schools in, 88–89, 260 (nn. 27, 28); churches in, 89–90, 114, 173, 219; Unionists in, 111–12, 114, 116, 121–22, 127; class conflict in, 177, 185, 190; change in, 211; Confederate morale in, 218–20, 222, 226–27

Gender relations. *See* Men, civilian; Women

General Order 100, 57, 63

Government, local: in garrisoned towns, 83–88, 160, 259 (n. 24), 260 (n. 26); on Confederate frontier, 95, 96–97, 162, 261 (n. 43); in no-man's-land, 105, 165; postwar restoration of, 231

Grant, Ulysses S., 66

Guerrillas: origins, motives, and modus operandi of, 21–22, 34, 47–49, 64–65, 181, 251 (n. 24); and Union army, 47, 49–50, 51, 63–67, 72, 75; and civilian men, 47, 126; and children, 49, 126; and communalism, 64–67, 72, 125; and Unionists, 66, 125–27, 129–30; and women, 126; and blacks, 166–67, 168–69; surrender of, 227, 231. *See also* Resistance, civilian

Hahn, Michael, 117–18

Halleck, Henry W., 27, 51, 67

Hard policy, 50–61, 74

Harrison, M. La Rue, 210

Hilton Head, S.C., 16, 60

Home guards: secessionist, 11, 15, 21–22, 23, 95–96, 123, 162; Unionist, 129–30, 192; organized to combat banditry, 209–10

Honor, 9, 41, 44–45, 47, 72–73, 159

Hopefield, Ark., 66

Hunter, David, 32

Huntsville, Ala., 44, 46, 88

Hurlbut, Stephen, 66

Invasion: initial reaction to, 13–24, 27–28, 30; psychological impact of, 20–21, 22, 211–13; secessionists' view of, 40–41, 47, 181

Jackson, Miss., 55

Jackson, Tenn., 103, 161–62

Jacksonville, Fla.: capture of, 17, 22, 23; Unionists in, 23, 110, 111–12; under Union occupation, 59–60, 85, 88, 110, 111–12, 176

Jayhawkers, 129, 268 (n. 56)

Johnson, Andrew, 110, 118, 119, 122, 156, 183, 203, 208, 209, 212, 224; as military governor, 43, 45, 117, 174; as president, 231, 232, 233

La Grange, Tenn., 57, 220

Lee, Robert E., 75, 225, 227

Leesburg, Va., 36, 80

Letcher, John, 123

Lincoln, Abraham, 15, 74, 112; election of, 9; and outbreak of war, 10, 26; and political reconstruction, 29, 114–18, 119, 120, 231; and slavery, 32, 54, 151–52, 157; assassinated, 228

Little Rock, Ark., 60, 117, 223

Louisiana: political reconstruction in, 29, 115, 117–18

Lovell, Mansfield, 21, 22

McClellan, George B., 51

McMinnville, Tenn., 22, 69, 198, 200, 208

Marietta, Ga., 57, 59, 179, 208

Memphis, Tenn., 63, 183; capture of, 16, 77; under Union occupation, 58, 70, 73, 81, 84, 86, 173, 182; Unionists in, 108, 109, 110, 111, 118, 119, 122

Men, civilian: and familial obligations, 6–7, 196–97, 199, 200; absence of, 19–20, 21, 196–97; and Union soldiers,

171, 180–86, 187, 189–94, 275 (n. 46); during early invasions, 20–21, 23; and Union army, 174–76, 177, 178–80, 190, 192; hardships of, 177–79, 185; opportunism of, 179–80, 184, 189–94, 205–6, 234–35, 275 (n. 46)

Pope, John, 54, 65

Portsmouth, Va., 62, 166; Union army's administration of, 77, 84, 86, 116, 121; conditions in, 81, 82, 158, 161, 200

Post colonies, 210

Privation: in garrisoned towns, 77, 79–81, 177; on Confederate frontier, 92, 94–95, 177–78; in no-man's-land, 99–103, 105–6, 177; among aristocrats, 177, 178, 186–87; among plain folk, 177–79, 185.*See also* Property, destruction and seizure of

Property, destruction and seizure of: by Confederate army, 17–18, 93; by Union army, 29, 30–31, 53–56, 65, 66–67, 150, 252 (nn. 41, 42), 253 (n. 45); in garrisoned towns, 81, 89, 90, 91, 190; on Confederate frontier, 92, 93, 191–92; in no-man's-land, 99–100, 103–4, 192–93, 263 (n. 56). *See also* Privation

Prostitution, 79, 85–86

Provost marshals, 84

Race relations. *See* Blacks; Slaveholders; Slavery

Radicalism. *See* Reconstruction, political; Reconstruction of Southern society

Randolph, Tenn., 66

Rape and sexual abuse, 19–20, 158–59, 197–98, 200–202

Reconstruction, political, 29, 110–11, 114–20, 182–83, 231, 232

Reconstruction of Southern society, 50, 53, 171–76, 181–83, 234

Refugees: aristocratic, 18–19, 20, 186; secessionist, 18–21, 60–61, 70, 254 (n. 59); plain folk, 19, 178–80, 189, 191; women, 19–20, 202–3; Unionist, 112, 114, 123–24

Relief efforts, 81–83, 96–97, 102–3, 105–6, 178–79

Religion. *See* Churches

Republicanism, 4, 41, 184

Resistance, civilian: lack of, during early invasions, 21–22, 34, 46; verbal, 31, 41–44; passive, 36, 44–46, 89; active, 46–49, 96; under hard policy, 69–73; end of, 226–28, 231. *See also* Guerrillas; Morale, Confederate

Ripley, Miss., 31

Rome, Ga., 90, 91, 92, 104, 190, 207

Rosewater policy, 25–27, 28–31, 32, 34–37, 81

Roswell, Ga., 191–92, 254 (n. 59)

St. Augustine, Fla., 20, 30, 44, 175

Savannah, Ga., 55, 159; Union army's administration of, 58, 77, 84, 190; conditions in, 190, 222

Schools, 88–89, 98, 104, 175, 179, 260 (nn. 27, 28)

Secession, 1, 7–10, 25, 40, 109

Shelbyville, Tenn., 111

Sheridan, Philip H., 65, 66, 95

Sherman, Thomas W., 28

Sherman, William T., 57, 62, 90, 91, 129, 173, 179; early conciliatory attitude of, 27; articulates hard policy, 51–52, 54; marches through Georgia and Carolinas, 55–56; administration of occupied territory by, 58, 65, 66, 82, 84; and Unionists, 111, 113; and blacks, 153

Slaveholders: attitude of, toward slaves, 2, 3, 9–10, 156–60, 167; during early invasions, 11, 14, 15, 21, 22–23, 31–33, 149; attempt to preserve slavery, 156,

children, 43; and civilian men, 43, 70–71; behavior of, in latter part of war, 52–53, 55–56, 58, 149–50, 152, 201–2; friendly relations of, with citizens, 218–20. *See also* Union army

Vicksburg, Miss., 57, 82–91 passim, 219
Virginia: political reconstruction in, 115, 116–17

Williamston, N.C., 92, 226
Wilmington, N.C., 77
Winchester, Va., 16, 27
Women: and familial obligations, 6–7, 21, 197–200, 202–3; and Union soldiers, 14, 19–20, 42–43, 43–44, 61–62, 71, 197–98, 199, 200–202, 218–20; and blacks, 14, 158, 198, 199–200, 201; rape and sexual abuse of, 19–20, 158–59, 197–98, 200–202; numerical predominance of, 19–20, 196; morale and resistance of, 38–39, 42–43, 43–44, 61–62, 71; and guerrillas, 126; and bandits, 206–7, 209

Yeomen: and aristocrats, 3–5, 9, 20–21, 171, 180–86, 187, 189–94; in antebellum era, 3–5, 9, 177; during early invasions, 20–21; and Union army, 174–76, 177, 178–80; hardships of, 177–79, 185; opportunism of, 179–80, 184, 189–94, 234–35
Yorktown, Va., 36

Finally, Ash shows that conflicts between
Confederate citizens and Yankee invaders were
not the only ones that marked the experience
of the occupied South. Internal clashes pitted
Southerners against one another along lines of
class, race, and politics: plain folk vs. aristocrats, slaves vs. owners, and unionists vs.
secessionists.

Drawing on a wide variety of published and
unpublished sources, this study adds another
dimension to our understanding of the Confederate experience.

Stephen V. Ash is assistant professor of history
at the University of Tennessee, Knoxville, and
managing editor of the *Journal of East Tennessee History*. His books include *Middle Tennessee
Society Transformed, 1860–1870: War and
Peace in the Upper South*.